DASHING TO THE END

HOLLYWOOD LEGENDS SERIES
CARL ROLLYSON, SERIES EDITOR

DASHING TO THE END

THE RAY MILLAND STORY

ERIC MONDER

UNIVERSITY PRESS OF MISSISSIPPI / JACKSON

The University Press of Mississippi is the scholarly publishing agency of
the Mississippi Institutions of Higher Learning: Alcorn State University,
Delta State University, Jackson State University, Mississippi State University,
Mississippi University for Women, Mississippi Valley State University,
University of Mississippi, and University of Southern Mississippi.

www.upress.state.ms.us

Frontispiece photo credit: Glasshouse Images / Alamy Stock Photo

Permission for "An Unnoticeable Star" by Tom Clark granted by Angelica Clark.

The University Press of Mississippi is a member
of the Association of University Presses.

Copyright © 2025 by Eric Monder
All rights reserved
Manufactured in the United States of America

∞

Publisher: University Press of Mississippi, Jackson, USA
Authorised GPSR Safety Representative: Easy Access System Europe -
Mustamäe tee 50, 10621 Tallinn, Estonia, gpsr.requests@easproject.com

Library of Congress Control Number: 2025931737

Hardback ISBN: 9781496831491
Epub single ISBN: 9781496856746
Epub institutional ISBN: 9781496856753
PDF single ISBN: 9781496856739
PDF institutional ISBN: 9781496856760

British Library Cataloging-in-Publication Data available

For my parents, Theo and Jesse, and my wife, Kathi

CONTENTS

INTRODUCTION: "X-Ray: Milland"................. 3

CHAPTER 1: The Child Who Saw Too Much (1907–1929).......... 18
CHAPTER 2: False Starts, True Romance (1930–1936)............ 38
CHAPTER 3: In the Shadow of Cary Grant (1936–1940)........... 69
CHAPTER 4: A War Begins . . . A Star Is Born (1940–1943)........ 101
CHAPTER 5: At Paramount's Peak (1944–1945)................ 124
CHAPTER 6: Downfall of a Homme Fatale (1946–1949).......... 149
CHAPTER 7: Shadows and Light (1950–1953)................. 177
CHAPTER 8: "For His Sin": Grace and Television (1953–1955)...... 198
CHAPTER 9: The Cold War Auteur (1955–1963)................ 219
CHAPTER 10: *Entr'acte* (1964–1970)........................ 253
CHAPTER 11: Babylon Revisited (1971–1977).................. 273
CHAPTER 12: The Long Voyage Home (1977–1986)............. 305

ACKNOWLEDGMENTS.................................. 329
APPENDIX 1: Feature Film Appearances................... 331
APPENDIX 2: Major Television Appearances and Made-for-TV
            Movies.................................. 335
APPENDIX 3: Major Radio Appearances.................... 338
APPENDIX 4: Major Stage Appearances.................... 341
APPENDIX 5: Directed by Ray Milland..................... 342
NOTES 343
BIBLIOGRAPHY 373
INDEX 379

DASHING TO THE END

INTRODUCTION

"X-Ray: Milland"

RAY MILLAND IS THE MOST CONSEQUENTIAL ACTOR—AND OSCAR WINNER— from Hollywood's Golden Age *not* to have a comprehensive biography.

Until now, the only two books about Ray Milland are his 1974 out-of-print autobiography, *Wide-Eyed in Babylon* (William Morrow and Company), a colorful collection of achronological anecdotes, and James McKay's 2020 filmography, *Ray Milland: The Films, 1929–1984* (McFarland & Company), a well-detailed monograph deliberately divorced from the actor's personal narrative.

One of the questions that inspired the writing of this book is: Why are there so few about Ray Milland when there are so many about other stars?

In most biographies, the author's assertion that the subject is complex has become not only *de rigeur* but a cliché. In the case of Ray Milland, however, the complexity is the point, and it helps explain why he has been accorded so few accolades in recent decades, let alone a complete account of his life story.

It is easy today to find almost any film on a streaming platform, but there might have been more attention paid to Ray Milland if Paramount Studios, where Milland toiled for two decades, had ever set up a proper venue for promoting its older titles. Meanwhile, for the last three decades, the dominant "old movie channel," Turner Classic Movies (TCM), has rotated its library of Warner Bros., MGM, and RKO films with regularity. Only once in thirty years did Milland rate a TCM "Star of the Month" celebration (in April 2011). The irony is that Ray Milland's jaded persona and multidimensional approach to his work would connect better to more recent generations of movie watchers than older "nostalgia-oriented" audiences if they had a chance to see him. Without a corporate incentive, though, the endeavor to (re)discover Ray Milland might take a while.

Bulldog Drummond Escapes (1937)

Still, there is no question Ray Milland was a major movie star—of the handsome, debonair variety—specifically from the late 1930s to the late 1940s, at a point when some of the complexity was airbrushed away; and for nearly six decades, from 1928 to 1985, he appeared in more than 135 theatrical releases, on top of dozens of radio and television programs (including TV movies, miniseries, special events, and two episodic series he produced). Additionally, he performed in the theater, even on Broadway, and directed a handful of feature films and many small-screen efforts. The voluminous size of Milland's canon across this time frame is remarkable, or downright astonishing, if one considers his lack of formal training, his belated start in show business in his twenties, and the fact he only lived to seventy-nine.

In a variety of genres, notably film noir, Ray Milland was reliably exemplary in everything from forgettable pictures to flawed gems to outright classics (in that last category, primarily Billy Wilder's *The Lost Weekend* [1945], for which Milland won his Oscar, and Alfred Hitchcock's *Dial M for Murder* [1954]). Occasionally, if the material was subpar, Milland went through the motions, yet even a bored Milland was more interesting than many other stars. Leonard Maltin recognized this in 1968, writing, "When an actor is consistently good, he receives a passing nod but little praise. . . . Milland was always good . . . [O]ne of the nicest things about Ray Milland is that he lacks all [the] pretentiousness and phoniness associated with Hollywood."

His tortured alcoholic in *The Lost Weekend* (1945) may or may not be Milland's finest hour-plus, but there wasn't anything phony about it, and the role elevated him, at least temporarily, from star to icon. Many movie fans today either forget or never knew that Milland was one of Hollywood's most popular—and highest salaried—actors *before* his Academy Award-winning triumph. Close to the peak of his fame, in 1942, he received billing above a post-*Stagecoach* John Wayne and the rest of the large cast in Cecil B. DeMille's epic *Reap the Wild Wind*, in addition to beating Wayne in a fight scene and running off at the end with the leading lady, Paulette Goddard.

The subsequent neglect of Milland stems from establishment critics and writers over the last few decades assuming much of his work is simply not worthwhile. This passage from *The VideoHound & All-Movie Guide Stargazer* in 1996 is typical: "[*The Lost Weekend*] was one of his last good films or performances ... [H]is later career was made up of mediocre parts in mostly bad films." Earlier, in 1975, respected historian Leslie Halliwell was only slightly more charitable in his *Filmgoer's Companion*: "[Milland] surprised many by becoming an actor and director of some repute before stepping on the inevitable downhill slope."

According to most critics of 1962, one of those "bad films" was Roger Corman's *Premature Burial* ("bad" by its very nature—a horror movie). Yet, just when a rigorous re-evaluation is expected in *The Movie That Changed My Life*, a 1991 compendium of famous writers' titular selections, Jayne Anne Phillips's choice of *Premature Burial* gives short shrift to Milland: in her chapter, the novelist spends twelve pages praising the underrated Gothic piece but never cites Ray Milland as a reason for this Poe adaptation changing her life. In fact, in one of her few mentions of Milland, Phillips curiously remarks that he "doesn't steal the film as [Vincent] Price would have ... [He] is distanced, rather vague." (Actually, Milland is quite superb as the emotionally paralyzed protagonist and far more appropriately cast than Price.)

Ray Milland would have more prominence in the public imagination today had he not passed up or been passed over for several landmark roles. Of the former, he rejected Howard Hawks's *Bringing Up Baby* (1938), which went to Cary Grant, and the original Broadway production of *My Fair Lady* (1956), which solidified Rex Harrison's place in theater and (later) cinema history. He was considered for both Ashley Wilkes in *Gone with the Wind* (1939) and the minister-hero of *How Green Was My Valley* (1941), and Paramount bought *Shane* (1953) with him in mind, those parts going to Leslie Howard, Walter Pidgeon, and Alan Ladd, respectively. For younger generations, he might have made an impression in the part played by Don Ameche in *Trading Places* (1983), but ill-health forced him to withdraw.

A deeper, more profound reason for both Milland's lack of recognition and the misreading of his contributions is that the actor upset the status quo and turned the notion of what it meant to be a matinée idol on its head—then paid the price for it.

According to historian Anthony Curtis, the original matinée idol was "an actor of outstanding presence and charm who commanded a huge and loyal following among leisured middle-class women who frequented the London theatre in the afternoon." Seymour Hicks and Ivor Novello in England and John Barrymore in America became preeminent ones. Later, the twentieth-century equivalent of this nineteenth-century masculine ideal could be best found in the cinema and was immaculately embodied by Cary Grant.

Both Grant and Milland represented the sound screen version of this archetype—the smooth, gallant, slightly roguish but always engaging hero. Their contemporaries who were similarly marketed and viewed this way included such Anglo actors as Ronald Colman, Herbert Marshall, Robert Donat, Leslie Howard, Brian Aherne, Errol Flynn, David Niven, George Sanders, and their pseudo-Anglo and all-American counterparts, William Powell, Douglas Fairbanks Jr., Robert Montgomery, Tyrone Power, Franchot Tone, and Fred Astaire, among others. (Though slightly modernized in more recent decades, the classical model has been maintained by Roger Moore, Pierce Brosnan, Hugh Grant, Daniel Craig and Henry Cavill.) The British-born James Mason came the closest to Milland during the same era in terms of challenging and revising the definition of this male species.

Significantly, though, Milland's Welsh culture should be seen as separate and apart from the British backgrounds of most of his friendly rivals. English was not even Milland's native language. Between his troubled upbringing in Wales and a Celtic desire for adventure, Ray Milland possessed an alternately moody and rebellious disposition well before he entered the movie business. With a military background and no stage experience, Milland got a job as a marksman on the British version of *The Informer* (1929). He then went to Hollywood, slowly proceeding to become an actor and American citizen, with many stumbles and setbacks along the way. Simultaneously, this mostly self-taught, intelligent young man found as much to like as not about commercial filmmaking. He followed orders (the military in him), but he also deconstructed the artificial, Old World concept of the matinée idol, partly by audacious design but mostly by his inherently Byronic nature, with no premeditation at all.

For a few years, in fact, Paramount attempted to mold new contract player Ray Milland into the "next Cary Grant," once Grant left the studio in 1936. Milland played along but eventually resisted this star-making manufacture

Cary Grant visiting Ray Milland on the set of *Dial M for Murder* (1954). Photo credit: Pictorial Press Ltd. / Alamy Stock Photo.

and established his own screen identity. At this point, around the late 1930s, he could be described as having the facade of Cary Grant with the inner spirit of James Cagney or John Garfield, those quintessential plebian "tough guys." Tellingly, his own idol as a youth was Ronald Colman, yet Milland declared in later years that the best actor he'd ever seen was Marlon Brando. Even during Milland's earliest career stages, a discerning viewer might have noticed that Milland was really the "anti–Cary Grant" (i.e. Milland's surreptitiously imperfect male vs. Grant's impossibly perfect male). Interestingly, writer O. B. Hardison cites both Milland and Grant as "Hitchcock's favorite male stars."

He was roughly the same age as Grant, but Milland aged faster. Grant nearly always photographed well; not so Milland, though they were both handsome. And Grant's sartorial sense was just that much classier and more neatly pressed. Both were superb with comedy, with Grant arguably edging out Milland as a physical comedian. Whether youthful or older, Milland's courtship techniques (at least on-screen) inverted Grant's tender earnestness. In *The Uninvited* (1944), a ghost story and not a comedy, the Milland hero's attempt to show off his sailing skills to Gail Russell's heroine finds him hitting his head on the sail and then getting seasick. Two decades later, in *X: The Man with the X-Ray Eyes* (1963), his scientist's idea of charming his female co-worker (Diana Van der Vlis) is to light their cigarettes with a Bunsen burner blowtorch; and, thus, in one fell swoop, dismiss Grant's romanticism and slyly immolate Paul Henreid's "continental" double-lighting bit from *Now, Voyager* (1942).

Most significantly, unlike Grant and his brethren, Milland embraced dark material and sinister roles, imperiling his methodically established hero image. Yet it wasn't that alone that set him apart. After all, several of those among the debonair set tried their hand at playing a psychopath once or twice (stunt casting, actually, which continues today with many popular leading men). Instead, Milland's greatest virtue was also his greatest vice: understanding his "shadow" self (after Jung), Milland's less theatrical, more cinematic, intensely personal style held up a mirror to viewers, showing them that his flaws and frailties were theirs, too. (Milland publicly doffed his toupée in 1970; Cary Grant never did.) This Brechtian betrayal of sorts to his large fan base, forcing uneasy self-reflection, was tempered by his charisma and ability to entertain.

There were indicators early in Milland's career. On paper, his tennis-playing, Long Island playboys of the 1930s were one-dimensional supporting parts, but Milland brought out the hidden depths in these stock types: from sad and soulful (*Next Time We Love* [1936]) to suicidal (*The Man Who Played God* [1932], *Menace* [1934]) to stealthily ruthless (*Bought!* [1931], *Blonde Crazy* [1931]).

Critic Frank Thompson observed in 2019, "Hollywood never quite knew what it had in Ray Milland, but he continuously showed himself to be an adventurous artist, always interested in exposing his established image to radical and surprising lights." In another recent analysis of the Milland paradox, a prabook.com author reflected that after *The Lost Weekend*, "Milland suddenly revealed himself as an actor capable of showing all the flaws in attractiveness. But that promise was not taken up by his employer [Paramount], largely because the bleakness of *The Lost Weekend* was so far ahead of its time." It was primarily after leaving Paramount at the end of a two-decade commitment (1934–1953) that Milland, the free agent, became a more overtly "adventurous artist," slowly losing his hold on mainstream audiences and, in exchange, becoming the cult figure of offbeat, low-budget fare.

While under contract to Paramount, Milland's riskiest move with the greatest payoff was accepting the lead in *The Lost Weekend*, originally rejected by the more cautious Grant. If Milland was only known for this Oscar-winning turn, he would still hold an important place in movie history and beyond. His selfish, suicidal barfly, a role antithetical to the matinée idol type, was proof to the world that this leading man of comedies (e.g. *Easy Living*

[1937]) and action adventures (e.g. *Beau Geste* [1939]) could be a superior dramatic actor. In fact, he was so good, many people believed for years that Milland had a drinking problem, which he didn't, ironically in a town full of artists trying to hide their addictions. This role and several others in his early career anticipate his foray into the horror genre, and as it turns out, Paramount, his place of employment, was built on top of cemetery grounds!

Toward the end of his Paramount years, Milland chose to play the Devil in seductive human form in the noirish *Alias Nick Beal* (1949), a personal favorite of his. While Cary Grant had just personified a guardian angel in the feel-good Christmas hit *The Bishop's Wife* (1947), Milland was unafraid of the career repercussions from appearing as the most heinous of all possible characters. Not surprisingly, the atypical undertaking lost money for the studio. Undaunted, Milland repeated the gig as an unbilled voice cameo in Nicholas Ray's *King of Kings* (1961) and several more times in projects of the 1970s and '80s.

It is worth remembering that in Milland's Catholic faith, Lucifer was a fallen angel and therefore a protean, dual-sided creature, every bit as much as the killers Milland would start portraying after World War II. *Alias Nick Beal* was sandwiched between two of Milland's most memorable homicidal cads, Mark Bellis in *So Evil My Love* (1948) and Tony Wendice in *Dial M for Murder* (1954). Despicable as they are, all three show moments of weakness and even a little regret. In the Hitchcock film, in particular, there are hints that Tony's motivation to kill his wife is as much out of jealousy, fear, and sexual dysfunction as it is about greed, yet the husband's avarice is the most clearly articulated incentive on the printed page of the screenplay. The extra layers are supplied by Milland's performance, the merits of which are easy to overlook because they are so subtle.

The different sides to Ray Milland on-screen manifest themselves as much within films as between films. At the same time he was playing killers, he was the perpetually absent-minded, bespectacled professor in *The Trouble with Women* (1947), *It Happens Every Spring* (1949), *A Woman of Distinction* (1950), and on his TV sitcom, *Meet Mr. McNutley* (a.k.a. *The Ray Milland Show*) (1953–1955), the last project airing concurrently with *Dial M for Murder*'s release. And just as Milland's killers had their unexpected virtues, these seemingly benign, genial heroes often revealed their negative attributes (obsessiveness, duplicity, narcissism, etc.).

The complexities and contradictions carried over off-screen. Was Ray Milland an orphic, sea-faring adventurer who traveled the world or a bookworm who enjoyed memorizing the encyclopedia? Was he the contented family man depicted in fan publications or the "irresistible lothario" in stories told by *Vanity Fair* writer Amy Fine Collins? Was he the kind if reserved gentleman so many colleagues fondly remembered (Billy Wilder said he was "nice ... maybe too nice") or the "total prick" described by Tony Curtis in Curtis's memoirs? Was he homophobic, as the unfortunate word choices in his own memoirs suggest, or was he completely comfortable working with such gay or bisexual directors as George Cukor, Curtis Harrington, and Mitchell Leisen, the last of whom he called a friend and his favorite director? Was he an actor who chose to play vulnerable men, often saved by a woman, or was he a writer who penned for movie magazines such misogynist essays as "Things I Wish Women Wouldn't Do"?

Though he needed a nudge now and then, one constant in the life of Ray Milland was his desire to take chances. Upon leaving Paramount, Milland took many more career risks than before, such as eagerly joining an independent company to make *The Thief* (1952), a low-budget film noir without any dialogue (!), about a spy having a nervous breakdown after killing an FBI agent. In this Cold War thriller, Milland upends the ostensible anti-Communist premise by creating a multifaceted portrayal of the villain. (He received a Golden Globe nomination for his performance.) Likewise, he regarded filming *Dial M for Murder* (1954) in 3-D an exciting new challenge, not a burden or gimmick, and he long yearned to be a director, finally starting in 1955 with the Western *A Man Alone*.

Over the years, a few perceptive writers and observers have distinguished Milland from his peers, noticing the different shadings of his characters, courtesy of the actor. In his seminal 1957 tome *The Liveliest Art*, historian Arthur Knight remarked that before *The Lost Weekend*, there never had been such a "sodden" hero. Jumping forward to the promos for Ray Milland month in April 2011, a TCM narrator declared, "No other star played the spectrum of roles from good to evil so successfully and convincingly." A decade later, in 2021, critic Charlie Largent wrote, "The most sinister light comedian in Hollywood, Ray Milland was never more charming than when he was fixing to cut your throat." In another essay, Largent noted that in *The Uninvited*, his 1944 ghost story, "[Milland] never looked so at home. But then the actor had always appeared haunted. Even in his comedies—and he made a lot of them—Milland delivered his lines like a condemned man, as if he understood the tragic implications of a pratfall."

The best parts of James McKay's 2020 filmography are McKay's detailed descriptions of the nuances Milland invested in his roles. About the brittle hero of Fritz Lang's *Ministry of Fear* (1944), McKay writes, "[H]is busy eyes [are] working overtime, emphasizing the uncertain, unsettled and suspicious nature of his character."

Given how much Milland controlled what he conveyed in his work, it is appropriate to apply the actor-as-auteur theory. In fact, there are several instances where Milland's off- and on-screen lives align, suggesting that he determined much of what he wanted audiences to see. Alfred Reginald John Truscott-Jones (born in 1907) literally authored his new stage name in 1928, when he chose "Milland" in honor of the mill lands of his birthplace in Neath, Wales. Later, Ray and Muriel ("Mal") Milland married in 1932 and had a baby boy, Danny, in 1940; after their adoption of a young girl, Victoria, in 1949, two Milland vehicles concerned themselves with the issue of adoption—the misbegotten comedy *A Woman of Distinction* (1950) and the unsung melodrama *Close to My Heart* (1951), the latter with the baby in question named Danny! As an older character actor, Milland's fathers often had conflicts with their sons, starting with *Love Story* (1970), something that was already a tragic undercurrent in his real-life relationship with Danny.

More generally, the cool distance Milland started projecting on movie sets during his peak years became downright chilly in his films, especially as he got older and his characters increasingly wary in a Cold War world of nuclear anxiety and existential dread. In *Alias Nick Beal* (1949), his humanized Devil frequently tells other characters how he doesn't like to be touched; in *A Man Alone* (1955), an apt title for his directorial debut, he plays a gunslinger who is indeed by himself in an Old West landscape, an outlaw hunted by both "good guys" and "bad guys" and, therefore, as modern day as any alienated protagonist of the 1950s. Milland's ever-devolving misanthropic persona seemed to mirror his own beliefs. In a 1962 interview to promote his sci-fi doomsday picture, *Panic in Year Zero!*, Milland was quoted saying, "[W]e go through life thinking we're very concerned about the other fellow, and in fact we don't give a damn for anybody but ourselves."

By the late 1950s, his on-screen nihilism expressed itself as out-and-out mental derangement, with Milland's psychopaths using charm and romance as a means to a nefarious end. He essayed these qualities expertly in Allan Dwan's little-known Acid Western, *The River's Edge* (1957), and, later, as a patient posing as the asylum doctor in the Caligariesque "A Home Away from Home" on the 1963 *Alfred Hitchcock Hour*. In the 1958 pilot for his TV noir detective show, *Markham*, he played hero again but one that describes himself as "cold, unemotional," and whom his best friend (Macdonald Carey) tells off by declaring, "You don't care about people. All you care about is matching wits—making a kill!" No matter the character, that glint in Milland's eye invites us to share vicariously in his character's misdeeds and then feel the guilt he betrays later.

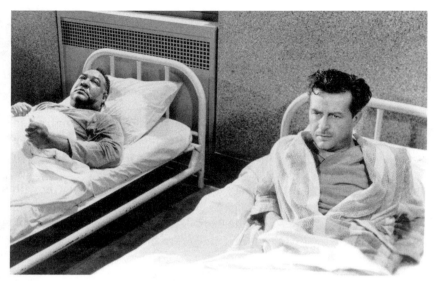

The Lost Weekend (1945), with Ernest Whitman. Photo credit: Moviestore Collection Ltd. / Alamy Stock Photo.

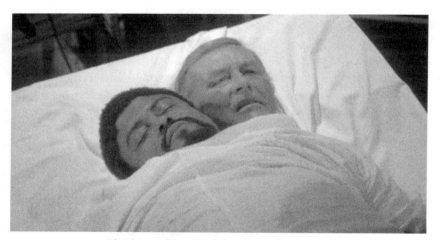

The Thing with Two Heads (1972), with Rosey Grier

Aspects of the Milland character can be found throughout his career, providing a throughline of sorts from his peak work to the supposed dreck of his last years. To wit, the infamous Bellevue sequence in *The Lost Weekend* (actually filmed in Bellevue's "drunk ward") contains an unusual shot—by 1945 standards—that seems to have inspired the 1972 *Thing with Two Heads*: Milland's Don Birnam lies in a cot situated next to an African American patient (Ernest Whitman), uniting them in proximity and egalitarian spirit as fellow travelers on an alcohol-fueled trip to hell and back; in *Two Heads*, Milland's racist Dr. Kirshner is more hostile than Birnam toward discovering an inclusionary utopia, but he is literally that much closer to his journey's "soulmate"—finding his head transplanted onto the body of Rosey Grier's Jack Moss, a prison inmate!

Though an industry insider, off-screen, Milland resisted playing the Hollywood game; over time, this hurt his career as much as any of the kind of parts he chose to play. Sometimes he even went beyond what were considered acceptable norms, certainly of a gentlemanly movie star. Frustrated with the condescending behavior of his *Beau Geste* (1939) costar, Brian Donlevy, Milland reportedly stabbed him in either the rib cage or shoulder during a fight scene, landing Donlevy in the hospital. Similarly, Milland didn't hold back talking acerbic smack in print about his fellow actors, including the popular, Oscar-winning Fredric March (in 1940): "I admired the frank theatricalism of March, and still do. His overacting is admirable. To overact as he does requires skill." In the same year of 1940, as Milland was becoming a major Hollywood player himself, he started feuding with the all-powerful gossip columnist Hedda Hopper; she waited more than a decade to exact her revenge and damage his reputation—by helping expose his affair with Grace Kelly during the shooting of *Dial M for Murder*.

At other times, Milland didn't help his cause at all by becoming a studio publicist's worst nightmare, uttering blunt and bracing statements for such articles as "Ray Milland Hates Acting" (in 1950), "The Man Who Hates to Act" (in 1953), "Ray Milland Hates Acting but Works at It" (in 1966), "Hollywood Has Become a Graveyard . . . and I'm Leaving It Forever" (in 1974), and of course, "Frankly, Ray Milland Is No Press Agent's Dream" (in 1985). As reporter Robert Cross has written, "Milland had a tendency to careen recklessly toward frankness in any of his off-screen appearances." It is amusing in retrospect that he was banished in the 1960s from *The Tonight Show* and *Hollywood Squares* for uttering "inappropriate" remarks, a risqué story on the former and a prudish diatribe about modern movies on the latter. Between the two, he probably sounded inconsistent, if not hypocritical, but it was his frankness that undergirded his behavior—and got him into trouble—in both cases.

It all caught up with Ray Milland in the 1970s, when he was either an aging, balding supporting player in a number of European co-productions or a guest star on such TV shows as *Columbo* and *Charlie's Angels*. He lost most of his older fans after his low-budget horror flicks, like the infamously campy *Thing with Two Heads* (1972), and emerged as a curiosity to younger

The Attic (1980), with Carrie Snodgress

generations. There were standout lead role exceptions along the way, like the disturbing thrillers *The Student Connection* (1974) and *The Pyjama Girl Case* (1978); and in *The Attic* (1980), Milland deftly criticizes both Americana and patriarchy via his portrayal of a cruel father who, in one scene, performs needlework on an American flag grid pattern while mercilessly needling his demoralized daughter (Carrie Snodgress).

Otherwise, most of Milland's other late career efforts were labeled schlock, prompting James McKay to write, "Perhaps, if he had retired in 1970 after *Love Story* his legacy and memory would have been better preserved." (Cary Grant retired in 1966, still the good-looking star of popular, big-budget studio films.)

By the 1980s, Milland's career impairment was a fait accompli. For a few nonconformist filmmakers and musicians, Milland was a cool inspiration; for many others, he was a has-been or a joke; for the rest, he was simply forgotten. The quiet surrounding Milland's death in 1986 was compounded by his instructions for a private family ceremony at sea (still the auteur, posthumously) and the fact that Cary Grant upstaged him one last time, dying a few months after him.

Even before his death, though, the Milland canon was forced "underground" (hence, his own "premature burial"), where his legacy was barely nourished by pockets of cultish enthusiasm. Reinforcing Milland's reputation today as a secretly venerated figure rather than a bona fide star, the pop culture homages over the last few decades have been oddball in nature and scattershot at best.

In 1982, director Carl Reiner's film noir parody *Dead Men Don't Wear Plaid* swiped clips of Milland from *The Lost Weekend* and of other Golden Age personalities (Bogart, Crawford, Cagney, et al.) for absurdist purposes within its whodunit narrative. To movie fans in the tri-state area of the Northeast in the 1980s, a Warholesque, digitalized Milland—standing in front of the clock from *The Big Clock* (1948)—began the televisual lead-in to every late Saturday night Public Broadcasting movie.

In 1985, an Argentinian alternative rock group, the Ray Milland Band (a.k.a. Raymilland), often referenced in their songs aspects of his 1963 horror tour de force, *X: The Man with the X-Ray Eyes*. In 1986, after Milland died, the band performed several tribute songs, including one with the following lyrics:

> A void will leave
> difficult to fill
> Ray Milland is leaving
> like an angel
> All heaven will cross
> Vincent Price will receive it
> Ray Milland is gone
> Goodbye, old Ray.

In 1998, on its *Heaven Forbid* album, the more mainstream rock group Blue Öyster Cult cited Milland by name in the song, "X-Ray Eyes," which comports with the themes of the same film. In 2003, Bruce Dellis directed the comic short *The Strange Case of Ray Milland*, depicting its antihero's struggle not with alcoholism but a cannibalistic appetite! Websites today devoted to Milland include a fanfiction and deviantart Facebook page called "Ray Milland: Actor and Spirit of Rain," created in 2015, and "Dial M for Milland: The Ray Milland Archive," a more traditional fan site created in 2022 by Matthew C. Hoffman.

Perhaps the most moving and meaningful tribute came from Tom Clark in 1990, as part of the late poet's volume *Fractured Karma*. In only a few stanzas, Clark touches upon Milland's multilayered, contradictory persona and the man's uneasy relationships with fame, commercialism, and mortality:

An Unnoticeable Star

just another pretty face
but behind that blank
and vapid mask

a supercilious nonchalance
with just a faint
undercurrent of malice

a safecracker hiding his
whiskey bottles in the chandelier
with a subdued flair
for dark emotional stories

both cursed and coolly
exploited his unnatural
gifts
    something disturbing
yet horribly true about
his mixture of extreme
irritation and disbelief
with almost gentlemanly disgust

something about reality
ray milland couldn't stand

The Lost Weekend (1945)

Ultimately, Ray Milland fell somewhere between a transitional figure and a transformational one and, thus, fell through the cultural cracks (the underground again). He took the voyage from the Old World to the New World and twisted the Matinée Idol into a Modern, Method-Tinged Actor, all the while maintaining his integrity as best as possible. Babylon didn't corrupt him, as it did so many, but it further disillusioned and dispirited him.

The great irony of the Ray Milland story is that the misanthropy he projected on- and off- screen is even more relevant in today's increasingly desensitized world than in his own, therefore further connecting him both to the very human condition against which he struggled and the audiences who don't know who he is.

CHAPTER 1

THE CHILD WHO SAW TOO MUCH (1907–1929)

MOST SUMMARIES OF RAY MILLAND'S BIOGRAPHY ARE SCANTY BUT FEW ARE identical. The inconsistencies include an incorrect birth location (Dragheda, Ireland) in William H. Kofoed's *Movie Diary*, an incorrect birth year (1905) in David Ragan's *Movie Stars of the '30s*, and an incomplete birth name (*Reginald Truscott-Jones*) in Ephraim Katz's generally reliable *Film Encyclopedia*.

The most definitive sources state that blue-eyed Ray Milland was born *Alfred Reginald John Truscott-Jones* on Thursday, January 3, 1907, "on a mountain called Cymla" in Neath, Glamorganshire, Wales. Years later, in 1939, he scolded a reporter, "And don't make it 1905 . . . They're always trying to pile on to me when I've got quite enough already."

As for his first name, Alfred was often called *Reginald* or *Reggie* during his childhood, which distinguished him from his namesake father. The name *Alfred* or *aelf* (in Welsh) means elf, a supernatural being, and *Reginald* or *raed* means counsel. Coincidentally or not, during the course of his acting career, Ray Milland played his share of legal advocates and embodied several metaphysical types, often with a deceptive elfin veneer.

Confusion over his name is understandable. There are as many names Milland acquired through the years as stories to go with them. For starters, as a youngster growing up in pre–World War I Wales, he was simply *Reggie*. Later, as an adolescent, Reggie took on the more masculine moniker of *Spike*, at the same point he was given his stepfather's last name, *Mullane*. By the time he entered show business in the late 1920s, he made up his own new last name of *Milland* (sometimes spelled *Millande*), and went along with a studio flack's suggestion to substitute *Raymond* for *Reginald*. Later, *Raymond* became *Ray*, and after he became a movie star, he tinkered with *Ray Milland* a bit more. When he started directing films in the mid-1950s, he billed himself as *R. Milland* and, as a producer, *R. A. Milland*. (The mysterious *A* stood for *Alton*, which was not part of his birth name in any way.) Some unfortunate, self-aggrandizing nicknames found their way into the mix, too: *Ray the Magnificent, Hollywood's Master Actor*, and *Ole Milland*. Finally, to his closest friends and family members he was simply known as *Jack*, a name he liked since he was a young adult.

Through it all, Ray Milland had a hand in most of his name changes, just as he took charge of his fate whenever possible, and he never seemed to lose touch with who he was—which had much to do with his upbringing in Wales.

Neath, a bustling seaport town on the Bristol Channel, was at the center of the world's tin-plate production during the industrial revolution at the turn of the century. Throughout its long history, Wales made various attempts to separate itself from England; whether clashing in combat or over political and religious differences, the "land of poetry and songs" always retained a distinct cultural identity. Both in reality and in folkloric portraiture, coal mining was regarded as the mainstay of the Welsh economy. For a middle-class family like the Joneses, however, mining was not a typical professional aspiration.

Reggie's parents were Alfred John Jones, born and christened *Alfredo* in Whitchurch, England, in 1876, and Elizabeth Annie Jones (née Truscott), born in Warwickshire, England in 1887, one of eight children of Anna Thick and Charles Truscott, the latter owning a British steamship business. Alfred Jones's chief exploit as a young man was joining the British army and serving as an officer in the Second Hussars. Jones participated in relieving the Siege of Mafeking during the Second Boer War, a colonial battle in South Africa that lasted from October 1899 to May 1900. In 1901, once he returned to Whitchurch, Jones established himself as a blacksmith.

In Whitechurch, Elizabeth met and soon married Alfred in 1905, and they had their first child that year, naming her Olivia. The young family then moved to Wales in 1907, where Reggie was born, a first-generation Welshman. In Neath, Alfred became a galvanizer in a steel mill, coating the steel with rust-resistant zinc, and in 1911 he was promoted to sheet millman, operator of the plant.

Alfred Jones's own father was James Jones, "a huge black-bearded man" whose mother was Spanish, which made him and his descendants "all rather suspect," wrote Milland in his memoirs. Alfred Jones's mother was Sarah Ann Jones (née Lewis), whose parents were William Lewis and Harriet Tilet. Reggie's fraternal grandparents divorced, as did his own parents, an act that was next to sacrilegious in the Catholic enclaves of Wales. Much later, Reggie would follow in his father's professional footsteps as an army officer (in the Welsh Household Cavalry), but no one in the family had ties to "show business," Reggie's ultimate calling.

By 1907, Alfred Jones had settled down to his day job at the steel mill, while Elizabeth Jones, eleven years his junior, was seen as a "typical well to do [sic] housewife of the period," or as Ray Milland would later recall, "a rather flighty and coquettish woman much concerned with propriety and what the neighbors thought." He would receive greater maternal comfort from Mary Catherine, the family housekeeper and laundress who may or may not have been a relative of his father.

CHILDHOOD

Raised Catholic, Baby Reggie was christened on March 15, 1907, at St. Thomas Church. Towards the end of the year, in November, Elizabeth had her third child, but the young, growing family experienced heartbreak four months later when Reggie's new baby brother, Leonard, accidentally drowned. (In March 1908, Reggie would have been one year and three months old when this happened.) Eventually, two more sisters arrived: Beryl, born three years after Reggie, and Enid, born four years after him.

The Jones family lived on 66 Coronation Road in Mount Pleasant, a semirural, westward part of Neath called Neath Port Talbot. Although today Coronation Road is called Dalton Road, no plaque exists near the Jones's house to mark Ray Milland's first dwelling. Among grown-up Ray's fondest childhood memories was of his playing in the lush, green hills and catching shrimp in the rivulets of Neath's picturesque landscape. Anticipating the film he made decades later, *Golden Earrings* (1947), he watched with great curiosity what he described as the "gypsies" camping around his boyhood wonderland. The same hills provided the neighborhood children with an opportunity for sledding during the winter months, and Christmas was always the most festive and eagerly anticipated holiday of the year, Reggie's personal "day of delights."

One of the Christmas rituals Reggie adored the most was attending the Panto shows starring such traveling pantomime actors as Maisie Gay and Seymour Hicks (already famous for touring as Ebenezer Scrooge). They interpreted loose musical fairy-tale adaptations he considered in retrospect "the bluest shows ever performed," with the men and women swapping roles and clothes. Thus, Ray Milland's first sampling of the theatrical arts was filled with adult, gender-bending sexual content by a matinéé idol (Hicks) with a penchant for self-parody.

THE CHILD WHO SAW TOO MUCH (1907–1929)

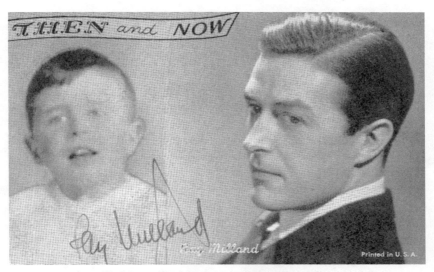

Alfred Reginald John Truscott-Jones and Ray Milland

This idyllic part of his childhood was further enhanced by his crush on a girl named Olwen, who lived in the neighboring village of Tongwynlais. Showing signs already of a roving eye, Reggie also made a point of getting his new clothes at Davies the Tailor, primarily because the owner had "a very pretty daughter," a different girl than Olwen.

Reggie's greatest respite came during the summer months, the time he visited his Aunt Luisa's horse farm in Cymla. At this "private paradise" in a suburb of Neath, he learned to ride ponies, then horses. Luisa and Emma were his father's older half-sisters, and little Reggie grew close to both of them, especially the unmarried Luisa. As Reggie matured, his visits to Luisa's farm became more frequent, and he later emerged a superior equestrian.

Yet, Reggie's childhood had its share of trauma and terror. The tragic death of his brother from drowning left him fearful of—yet fascinated by—water, particularly the mysteries of "what lies beneath." Similarly, he learned at a very early age that every Welsh village is inhabited by a witch and that "people go to the witch for the fulfillment of strange and devious desires." Milland later elaborated, "For the Celtic mind in its lonely moments is a tumbling sea of love and compassion and romanticism and neurotic hates."

When he was six, Reggie heard a revivalist visiting the town say, "Death comes to us all," a pronouncement that scared him. Soon after, he summoned the courage to visit his own village's witch, Bronwen Madoc. One day, he nervously approached her cottage, asked if he could enter, then inquired once inside, "Bron, must I die?" Her pithy, quiet response, "Death will come when you are ready for her," was hardly reassuring to little Reggie, so he bolted from the cottage, feeling spooked. (A few years later, he revisited Bronwen; her new bromide, "Life in the new world becomes you," was a more welcome message, and he thanked her this time before he left.)

As a youngster, Reggie was already developing an adventurous streak. He pulled a stunt that led to a harsh, sober outcome and "the moment that [he] started to grow up." With his best friend, Donald Hope, he sneaked onto a freighter in the Briton Ferry Yard to experience what it was like to stowaway on a commercial ship (albeit a docked one) for a whole weekend. But during the first night's stay, he overheard some of the ship's crew start to suspect they had young interlopers on board. Reggie realized he and his friend should quickly depart. Donald began crying inconsolably, yet the boys managed to escape without incident. On the way home, Donald admitted to Reggie he had left a note for his parents disclosing where they had gone. He also guessed his parents had probably informed Reggie's. Sure enough, arriving home, Reggie encountered his father's wrath. His punishment was supposed to have involved a nasty-looking toasting fork, but the painful beating was thwarted by his mother, who, instead, hit her son in the mouth. Mary Catherine tended to his wounds, and he went to bed without any dinner. Considering the harsher possibilities, Reggie felt lucky he survived the ordeal. As further penance, though, his father forced him to give away his favorite companion, Gypsy, a large and lovable pet dog.

Reggie's formal education was affected by both his incipient devilry and the chaotic Jones family dynamics. He and his family spoke only Welsh, but once he entered Gnoll Hall, his primary school, Reggie finally learned English. His favorite adults at Gnoll were Gomer Jenkins, the well-respected headmaster, and Miss Griffiths, one of his teachers. Unfortunately, a naughty prank placed him in low esteem with both of these supportive authority figures. During a class exercise, Reggie tricked a Belgian refugee child named Victor into spelling aloud for Miss Griffiths the word *cake*, but he whispered to Victor the wrong letters, so the poor boy ended up spelling *caca*, a verboten expression that means excrement. Since Mr. Jenkins was present for this dismaying bit of immaturity, he immediately figured out that Reggie was the instigator; he ordered him to his office for a caning on both hands, followed by a lecture and a command to apologize to both Victor and Miss Griffiths. A sheepish Reggie was spared having to atone for his sins in front of his peers, but he learned an important lesson in thinking about others' feelings more than his own. In fact, he was so moved by the experience, as an adult he attended Mr. Jenkins's funeral during one of his trips back to Wales.

At least temporarily, Reggie became a better student. He was particularly avid about reading, and his favorite books were *Alice in Wonderland* and *Treasure Island*. One of the activities he enjoyed the most was singing in the boys' choir at school. He was a boy soprano until his voice changed—then the vocalizing had to stop. He also looked forward to his Saturday afternoon piano lessons from Professor Balaclava Evans.

As World War I began in 1914, Reggie was alarmed by a new incident involving water. On a sunny day, during a swim in a canal with friends, he encountered and briefly touched the bloated corpse of a woman in a heavy coat, a casualty of the war. "I screamed as I reached the air and tore for the bank and climbed out shaking with horror," he later recalled. This episode forever reinforced his conflicted attraction-repulsion to water: "I am fascinated by water.... But I am terrified of it. I fear it.... [F]ear and horror were born on this day."

Once he reached safe ground, the police were called, and Reggie was taken home, still shaking; he could barely sleep for a week! At the point Reggie calmed down, his father informed him he was separating from his mother. Then he asked if Reggie would like to spend the next few weeks at Aunt Luisa's farm. His parents' clumsy, ill-timed announcement floored Reggie, who hadn't fully processed his nerve-shattering previous few days, but he was glad to have the chance to return to his favorite aunt and her horses.

Soon after Reggie settled in at the ranch, Luisa gently clarified that his parents' separation would be permanent: his mother was actually divorcing his father. A short time later, as Reggie was still reeling from Luisa's revelation, both his parents found new partners. Reggie's mother eventually married a local steel-mill superintendent named Mullane, who adopted Reggie and gave him a new last name. At the age of eight, while shuttling between his mother and father's households, "Reginald Mullane" felt increasingly alienated and did not get along with either of his stepparents. Among his parental figures, he remained closest to his father, a quiet man and "incurable romantic," who was "a little afraid of his emotions." For his part, Alfred Jones later remembered how his son showed early signs of "wanderlust," when, more than once, he ran away and got lost for days at a time.

In the midst of World War I, around 1916, Reggie started to make friends with mischievous youths and joined them in committing practical jokes or the outright bullying of innocent strangers. Years later, Ray Milland expressed deep regret for his behavior. In other, somewhat more positive ways, his time spent with these fellow miscreants unleashed his daring inner spirit. After attending a movie matinée of an adventure serial, Reggie (at age nine) and his friends dared each other to lay on a track while a local train rode over them, missing their bodies by mere inches. This life-threatening event actually planted a seed in his head about becoming a movie actor, which, at the time to him, meant stuntman. (During his Hollywood career, Milland would almost always perform his own stunts.) Around this same time, and foretelling some of his late-career horror films (e.g. *Terror in the Wax Museum* [1973]), he relished visiting the ghoulish waxworks museum on St. Mary Street in Cardiff.

ADOLESCENCE

When his parents mutually decided it would be best for Reggie to live permanently with his mother, he was forced to leave Gnoll. Since his stepfather had to travel for his job, Reggie moved from school to school until the age of sixteen in 1923. Gaps in his learning resulted, which he filled through self-teaching, though he felt painfully inadequate about the extent of his knowledge. He later admitted that he had been a poor student and found his studies tiresome. Over the years, he compensated for his educational lapses by reading voraciously, particularly the encyclopedia. As he became a teenager, he suffered further embarrassment because he was so much taller than the other males his age (at fifteen he was already six feet tall, though weighing only 140 pounds).

Aunt Luisa's ranch was his place of refuge. Reggie took a formal job with her for a year as a breeder of horses, training and exercising jumpers and racers from six in the morning to six at night. Soon, Reggie himself was entering contests, though there is some dispute as to whether he won any cups or medals; still, he became the first "gentleman rider" in the United Kingdom to ride the Grand National course at Aintree without being thrown from his saddle. When Luisa felt her nephew needed more rigorous instruction, she sent him to a nearby riding school.

It was at this school that Reggie met a fellow student named Penelope who invited him to her parents' country house for a party. During the festivities of the evening, another young lady, a seventeen-year-old blonde, lured fifteen-year-old Reggie to the horse stables where he had his first sexual experience. But instead of elation afterwards, he felt degraded, a sense of "postcoitus melancholia," and vowed never to visit that house or those people again.

It was sometime following this dispiriting interlude that Reggie and his family moved yet again. While staying with his mother, stepfather, and oldest sister, Olivia, Reggie attended Radyr, a school he liked, located in Taff Vale, near Cardiff, the capital of Wales. At Radyr, he realized by chance that he had an amazing capacity for memorization. Of course, this achievement was more helpful to him later in life, especially when having to remember long passages of dialogue.

In 1922, Reggie had pressing matters to consider: his ambition to travel by sea—water phobias aside—were stimulated by living next to the rough-and-tumble Tiger Bay docks. He even tried to obtain a berth on a deep-sea vessel, but that plan fell apart. For a while, Reggie left school to work short stints on a potato boat near Bristol—boiling and peeling potatoes—then at a steel mill; when his parents demanded he return to Radyr, he found a part-time job on Fridays and Saturdays as a shipping clerk at a company owned by his mother's relatives. Years later, in 1939, his mother told reporter Max Breen, "Even at a very early age I always felt that he was reaching out for something beyond his grasp—something he might never reach; but that didn't matter so much as the attempt."

Eventually, the clerk position led to sailing with the engineer crews on any one of three ships. Most of the junkets were to the Mediterranean. His main task was to run down with manifests and bills during the loading of the ships. All this activity meant missing classes again, but Reggie was at least starting to live his dream to see the world. To sound more masculine and working class, he renamed himself *Spike*, though to his family he was now formally *Reginald*.

Along the way, he experienced a particularly painful and unfortunate excursion. At a port sinkhole in Alexandria, Egypt, in an impetuous moment, he allowed himself to get tattooed on his upper right arm with the image of a snake twisting through the eye of a skull. (The tattoo artist stabbed Reginald "at the rate of a hundred and fifty times a minute.") He would later lament having the tattoo, but at the time he mainly regretted the faulty, unhygienic procedure itself: Reginald became deathly ill with septicemia and was forced to stop at a port in Spain to be treated. The doctor, named Cantu, told him he was lucky he didn't have to have his arm amputated, and he allowed Reginald to recuperate at his home for several weeks. The only upside to this wretched adventure was that the Cantu family taught him how to speak Spanish, his great-grandmother's native tongue. (Over the next few years, Milland had an innate gift for picking up languages and learned French and German as well.)

According to ancient Welsh culture, St. Patrick was neither Scottish nor English but Welsh, and the venomous snake represented the dangerous world wherein St. Patrick lived—as well as an animal he wanted to banish. The skull was a symbol for the seat of power and the soul, which must be sacrificed by tossing the skeleton's head into a body of water as a gesture of purification. How much young Reginald knew of these myths is uncertain, but he believed having this particular tattoo would be considered a sign of manhood. It was also a "cool" emblem in his teenage mind.

After Reginald's near-death sailing disaster and long trip home, his concerned parents prodded their son to study architecture, which didn't interest him anymore than returning to his formal education. Instead, following his maritime clerk job, he briefly tried his hand as a shooting-gallery attendant and then a bond salesman, both unfulfilling stints. He finally agreed to attend Monks Preparatory School. By the fall, though, with Luisa's encouragement, Reginald applied for a term at King's College in Cardiff, where he was accepted, and he learned typing, shorthand, and bookkeeping. During his winter break in 1924, Reginald returned to the horse farm and more racing.

It was in Galloway in Scotland at a county fair that he was asked to "throw" a race, which angered him tremendously. Since Reginald tried but failed to legitimately win, the man who asked him to cheat was delighted in his loss. Shortly after the race, a furious Reginald punched him several times, which turned the teenager into an instant pariah among the local racing enthusiasts.

In the wake of this unsettling experience, it was Reginald's idea to attend the Cardiff branch of the University of Wales, with the ultimate intention of going to Cambridge. But depression and boredom led to a year of aimless wandering. He joined a cousin named Frank, his father's nephew, for many months of picking up women at dance halls, among other wayward pastimes, like learning how to box. This latter talent came in handy during fight scenes in his movies, where he looked very convincing beating up his opponents (even Clark Gable and John Wayne). Another troubling incident forced Reginald out of his directionless rut, as he later related: "A local dentist, a pillar of the Church, furtively dropped his hand onto my crotch while he was examining a wisdom tooth. . . . In shock and horror, I lashed out and kicked him in the stomach and ran out of there. In my ignorance, I was terrified."

MILITARY SERVICE

During a visit with his father, who had become noticeably withdrawn from the world, Reginald announced he wanted to join the cavalry. His father was not as enthusiastic as he expected him to be, but he recommended the elite Household Cavalry division and gave him the name of Major Ramsey as a contact. Reginald immediately wrote to Ramsey and applied to join the Blues Regiment of the King's Royal Guard. At the time, he felt a sense of upbeat urgency, but later, as an older man, he thought of his application as "the death of [his] innocence" and a betrayal of his Welsh heritage, given that he was aspiring to guard the British royal family.

Nevertheless, the reply from Ramsey was positive. All Reginald needed to do was take a physical exam in London, followed by a trial assessment, and, if accepted, prepare for a four-year stay. During his initial visit, he was asked to ride a horse, his specialty, yet he experienced an unexpected glitch: during the trot test, it was bitingly ironic to Milland that he had so much difficulty maneuvering the uncooperative animal (he called "a big bastard")—but he ultimately passed.

As a serious candidate for the King's Royal Guard, eighteen-year-old Reginald relocated to London in 1925, mainly with the help of his loving Aunt Luisa's gift of $17,000 (the cavalry did not pay for expenses). Now the emphasis of Reginald's education was less on academic studies and more on active tasks. His first eight weeks were especially challenging, a training period to become officially confirmed. He had to learn sword play, rifle discharge, machine-gun shooting and landline signaling, the last while positioned on another uncooperative bastard! He was also responsible for the care and feeding of his own two horses, maintaining their harnesses, and memorizing drills and map locations. Even negotiating his four separate uniforms and all his heavy equipment was a burden, though the seventy-pound uniform provided a certain degree of kinky allure—from the epaulets to the jackboots to the tight breeches, the last of which made him "continually numb from toe to belt."

Reginald's most sickening and frightening episode during this initiation stage was having to watch a corporal demonstrate how to use a sabre by slicing four live sheep in three seconds.

After the eight weeks, Reginald was given another four weeks to work on his deficiencies. George Gillam, an older fellow applicant who shared Reginald's "wicked and subtle sense of humor," was of great help, and they formed a friendship that lasted for the next thirty-five years (until Gillam's death). Once he emerged from this baptism by fire, Reginald had a final test, a demonstration of his many skills in front of the military brass. With great relief, he graduated to full-fledged trooper on what was amusingly called "Passing Out" day.

During his years in the Cavalry, while stationed at the Albany barracks, Lieutenant Mullane realized he was particularly adept at marksmanship, winning many contests against his comrades. Along with these teammates, he won the coveted Queen's Prize at a Bisley match, the annual International Imperial Shooting Competition.

Reginald in the Household Cavalry (1925)

Milland also regained his standing as an expert horseman, sharpened his boxing techniques, and learned to pilot planes, which became a future hobby. The highlight of his regular duties was acting as a posted guard for George V and Mary of Teck, the King and Queen of England, for which he received fawning attention from the crowds whenever he participated in the Changing of the Guards at Buckingham Palace. When not fulfilling his functions for his division, he was making friends and overcoming any shyness he had left. He regularly enjoyed dating the women he met at nightclub parties in London. (His six-foot-one frame, thick, straight black hair, and developing good looks made him a "catch" at twenty.)

In 1927, during a leave from the cavalry, Reginald signed up for a ballroom dance contest in London. His partner was a lovely young woman named Margie Roberts. They danced exceedingly well together considering that they didn't know each other and neither had any professional training. By the end of the night, they took first prize, having no idea that each would become a major movie star the following decade, she by the name Anna

Neagle, or that they would be costars one day (in *Irene* [1940], in which they would dance in Technicolor, and in *Forever and a Day* [1943]).

There were low times as well. At a certain point, a boxing opponent caused the loosening of several of Milland's teeth, necessitating a dental bridge replacement. Years later, Milland reflected about a more serious accident: "One winter's morning, I was escorting the King and the Premier of Afghanistan to the Guild Hall when my horse slipped on the ice. I was thrown and knocked unconscious. When they got me to the hospital, I was bleeding internally." The surgeons mended him, but Milland was laid up for several weeks.

ENTERING BRITISH FILM

So how did a Welsh Cavalry officer become a Hollywood studio contract player? Alfred Reginald John Truscott-Jones never planned for a career in show business, but once he stumbled into it, he was hooked.

The first "stumble" came about during the last half of 1928, when, after nearly four years in the cavalry, he grew restless again. Neither his father nor his stepfather were in the position of helping him financially, so he spent his remaining $2,000 from Aunt Luisa's inheritance gift to be honorably discharged from the army and continue his love of travel. Yet, after a few weeks visiting European cities, he didn't know what to do next.

One day, he called a friend, Estelle Brody, an American actress he had met through dancer Margot St. Leger at a club party during the end of his army tour. He invited Brody to Ciro's where he admitted over dinner that he was practically broke. Brody paid for dinner and promptly arranged for him to come a few days later to London's Elstree Studios commissary. She thought they could talk over lunch about the possibility of a career in the cinema, starting as an extra. The date turned fortuitous, leading to Reginald's unplanned film debut.

In production at Elstree at that time was the very prestigious and expensive *Piccadilly*, one of the last of the British silents. Upon his arrival, while looking for Brody and the location of the commissary, Reginald accidentally walked onto the elaborate nightclub set—designed by the renowned Alfred Junge—central to *Piccadilly*'s story. Taken aback, he witnessed a rehearsal between two of the stars, Anna May Wong and Jameson Thomas, while a crowd of extras in dinner dress sat at their appointed tables. Reginald was overwhelmed by the authentic-looking display.

When he finally found Estelle Brody, she invited *Piccadilly*'s casting director to meet Reginald (later, he only remembered the name of the man was *Mr.*

Allen). During lunch, an impressed Mr. Allen invited him to report in fancy dress to the set the following morning and join the 150 other "nightclub" denizens. Reginald happily agreed and spent the better part of the next few days on set in costume and makeup.

Today, you have to keep your eyes peeled to find Milland in the film, but another actor making his debut was Charles Laughton. The British theater star's comedic "bit" is memorable, playing a diner who informs the wait staff of his dissatisfaction with the food and service. Within a few years, Laughton and Milland were in another movie together, *Payment Deferred* (1932), and nearly two decades later, they were paired again, with both actors in peak form, in *The Big Clock* (1948). But Milland's *Piccadilly* experience was hardly gratifying and brought him no attention at all, despite the fact that E. A. Dupont's melodrama was entertaining and demonstrated the German-born director's skill with expressionistic design. Milland's memory of the episode was mostly shaped by his awe of Anna May Wong, the Chinese American actress who, as part of the narrative, plays a kitchen maid who becomes an overnight star at the Piccadilly Club.

While technically Reginald was making his debut in *Piccadilly*, the film was released twice, first in silent form in February 1929, then again with sound effects added almost a year later. In the meantime, he became involved in a few other films, also produced by British International Pictures (BIP), and some of these were released in between *Piccadilly*'s two separate premieres. In fact, soon after *Piccadilly* wrapped, Reginald appeared as a theater patron, again uncredited, in *Moulin Rouge*, another excellent E. A. Dupont melodrama, set in a different famous nightclub—the titular Parisian landmark. The silent *Moulin Rouge* premiered in May 1928, which predated *Piccadilly*'s release, establishing *Moulin Rouge* as Ray Milland's first cinematic appearance before the public (the sound reboot premiered in January 1929).

On the last day of shooting in the *Piccadilly* nightclub, Reginald was noticed by an American casting director who asked if he would like to appear in a film starring Nigel Barrie being produced in Scotland. He eagerly agreed and boarded a train the next morning. But the film he appeared in was something he later described as forgettable and never released. This disappointment was followed by a fellow struggling actor's suggestion he acquire representation. While still in Scotland, Reginald made his first attempt by visiting an agent named Dan Fish, but Reginald bumbled his way through his interview and was politely shown the door. The next day, he tried again with another agent, Frank Zeitlin, who was similarly unimpressed with Reginald but reluctantly agreed to take him on as a client. After about a month of waiting for a part, he became suddenly in demand.

Zeitlin knew that the producer of *The Informer* needed an expert marksman to replace the man who had been hired to do the job—a German sharpshooter who was injured on the way to the set. Since Reginald had wisely listed shooting skills on his resumé, Zeitlin immediately sent him to Elstree Studios back in London to meet with the German director, Arthur Robison, and several of the crew members. His "audition" took place when Robison and Joe Grossman, the studio manager, told him to fire at a target they had set up at one end of a conference room. Reginald made eleven shots in a row, all of them hitting their marks. Everyone in the office was dazzled by what they saw, and Reginald was told to report to the exterior location to replicate his feat for the camera the next morning.

John Ford's 1935 sound version of *The Informer*, made in Hollywood, is the one most people remember today, but the 1929 silent version is equally worthwhile, or, as historian Jack Lodge has written, a "neglected and excellent" adaptation of Liam O'Flaherty's story about an IRA member (Lars Hanson) who betrays a friend for reward money. Like *Piccadilly* and so many films of this period, sound effects and postdubbed dialogue were added for *The Informer*'s later re-release.

Though Reginald's part in *The Informer* was not initially much bigger than his *Piccadilly* debut, his contribution grew over time when Robison realized he needed someone skilled with a rifle for other scenes. One especially tricky and dangerous stunt involved his shooting a mirror out of the hands of the leading lady, Lya De Putti, which he carried out perfectly.

Reginald stayed on for several weeks, and BIP wanted to use his services further. BIP was simultaneously filming *The Plaything* in Scotland, a comedy starring his friend, Estelle Brody, which meant a return trip "north of the border"; Reginald arrived to play another minor bit, though an actual character in a party scene. He finished the job quickly and got back to the set of *The Informer* in London.

By the time *The Plaything* was released, Reginald chose to be billed as Spike Mullane. The other significance of *The Plaything* was that its director, Castleton Knight, would soon champion Reginald as a leading man.

SHORT-LIVED STARDOM

Once again, the case of a performer's accident led to Reginald's next role, which was comparatively plum-sized in a partial talkie. During a break in *The Informer* production, Reginald was approached by the casting director, Mr. Allen, who told him that another movie on the lot, *The Flying Scotsman*,

The Flying Scotsman (1929)

needed a young male lead—immediately! Apparently, the actor who was set to play the part, Cyril McLaglen, the brother of Victor McLaglen, broke his leg on his way to the studio. Reginald met with the producer, Ed Newman, and the director, Castleton Knight, and they both agreed to hire Reginald if he would consent to a screen test.

He was not even sure what a screen test entailed, thinking it might involve urinating into a bottle, but he cooperated fully. His assignment was to smear dirt on his face and walk through a door while swearing. Reginald's days in the cavalry trained him well for the swearing part, so his casting was secured, which meant leaving *The Informer*'s director without his marksman.

For the next eight weeks in early 1929, Reginald played Jim, a cocky Scottish train stoker who replaces a recently dismissed older engineer, Crow (Alec Hurley). The action takes place on the actual train called the Flying Scotsman, not a set. Before his first ride on the famous locomotive, Jim meets and falls for a young lady, Joan (Pauline Lord), not realizing she is the daughter of the very conductor, Bob (Moore Marriott), he is about to assist.

The genuinely exciting, edge-of-your-seat climax depicts how Joan saves her father and boyfriend from a vengeful plot by Crow, and even manages to save the train itself by pulling the correct railway switches to avert a crash.

As the central figure of so many scenes, Reginald may have felt ill at ease in front of the camera, but director Knight was patient and tried to help the neophyte actor. Thus, Reginald's nerves never showed, and *The Flying Scotsman* emerged as both a superior film and the first showcase of his talents.

Even today, *The Flying Scotsman* is not harmed by what can only be called gratuitous and poorly recorded dialogue half-way through. The climax is truly a tour de force for everyone involved: it is shot entirely in or on the fast-moving train by cinematographer Theodor Sparkuhl, and the actors do their own fights and stunts. Knight, a specialist in documentaries, details the nature of train travel from the point of view of the engineers, and A. C. Hammond's editing is seamless. It is no surprise that Warner Bros. chose this BIP film over several others to distribute in America.

During the making of *The Flying Scotsman*, Alfred Reginald John Truscott-Jones officially became Ray Milland or, more accurately, a third-billed "Raymond Milland." When producer Newman asked how he wanted to be listed in the credits, having already rejected the idea of using *Mullane* or *Truscott-Jones*, Reginald thought awhile about it, then realized he greatly missed the homeland of his youth, or the mill lands; thus, he came up with *Milland*.

For his first name, Reginald wanted to use *Jack*, the informal, medieval variation of his middle name, *John*: hence, Jack Milland. Newman and his assistant dismissed *Jack* by claiming that in Hollywood, "only dogs are called Jack," so they thought of Raymond to replace Reginald, and he agreed to it (or, in a separate recollection, Milland himself picked it from a list of choices). Raymond wasn't Reginald's first choice, but if he couldn't be Jack, he wanted to retain the initial of his given name because his mother had engraved his luggage with a large *R*. Since he still preferred *Jack* to *Raymond*, he decided at this point that only his best friends would call him *Jack*—and that arrangement stuck for the rest of his life.

In 2011, thanks to its status as the first British "talkie," *The Flying Scotsman* was digitally restored at great expense and shown for the first time in many years at the Glasgow Film Festival (a DVD release followed). Bob Flynn wrote in the *Times of London*, "Historians regard the film as one of the most remarkable achievements of the pre-war British movie industry. Most films of the era were shot in studios, but Milland's screen debut [sic] was made at Waverley Station in Edinburgh, London's King's Cross and on the train itself."

At the time of the 1930 sound release, the reviews were slightly more muted, but a few publications singled out Milland: *Kinematograph Weekly* thought *The Flying Scotsman* was "pleasant entertainment," while "Raymond Milland is quite one of the most attractive juveniles we have seen on the English screen; moreover he is a very good actor."

The director, Castleton Knight, "a very kind and understanding man," according to Milland, thought well enough of this new face to suggest BIP sign him for a six-month contract. He was paid twenty pounds a week for twenty-four weeks, during which time he made only one more feature. When he wasn't working, Milland enjoyed going to the movies and attending tea dances at the Savoy Hotel. Milland later reflected, "Life was just a bowl of cherries in the early days.... But it all happened by luck, and I was just in there at the right place and at the right time."

Knight's *The Lady from the Sea* (a.k.a. *Goodwin Sands*) gave Milland another starring role (and again third billing) in his fourth film. The taste of stardom was elusive, however, since it would be many more years before Milland would again have a chance to be a leading man. But in this low-budget "quota quickie" (at a mere fifty-six minutes), Milland seized most of the attention.

Joe Grossman's original story concerns a seemingly happy young couple, Tom and Rose (Milland and Eugenie Amami), whose engagement is halted after Tom, a fisherman, rescues a beautiful French woman, Claire (Mona Goya), from a shipwreck at Goodwin Sands, off the east coast of England. Soon, Tom falls for Claire, which naturally upsets Rose, so his brother, Dick (Bruce Gordon), tries to reason with him. But during their heated exchange in a cave-like dwelling, an accident occurs, and Dick is killed. Tom leaves his family home in disgrace but later tries to redeem himself by working on a rescue lifeboat. He finally reunites with Rose and his family.

The original silent version of *The Lady from the Sea* is a lost movie. What exists today is a crisp print of the postsynched sound "upgrade," created by the same filmmakers both on location off the Deal coast in Kent and in Elstree's London studio. Milland dismissed *The Lady from the Sea* in his autobiography, saying he never saw the finished film and doubted (incorrectly) that it was ever released.

But Milland is unfair to the picture. What makes *The Lady from the Sea* rewarding today is its look. More so than with *The Flying Scotsman*, cinematographer Theodor Sparkuhl sets up some beautiful compositions—especially during the exterior scenes on the shore—a link to the German Expressionist movement of which Sparkhul was part. (After he emigrated to Hollywood, he worked with Milland five more times.) Otherwise, most of the actors seem stiff, which is either because they were working around the primitive sound equipment or because on one of the days (May 29, 1929), the Duke and Duchess of York visited the set, which was no doubt distracting, if not intimidating.

When they weren't in front of the cameras, Milland and Mexican-born French actress Goya had a tense relationship. Milland was pleased with the

The Lady from the Sea (1929), with Mona Goya

long pauses between takes, giving him the excuse to leave the set. On one such occasion at Elstree, he visited the next-door production of *Blackmail* and met Alfred Hitchcock for the first time. It was a brief introduction, but it might have planted a seed in Hitchcock's mind. A full twenty-four years later, the two worked together on *Dial M for Murder*.

As with *The Flying Scotsman*, it is somewhat remarkable to see Milland as a young man (only twenty-two when the film was shot): tall, gangly, and downright skinny! Unfortunately, his performance this time is uneven, hampered by the added dialogue insertions.

Unlike *The Flying Scotsman*, *The Lady from the Sea* was barely covered by the press and not widely distributed.

THEATRICAL FIASCOS

Once Milland completed his back-to-back leads in *The Flying Scotsman* and *The Lady from the Sea*, he decided he needed more training or would be forever known for what he considered his poor performances. An actress friend, Norah Howard, recommended he join a new theatrical touring company sponsored by Bobby Page, the club owner. Somewhat easily, Milland won the second lead in the perennial murder mystery *The Woman in Room 13*, written by Sam Shipman, Max Marcin, and Percival Wilde.

After three weeks of rehearsal in London, the company traveled to Southport in Lancashire for the opening. Everything seemed fine, including a relatively smooth first night performance. But on the second night Milland tried to calm his nerves with a couple of drinks and unintentionally turned the mystery-drama into a slapstick mess: early on, during a stage exit, he tripped, fell face down, and lost his bridge. When he heard the laughter from the audience, he cringed. Later, he tried to repair his missing bridge backstage with a temporary one, but during the play's climax, when he uttered his final line, he accidentally spit out the makeshift mouthpiece across the stage. At this point, the audience was roaring uncontrollably, as were most of Milland's castmates. After touring five more towns over two week's time, the producers fired Milland three weeks before the end of the run, though he stayed on a little longer until a replacement could be found.

Milland's next attempt to improve his acting was to hire a drama coach in London. Kate Rorke had respected credentials, but she was an imperious older woman who made Milland nervous. His recital of a Richard of Gloucester soliloquy from Shakespeare's *Richard III* was so disastrous, she recommended he go back into the military. ("You better get mounted again," was her farewell piece of advice.) A very discouraged twenty-three-year-old Milland told Norah Howard he was thinking of giving up the profession, but she talked him out of it.

Milland's only remaining theater training was in the dance classes at the Max Rivers School of Dance. During one lesson, as he was starting to learn soft-shoe and tap dancing, the famous French impresario André Charlot stopped by the rehearsal hall. Not knowing who Charlot was, Milland made the blunder of dismissing him from the room before learning that Max Rivers had invited Charlot to the school to look for new dancers. Rivers had Milland particularly in mind to be cast in the annual musical show *Charlot's Revue*, the 1930 edition starring Beatrice Lillie. The dance master quickly clarified the misunderstanding, and Charlot charitably offered Milland a second chance, inviting him to audition the next morning at the Hippodrome Theatre.

Though feeling foolish about his faux pas, Milland showed up to do a passable job of singing and dancing, and he was offered a contract to play the "leading juvenile." The next thing he knew, Milland was having a celebratory lunch at the Carlton Hotel with Norah, her fiancé, Stuart Rodney Ross, a young actor (and later star) named Louis Hayward, playwright Noël Coward, and, of course, Monsieur Charlot.

Unexpectedly, during the Carlton lunch, a man from another table walked over to greet the fabled theater celebrities but focused most of his attention on the lesser-known Milland. He had just seen *The Flying Scotsman*, liked him in it, and asked Milland to call him the next day. The man was

Metro-Goldwyn-Mayer (MGM) producer and talent scout J. Robert Rubin, later a vice president at the company. The following morning, Rubin invited Milland to sign with the famed Hollywood studio for a short-term (nine-month) contract at $175 per week, a considerable amount more than his British International income or what Charlot was offering. Milland felt torn but accepted Rubin's offer. The esteemed author and MGM screenwriter Anita Loos (*Gentlemen Prefer Blondes*) was asked to negotiate the termination of his *Charlot's Revue* contract.

Within two weeks of signing with MGM, on July 28, 1930, Milland cheerfully began his first-class trip on the SS *Majestic* to New York. After a few days, he arrived in Manhattan, and a studio representative treated him to some Broadway plays, an evening at the famed Central Park Casino, a visit to the Algonquin Round Table (where he met and immediately befriended Robert Benchley), and a final night on the town—this time at the Cotton Club in Harlem. From New York, which the increasingly jaded Milland found depressing in its "dinginess of squalor," he boarded the *Twentieth Century Ltd.* and traveled cross-country to MGM, the mecca of movie entertainment.

Though many more unforeseen gaffes and disappointments lay ahead, Ray Milland was excited about his latest adventure.

CHAPTER 2

FALSE STARTS, TRUE ROMANCE (1930–1936)

ONCE RAY MILLAND STEPPED OFF THE CROSS-COUNTRY TRAIN FROM NEW York and arrived in Hollywood on August 17, 1930, he was on yet another expedition, one that offered the potential rewards of fame and money as part of the bargain.

Hollywood in 1930 was just starting to feel the pinch of the Great Depression, meaning that the so-called Dream Factory would have to adjust to cost-cutting measures over the next decade but still try to deliver expensive spectacles to a movie-hungry public. One ever-lasting, simultaneous change was that all films were shot with sound. Silent picture-making was halted, and mastering the technique of sound recording, not to mention exhibiting "talkies" in theaters, proved a great challenge.

Ray Milland was enthusiastic but nervous about his uncertain future. His contract with MGM was a short-term one with no guarantees that he would advance beyond bit player or that his starting salary would ever increase. Ominously, too, the studio had issued him a round-trip ticket.

California, from its sunny weather to its extroverted citizenry, offered quite a contrast to Wales or London. Yet one particular area would eventually remind him of home: according to David Niven, Beverly Hills was welcoming to those from "across the pond." Niven, a younger debonair émigré, observed,

> [The suburb] had gone against the haphazard planning of Greater Los Angeles, and when the Rodeo Land and Water Company decided to develop its gently sloping acreage, it had the great good taste and foresight to send for an expert from Kew Gardens, London, who planted a different species of tree for every street.... A home in Beverly Hills

was the status symbol of success in the prewar motion-picture industry, and the area boasted more private swimming pools and detectives to the square mile than anywhere else in the world.

Milland was greeted at that train station by MGM publicity flack Jerrold Asher, who escorted him to the Ambassador Hotel for a week's stay. During the seven-day whirlwind, MGM talent scout Robert Lisman gave Milland a tour of Hollywood, highlighted by a Greta Garbo movie premiere and dinner at the Brown Derby. Milland knew his brief taste of Ambassador luxury would end as soon as he could find an affordable place to live, which had to be close enough for him to commute to the studio. With Asher's help, Milland rented a walk-up apartment on busy Sunset Boulevard, off Laurel Avenue, for forty dollars per month. (He also bought a used car.) It may have been a far cry from glamorous Beverly Hills, but at least Milland could aspire to dwell in that coveted nearby pasture.

MGM

As he was promised, Milland officially became a working contract player at MGM, the "Tiffany of the Studios," which was known for having "More Stars Than There Are in Heaven," its unofficial motto. Indeed, MGM had a very large stable of stars, and Milland arrived at the studio after the release of *The Hollywood Revue of 1929*, a classy vaudevillesque showcase for Norma Shearer, Joan Crawford, Buster Keaton, Lionel Barrymore, Marion Davies, John Gilbert, and Laurel and Hardy, among others.

With so little stage or screen experience, Milland was slightly overwhelmed by both the star power and the studio's vast expanse, covering, as it did, a large portion of Culver City. Historian John Baxter once described the place:

> Greatest of all the studios was Metro-Goldwyn-Mayer. It was the richest, the biggest, the most productive. Tied to the extensive theatre chain of Marcus Loew, it had access to the largest film outlet in the world, while its financial associations with the Chase National Bank gave it capital so extensive that no production, however elaborate, was a risk. At its peak, the twenty-two stages of Metro and its hundred acre back-lot of standing sets produced forty-two feature films a year, the biggest output of any studio in the history of the cinema.

Actress Marsha Hunt's experiences concur with Baxter's claims. (Hunt went from Paramount to MGM, whereas Milland went from MGM to Paramount, and she appeared in two Milland movies along the way.) At 104, Hunt remembered in an interview that "both studios were friendly and helpful to me, generous and kind, [yet] all [my] Paramount impressions were 'first' ones,'" while "Metro was the colossus. . . . It was bigger and less personal. [Paramount] was busy, but Metro was [the best]."

Despite MGM's fabled reputation, Ray Milland felt let down once he saw the building interiors up close for the first time. MGM's official motto was "Ars gratia artis," Latin for "Art for Art's Sake," which was emblazoned on its roaring Leo the Lion logo, but Milland's mostly self-taught knowledge of architecture and fine art clashed with a disheartening discovery. He would later write that the building structure looked "rather tacky and broken down," and much of it was "painted the color of a dead mouse."

Nevertheless, Milland was determined to do well at the most illustrious of the major studios, and he learned quickly who was really in charge. According to Thomas Schatz, the all-powerful studio cofounder, Louis B. Mayer, was a mere figurehead who spent weeks, sometimes months, away from MGM (a.k.a. Metro). The true driving forces were Eddie Mannix, Mayer's thuggish chief lieutenant, and Irving Thalberg, the hands-on "Boy Wonder" producer-turned-head-of-production.

Milland had a persistent problem from the start: he was overshadowed by Robert Montgomery, another contract player who had already caught on with the public in the kind of roles Milland could just as easily have handled had he felt more confident (*The Flying Scotsman* proved he had the talent). Like Milland, Montgomery was a tall, dark, and handsome type, with a gentlemanly quality that served him well playing patrician characters (unlike the sexier but more proletarian newcomer Clark Gable). Milland felt additionally "dime a dozen" since other studios boasted their own British or pseudo-British matinée idols, like Sam Goldwyn's Ronald Colman and Warner Bros.' Douglas Fairbanks Jr., who was actually born in New York but a dedicated Anglophile with a continental accent.

Robert Montgomery himself was born into privilege in New York in 1904, and he was near the same age as the slightly younger Welshman, but he had the advantage of greater stage experience and a much cockier attitude. At the point Milland started at MGM, Montgomery had already amassed a fan base.

By contrast, Ray Milland never achieved stardom at MGM, nor did he even get a chance as a leading man. If anything, what he made on loan-out to other studios gave him much more to do than any of his MGM assignments.

Apart from Milland committing his own series of missteps, it is inarguable that Metro's upper management always had more invested in the rise of Robert Montgomery.

Thus, Milland started at the lowest tier possible. His earliest chore for the studio was in the screen-test department, feeding lines—with his back to the camera—to test subjects, often fellow newcomers. One of the first of these tests was directed by a young man named Mitchell Leisen, Cecil B. DeMille's principal art director. The test was arranged by DeMille himself, not to evaluate the actors but to see if Leisen was filmmaker material. According to Milland, both he as actor and Leisen as director were nervous but finally calmed down and shot a scene chosen from DeMille's upcoming 1931 version of *The Squaw Man*. That day, neither Milland nor Leisen could possibly have predicted that within the decade Leisen would be directing Milland in eight films during their Paramount years (plus five episodes of Milland's *Markham* TV series in the late '50s). Milland would also later call Leisen his favorite director.

One of Milland's other apprenticeship requirements was to take classes with the house drama coach. Like his experience with the predatory college dentist, he felt uneasy around this male instructor, who made no secret of his sexual attraction to his new pupil. For the most part, Milland managed to find ways to avoid these sessions.

Several weeks went by before Milland was given a chance at an on-screen role, albeit an uncredited one. *Way for a Sailor* (1930) was built around John Gilbert, the silent-screen heartthrob who was having a difficult time transitioning to sound films.

Directed by Sam Wood, *Way for a Sailor* was a typically mediocre Gilbert movie at this stage: the story centered around a sailor who is broke, just out of jail, and unkempt in appearance. Released towards the end of the year, the film was mostly panned: Richard Watts Jr. in the *New York Herald Tribune* called it "a tedious attempt to provide a roystering comedy."

Ray Milland made his inauspicious MGM debut as a Canadian ship's officer who speaks briefly with the heroine (Leila Hyams). He was on-screen for mere seconds and had to wear a false mustache.

Milland's next film, *Passion Flower*, directed by William C. DeMille, was somewhat better, though Cecil B. DeMille's older brother was uncomfortable with the new sound apparatus and soon became strictly a writer-producer.

Likewise released late in 1930, *Passion Flower* concerns a love triangle between two wealthy cousins (Kay Johnson and Kay Francis) and a handsome but rough-hewn chauffeur (Charles Bickford). Ray Milland was not credited but had a memorable bit playing an inebriated party guest who is searching for his missing hat. Made while Prohibition was still in effect (1920–1933), this marked Milland's first of many "drunk" scenes in films leading up to *The Lost Weekend* fifteen years later.

Again, Milland was ignored by the critics, but the film was given a slightly better reception than *Way for a Sailor* and made money for the studio. *Variety* asserted that *Passion Flower* "has so many good points that it's something of a problem to figure out how it resulted so indifferently."

The Bachelor Father, a January 1931 release, at last gave Ray Milland his first MGM credit—and it was Milland's own idea to slash the name *Raymond* to *Ray* for the occasion. It also afforded him a much larger role than his first two efforts. Shot by the reliable Robert Z. Leonard, the film was produced by William Randolph Hearst and Marion Davies through their independent Cosmopolitan Pictures, which had an arrangement with MGM to distribute its films.

In this star vehicle, Davies plays one of three grown children who gather to be with their British patriarch (C. Aubrey Smith) at his Surrey manor house. They may or may not be "illegitimate," but each one hopes to inherit wealth from their "bachelor father." Though the industry's new watchdog, the Production Code Administration (PCA), developed by the Motion Picture Producers and Distributors of America (MPPDA), was not yet in full effect, the PCA censors demanded that dialogue be added to make it clear that the bachelor father did not have his children out of wedlock but, rather, was married three different times.

Fourth-billed Milland portrays Geoffrey, one of the other three children (Nina Quartero is the third). His presence is conspicuous in the early scenes when the children meet their father for the first time. In a lively moment, Milland plays the piano while Davies tap dances and Quartero sings. Here and elsewhere, Milland shows hints of the comic timing he would perfect over the years, although he and Quartero have less camera time as the story proceeds.

For whatever reason, Milland's handsome facial features were obscured in *The Bachelor Father*. While nicely dressed in a double-breasted suit, he looks as if he is wearing lipstick and white face powder. In his memoirs, under a still photo, Milland joked about his peculiar appearance, writing in the caption, "I'm the girl on the right." (It is possible his character was meant to be gay or queer.)

At least the experience was enjoyable for Milland, who made friends with Davies and was able to unwind during a two-week rehearsal sojourn at Hearst and Davies's famous mansion in San Simeon. As it turned out, there was more partying than rehearsing during Milland's stay at "the Camelot of California," where more than two dozen guests who had nothing to do with

Ray Milland in the early 1930s

The Bachelor Father reveled in the luxurious surroundings. Later, Milland was invited back for other retreats and ended up adoring Davies, but he always thought of Hearst as "strange and forbidding." In her memoirs, Davies wrote, "Milland used to talk about England and Ireland. He was very pleasant," then added cryptically, "We never had any trouble at all."

The Bachelor Father was shot in twenty-two days, and Milland got along well with "Pop" Leonard, whom he considered "well-mannered and patient." The reviews were mostly positive, and more than one critic pointed out the new actor. In the *Hollywood Daily Citizen*, Marjorie Ross wrote, "[Milland] gives an effective portrayal."

Just as *The Bachelor Father* reached the screen, Milland was called upon by his MGM bosses to report to the set of *Strangers May Kiss*, directed by journeyman George Fitzmaurice throughout January 1931 and released in early April. Whatever complaints MPPDA president Will Hays had about *The Bachelor Father* paled next to this new picture, a melodrama based on a racy Ursula Parrott novel.

A p.r. official aligned with Hays wrote in a memo to MGM, "[I]t would be difficult for me to exaggerate my revulsion at this picture and my sense of horror that our present setup is permitting product of this type to go through . . . [*Strangers May Kiss*] is a reflection of the initiatory stages of the degeneration of a people. It embodies and personifies the warped moral sense which has disintegrated every previous civilized nation."

Milland's role is insignificant. Late in the story, in a Spanish casino, the unbilled Milland plays a friend of Robert Montgomery's Steve, the one-time fiancé of Norma Shearer's Lisabeth. Milland's only function is to reintroduce these characters to each other, though the flirtatious Lisabeth prefers her new lover (Neil Hamilton). The single interesting thing about Milland's arrival is that for the few moments he stands side by side with Montgomery, they look as though they could be brothers. It is even possible to imagine Milland playing Steve, but he vanishes before we get to know his character at all.

Audiences loved *Strangers May Kiss*, the critics were approving, and Milland was lost in the mix.

For most of March and April, Milland worked on *Just a Gigolo*, released in early June. The romantic comedy concerned a wealthy playboy (William Haines) who makes a bet with his uncle and benefactor (C. Aubrey Smith again) to test the virtue of a young heiress (Irene Purcell).

Briskly directed by Jack Conway, the sixty-six-minute feature was one of the best in which Milland appeared at MGM. The screenplay had to be altered due to Hays Office objections, yet the technical aspects were first rate. (*Just a Gigolo* was still banned in a few regions, including Ireland, Nova Scotia, and British Columbia.)

Once more, Milland was not billed, showing up briefly in several scenes as "Freddie," one of the heroine's many male admirers. The reviews were mixed, but the *Hollywood Reporter* called it "light, sophisticated, clever entertainment."

Milland's next opportunity to be seen in an important film turned into an outright fiasco, preventing him from any real chance of advancement at MGM. In late April 1931, Milland was assigned to *Son of India*, a Ramon Novarro epic directed by Belgian-born auteur Jacques Feyder. It was only another bit part, but Milland fouled up his single moment in this large-scale production. As Milland tells it, he was selected to play a British soldier in a scene set in a maharaja's palace ballroom. Surrounded by two hundred extras, he was required to dance with the leading lady (Madge Evans), walk her to a nearby bar, and start flirting with her. But Milland was so nervous during a rehearsal run-through, he barely made it to the bar before Feyder yelled for everyone to stop. Feyder proceeded to loudly upbraid Milland in front of the entire cast and crew, asking, "What clown in the casting office had been responsible for foisting on [me] such a cretinous imbecile?"

Unexpectedly, breaking through a painfully long silence on the gigantic soundstage, supporting player Marjorie Rambeau came to Milland's defense, berating Feyder to the roaring approval of the extras. Milland chose to slip away to his apartment after the incident, feeling as though he could murder Jacques Feyder but also aware he would be replaced on *Son of India*. The next day, Milland received a visit at his flat from casting director Benny Thau's assistant, who reassured him that Feyder was notorious for such unpleasant outbursts; further, Milland was told not to worry about it and take a week's vacation before coming back to the studio. He spent much of the next several days near the beach, riding horses at the Riviera Stables.

When Milland's respite ended, he returned to the lot and met with Benny Thau himself. Thau advised him to become "more American" as a way to open up casting opportunities, and he recommended getting help from the head drama coach. Milland reluctantly had to explain to Thau about his discomfort around the lecherous mentor, so with Thau's permission, he picked his own private tutor.

Milland made the mistake of choosing a friendly acquaintance named Bernadette Conklin to train him in American diction and slang. A few weeks later, Milland and contract player Mary Carlisle were given a dramatic scene to perform live for Thau and several executives. Shortly after the actors started, the staid "suits" bursted out laughing. Milland's American accent was almost unintelligible, and the results were unintentionally hilarious. It turns out that Conklin hailed from Pine Apple, Alabama, and had taught him how to converse in a deep southern dialect. He wasn't fired, but following this latest humiliation, Milland decided to listen carefully to actors like Ronald Colman and Walter Huston as the best way to modulate his British intonation and unlearn his Alabama cadence. (In his memoirs, Milland admits to inventing the Bernadette Conklin name to protect the identity of the young woman who, years later, he saw working in a Panama bordello.)

Despite all the blunders, MGM gave Milland another chance by loaning him to Warner Bros. during May and June 1931 for *Bought!*, a downbeat melodrama released in August.

Thankfully, with *Bought!*, Milland captured some of the spotlight in an A picture and secured fifth billing (back to Raymond Milland). The star attraction was Constance Bennett, earning a then-record $30,000 a week for this one film. Another sign of *Bought!*'s prominence was behind the camera: Archie Mayo as director and Ray June as cinematographer.

Bought! focuses on Stephanie (Bennett), who pulls herself out of poverty by winning a job as a fashion model and landing in the company of Newport society. She falls for the playboy Charles Carter Jr. (Milland), and they eventually plan to marry. But Charles calls off the wedding when he discovers Stephanie's parents were never married. Branding Charles and his crowd as snobs, she returns to Nick (Ben Lyon), a former boyfriend.

Milland's role is quite substantive. Initially, we see him in his ritzy apartment wearing well-tailored attire and holding a cocktail shaker. This would become Ray Milland's most indelible image for the next several years in a variety of pictures. His other frequent "look," appearing in white tie and tails, occurs in *Bought!* during a nightclub sequence. Later in the decade, his characters would be less pompous, but even here he is quite appealing, so it is understandable that Stephanie would overlook Charles's flaws.

Bought! would give audiences the first real inkling of Ray Milland's charm and talent. Perhaps inadvertently, it also introduced his career-long darker side: in one particularly disturbing scene, out of camera range, Charles sexually assaults Stephanie.

Bought! made money, but the reviews were mixed and very few mentioned Milland. Only Jimmy Starr in the *Los Angeles Evening Express* showed insight: "A new idea in villains has been introduced. It isn't a new gesture, but Raymond Milland, unknown to screen fans, puts what might have been the typical movie villain in a new light, and the result is most gratifying."

Warner Bros. immediately asked to borrow Milland again from Metro. This time it was for *Blonde Crazy*, his only collaboration with James Cagney, who was quickly becoming one of Warner's biggest stars. Milland had another key supporting role and was again billed fifth. Shot in June 1931, it was released in November, making the overlapping shooting and release schedules a confusing matter the actor would have to get used to over the years.

Unlike *Bought!*, *Blonde Crazy* was more typical of early pre-Code Warner's product—fast-paced comedies and dramas with lots of action. During this period, Cagney made a string of these films. It was one of six he headlined in 1931 alone (with *The Public Enemy* his break-out hit). In the story, Cagney and Joan Blondell play con artists who are swindled by one of their marks (Louis Calhern). Milland shows up late in the story as Joe, a gallant stockbroker whom Blondell's character marries once rejected by Cagney's unreformed rake. Joe, then, turns out to be a scoundrel himself!

Milland did not enjoy his experience at Warner's this time. Director Roy Del Ruth was a taskmaster intent on finishing his films on schedule. Dorothy Kingsley, a screenwriter who worked with Del Ruth, remembered that "Del Ruth would really talk to you a lot, and would often say, 'That stinks!' He really drilled you until he got something he liked."

Right from the start, Del Ruth was incensed by how fast-paced Cagney and Milland were speaking in their joint scene. During rehearsals, what should have lasted three minutes was completed in one. Del Ruth told the actors to practice at home, not on his time, calling them "a couple of goddam woodpeckers." This altercation brought about an unlikely friendship between Milland and Cagney, though they bonded over boats, not show business. The two shared a mutual love of watercraft but rarely traveled together on any. Apparently, Cagney would become seasick before getting out of the harbor!

Despite Del Ruth's contempt for his actors, *Blonde Crazy* was finally completed. Mordaunt Hall of the *New York Times* called it "lively and cleverly acted." Only a few critics mentioned Ray Milland, and then only in passing.

On another loan-out, this time to Fox Studios, Milland was given his first Hollywood "hero" role, though far from the lead. *Ambassador Bill*, shot in August and September 1931 and released in November, was a showcase for comic Will Rogers.

Rogers had already made the similar *The Truthful Liar* in 1924, in which he played an American ambassador to a mythical kingdom, trying to calm the roiling discontent among the masses. By 1931, such a movie subject was even more topical given the growing unrest in Europe. But *Ambassador Bill* was meant to be purely comedic in its tone; sadly, despite the presence of an individual many at the time considered the greatest American humorist since Mark Twain, the political jokes were mild at best.

Milland is the king of a Balkan country, Sylvania. The story starts with his highness abdicating his title because he mistakenly believes the queen (Marguerite Churchill) has been unfaithful. Thus, their young son (Tad Alexander) becomes the de facto king. When Rogers's Bill Harper of Oklahoma arrives, he uses his diplomatic skills on the eight-year-old boy but soon realizes that a palace coup is afoot.

Apart from wearing another fake mustache (as he did in *Way for a Sailor*), Milland looks more self-assured than he had in any prior film. The opening takes place in a cockpit and finds Milland as a pilot incognito, transporting Ambassador Bill to his destination. This lighthearted sketch is slightly morbid in retrospect, given that Rogers would die in a plane crash in 1935. In any case, it is the first of Milland's many aviator roles. A later scene with Marguerite Churchill reveals Milland in romantic mode, close-ups included, though he is a little stiff in the clinches. Milland appears just right in the finale, wearing his royal regalia (which resembles his cavalry uniform), his highness having been restored to the throne.

Ambassador Bill comes across today like a family-friendly picture created for the post-Code era. In fact, when the Fox Film Corporation merged with Twentieth Century, the new outfit rereleased it in 1936, capitalizing on both the news surrounding Rogers's sudden death and Milland's growing ascendancy as a box-office attraction. But in 1931, *Variety* found the "wilting yarn" wanting and called *Ambassador Bill* a "hokum piece."

Towards the end of 1931, following the releases of *Blonde Crazy* and *Ambassador Bill*, Milland briefly returned to the United Kingdom, his MGM salary suspended. Whether it was due to homesickness or disillusionment about his Hollywood career, he thought he would start over, perhaps in another line of work. He took the long ocean voyage back to London, where he could only find jobs pitching products in filmed advertisements. But acting was something he had come to appreciate, and during his stay in England, he chose to continue in Hollywood: "I came back the cheapest possible way. On a passenger freighter through the Panama Canal. The [ad] company let me keep the modern wardrobe I'd used in the commercials, and I arrived back with $150 in my pocket."

By the time he returned, however, Metro had nothing planned for him to do, so, as he put it, "For months I made a living playing bridge and practically starved," barely able to afford his Sunset Boulevard apartment rent. It was a card game, indirectly, that led to Ray Milland falling in love with the woman who would become his wife.

"MAL"

In December 1931, a resettled Milland was invited to a brunch and bridge garden party at the Beverly Hills home of millionaire J. J. Murdock. During the busy and crowded gathering, Milland was in the middle of a bridge coup when he was introduced to a beautiful, dark-haired young woman. The meeting was brief, and he couldn't hear her name, but he was stunned by her looks and presence. He noticed two particularly striking features: at five feet nine and one-half inches, she was close to his height, and though college age, she had a grey streak in her hair. Later that morning, he saw her again, moving quickly about at a distance. After he left the party, he plotted to reunite under more favorable circumstances.

By providence it seemed, Milland didn't need to plot at all. Janet MacLeod, his socialite friend who had introduced him to the mesmerizing woman, phoned the next week. She invited him to a party at a different Hollywood residence, this time only a block away from Milland's apartment. At first, he was hesitant to attend yet another noisy Sunday brunch, but he finally acquiesced. Either by chance or someone's design, the house turned out to be the elusive beauty's family home. Milland could hardly believe he was getting a second chance to reacquaint himself so soon and so easily.

He learned her name was Malvina Muriel Weber, a twenty-two-year-old student at the University of Southern California, who was taking courses to be an elementary school teacher. She gave the official house tour, and he also got to meet her entire family, originally hailing from the South Side of Chicago—her sister, her brother and his wife, and her mother and father, the last of whom he found very intimidating. (Milland later learned Papa Weber was an influential theatrical agent, yet he never helped Milland or signed him as a client.) It was a nervous but exciting morning that ended with a tentative plan between Ray and Mal, as she liked to be called, to meet again.

What Milland did not expect was that it would take two weeks before Mal agreed to a specific rendezvous—a night at the movies. In preparation, he rented a fancy car meant to impress her, but when he arrived at her door, he was taken aback to discover they would be joined by her older brother, Herbert, and a family friend named Eddie. The foursome watched the movie with poor Ray not even permitted to sit next to his date! The courtship continued for a while this way before Mal allowed Ray to date her without chaperones. Years later, Mal recalled these early days: "A friend introduced me to this very polite, quiet Englishman. He was mannerly and soft-spoken—not at all like the boys I'd been going out with. I remember how impressed I was by the fact that he actually listened to what I had to say. And I was really impressed by the wealth of knowledge he had stored in his head."

Back at work, Milland was loaned out again to Warner Bros., which needed a sensitive gentleman-type for *The Man Who Played God,* shot in December 1931 and released in February 1932. This "prestige" film starred distinguished British actor George Arliss as a concert pianist who loses his hearing. By reading the lips of the people sitting in the park below his penthouse, the man discovers how to become a useful part of society as an anonymous philanthropist. Milland was cast as one of the people whose life the pianist changes.

Directed by John G. Adolfi, *The Man Who Played God* was the most popular of Arliss's string of films for Warner Bros. as well as one of the most financially successful releases for the studio in 1931 and '32.

Through the urging of Arliss, a young Bette Davis was cast as the pianist's protégé-fiancée. Ray Milland later recalled that "[Davis] was a very pretty and pleasant creature. . . . No sign of her later arrogance and imperiousness." Milland greatly admired Arliss, especially the veteran's disciplined and professional approach to his craft, though he shared no scenes with either Arliss or Davis.

Unbilled, Milland has a memorable vignette as Eddie, the male half of a desperate couple (Dorothy Libaire is his wife, Jenny). *The Man Who Played God* illustrates an early example of how Milland could appear both elegant and vulnerable, even close to suicidal, a rare combination not seen in his slicker debonair peers (e.g. Robert Montgomery and William Powell).

Just before the release of *The Man Who Played God*, Mal accompanied Ray to begin the pro forma step of petitioning for him to become a naturalized citizen. After ringing in the New Year, the couple went to the Los Angeles courthouse—joined by the studio's J. Robert Rubin as a signing witness—and filled out the necessary paperwork. Oddly, Milland cut down and transposed his birth name on the form to *Reginald Alfred Jones* and altered his stage name yet again to *Raymond Alton Milland*.

As for *The Man Who Played God*, the *Hollywood Reporter* summarized the overall critical reaction: "It is very clean, very wholesome, and rather dull." Regrettably, the reviewers did not mention Milland's standout performance, but he later experienced a taste of Hollywood glitz when Mal joined him for the showy premiere at Warner's Western Theater in Los Angeles on Valentine's Day, 1932.

Returning to MGM, Milland was assigned to *Polly of the Circus*, his second Marion Davies film. For those keeping score, it was also his third pairing with C. Aubrey Smith, though unlike *The Bachelor Father* or *Just a Gigolo*, they shared no scenes.

Polly of the Circus was a major step backward for Ray Milland. Not only wasn't he credited, his contribution was fleeting—playing an unnamed church usher who utters a single line of dialogue.

Based on a novel and 1907 play by Margaret Mayo, *Polly of the Circus* went into production in December 1931. Every version of the story up to this point concerned the awkward alliance between a hot-tempered but injured circus performer and the kindly priest who cares for her. Clark Gable insisted on changing the priest to a minister, though he still thought the assignment was a mistake given his image as a virile leading man. Ray Milland's few seconds show him keeping Polly's nemesis (Raymond Hatton) from disrupting a church service. In a dark suit, Milland looks nice but barely registers in the viewer's mind.

In an unusual move, and one that turned out to be another mini-disaster for Milland's fledgling career, director Alfred Santell cast Milland in an additional and separate part. Early in *Polly of the Circus*, in a boys' club gymnasium, he plays a boxing opponent to Gable's preacher, his face hidden. Obviously, Milland was called upon for this extra duty because of his professional-level fighting skills. What went terribly wrong was that he accidentally knocked a partial bridge out of Gable's mouth during their match. Gable then needed time to recover, shutting down production for two days. Consequently, Milland and Gable socialized over the years, but Gable never quite trusted his one-time "opponent." At least Milland thought that Gable always acted somewhat wary around him. The more immediate result of the episode was that Milland was again held in low esteem by the studio brass.

In late February 1932, *Polly of the Circus* earned a modest profit, thanks to Davies and Gable's marquee pull, but the reviews were deadly. Richard Watts Jr. put it bluntly in the *New York Herald Tribune*: "The picture at the Capitol is that disturbing phenomenon, a work from the usually expert Metro-Goldwyn studies [*sic*] that is totally lacking in a professional quality. . . . The acting is surprisingly bad."

Away from MGM's artificial recreation of romantic courtship, Ray finally found the courage to ask Mal's hand in marriage and was delighted by her answer; they decided on a short summer engagement with a September wedding to follow.

At the same time *Polly of the Circus* was grilled by the critics in February 1932, Milland was cast in another bit part, lasting a few seconds and without any lines at all this time.

But the Flesh Is Weak was MGM's adaptation of Ivor Novello's play *The Truth Game*, a romantic farce about grifters invading British society. The film's primary purpose was to affirm Montgomery as a bona fide leading man.

Milland appears less than ten minutes into the action, during a party scene. Attentive viewers should be able to spot Milland in the background smiling and laughing. Like Montgomery, he is dressed in white tie and tails and, as in *Strangers May Kiss*, they are so similar in appearance, they could pass for siblings. An extremely sharp-eyed viewer will notice that Mitchell Leisen, Ray Milland's friend and future director, is also on hand in this party scene.

The April 1932 release drew Montgomery fans but disappointed critics. Again, Richard Watts Jr. of the *New York Herald Tribune* wrote scathingly, "*But the Flesh Is Weak* emerges as a feeble attempt at English whimsy, in which some of the best of Hollywood's London exiles are wasted on a makeshift comedy."

In July, Mal finished her studies at USC and celebrated with an engagement party at her family home. A *Los Angeles Times* article on the engagement incorrectly named Ray "Harry Milland" (Harry was her father's name) and identified Milland as a "business man," which must have amused Ray but appalled Mal's father.

Milland's next picture for MGM, *Payment Deferred*, turned out to be his last under his contract. Symbolically, he was playing the murder victim, killed off early in the story.

Payment Deferred showed potential—a thriller starring Charles Laughton, based on a 1926 C. S. Forester novel that became a West End and Broadway hit in 1931. Ray Milland was given a more substantial role than usual, at least compared to his previous MGM efforts, and a pre-*Tarzan* Maureen O'Sullivan played Laughton's daughter.

Charles Laughton, Ray Milland, and Maureen O'Sullivan in *Payment Deferred* (1932)

But *Payment Deferred* flopped badly. Somehow, what had been suspenseful on the printed page and in the theater was slow moving on celluloid.

The story concerns a London banker, William (Laughton), who is in desperate need of money. When his wealthy Australian nephew, James (Milland), arrives unexpectedly one night, William poisons the young man, steals his money, and buries the body. William makes a fortune on the stock market, but all his suspicious activities lead to his wife's suicide and his own downfall.

Through the late summer shoot in 1932, Milland came to admire director Lothar Mendes, while Mendes in turn grew impatient with Milland's nervousness and later recommended MGM's executives drop him from their roster.

In spite of his jitters, Milland gives the best performance. His demeanor is more natural than Laughton's, and he stands considerably taller than everyone else. The horror movie aspects of the murder sequence also present a harbinger of things to come in Milland's canon.

When *Payment Deferred* was released in November, the critics had mixed reactions. *Variety* thought it a "notable achievement" yet "depressing," while Irene Thirer in the *New York Daily News* was rapturous over Laughton but ended her review, "Mendes' direction is painful and plodding as befits the continuity."

Despite his tenuous job situation, on September 30, 1932, Ray Milland married Malvina Muriel Weber during a ceremony at the historic and beautiful Mission Inn Hotel and Spa in Riverside, California. Two hundred and fifty guests were in attendance, including a young usher named John Wayne, one of Milland's new Hollywood friends (and a future costar). Following the ceremony, the entire wedding party went back to the Weber home for the reception. The newlyweds capped the very long day with an extended car trip up the coast for their honeymoon in Carmel.

The Milland wedding was a joyous occasion, though somewhat dampened first by Mal's disapproving father, who never allowed Ray to feel completely welcomed into the family, and later by news from MGM.

As soon as they returned from Carmel, Milland learned his studio option was not renewed. For the next few months, without any work in sight, Milland grew frustrated, and both he and Mal became depressed. Feeling at a crossroads, they agreed to quietly divorce while he would return to England and look for work there. Milland had no offers pending but felt he could start over more favorably in England than Hollywood. The Millands' decision to divorce, rather than separate, seems like a drastic move that remains a mystery. In a 1939 *Picturegoer Weekly*, the interviewer tried but failed to clarify what happened: "I've heard it said that you insisted on divorcing [Mal] because you were so hard up that you knew that she'd eat more regularly at home with her folks," to which Milland countered, "That's rot . . . [W]e were fed up with each other, that's all."

THE RETURN TO THE UNITED KINGDOM

Milland's journey back to England this time was long and arduous. It encompassed a detour to the Gulf of Mexico, where he was severely injured while he impetuously took a dip at a port of call and was stung by a smack of jellyfish. On the same voyage, while recovering, Milland met someone who became a good friend with professional connections. The man was publisher Arthur Barker, and during their travels to Liverpool, the last leg of Milland's trek, Barker told Milland about his brother, Vere Barker, a partner in a major theatrical agency.

As soon as Milland found a place in London to stay, a flat at Earl's Court, he made an appointment with Vere Barker, then took a week to visit his family in Wales. His reunion with his father and his father's new wife was sad and awkward since it was clear his father had become more reclusive than ever. Milland also managed to fit in a short visit to his Aunt Luisa, but he chose not to visit his mother, who had married a third time (to an art dealer in Cardiff), sensing she would look down on his lack of employment. Instead, he found solace walking around the neighborhoods and visiting his old haunts.

Back in London, Milland was ready to meet with Vere Barker, whom he discovered to be shy and retiring. It was actually Barker's partner, one "Miss Connie," who interviewed Milland and decided to take a chance on the inactive actor. It took a number of weeks before Miss Connie found Milland work. To earn needed funds, he entered himself in a series of steeplechases twice a week.

At last, an opportunity presented itself, a supporting part in a Gaumont British Picture Corporation production. The farce, *Orders Is Orders*, would be directed by Walter Forde at Lime Grove Studios in early 1933. The story concerned an American film crew embedding itself with the British army in order to shoot a movie—with comically disastrous results. The tenth-billed, Milland played the only soldier with a romantic interest.

Yet, for all the high expectations, critics were divided about *Orders Is Orders*. The *New York Daily News* stated, "The jokes don't joke," yet *Life* magazine called it "swell fun."

Waiting for his next assignment, Milland became part of steeplechase lore when he entered the Sandown Park event in Esher, Surrey, which required thirty-two jumps. According to James Robert Parish and Don E. Stanke, "At the three-and-a-quarter-mile jump, his horse stopped dead in its track while seven other horses and riders crashed into him. Newsreel cameras captured for posterity one of the most spectacular equestrian entanglements in the history of the steeplechase."

Mild injuries and embarrassing headlines aside, Milland was tapped by British Lion for *This Is the Life*, another farce with an American angle, shot at Beaconsfield Studios in midsummer. In Clifford Grey's story and screenplay, Brighton tea shop owners Sarah and Albert Tuttle (Binnie Hale and Gordon Harker) receive a massive inheritance and try to enter high society. When Chicago gangsters show up, the Tuttles end up losing their fortune and returning to the tea shop. Ray Milland plays a young artist engaged to the couple's daughter (Betty Astell).

This Is the Life had less stature than *Orders Is Orders* but at least as much to recommend. Hale and Harker are a boisterous team, especially in their lampooning of both a rumba and an opera duet (from *Il Trovatore*). Fourth-billed Milland exhibits some of his charm in a role that adds the sweetness to the bittersweet ending.

The critics generally liked the effort. *Kinematograph Weekly* called it a "Rollicking social comedy . . . This is just the stuff to give the masses."

Despite the mostly positive reception for both British films, Ray Milland was missing Mal and the life they had just started in California. Homesick for Hollywood, of all places, and distressed by the high prices brought on by the weak American dollar, Milland opted to return to Los Angeles and take his chances again on the bustling studio system, hoping this time to acquire better representation from a casting agency.

Before catching a cruise ship back to the states, Milland vacationed in a few European cities along the way. He went skiing in Garmisch, Germany, and then headed to Munich. In the Bavarian capital, Milland enjoyed an afternoon tea at the Regina Palast. While there, he noticed "professional" dancers, both male and female, were engaging the clientele. One of the male dancers, he was told, was an aspiring Viennese writer named Wilder. By a complete coincidence, a decade later at Paramount Studios, this escort-turned-writer-turned-director, Billy Wilder, joined forces with Milland for two of Milland's best-remembered movies, *The Major and the Minor* and *The Lost Weekend*.

PARAMOUNT

Ray Milland's return to Hollywood in the early autumn of 1933 felt even riskier than his first trip to America. For one thing, he had no job prospects this time. He was certainly unable to afford a house for Mal, whom he was courting all over again, much to Harry Weber's chagrin. While she lived at her family home, Milland rented a room at the Orange Grove Apartments on Sunset Boulevard. One night, an earthquake and its after-shocks startled Milland, who had gone to bed in the nude, as he was wont to do. He quickly got up, threw on a pajama top, and ran out of the building into the streets. When he realized he was naked from the waist down, he jumped into a nearby water fountain before the crowd outside became the people that saw too much!

In one attempt to reingratiate himself into the film community, in September, he attended a concert given by Ramon Novarro at the former silent star's home. Though Milland was mingling with Irving Thalberg (his ex-boss), Cedric Gibbons, Adrian, Myrna Loy, John Gilbert, and Cary Grant (meeting him for the first time), his appearance at the exclusive event didn't lead to anything.

Soon enough, Milland was on a mission to find work, any work, at one of the studios. Without any helpful contacts at MGM, he was not in a very different position than most of the unemployed during the depths of the Depression. His pavement pounding took so many months, Milland was forced to ask friends—including a young John Carradine—for loans to help him pay for food and rent.

While new US president Franklin D. Roosevelt promised greater prosperity, the economy was still suffering. With resignation, Milland resolved he would look for a job outside the movie business. Briefly, he assisted a bookie before learning about an opening for an assistant manager at a Shell gas station. By a stroke of good luck and better timing, he was coming back from his successful eight a.m. interview at the Shell garage, situated near Paramount Studios, when a Paramount casting director named Joe Egli grabbed him off the street. Egli told Milland he wanted him to play a part in an upcoming picture called *Bolero*. (The actor he would be replacing had been "stabbed by his boyfriend the night before," according to Milland.) Egli was aware of Milland's prior work and thought he would be perfect as an English lord in the new George Raft–Carole Lombard film to be directed by Wesley Ruggles.

Egli's prediction paid off. In December 1933, Milland was hired right away, reporting for the first time to Paramount Studios for a one-picture deal at $300 a week (for two weeks), even though this was less money than the gas station job.

Milland's first day was intimidating from the start: he had to pass through Marathon Streets's enormous and ornate Bronson Gate—emblazoned with "Paramount Pictures"—in order to enter the studio grounds. Shortly thereafter, he got anxious meeting the stars, Raft and Lombard. In the film itself, like so many times before, his part would be relatively minor, but *Bolero* was an unexpected box-office winner (i.e. "a sleeper") when released in February 1934, and, indirectly, it helped pave the way to what would become the actor's twenty-year association with the studio.

Bolero is a peculiar hybrid of the pseudo biopic, romantic melodrama, and dance musical. The surprise is that Raft and Lombard, an odd couple to begin with, are cast as dance partners. Their dances together are actually quite accomplished, though in some long shots dance doubles were used.

The Horace Jackson screenplay is loosely based on the true story of Maurice Mouvet, an overly ambitious American dancer who emigrated to Europe before World War I and became as well known for his hoofing abilities as his penchant for discarding dance partners. Raft plays Raoul De Baere and Lombard is Helen Hathaway, the one woman he truly loves. Ray Milland (billed again as Raymond Milland) plays Lord Robert Coray, the British officer Helen abandons to be with the self-centered Raoul. In the end, Raoul eventually dies from a heart attack, and Coray wins her back.

Bolero rarely lags, and if the dance sequences hardly rival those of Astaire and Rogers, they are stylishly concocted. The highlight, naturally, is the climactic dance to Ravel's title composition, directed by an uncredited Mitchell Leisen.

Milland's character is anemic—and he is hindered by having to wear yet another paste-on mustache, a bushy one this time (not unlike his father's real one). For wardrobe, John Carradine again came to the rescue, loaning Milland a pair of dress gloves needed to complete his attire as the titled officer.

Critics were less impressed than audiences. *Life* magazine's reviewer wrote, "[T]he idea sounds like glamorous entertainment. I assure you it is not. Fair, and that's stretching it." Milland didn't care so much about the reviews. His instant friendship with the attractive, down-to-earth Lombard was more important: it was Lombard who recommended he be cast in her next film, again at Paramount.

As with *Bolero*, Milland had little to do in *We're Not Dressing*, another "sleeper." This musical-comedy take on James M. Barrie's 1902 play, *The Admirable Crichton*, is about a haughty heiress (Lombard) who is rude to a sailor (Bing Crosby), but when they are shipwrecked on an island, he is the only one who possesses the know-how to survive.

The overall production is well cobbled together by director Norman Taurog, who divided the shoot between Santa Catalina Island and Paramount's soundstages. Charles Lang Jr., who would later photograph a few other Milland films, expertly blends the location shots with the studio portions. *We're Not Dressing* is amiable, but the excess of music and physical comedy blunts whatever class-conscious critique Barrie intended, leaving only the sexist undercurrent of the male becoming superior to the female. To wit, Lombard was so incensed about having to play a scene in which Crosby slaps her, she slapped him back and knocked him over, tearing off his toupée in the process!

Musically, Crosby hogs the wealth of the songs—eight in a mere seventy-seven minutes (Edwin Schallert of the *Los Angeles Times* described the film as "a Crosby song recital"). The comedy ranges from slapstick bits involving a pet bear aboard the yacht to some better routines with George Burns and Gracie Allen as botanical explorers.

Ray Milland (seventh-billed as Raymond Milland) is mostly sidelined as a priggish, Euro-trash "prince" who dotes upon Lombard's character. He has no funny moments but fits his part well. During a scene with Burns and Allen, Milland ad-libbed a line, impressing director Taurog enough for him to join Lombard in urging Paramount hire Milland long-term. It didn't immediately change his status, but Milland had job security again. On February 14, 1934, he signed his contract, with a starting salary of $300 per week and the understanding that his option could be dropped following a six-month period.

Finally, in the wake of their many months apart, Ray convinced Mal that his Paramount deal would lead to a bright future and that they should remarry and live together. This time, they got hitched at the LA County courthouse on March 18, 1934, without fanfare. Only Mal's parents were present as witnesses. The re-newlyweds next looked for an affordable place and eventually found a modest-sized duplex rental on King's Road, in a building called Les Maisonnettes, part of a residential section near Santa Monica Boulevard. In addition, Milland repaid the friends who had helped him through the lean times.

While the reviews overlooked Milland, *We're Not Dressing* was at least well-received. Mordaunt Hall in the *New York Times* called it a "thoroughly satisfactory picture, whatever one may think of Mr. Crosby's singing." In February, the studio announced Milland as a supporting player in *The Great Magoo*, starring Jack Oakie and rising star Dorothy Dell, but the comedy was never filmed. (A few months later, in June 1934, the nineteen-year-old Dell was killed in a car accident.)

It took time for Milland to adjust to his new environment. Paramount was almost as prestigious as Metro, but there were some key differences, according to Jack Lodge:

> Most of the big studios developed a distinctive style. MGM spent the most money, and it showed in their richly furnished sets and elaborate spectacles . . . [T]here was a prevalent blandness and unwillingness to take chances, but no MGM film was ever careless or tatty. . . . Paramount was the most sophisticated of the majors. Originally known as Famous Players-Lasky (Paramount itself was once a distribution company), it went back almost to the earliest days of West Coast production, and throughout the twenties led the field [as supervised by Adolph Zukor]. In the thirties the Paramount "look" became famous. Dazzling, often fantastic sets, camerawork that seemed to have a peculiarly luminous quality and acting with a casual elegance all contributed to a series of visual successes. The main contributor was Paramount's art director Hans Dreier, who came from German films in the twenties. . . . In its directors, too, Paramount was unequalled, with Ernst Lubitsch, Rouben Mamoulian, Josef von Sternberg and Mitchell Leisen all working for that studio during the period.

Actually, Lodge considers *We're Not Dressing* an exception to the Paramount output, calling it one of the studio's few "creaking horrors" of the 1930s. What Lodge does not mention is that since 1932, Paramount had reported annual losses and eventually filed for bankruptcy. (The costly implementation of sound equipment into its nine hundred theaters had been one of the causes.) The studio rectified its financial situation over time by producing more middle-brow titles like *We're Not Dressing*.

As for Ray Milland, if he couldn't be at MGM, Paramount was an ideal substitute, probably the best studio to accommodate his gentility, wit, and good looks. His only problem in the mid-1930s was that Paramount already had another actor under contract who conformed to that type: Cary Grant. Thus, Milland, who was ignored at Metro in favor of Robert Montgomery, was about to have a similar dilemma at his new digs. Milland's minor-league stature was made immediately clear to him when he was appointed his place on the second floor of the three-story Dressing Room Row. Only the top stars (Grant, Bing Crosby, Mae West, George Raft, Carole Lombard, et al.) were given rooms on the first floor, and the third floor was reserved for character actors. On the other hand, Milland had full access to the gym, barbershop, doctor's clinic, and cafeteria.

He officially started his long-term Paramount contract with *Many Happy Returns*, another musical-comedy featuring Burns and Allen, shot from mid-March to mid-April and released in June 1934. Milland's part was even smaller than the one in *We're Not Dressing* (now sixth-billed as Ray Milland). The good news was that the back-to-back profits from both movies meant Milland's contract would be renewed, and he was expected to fulfill the type of standard seven-year agreement signed by actors at all the major studios. (One other benefit of Milland's participation was that he again enjoyed the spirited friendship of Burns and Allen.)

Directed by Norman Z. McLeod, *Many Happy Returns* blends comedy sketches and musical numbers into a mindless Hollywood studio story. Oddly, most of the jokes fall flat—even George and Gracie cannot salvage them—and the musical segments are bland, the majority of them supplied by top-billed Guy Lombardo and his Orchestra.

Many Happy Returns did well enough at the box office but gave Milland a paltry stint playing an aspiring actor in the story. The critics overlooked him again and didn't care for the movie. Grace Kingsley in the *Los Angeles Times* was blunt: "Of course *Many Happy Returns* was tailored for Gracie. In fact, there are places which fit too tight! A little more plot and little less Gracie, after the first twenty minutes, would have improved the picture."

As soon as *Many Happy Returns* finished shooting, Milland applied for his Declaration of Intention for Naturalization. On May 4, 1934, Milland submitted his form to the Los Angeles chapter of the District Court of California. This continuation from his 1932 petition meant he intended to remain an

American citizen, although his actual citizenship would take another four years to be finalized.

Milland witnessed his art nearly imitate his life when Paramount screen tested him for a major role as a Household Cavalry officer in the action-adventure *Lives of a Bengal Lancer*. He was sorely disappointed when he was passed over for the more familiar Franchot Tone. In 1935, *Lancer* was a tremendous hit with audiences and surely would have helped Milland's career.

Instead, Milland was rushed through a series of B programmers, with barely a break between them. He could hardly take comfort in the fact that Paramount was not giving Cary Grant very decent assignments, either. Between 1934 and 1935, Grant appeared in such forgettable pictures as *Thirty-Day Princess, Kiss and Make-Up, Ladies Should Listen, Enter Madame!, Wings in the Dark,* and *The Last Outpost*.

As for Mal, one of the duties of a "Hollywood Wife" was throwing parties. In mid-August, she and her sister-in-law, Mrs. Herbert Weber, gave a surprise baby shower at the Bel-Air Country Club for both Mrs. John Wayne (a.k.a. Josie Saenz) and Mrs. W. L. Marxer (a.k.a Lenore Bushman), the latter an actress and fellow extra with Ray in *Just a Gigolo*, which her brother-in-law, Jack Conway, had directed.

Around the same time, Milland learned the heartbreaking news that his beloved Aunt Luisa had died from injuries sustained by a kick from a mare she was trying to shoe. Sadly, he would be kept too busy by his new studio to travel to Wales for her funeral.

In what seemed like a rerun of his demeaning MGM experience, Ray Milland was loaned out by Paramount to Fox Studios for a serial entry, *Charlie Chan in London*, shot in July and released in September 1934. At least he was billed third and had more screen time than in his last several films.

Charlie Chan in London was Fox's sixth film in a series that started in 1931 with Swedish-born Warner Oland as the polite but persistent Asian detective invented by author Earl Derr Biggers.

Charlie Chan in London is lightly entertaining with a genuinely challenging mystery. In this installment, the famous detective is asked to help an heiress save her brother from execution when it becomes clear that the young man was not responsible for a murder.

Ray Milland plays a lawyer and the fiancé to the heiress (Drue Leyton). Milland disappears for a few stretches but shines when on-screen, showing his gentler side in his scenes with Leyton and an early version of his sharper, inquisitive side as he becomes the temporary sidekick to Charlie Chan.

The reviews were highly complimentary for a B movie. Even the *New York Times* was pleased: "The plot is sufficiently baffling . . . [Eugene] Forde's direction is rapid and intelligent and the photography is uniformly fine." Ray Milland was mostly ignored by the critics, but he stood out more prominently than usual to audiences.

Back at Paramount, *Menace* was shot quickly in August and released in October 1934. Milland returned to filling a small part—dominating the first reel with his presence but, as in *Payment Deferred*, dying early on (he is billed fifth as Raymond Milland). At just under one hour, *Menace* is a nicely plotted mystery with a comic edge.

In the prologue, Milland plays a Gable-like mining engineer overseeing the construction of a dam in Kenya. When he is called upon to help during a storm, he flies a plane to the bursting dam but realizes he cannot protect his workers and decides to take his own life by crashing his rickety aircraft. Ostensibly, "The Menace" is the unseen brother of Ray Milland's character, seeking revenge on the three people he feels are responsible for his death—especially the brother's wealthy fiancée (Gertrude Michael). One truly mourns losing Milland so early in the story after such a memorable introduction as the angst-ridden supervisor. Counting *Ambassador Bill*, *Menace* gave Milland his second chance to play a pilot, a hobby he had taken up recently and loved in real life.

Even if Milland was again neglected by the critics, the reviews were favorable. The *New York Herald Tribune*'s Marguerite Tazelarr called *Menace* "a brisk murder mystery with an excellent quality of suspense and a reasonably diverting story."

Up next: *One Hour Late*, a programmer filmed in September and released in December 1934. Pitifully for Milland, he did not receive a credit in the opening titles (he was billed tenth as Raymond Milland at the end titles). The tepid B picture was meant to turn radio singer Joe Morrison into a Bing Crosby-type of star.

The story revolves around Morrison's character, Eddie, trying to win over Betty (Helen Twelvetrees), both of whom work as assistants at a radio station. By the end, Eddie becomes a radio star with Betty at his side.

Milland has a small role as Tony St. John, a man who is in love with the station owner's wife, Eileen (Gail Patrick). His main scene, set in a fancy restaurant, has him reasoning with Eileen to divorce her husband and marry him. He says his few lines in close-up shots, but the brief interlude hardly stands out and is entirely tangential to the central narrative. Not too many reviewers took notice, but the *Hollywood Reporter* at least thought *One Hour Late* was "very amusing." Six years later, Milland and Patrick reunited in *The Doctor Takes a Wife*, by which time Milland was a much bigger star.

ONE STEP FORWARD, TWO STEPS BACK

When Franchot Tone proved unavailable, Paramount boosted Milland's standing with a meaningful role in an A picture: *The Gilded Lily* was shot from early October to early December 1934 and released in January 1935. Though Milland's character didn't "get the girl," it hardly mattered since "the girl" was Claudette Colbert, and Milland was essential to a widely seen love triangle. For his third billing, he was Ray Milland in the opening credits but Raymond Milland in the closing credits.

The Gilded Lily inaugurated the first of seven screen pairings between Colbert and Fred MacMurray, who was elevated to major stardom with this romantic lead. It was also one of several collaborations between writer Claude Binyon and *Bolero*'s director, Wesley Ruggles, whom Milland later described as "somber-visaged" and "more morose than ever" during production. (Ruggles was in the midst of a divorce.) Despite Ruggles's moodiness, *The Gilded Lily* turned out to be a bright, fun movie and a pleasant experience for Ray Milland. At the start of the shoot, he was too awestruck to speak with Colbert between takes, but by the end of production, he became friends with both of his costars. Milland later reflected, "Fred and I had been signed by Paramount about the same time . . . [The MacMurrays] were our closest friends, and we hung onto each other like four Christians in the Colosseum."

In Binyon's story, Colbert plays Marilyn, a Manhattan stenographer who enjoys her platonic friendship with Peter, a reporter (MacMurray), but falls in love with a British royal, Charles (Milland), traveling incognito as an out-of-work commoner. When Charles's father (C. Aubrey Smith in his fifth Milland movie) summons Charles to England, Peter twists her story into an exclusive about how *she* rejected royalty. Capitalizing on her press coverage, Marilyn becomes an unlikely nightclub sensation. On tour in London, she reunites with Charles but is disillusioned again when Charles turns out to be a celebrity chaser. She returns to New York and to Peter, her true love.

Though the contrived ending weakens *The Gilded Lily*, most of the film is a treat. Binyon takes sharp satiric swipes at celebrity-for-its-own-sake, and Colbert is at her best as the modern-day Cinderella; in the nightclub sequence, she wisecracks and ad-libs her way through a deliberately clunky song-and-dance routine. MacMurray holds his own as the newsman who conceals his true feelings with a tough-guy cover.

Milland is a revelation, too, here playing a sensitive love interest, following so many less-rewarding roles. Whether showing exultation after a Coney Island roller coaster ride or telling Colbert's Marilyn about his deep affection for her, Milland gives his most emotional and appealing performance to

On the set of *The Gilded Lily* (1935), with Claudette Colbert

date. Similar to his characters in *Bought!* and *Blonde Crazy*, Milland's likable character reveals his dark side late in the story, yet the conclusion rings false this time: it makes no sense for Charles to be suddenly starstruck by Marilyn, and her overreaction—leaving him and London to be Peter's wife—is a speciously tidy way to end the love triangle.

Flaws aside, *The Gilded Lily* garnered good reviews, as did Milland himself. The *New York Times*' Andre Sennwald called it a "bright-faced romantic lark. ... Mr. Milland is handsome and personable," and Mae Tinee in the *Chicago Daily Tribune* thought *The Gilded Lily* "a bright, actionful little comedy drama. ... There are two honest to goodness he-man heroes—Fred MacMurray and Ray Milland. Either of 'em could give Clark Gable a run for his money."

Riding high from his *Gilded Lily* accolades, Milland was awarded the lead in *Lightning Strikes Twice*, as a reporter who helps a nurse accused of poisoning a patient. Milland's costar would have been Sylvia Sidney, but Paramount sold the property to Fox, where it was filmed as *Half Angel* (1936), with Brian Donlevy and Frances Dee.

Milland was next relegated to a much smaller role in an unusual urban drama. At seventh billing, Milland had little to do in *Four Hours to Kill!*, which was shot in February and released in April 1935.

Norman Krasna's screenplay, based on his play, has a multistory structure and is set in a Broadway theater on a single night. Richard Barthelmess plays an escaped killer handcuffed to a detective (Charles Wilson), and he spends "four hours to kill" before the authorities are expected to pick him up and return him to prison. Joe Morrison is a cloakroom attendant who loves his girlfriend (Helen Mack) but had a tryst with a gold-digging usher (Dorothy Tree), who is extorting money from him for an abortion. Lastly, Ray Milland plays a "kept" gentleman having an affair with a married woman (Gertrude Michael). It is her stolen brooch that ties together the disparate subplots.

In this *Grand Hotel* meets *La Ronde* scenario, director Mitchell Leisen shows more of his skill at juggling the various storylines than he does at his true forté, creating a polished mise-en-scène. Leisen and cinematographer Theodor Sparkuhl shoot in the different theater locations with an adept sense of intimacy—backstage, in the seats, by the cloakroom—and in a postmodern touch, Leisen leaves out the stage and its performers, turning the audience members and theater workers into the "stars."

Leisen grants Milland and Michael numerous close-ups in their individual playlet, but their characters' extramarital misery is less interesting than the Barthelmess and Morrison dramas. Milland's episode best serves its purpose to link together the other, more exciting action, and in white tie and tails, the actor looks classy while displaying hints of his charisma—with an added touch of ennui. Still feeling awkward during kissing scenes, Milland needed some prodding for his momentous smooch with Gertrude Michael. Apparently, Leisen privately coached Michael to give Milland a surprise French kiss. "I thought my collar button would rip off. I was terribly shocked," Milland later recalled.

Four Hours to Kill! received mixed reviews. *Variety* wrote, "Picture is melodrama, but as entertainment [it] happens to be a time-killer and not much more," but the *Hollywood Reporter* thought it "a thriller that will grip any audience.... Gertrude Michael and Ray Milland, as a pair of surreptitious lovers, do excellent work."

Milland took a further step backward in another minor role as another murder victim in *The Glass Key*, filmed throughout March by Frank Tuttle and released in May 1935.

Based on Dashiell Hammett's 1931 novel, this first film adaptation is not as well known today as its 1942 remake, thanks to the latter's fire-and-ice pairing of Alan Ladd and Veronica Lake. Here, George Raft plays the second lieutenant to a crime boss (Edward Arnold) who is attempting to go straight by entering politics and marrying a rival politician's daughter (Claire Dodd). When the woman's brother, a gambler in debt played by Milland, is found murdered, suspicion falls on the reforming crime boss. Raft's glorified bodyguard infiltrates a rival syndicate as a way to uncover who killed the gambler.

Raft was more at home in *The Glass Key* than in *Bolero*. This represented the actor's peak as a pin-stripe-suited gangster despite the fact the gangster genre was considerably less potent than it had been before the PCA became strictly enforced in 1934. As with *Payment Deferred* and *Menace*, Milland takes advantage of his few scenes before his character is killed (within the first twenty minutes). He expresses sincere affection for the head gangster's daughter (Rosalind Keith) while also indicating his desperation to amass enough funds to pay off his crooked creditors. Milland only shared one short scene with Raft, in which Raft's character knocks him over with a kick to his leg. Still, he was able to study Raft's smooth yet tough acting style up close, which Milland found instructive.

The Glass Key was highly profitable, even if the critics were not impressed. *Variety* stated, "It just misses providing the basis for a screen outstander." Thankfully, *Billboard* noticed that Ray Milland "is showing more promise with each succeeding picture."

Previously, Milland's loan-outs were a way to keep the actor busy and give him needed experience. Now, loaning out an up-and-coming star like Milland was a way to take a large fee from a rival studio for the actor's services. Paramount did this several times in the 1930s with Milland. One of his 1935 titles, *Alias Mary Dow*, was produced at Universal's B unit. Again billed as Raymond Milland, he was at least given a true leading man role, even if the picture was largely monotonous.

In the screenplay by five writers(!), Sally Eilers plays Sally, a waitress who is recruited by a wealthy man, Henry Dow (Henry O'Neill), to impersonate his long-lost daughter, Mary. Dow's goal is to accommodate his sickly wife's wish to see her again. During her masquerade, Sally meets and falls for a playboy (Milland), while a blackmail scheme is started by a Dow family servant. In the end, the truth comes out that Sally is not Mary, and the facts about Mary's disappearance are revealed.

Shot in March and April and released in May 1935, *Alias Mary Dow* topstarred Eilers, who plays her dual role with energy. By contrast, the others in the cast are just adequate. Even Milland, who would portray so many playboys in his early career, seems bored at times (perhaps appropriate for a playboy!). Here and there, Milland shows off his droll qualities, such as in his comical introduction wearing silk pajamas in his penthouse bedroom, and he has on-screen support from his friend, an uncredited John Carradine, as a nightclub drunk. Otherwise, *Alias Mary Dow* is routinely directed by Kurt Neumann.

Happily, most reviewers noticed Milland this time. *Variety* was typical: "Because of lack of story strength and a cast that isn't strong enough, the picture misses being a winner. . . . The romantic side of the story is built up well, with Raymond Milland turning in a fairly good job as hero opposite Miss Eilers." For its 1948 rerelease, exploiting Milland's superstar status at that time, Universal retitled the movie after its originally planned name, *Lost Identity*.

One of Milland's greatest professional mistakes during his slow climb to stardom at Paramount was to turn down the lead in *Hands across the Table*, a Carole Lombard screwball comedy. In the summer of 1935, amid preproduction, director Mitchell Leisen learned that Lombard's proposed costar, Gary Cooper, was too busy, so Leisen suggested Ray Milland, thinking him sexier than Cooper, anyway (Lombard herself wanted Cary Grant). But despite his high regard for Lombard, Milland did not feel adequate in the area of comedy and "begged off"; his *Gilded Lily* costar and friend, Fred MacMurray, got the part and raised his own profile in what would be the first of his four teamings with Lombard.

One wonders what would have happened to Milland's career had he played the romantic hero in this very popular, critically acclaimed movie. For the time being, it meant continuing with supporting roles and loan-outs. Seeking relief from his career doldrums, Milland amassed enough funds to purchase a single-seater plane. For the next few years, until his bosses stopped him, he would escape from his personal and professional woes by taking solo flights.

At Universal, Milland replayed the rejected "other man" in another A picture, *Next Time We Love*. In fact, the narrative was similar to *The Gilded Lily*, only this film was considerably more somber.

The January 1936 release starred Margaret Sullivan and James Stewart, the latter in his first major role as a leading man. It turned out to be a box-office flop, but Sullivan and Stewart would go on to team up three more times between 1936 and 1940.

Next Time We Love was based on a serialized novel by Ursula Parrott, the *Strangers May Kiss* author, and the adaptation was a haphazard affair. When shooting began in October 1935, only part of Melville Baker's screenplay had been finished. Other writers worked on the script during filming, including an uncredited Preston Sturges. Athough Edward H. Griffith was the credited director, first assistant director (AD) Ralph Slosser shot extensively,

Next Time We Love (1936), with James Stewart and Margaret Sullivan

both on location in San Francisco (using doubles for the stars) and some studio scenes back in Hollywood. Production dragged on until the end of December 1935.

In Parrott's story, Sullivan and Stewart are happy Manhattan newlyweds until their careers begin to keep them apart. Christopher, a reporter, is assigned to overseas posts for long stretches. Cicely initially puts her acting pursuits on hold when she becomes pregnant, but once the baby is a toddler, she resumes performing and skyrockets to stardom. Throughout Christopher's absences, Tommy (Milland), a fellow actor and family friend, comforts Cicely. Eventually, Tommy confesses his love for her, despite the fact he himself is in a failed marriage. Cicely rejects Tommy and reunites with her husband but, shortly after, learns Christopher is dying from a fatal disease contracted in China.

Next Time We Love is a skillfully crafted melodrama. Its problem is that one episode jumps abruptly to another, compressing a nine-year time frame too quickly. The last reel is especially histrionic, as it includes the tragic tag involving Christopher's fate. Still, the story is directed with such care, it almost seems fresh and original, especially early on.

Best of all are the three leads. Margaret Sullivan and James Stewart are convincing in their roles and exude a special rapport in their first film together. Ray Milland is even more impressive, exhibiting a tender side similar to his work in *The Gilded Lily*, and his synergy with both Sullivan and Stewart is natural and effortless. Milland deserves credit for creating a "third-wheel" character we care about, mainly because he is able to hide Tommy's anguish under a façade of forged jocularity, apart from his poignant scene declaring his love to Cicely.

Critic Mae Tinee of the *Chicago Daily Tribune* remarked, "[In this] peculiar triangle . . . [Ray Milland] gives a performance that's a decided contrast to that of the other two principals. He is the still, silent sufferer. The uncomplaining and always dependable bulwark. . . . You hope, as the film ends, that the future may offer him some recompense—as husband to Cicely and step-papa to their little son—but you doubt if it will." *Billboard* magazine also singled out Milland: "Sullivan, Stewart and Milland are excellent, tho Sullivan has a weepy role and Stewart has to grow on you. Milland is superb."

Looking forward, Ray Milland would be waiting in the wings when Paramount's top star in the debonair matinée idol mold, Cary Grant, suddenly departed. This impending career turning point would be initially advantageous for Milland, who, with *Next Time We Love*, would see his very last billing as Raymond Milland.

CHAPTER 3

IN THE SHADOW OF CARY GRANT (1936–1940)

CARY GRANT'S PARAMOUNT FILMS FOLLOWING HIS TWO 1933 HITS WITH MAE West (*She Done Him Wrong* and *I'm No Angel*) were not box-office winners, and Grant was becoming frustrated. As Jerry Vermilye writes, "By 1935, Cary Grant's willingness to continue at Paramount in the tall shadow of Gary Cooper had dwindled considerably. No longer was Cary Grant a picture novice in need of cinematic exposure. Yet, it seemed his career might continue as a never-ending succession of Cooper rejections and hand-me-downs. He was champing at the bit, beginning to kick up his own heels." When Paramount and Cary Grant mutually parted ways in 1936, Grant moved onto a spectacular freelance career for the remainder of his days in Hollywood. Yet Paramount was stuck without a debonair leading man or matinée idol of Grant's growing stature.

Paramount's answer to its "Cary Grant Problem" was to groom contract player Ray Milland "to continue in the footsteps of Cary Grant," according to historians James Robert Parish and Don E. Stanke. The studio had many actors but no others that fit the tall, dark, and handsome prototype—with a transcontinental accent as well. Soon enough, rival studios created their own versions of Grant by elevating the profiles of imports like David Niven and Louis Hayward.

Milland secured his own spot in this group primarily due to the surprise successes of *The Jungle Princess* (1936) and *Easy Living* (1937). Between 1936 and 1937, he appeared in ten feature films and quickly became a "name." In the first of his 1936 releases, *Next Time We Love*, Milland was a supporting player; by the end of 1937, with the release of *Wise Girl*, he was a genuine leading man, though not nearly the star he would become in the 1940s. Yet, the entire time, Ray Milland inherited the same dilemma Cary Grant had endured with Gary Cooper: now Ray Milland was standing in the shadow of Cary Grant.

Paramount had a much bigger concern at this point: the Banking Act of 1935 reversed many of the gains of the recovery. By 1936, the Great Depression worsened, and Hollywood felt the impact. Paramount was not the only studio having troubles, but the situation was exacerbated by the exit of major stars like Cary Grant and, later, Marlene Dietrich and Gary Cooper. In an ill-fated move in 1935, the front office put its most esteemed director, Ernst Lubitsch, in charge of all movies.

As the only Hollywood director in the position of production manager, Lubitsch oversaw sixty different films and found the job difficult, particularly when it came to delegating authority. Within a year, he was fired and went back strictly to filmmaking and then departed Paramount as well. Meanwhile, new president Barney Balaban's cost cutting was starting to show, making the studio best known for luxuriant entertainment look somewhat bargain basement.

Milland's next film was indeed low budget and the studio's first attempt to mold Milland in Cary Grant's image. With *The Return of Sophie Lang*, a July 1936 release made earlier in the year, Milland had his first leading man role at his home studio. Not by chance, Milland was reteaming with his *Four Hours to Kill!* paramour, Gertrude Michael, who had been memorable in *I'm No Angel* with Grant and was Grant's leading lady in *The Last Outpost* (1935). Though Milland is billed below both Michael and Guy Standing, he has at least as much screen time and shines in every scene in which he appears.

Directed by B stalwart, George Archainbaud, *The Return of Sophie Lang* was the second film in a trilogy all starring Michael as the title character, a glamorous "lady jewel thief," a gambit conceived by author Frederick Irving Anderson.

Unlike Marlene Dietrich in *Desire*, Paramount's better 1936 jewel-thief comedy-adventure, Gertrude Michael is too unassuming to portray an alluring heroine. However, Milland registers strongly as an intrepid reporter, not only with his sharp delivery of dialogue but also with his polished yet street-smart demeanor (patterned after Cary Grant but also influenced by his having worked with James Cagney and George Raft).

The critics approved of this "new" leading man. Frank S. Nugent of the *New York Times* thought *The Return of Sophie Lang* was "lively, engagingly played and amiably agile," adding "Ray Milland, too, is of vast assistance . . . he has a knack of rallying 'round when he is most needed, and that is justification enough for his presence."

Along with his other activities early in the year, Milland was sent over to David O. Selznick's new studio to test for the supporting role of Captain de Trevignac in the Technicolor sound remake of *The Garden of Allah*, starring

Dietrich and Charles Boyer. David Niven and Cesar Romero also tested for De Trevignac, but Selznick chose Alan Marshal, Milland's future *Irene* costar. (Milland's near-miss appearance with Dietrich would be rectified a decade later by *Golden Earrings*, but the pairing ended up a fraught one.) By midyear, the studio announced Milland would team with Ida Lupino in Graham Greene's crime thriller *This Gun for Hire*, but the film wasn't made until 1942, when Alan Ladd and Veronica Lake stepped into the parts.

Milland's October release, *The Big Broadcast of 1937*, shot during the summer of 1936, represented a slide backwards. It was the third of four films in another Paramount series—this one starting with *The Big Broadcast* in 1932. It marked the second time Milland was working with director Mitchell Leisen and the third time with his friends George Burns and Gracie Allen, but he was lost in the movie's shuffle.

Despite all the talent in front of and behind the camera, *The Big Broadcast of 1937* turned out weak. It gave Milland little to do but be a spectator within his own movie—reacting to the comedy lines of others or passively watching song-and-dance numbers. Wisely or not, Paramount stinted on the production values, such as rejecting the use of Technicolor, which helped the bottom line but not the entertainment value. The studio's financial strain during this period was keenly on display: for an on-the-town montage sequence supposedly featuring Ray Milland and Shirley Ross, Leisen culled footage from his 1934 *Murder at the Vanities*; and the musical offerings, ranging from Leopold Stokowski to Benny Goodman, were designed with shadowy effects in order to conceal the sizes of the sets and the number of background dancers.

In the story and screenplay by a gaggle of writers, Milland plays an agent to a pompous radio star (Frank Forest), even though he would rather help an aspiring singer (Ross). Deferring to the sponsors of a network program (Burns and Allen), the agent sidelines the newcomer. In the end, though, she forgives him, and they get married on the air.

Like other radio-themed movies of the era, this *Big Broadcast* takes an ambivalent attitude toward cinema's entertainment rival. It honors what would have been "free" to Depression-era audiences, yet it demonstrates the humorous limitations of the audio-only medium with sketches starring Bob "Bazooka" Burns, the worst parts of the film.

Ray Milland is merely a handsome straight man to the comic crew (Jack Benny, Burns and Allen, Martha Raye), as indicated when Allen first meets him and gushes, "Isn't he pretty?" Yet his talent agent's devious plotting against the very woman he loves (Ross) presages Milland's emerging screen persona—the matinée idol with a warp. Of greater importance at the time,

The Big Broadcast of 1937 gave him another romantic lead in a widely seen movie. And the reviews were generous: the *Boston Daily Globe* loved the entire film and singled out Ray Milland as "personable and charming."

B-MOVIE STARDOM

One month later, in November 1936, Milland's place in the business was heightened considerably by the release of *The Jungle Princess*. Milland got the assignment by default: during the summer, he was the screen-test partner to a series of actresses vying to be the heroine. When the little-known Dorothy Lamour was chosen, she insisted Milland be her costar, though he had not been considered up to that point. Thanks primarily to Lamour, he looked forward to the assignment.

Paramount's counter to MGM's lucrative Tarzan franchise promoted a gender twist: in *The Jungle Princess*, it is a beautiful young woman raised in the jungle who saves and falls in love with a "Great White Hunter." Milland is the hunter and Lamour the title character, and one memorable *Tarzan* send-up line has him teaching her English with, "Me Chris, You Ulah" (though she thinks "Chris" means "kiss").

During preproduction, *The Jungle Princess* was the subject of much concern by the censors. The screenplay received many objections from Joseph Breen, the new head of the Hays Office PCA. The biggest issue was the implication that there existed an "illicit sex relationship between Ulah and Christopher."

The tale concerns the American, Christopher, who is separated from his hunting party in the Malaysian jungle. The native Ulah rescues Chris from an attack by her beloved tiger, and eventually Ulah and Chris fall in love. Later, a tribal chief captures Ulah's tiger, and in her attempt to retrieve her pet, Ulah and Chris's hunting party is trapped. Chris saves everyone by shooting the chief, and, in the end, when the others depart, he stays behind to live with Ulah.

Production commenced in July 1936, with parts of the San Fernando Valley doubling for the jungle. On location, Milland was present during a series of mishaps. One especially unfortunate incident involved "Bogo," Ulah's pet chimpanzee, attacking a crew member, who later died from his injuries. Next, while washing Lamour's hair to keep it looking straight, an assistant poured a liquid dry cleaner over the actress's head. When the solution seeped into her eyes, Lamour felt excruciating pain and ran around hysterically until Milland slapped her and then plunged her under a waterfall to dilute the chemicals. Nevertheless, Lamour had only pleasant memories of her costar:

The Jungle Princess (1936) poster art, with Dorothy Lamour

Ray was a genuinely unselfish actor—a rarity in the film business. One of the first scenes we did involved a big close-up of me, shot over Ray's shoulder. What did I know about camera angles? After all, other than my screen test and the family Brownie, this was my first experience in front of a camera. I kept turning my face away, but Ray would gently take me by my shoulders and adjust me so I was facing the lens. Sometimes Ray would even sacrifice his own scenes to get my face in the proper position. That's really something when a performer does that for a colleague! I think he taught me more about the technique of motion picture acting than anyone I knew.

Lamour would remain a good friend for the rest of Milland's life, calling him "My Jungle Prince."

Once the completed film was submitted for censor approval, Breen was outraged and wrote to the studio that it must delete "all business of Christopher carrying Ulah into the cave" and "the physical contact between them in the cave." Dialogue that Breen found offensive included Chris telling his friend Frank (Lynne Overman), "All she knows about civilized ways is just what I've been able to teach her myself," and Frank's response, "That ought to make her quite a girl!" Audaciously, Paramount cut very little of what bothered the right-wing censor but received a seal of approval anyway. Paramount even used fleshy cover art of Dorothy Lamour in its advertising. For a post-Code picture, *The Jungle Princess* was as sensuous as it got!

This *Tarzan* rival was met with great approval by audiences, and top-billed Lamour—as the first of her many sarong-wrapped heroines—became an overnight star at twenty-two. During one of the film's interludes, she crooned to Milland "Moonlight and Shadows" in a distinctive, sexy contralto, helping it reach number one on the "Hit Parade" radio show.

Now, Milland was seen in a new light. Baring much of his skin, he and Lamour cavort through their initial scenes together with evident joy, especially in a lively swimming sequence, and they approach the more melodramatic second half of the story with the right degree of mock seriousness. Director Wilhelm Thiele shows a knack for both humorous bits and large-scale action.

Most critics were "above" enjoying *The Jungle Princess* and had predictable responses. The *New York Times* called it a "charmingly spurious [item] attracting the customers in herds." Marguerite Tazelaar in the *New York Herald Tribune* thought the story "foolish" but did admit, "Ray Milland touches his Chris up with subtle comedy and a performance authentically childlike." It didn't really matter what the reviewers said: *The Jungle Princess* was critic-proof, and a quasi-sequel was later made with Lamour and Milland.

As part of his glorified grunt work, and in advance of his studio's silver jubilee, Milland traveled to the Boston premiere of *The Jungle Princess*, stopping at Harvard University on the way to deliver fifteen hundred Paramount photo stills to the school's library theater collection. Additionally, he took a short trip to New York for the opening at the Rialto. At least the studio recognized Milland's potential, rewriting his contract and tripling his salary to more than $900 per week. With greater income, he and Mal started visiting Los Angeles auctions, bidding on artworks, and over time, amassing an impressive collection.

The Jungle Princess was followed by another "sleeper" a month later, December's *Three Smart Girls*, which Milland filmed on loan-out to Universal (from September through October 1936). Though he was back to featured player status, Milland definitely enhanced a film meant to showcase its young leading lady, fourteen-year-old operatic sensation Deanna Durbin. Harpist Louise Steiner Elian (Mrs. Max Steiner at the time) remembered that the Universal orchestra and sound system were not as grand or state of the art as those of the other majors but that Durbin was in perfect pitch no matter the circumstances.

Thanks primarily to Durbin, *Three Smart Girls* helped save the cash-strapped studio from bankruptcy. As the youngest of the "three smart-girl" sisters of the story, Durbin was hailed as a fresh screen talent by critics and audiences. Even the Academy of Arts and Sciences took notice of the film, nominating it for Best Original Story, Best Sound, and (most astonishingly) Best Picture.

Milland's casting resulted from good fortune again. Louis Hayward, who was also compared to Cary Grant at the time, had been set to play Lord Michael Stewart, but either fell ill just before the start date or, according to director Henry Koster, was too nervous and "didn't think it would help his career at all." Looking for another British type, casting director Dan Kelly suggested to producer Joe Pasternak he borrow Ray Milland from Paramount. In terms of attaining greater fame, Milland was lucky to appear in a very popular movie. Simultaneously, he contributed something unique, even if most of the accolades went to Durbin.

Milland plays the titled suitor to one of the older sisters of the story (Barbara Read) as he amuses himself in his attempt help the youngest sister, Penny (Durbin), reunite her estranged parents (Charles Winninger, Nella Walker) and stop the impending marriage between her father and the scheming Donna (top-billed Binnie Barnes).

Director Koster would soon become known for his sentiment, but here he keeps the schmaltz in check when Durbin is off the screen, particularly during Milland's more puckish moments. Graham Greene wrote in *The Spectator* that the second half of *Three Smart Girls* was where "some welcome humour of an adult kind creep[s] tardily" into the film, praising the work of Barnes, Alice Brady, Mischa Auer, and Ray Milland.

Off screen, as a sign of his increased acceptance in Hollywood, Milland was invited into a large assemblage known as "The British Colony." Though he and Mal were not frequent partygoers, they did enjoy the company of other British émigrés. In his biography of Laurence Olivier, Donald Spoto put the clannishness in its worst possible light by saying Olivier and, later, Vivien Leigh

> were not intimately attached to the clubby British contingent in Hollywood, a group that met for cricket at the home of C. Aubrey Smith and for tea at Cedric Hardwicke's. These and others of the clique (among

them Basil Rathbone, Claude Rains, Aldous Huxley, Ray Milland, Ronald Colman and Herbert Marshall [plus Cary Grant, Charles Laughton and James Whale]) Olivier regarded somewhat disdainfully, considering them professional Englishmen who privately hated Hollywood while luxuriating in fat salaries and comfortable southern California living.

Joan Fontaine, a future Milland costar with British roots, had a similarly derisive view of "the Beverly Hills British Colony . . . [Ronald Colman was] the self-appointed King-of-the-colony, while the self-appointed queen was Basil Rathbone's wife [Ouida]. . . . To be invited to the Colman's 'house on the hill' was considered the stamp of approval." If nothing else, Milland found specialty shops through his British Colony contacts. Unique clothing stores on Beverly Drive provided a range of British-made attire, which was his preference.

Milland returned to Paramount at the end of 1936 to star in *Bulldog Drummond Escapes*, released in January 1937. Though lower budgeted and less recognized than either *The Jungle Princess* or *Three Smart Girls*, this B picture gave him top billing and his first opportunity to play a title character.

Debuting in 1920, Hugh "Bulldog" Drummond was a British detective in a string of novels by H. C. "Sapper" McNeile. Later, plays, radio programs, and several films followed. Paramount eventually bought the franchise to launch a series.

Bulldog Drummond Escapes was the first of the studio's entries and the only one headlined by Ray Milland. The next seven (lasting until 1939) starred John Howard. In the story, Milland's detective gets involved with a "lady in distress" (Heather Angel), an heiress kept prisoner in her manor home. Drummond works both with and against Scotland Yard to figure out who at the estate is behind driving the heiress mad and trying to steal her fortune.

Director James Hogan gives this *Bulldog Drummond* the right fog-bound atmosphere and turns Paramount's backlot into a convincing substitute for current-day London. Edward T. Lowe's screenplay combines suspense and humor well, providing Milland witty banter with both Heather Angel as his love interest and E. E. Clive as his valet. Milland had first met Angel during his days in London and was delighted to have her on board. They remained lifelong friends and reunited for the 1962 horror film, *Premature Burial*, playing siblings.

The reviews, such as the one in the *Hollywood Reporter*, gave the film and Milland high marks: "Ray Milland is so breezy, debonair and likable as the new Drummond that he successfully holds his own in a strong British cast."

As spot on as he was as Drummond, Milland was becoming too big a star to continue in the series. Paramount had other plans for him, such as co-starring in a remake of the classic *Beau Geste,* but that didn't pan out for another two years. In the meantime, the loan-outs persisted.

Milland was sent back to Universal for *Wings over Honolulu,* a May 1937 release (shot in January and February). This specific loan turned out to be a "trade" for Universal's Roscoe Karns and at least spared Milland from wasting his time in Paramount's inferior *Murder Goes to College* (1937). *Wings* simultaneously cost Milland a leading role in Wesley Ruggles's *I Met Him in Paris,* a comedy starring Claudette Colbert, Melvyn Douglas, and Robert Young (filling in for Milland).

A B romance with a military background, *Wings over Honolulu* was influenced by the public fascination with aviator celebrities (e.g. Charles Lindbergh, Amelia Earhart). In it, Milland plays a daredevil navy lieutenant-pilot, Sam "Stony" Gilchrist, stationed in Pearl Harbor with his new bride, Lauralee Curtis (top-billed Wendy Barrie). When Stony is called away on a secret mission, the lonely Lauralee accepts an invitation from a former boyfriend (Kent Smith) to a nightclub. That innocent date prompts a clash between the newlyweds, forcing Lauralee to leave Stony. But after she learns he is hurt in a plane crash, she returns to him.

Though the material is trite, director H. C. Potter infuses *Wings over Honolulu* with pleasurable touches. Stony landing his plane in Lauralee's backyard leads to their love-at-first-sight moment, a full year before a similar scene with Clark Gable and Myrna Loy was staged by Victor Fleming for *Test Pilot.* Mary Philips, who would later appear with Milland in *Lady in the Dark* (1944), adds welcome humor as an aviator's wife. Best of all, there are some beautiful shots of planes in the air, with the North Island naval base in San Diego a credible substitute for Honolulu. Joseph Valentine was nominated for an Academy Award for his cinematography (the film's only nomination), and Valentine had already worked with Milland on *Alias Mary Dow, Next Time We Love,* and *Three Smart Girls.* It is only too bad that *Wings over Honolulu,* their last together, could not have been shot in Technicolor, as would be the case for Milland's next skyward drama, *Men with Wings* (1938).

The reviews were highly complimentary. Edwin Schallert of the *Los Angeles Times* considered *Wings over Honolulu* "fascinating ... [T]here is style in [Potter's] work, warmth and spontaneity.... Miss Barrie and Mr. Milland seem exceptionally en rapport, and the development of the story depends on them almost entirely at the outset."

Watching *Wings over Honolulu* today could trigger uneasy feelings given the Pearl Harbor location (four years before the bombing). The film also counts as one of the earliest Hollywood films to promote the engagement of aerial "war games" prior to World War II. At the time, Milland's only disappointment was that the production schedule conflicted with his invitation from the Household Cavalry to return to England for the Coronation of George VI and participate in the parade with his old school comrades. He soon overcame any regrets, realizing he preferred being in a military movie rather than showing off his actual military credentials.

Milland next tested for a part at Warner Bros. that he didn't get. During March 1937, many actors tried out for the role of the school teacher falsely accused of murder in Mervyn LeRoy's *They Won't Forget*. Milland was in a good company of rejects, including Jimmy Stewart and Tyrone Power. Newcomer Edward Norris was selected over all of them for the powerful drama.

Returning to Paramount, Milland was compensated with a leading-man assignment in a major production titled *Easy Living*. He was nervous attempting a screwball farce, but director Mitchell Leisen convinced him he possessed the requisite comic gifts. Designed as a showcase for Jean Arthur, the film became hugely profitable, and Milland continued ingratiating himself with critics and audiences.

This first official Paramount writing gig by *wunderkind* Preston Sturges, based on Vera Caspary's original story, follows an innocent young woman, Mary Smith (Arthur), after a mink coat falls on her head while she is commuting to her job. Mary finds the coat's owner, bank president John Ball (Edward Arnold), who threw it off his apartment roof to teach his wife a lesson in thrift. Thereafter, people assume Mary is John's mistress just as she becomes smitten with the son of the banker, John Ball Jr. (Milland), not knowing the two men are related. Matters are smoothed out at the end, with the various characters realizing Mary deserves to wed John Ball the younger.

Milland's scenes shift from drama to comedy to romance, starting with his argument over breakfast with his father about his lack of independence. This sober opening leads to the famous set piece in an automat, where John Ball Jr. takes a job as a busboy and meets Mary. During a subsequent free-for-all, as the many patrons fight over the restaurant's scraps, John treats fur-clad Mary to a bountiful spread. Critic Bernard F. Dick spells out the underlying message of the wild slapstick: "By highlighting the extremes of affluence and poverty, it defines the Great Depression as a time of sable for the lucky and rags for the luckless." Later, in an ostentatious apartment set, Milland exhibits his playfully amorous side as he and Arthur romp through an enormous bathtub water fountain. (The moment he slips and gets stuck in the tub was unplanned but kept in the final cut.)

During production, Milland restricted his whimsical antics to time in front of the camera. Apparently, his anxiety had as much to do with his lack of training in comedy as it did the relative importance of the undertaking.

A publicity photo for *Easy Living* (1937), with Jean Arthur

While Jean Arthur's actor-producer husband, Frank Ross, quietly helped Milland calm himself between takes, all the cast and crew members ever saw was Milland's polite but reserved comportment. Actress Marsha Hunt, a new arrival to Paramount, appeared in the final reel of *Easy Living* and remembered that "[Milland kept] pretty much to himself but [was] cordial when questioned or chatted with." She found him the same way when they appeared together in *Irene* three years later.

Easy Living received mixed reviews (*Variety* called it "uneven, uninspired") but audiences loved it, allowing Milland to better his prospects within the studio. Now, Paramount requested he be interviewed on a live radio broadcast (Warren Stokes' show on KEHE) about his upcoming release. Later in the year, in November 1937, Milland made his radio bow as a guest star on NBC's music-variety Kraft Music Hall show. Ominously, like many stars, Milland was paid by Lucky Strike a $2000 lump sum—the first of many—to hawk the company's cigarettes in print ads. At the same time, a photo of Milland's mug graced the Diamond Match Company's matchbooks. (Milland's smoking habit was the likely cause of his lung cancer in the 1980s.)

During the summer of 1937, in a turnabout from Paramount's attempt to transform Milland into "the next Cary Grant," it was Milland who rejected a part ultimately played by Grant. Sensing the material would not suit him, Milland declined Howard Hawks's invitation to star opposite Katharine

Hepburn in RKO's *Bringing Up Baby* (Robert Montgomery and Fredric March also turned Hawks down). Today, this career move might sound suicidal since *Bringing Up Baby* is considered one of the all-time great (and screwiest) screwball comedies. But it is often forgotten that in 1938 it was a failure at the box office.

IN DRY DOCK

Ebb Tide, a summer shoot and November 1937 release, put Ray Milland back in Cary Grant's shadow. Frances Farmer had just appeared in RKO's *The Toast of New York* opposite Grant, so Paramount reasoned teaming her with Milland would be a natural—both films are even set during the nineteenth century. Instead of the nightclub settings of the Grant picture, though, Milland and Farmer would find themselves on a decrepit vessel in the South Pacific.

Based on the 1894 novel, *The Ebb-Tide*, by Robert Louis Stevenson and Lloyd Osbourne, the adventure tale was filmed in Technicolor, and Paramount publicized it as the first major film to use color photography at sea. The studio heads touted not only Farmer, whom they billed above Milland and were christening "the new Garbo," but also Oscar Homolka, the acclaimed Austrian actor in his Hollywood debut. Homolka, who is best remembered today as a character actor, was given billing over both Farmer and Milland.

But Milland's first time in color was doomed before it began. When Henry Hathaway was detained on another film, producer Lucien Hubbard replaced him with James Hogan, Milland's *Bulldog Drummond Escapes* director. Despite the efforts of Technicolor expert Ray Rennahan as co-cinematographer (with Leo Tover), Hogan was unable to capture the visual splendor of the exterior settings (granted, Catalina Island was a poor substitute for the South Seas locale), and the action scenes, including a powerful typhoon, were not properly covered, though Milland impressively performed an Errol Flynn-like leap from the mast to the ship's deck.

Bertram Millhauser's adaptation is a creaky affair. In 1890, three beachcombers (Milland, Homolka, and Barry Fitzgerald) stranded on a South Pacific island are given a chance to leave if they agree to man a rickety freighter. The three drifters are surprised by a mystery woman on board (Farmer) and encounter troubles along the way: the anointed captain (Homolka) struggles with a drinking problem, and when the typhoon nearly destroys the ship, the crew finds itself on yet another island—where a religious fanatic (Lloyd Nolan) seeks to kill his guests!

Ebb Tide is a mess, and the cast doesn't help. The dialogue uttered by both Fitzgerald's drunken "Cockney" sailor and Homolka's haunted Dutch captain is literally difficult to understand, and the inevitable romance between Milland and Farmer is strained by Farmer's one-note performance as a British stiff-upper-lip heroine. (Farmer called her *Ebb Tide* character, "an ill-defined bit of nothing.")

Paramount was happy enough with the box-office returns, but the bloated $1 million budget dampened some of the enthusiasm—the typhoon sequence alone cost $100,000. *Newsweek*'s review was typical of the critics' reactions: "[The] adventures might have made an absorbing film. Instead, the director, James Hogan, subordinates a realistic storm at sea, death and horror on an island ruled by a madman, to assorted close-ups of characters in interminable conversation."

As *Newsweek* intimated, a minor but not insignificant aspect of *Ebb Tide* is that the last reels involving the threatening religious zealot pinpoint one of Milland's earliest incursions into the horror genre. Though bright Technicolor and the tiresome Lloyd Nolan blunt the creepy *Island of Doctor Moreau*-cum-*Most Dangerous Game* aspects of these scenes, *Ebb Tide* hints at something much better to come for its star. (Coincidentally, MGM considered loaning Milland to RKO for a small part in the original *Most Dangerous Game* in 1932, but scheduling problems prevented it.) The only constructive way of viewing Nolan's casting is that it embodies "the banality of evil," and former silent star, Lina Basquette, as the psychotic man's slave, supplies the real sense of horror through her terrified reactions to his commands.

In any case, at this stage, Milland was more associated with comedy, and he stayed in that lane with his next project, a loan-out first rejected by Cary Grant. Despite *Easy Living*'s everlasting reputation as one of the era's great screwball comedies, Milland's *Wise Girl* is nearly as good. Without having any of the caché of the Paramount film, *Wise Girl* was afforded little of the same fanfare by RKO and is barely remembered today. But *Wise Girl*, shot from September to October, became Milland's final 1937 release and gave the actor more material with which to work. Arguably, too, Milland's top-billed leading lady, Miriam Hopkins, was a better romantic foil than Jean Arthur.

In Allan Scott's screenplay, Manhattan socialite Susan (Hopkins) masquerades as a struggling actress living in Greenwich Village in order to wrest away her late sister's two young daughters from John (Milland), the ne're-do-well artist-brother of her late brother-in-law. Eventually, after many misunderstandings, Susan and John end up together, with the children in tow.

Director Leigh Jason's technique is merely adequate, but Scott's screenplay puts a bright spin on the familiar premise of a wealthy woman "slumming it." For Milland, there are remnants of Cary Grant-type moments, particularly his introductory scene selling a woman's hat to a customer by modeling it first. Otherwise, Milland makes the part his own, a more variegated interpretation than Grant's typically slicker approach. He and Hopkins are surrounded by stock screwball characters of the "loony" or vaguely "foreign" variety, but the stars maintain a solid center, first as antagonists and then as romantic partners. In one risqué early scene, for which director Jason ordered a closed set, John refuses to let Susan bathe peacefully in a tub. Off camera, Milland and Hopkins got along well and reunited three years later for a radio adaptation of *Morning Glory* (1940), then eighteen years later when Hopkins accepted Milland's appeal to be a guest on his television sitcom, *The Ray Milland Show* (1955).

Both the negative and positive reviews of *Wise Girl* recognized Milland's contributions. *Variety* stated, "It's a better picture for Milland than for the femme star opposite him. The actor disports himself as well as any one might, considering the material and the plot's irregularities." The *Hollywood Reporter* went further: "Deft treatment makes this top program comedy a thoroughly enjoyable affair . . . [T]here is fine comedy . . . and unforced sentiment in Milland's drawing of the manly artist. This is his best to date."

With his growing popularity and satisfying notices, Milland received more consideration from Paramount. In early October 1937, independent mogul Hal Roach pitched a nonstarter, teaming Milland and Margaret Sullivan in *Roadshow*, a low-budget screwball comedy. It was rejected by Milland's bosses, so Roach produced *Roadshow* in 1941 with Adolph Menjou and Carole Landis.

As if Milland wasn't busy enough in 1937, he was obligated to take a sixteen-day trip to his family home in Wales, not so much for a reunion but to "keep title to the property" since he was recently named the family's land-grant owner. His only duty in this position (as decreed three hundred years earlier by Sir Henry Morgan, the original proprietor) was to spend two nights in a row at the estate annually. In the fall, Milland flew to New York to catch a steamer to England and did the same in reverse after his sojourn. He would repeat this trek every year, except during World War II. As for Alfred Jones, his pride in his son was evident: he attended Ray Milland movies whenever they played Neath's Empire Cinema, where he retained a special seat and was always served a complimentary cup of tea by the management.

By December 1937, Milland was in the United States to begin the long-delayed follow-up to *The Jungle Princess*. Nearly two years after that "sleeper," Paramount commissioned *Her Jungle Love*, released in April 1938.

With the jungle setting and the love story between the white man and native woman, *Her Jungle Love* repeats the basic premise of *The Jungle Princess*. Milland and Lamour have different names, but their characters are practically the same. Also, Lynne Overman, who had been a fellow hunter in *The Jungle Princess*, is along for the ride. The plot device of the hero giving up his "civilized" life and conventional love interest in favor of jungle life is likewise replicated, as is the third-act threat from a tribal chief.

The expensive modifications were clearly meant to assure a larger box-office return. Most distinctly, Paramount lensed *Her Jungle Love* in Technicolor. But the bigger spectacle meant bigger mishaps this time. A huge cavern set used early in the story was destroyed during the shooting of an earthquake scene, which injured thirty-seven extras. Taking dangerous chances of their own, Dorothy Lamour threw a Malay knife at Ray Milland in another scene—without any stunt doubling!

Continuing the gender-bender spirit established in the earlier film, it is Milland who is the sex object of the story. A cute scene has Tura (Lamour) calling Bob (Milland) "pretty," and he initially bristles at the idea before resigning to it. As in *The Jungle Princess*, Lamour sings (only more often), and Milland even joins her briefly for "Coffee and Kisses." Further, Milland fans could catch the single time his arm's snake-and-skull tattoo was ever clearly captured on film.

Ultimately, *Her Jungle Love* is not as entertaining as *The Jungle Princess*, mainly because it prolongs the same story and features less humor and more melodrama. George Archainbaud, director of Milland's *Return of Sophie Lang*, does a strictly yeoman job. Audiences approved, as the studio had hoped, but the critics were unimpressed. Frank S. Nugent in the *New York Times* considered it a "clownish film.... Mr. Milland and Miss Lamour make themselves quite ridiculous by trying to play it straight."

Technicolor would have vastly improved *Tropic Holiday*, a near-immediate reunion for Milland and Lamour, with Milland replacing an unavailable Don Ameche. Shot from January to March, the July 1938 release was their third and final film together, directed without distinction by Theodore Reed. Unlike Milland and Lamour's first two films, there is no jungle setting, and while Lamour is "exoticized," she has full command of English as a Mexican beauty who falls for a Hollywood screenwriter (Milland) staying at a Mexican hotel while struggling to finish his latest script.

Inexplicably, Paramount used *Tropic Holiday* to make a star out of Bob Burns, the folksy comic who helped spoil *The Big Broadcast of 1937*. Thus, both Lamour and Milland are billed below not only Burns but also his comedic vis-à-vis, Martha Raye.

For Milland, his partnership with Lamour remains pleasurable but turns blandly decorous by the frequent musical-comedy distractions. The actor's best moments come early on, as he tries valiantly to overcome his writer's block. Milland's on-screen frustration is both funny and authentic, fueled by his feelings about his real-life two-steps-forward, one-step-back career path, including his fourth-billed place in this very production.

Few reviewers even mentioned Ray Milland. *Variety* called *Tropic Holiday* "a hokey comedy with music which has some good points but on the whole hasn't got what the boxoffices presently require."

Just before *Tropic Holiday* was released, Milland and Lamour participated in the massive Motion Picture Electrical Pageant. As part of the Paramount contingent, they joined dozens of stars and government officials at the Los Angeles Memorial Coliseum to celebrate Hollywood and plug their latest movies, circus style.

Between all the filming and publicity stunts, Milland was exceptionally active throughout the 1930s, yet he always found time to read. His latest book, *Serenade*, the newly published, controversial James M. Cain novel, was one that intrigued him.

Following the Lamour teamings, Paramount planned casting Milland opposite Madeleine Carroll as a reporter tricked into marriage in *Cafe Society*. By the time the romantic comedy commenced months later than scheduled, Milland was unavailable, and Fred MacMurray replaced him.

As Milland's's screen status grew, recognition by Hollywood's elites extended beyond "The British Colony." In March 1938, the Millands were invited to a surprise birthday party for Joan Crawford. At the Trocadero, Ray and Mal mingled with Crawford and Franchot Tone, her then-husband, Barbara Stanwyck and Robert Taylor, and Irving and Ellin Berlin, among many others. The Crawford relationship grew over time, with Mal and Joan starting a fad to knit together in fancy restaurants around town. Still, the Millands were too smart not to realize most of their friendships were predicated on snobbery, but they played the game wisely, if cautiously.

Later that spring, the Millands returned to the Los Angeles County Courthouse to submit his Petition for Naturalization. It was no longer a question whether they would be staying in the United States: Ray Milland was very much an American movie star. On May 17, 1938, the court received the petition, and on August 26, it was officially approved. In between, in June, gossip columnist Erskine Johnson wrote a curious one-liner: "The Ray Millands, who should know, insist that divorce gossip is untrue."

AIRBORNE

Milland started work in the spring on *Men with Wings*, an October 1938 release and another Cary Grant castoff. Like *Wings over Honolulu*, *Men with Wings* focused on societal interest in flight history, as commuter aviation was becoming increasingly accessible to the masses. For Paramount, the film was an answer to MGM's *Test Pilot* starring Clark Gable and Warner Bros.' *Dawn Patrol* starring Errol Flynn, both released in 1938 as well. When Paramount executive Jeff Lazarus conceived the idea in 1936, he had hoped to team Cary Grant with Randolph Scott. But by the time of production, in May of 1938, Grant was long gone from Paramount, and Ray Milland was set to take his part opposite top-billed Fred MacMurray in the Scott role.

Robert Carson's screenplay blends real-life events with a fictitious story about three Midwesterners—Patrick Falconer (MacMurray), Scott Barnes (Milland), and Peggy Ranson (Louise Campbell)—helping the World War I cause by designing and flying planes that are specially equipped for combat missions. At the same time, both men love Peggy, and she is torn between them. In a climactic air flight, Pat is killed, and Scott and Peggy honor his legacy.

There are many plot detours, but the unquestionable highlights are the aerial sequences, the first of their kind to be photographed in Technicolor. Director William A. Wellman had flown a combat plane during World War I and had already directed *Wings* (1927), the first Best Picture in Oscar history, yet it was stunt flyer Paul Mantz who directed most of the exciting aerial shots. Similarly, despite his flying prowess, Ray Milland was never once aloft for what were the best parts of the movie.

The character of Scott allowed Milland to show some unanticipated vulnerability, especially in the scene when he first hears that Peggy has married the more adventurous Pat. In fact, Scott's eternal devotion to Peggy following her marriage is one of the few honestly moving aspects to the drama. MacMurray and Campbell are merely passable in their roles, and the supporting cast adds predictable flavor—Andy Devine's "yokel" humor as a friend to the flyers is typical.

Variety singled out Milland's contributions: "It may not match *Test Pilot*, which it parallels in a somewhat distant manner, but it won't be far behind that epic of the air.... Milland plays his part with fine restraint, understanding and poise." Milland rendered his obligatory studio flacking by turning up at the Cavalcade of Aviation airshow in mid-September, a few weeks before the premiere of *Men with Wings*.

It was around this time that independent producer David O. Selznick considered Milland for the role of Ashley Wilkes in his upcoming blockbuster,

Gone with the Wind. According to one of Selznick's famous memos, he favored the idea of Milland because the actor possessed a sensitivity and "enormous attractiveness" but also a "weakness" that is more appealing to both strong heroines (Scarlett and Melanie) than the arrogant preening of Rhett Butler. Milland even screen-tested for Selznick. In the end, though, classically trained British actor Leslie Howard, who was fourteen years older than Milland, won the part.

Milland's November 1938 release, *Say It in French*, was only a programmer comedy. It had a lengthy production schedule (mid-August to mid-October), presumably because of some extensive filming in New York City by director Andrew L. Stone, later known for his thrillers shot entirely on location.

Say It in French is a screwball romance filled with complications. In Frederick Jackson's screenplay, Milland plays Richard Carrington Jr., a New York playboy. When Richard arrives home from a trip abroad with his new French bride, Julie (Olympe Bradna), he discovers his father is in a financial bind, so he must pretend to be engaged to his wealthy former fiancée, Auriol (Irene Hervey), while Julie takes a job as Richard's mother's maid. Many more plot developments occur before Richard finally tells his family Julie is his wife.

Though Ray Milland was top-billed, Paramount hoped *Say It in French* would be a great introduction to Parisian-born Olympe Bradna, who was in line to replace the departing Marlene Dietrich. The studio's publicity campaign included a special emphasis on how to pronounce Bradna's first name: "O-lamp." Critics and audiences were not responsive, however, and Bradna was let go by Paramount after one more minor effort.

To be fair, Bradna should not be blamed for the failure of *Say It in French*. The problem is that the film tries to impose humor where it doesn't exist. In one such bit, Richard slings a drunken Auriol over his shoulder and removes her from the Rainbow Room, much to the supposed amusement of the restaurant patrons. The reviewers wrote off the whole thing. Frank S. Nugent of the *New York Times* complained, "The film freezes into conversational attitudes altogether too frequently and makes the mistake, here and there, of laughing too heartily at its own jokes."

At least Milland makes Richard an appealing character, and he was pleased to be cast as a golf pro, having recently taken up the sport. His funniest moments come from having to pretend the new maid of the house isn't his wife. One other plus is that Milland shows off his fluency in French (with perfect accent) during Richard's shouting match with Julie.

The biggest laugh comes at the very end. Richard is hoisted onto a ship heading back to France, thinking Julie is aboard, but she is still on the dock as the ship sails away—under the "end title" card. Defying the romantic comedy tradition of having the two leads embrace at the conclusion, *Say It in French* provides a hint of Ray Milland's more distant screen persona to come.

Without delay, Paramount used Milland to support another European import designated to be the next Dietrich. The actress this time was Italy's Isa Miranda, who had made a great impression in Max Ophuls's *La signora di tutti* in 1934. How she ended up in a part planned for Dietrich is an intriguing story in a production that was cursed from the start.

During his brief reign as a mogul, Ernst Lubitsch green-lit remaking the 1927 silent classic *Hotel Imperial*. With a new title, *Invitation to Happiness* (then later, *I Loved a Soldier*), production got underway in January 1936 with Marlene Dietrich as a Polish World War I entertainer who poses as a chambermaid at the Hotel Imperial. The character's goal is to discover who killed her sister within the famous establishment, situated near the Russian-Austrian front. She is helped by an Austro-Hungarian officer hiding from the Slavs inside the hotel. Charles Boyer was cast as the officer, and the efficient but demanding Henry Hathaway was hired to direct.

Yet, only a few days into filming, a gun went off, the bullet almost hitting Boyer. Next, Hathaway and Dietrich clashed over the deglamorized way he wanted her to appear, which drove the frustrated producer, Benjamin Glazer, to quit. Lubitsch stepped in and backed Hathaway over Dietrich, leading Dietrich herself to bolt the production and, eventually, Paramount, her home studio since 1930. With the unrealized movie already costing nearly $1 million, upper management fired Lubitsch from his executive post. In order to proceed, the studio borrowed Margaret Sullivan from Universal, but during rehearsals Sullivan broke her arm, so *I Loved a Soldier* shut down seemingly for good.

Two years after the debacle, new production chief William LeBaron decided to revive the project again—this time using the original title, a new script, and a tighter budget. Isa Miranda was given the full star build-up, and Ray Milland was cast as the officer, getting second billing. Under the direction of Robert Florey, production began in late October 1938, ending in early December.

NEAR DEATH

Calamitous bad luck returned toward the end of shooting *Hotel Imperial*. During the final sequence showing him riding off with his troops, Milland was supposed to jump from one horse to another. He insisted on doing the stunt himself, but as he started the jump, his saddle came loose, sending him crashing headlong into a pile of broken masonry. Bloody and gravely injured, Milland was rushed to the Santa Monica Hospital, where he laid unconscious for twenty-four hours while Mal sat at his bedside. With multiple fractures and lacerations, including a three-inch gash to his head, he was lucky to be alive and had to spend several weeks recuperating. But the studio did not replace him since so much of the film had been completed, and he resumed his role once released from the hospital.

The jinxed *Hotel Imperial* turned out to be a box-office and critical dud, yet the film is better than its reputation. It maintains a quirky Mittel European flavor and boasts a colorful bunch of character actors: Reginald Owen, Gene Lockhart, J. Carroll Naish, Albert Dekker, and Curt Bois. Only Miranda, *impassif* in a literally pale imitation of Dietrich, is off-putting.

Milland condemned the film, sarcastically calling it "a little gem," but he is well cast as the adventurous lieutenant, a facsimile of his earlier life in the Household Cavalry. Milland's hunted and isolated man would later become a distinct character type (notably in *The Big Clock*, *The Thief*, and *A Man Alone*), and he injects absurdist humor into a sequence when his character poses as fancy-dress hotel waiter, hiding in plain sight of the buffoonish Russian general (Owen).

The French-born Florey had a checkered career going back to the 1928 avant garde short, *The Life and Death of 9413: A Hollywood Extra*, a stinging indictment of the studio system and its mistreatment of actors. In *Hotel Imperial*, Florey's visual flair enlivens the narrative. Despite Milland's dismissal of the film, he had enough faith in Florey's abilities to hire him two decades later to direct nine episodes of his noirish TV detective show, *Markham*.

Reviewers of the day panned this now-forgotten oddity. The *Los Angeles Times* griped, "Elements of the antique and a comic opera flavor are scarcely absent from the completed version, which suffers also, at times, from a pervading dullness."

Following the treacherous *Hotel Imperial* shoot, Milland went on his annual pilgrimage home to Neath. He visited his father for Christmas in 1938, having dinner with him at the Port Talbot Hotel before a short stay in Newport.

By the time he returned to Hollywood for the New Year, Milland started a new hobby: making furniture. The studio was now prohibiting Milland from flying planes as a diversion, so he thought setting up a machine shop would be a safe alternative. Disastrously, in the midst of cutting wood with a power saw one day, he severely wounded his left hand—within a month of the *Hotel Imperial* calamity! The bloody, mangled tendons and missing part of his left thumb required an immediate return to the hospital, where he had just been treated for his on-the-set injuries.

Ray Milland, Gary Cooper, and Robert Preston on location for *Beau Geste* (1939)

Undaunted, Milland didn't give up on wordworking, but he soon added a relatively harmless downtime activity; before wartime "victory gardens" were in vogue, he began growing his own vegetables in the backyard of their home.

Milland's painful accidents were followed by his most significant title to date: *Beau Geste*, the classic about three British brothers joining the Foreign Legion.

Like *Hotel Imperial*, *Beau Geste* was a knockoff of an earlier Paramount silent, based on P. C. Wren's novel, but this time the overhaul was well received by audiences and critics alike. The inspiration first emerged in 1936, when Paramount had planned to make it the studio's initial three-strip Technicolor production, with Henry Hathaway assigned to direct and Milland announced as part of the cast. The Hathaway version was dropped, but the idea came about again in 1938, when Paramount caught wind of RKO's intention to film *Gunga Din*, based on the Rudyard Kipling poem, also about three British sergeants fighting in foreign territory. That George Stevens production had all the makings of a hit, with a cast headed by Cary Grant, Douglas Fairbanks Jr., and Victor McLaglen.

Paramount's response was to revive their own take on the three-comrades-in-arms formula, plugging in Milland for Grant, though *Gunga Din* takes place on the Northwest Frontier of India around 1880, and *Beau Geste* is set in French Morocco just before World War I.

For this new *Beau Geste*, in less costly black-and-white, William A. Wellman was selected after the success of *Men with Wings*. Paramount had already considered reuniting Wellman and Milland for a different production based on a Kipling novel, *The Light That Failed*, costarring Ida Lupino; instead, Wellman mounted the painter-going-blind story in 1939 with the older, more genteel Ronald Colman.

Milland and the rest of the cast and crew spent most of early 1939 (mid-January to early April) near Yuma, Arizona, where a team of engineers built an entire desert city with 136 tents designed to house one thousand men. What had been known as Buttercup Valley was now branded Beau Geste Valley, and it even had its own movie theater.

Though Wellman was known to be temperamental, *Beau Geste*'s production ran smoothly—with one exception. It was Brian Donlevy who acted rudely toward his fellow cast members, much like the character he was playing. Fed up with Donlevy's behavior one day, Milland actually stabbed him in the lower left rib cage during a fight scene. This fracas landed Donlevy in a Yuma hospital for nearly a week, while Paramount's p.r. department worked overtime calling the fight an accidental wounding to Donlevy's shoulder. (Donlevy was later compensated, figuratively, with a Best Supporting Actor nomination.)

Gary Cooper, Ray Milland, and Robert Preston play the Geste brothers. Their reason for joining the French Foreign Legion involves family pride and a stolen "Blue Water" sapphire. It is conspicuous that Milland plays the only brother who survives, the brother who kills the sadistic commander, Sgt. Markoff (Donlevy), the only brother with a love interest (Susan Hayward as his fiancée), and, frankly, the only brother who sounds remotely British. With Gary Cooper as the nominal star, this emphasis on Milland's character could have been seen as a cinematic changing of the guard—at least as far as Paramount viewed the two actors.

The highlights of *Beau Geste* are the various battles and skirmishes. However, the most memorable sequence is the very first we see—another preview of Milland's later horror pictures: a tour of a ghostly fort inhabited by the dead soldiers, propped up by Markoff to fool the Arab army into thinking they are alive. According to author Ralph Schiller, composer Alfred Newman deserves the most credit for the strength of this startling opening: "Newman's eerie, haunting music ... is more frightening than anything ever composed for a Universal horror film."

As with *Gunga Din*, *Beau Geste* asserts a Royalist message—the British Empire is represented majestically, while the invaders (in this case, the Arabs) are purely evil and never defined as individuals. Wellman was not known for revisionist ideas; thus, *Beau Geste* is a well-made but ideologically backward film.

For Milland, *Beau Geste* signaled an advancement from the kind of generic farces and smaller-scale adventures he was making up to this time. In early 1939, Paramount rethought loaning Milland to Twentieth Century-Fox for *Elsa Maxwell's Hotel for Women*, a minor-league melodrama. Around the same time, though, a real chance at a promotion didn't work out. Mitchell Leisen wanted Milland as the romantic lead in *Midnight*, opposite Claudette Colbert, which turned out to be one of Colbert's best films of the decade, but Milland's commitment to *Beau Geste* conflicted with its shooting schedule. Don Ameche got the part.

Then, melancholy cast over the Milland home on March 8, 1939: Harry Weber, Mal's father, died at age fifty-eight, following his third stroke in a year. The family arranged for and attended his burial at the Hollywood Memorial Cemetery.

THE BATTLE OF LONDON—AND THE SEXES

Soon after, Milland was told by the front office he would be traveling to England to make *French without Tears* for Paramount's Two Cities Films Ltd. The only issue was that his left hand was not fully healed, so without telling the studio, he disguised his damaged digits and went about arranging his itinerary with his grieving wife and her mother, Elaine Weber.

Before departing, the Millands employed architect Robert Woolf and his crew to build a nine-room home in the pricey Coldwater Canyon area. Tired of renting a house and wanting something larger, they instructed Woolf to use a Georgian Cotswolds and Tudor style for their new place. (And yes, Woolf had previously designed and built Cary Grant's house.) Given his injuries and upcoming trip, Milland was glad not to be part of the construction team and left everything up to the general contractor. Later, after moving their belongings from their last rental, Ray and Mal hired Loretta Young's mother, Gladys Belzer, a renowned interior decorator, to accessorize each room.

Ray Milland and Gilbert at the Coldwater Canyon house (1941). Photo credit: Album / Alamy Stock Photo.

A sign that Milland had "made it" was that he was finally living in Beverly Hills (across the street from Mitchell Leisen). He and Mal adopted a big, affectionate English Setter, naming him Gilbert after a dog hero of Welsh history, their first pet dog but not their last.

Ellen Drew, Milland's new costar, joined the Milland family on the *Aquitania* ocean liner. Soon after their arrival in late March, *French without Tears* went into production at Sound City Studios in Shepperton, London. With the impending war in both England and France, the title might have suggested a war drama, when, instead, it was a lightweight farce without any war references. Terence Rattigan adapted his 1936 play for the screen with Anatole DeGrunwald, Ian Dalrymple, and the uncredited team of Billy Wilder and Charles Brackett.

The story is set in a school in the South of France, where British gentlemen go to learn French. When one of the student's sisters arrives for a visit, the young woman, Diana (Drew), turns out to be a glamorous flirt. Most of the men are attracted to her, but Allan (Milland) is simply annoyed, seeing through Diana's teasing ways. Of course, Allan and Diana end up together.

Though some of the social satire was softened for the film, *French without Tears* turned out to be a treat. Anthony Asquith, who had recently codirected Shaw's *Pygmalion* for the screen, did another laudable job of making a talky play feel cinematic. By sheer coincidence, during his cavalry days, Milland guarded Asquith's father, H. H. Asquith, who had been prime minister of the British Empire.

French without Tears mostly relies on the talents of its ensemble. At first, Missouri-born Ellen Drew seems wrong for the British heroine, which would have been better suited for the irresistibly beautiful Vivien Leigh, yet Drew becomes increasingly alluring to the viewer, just as she does to our crabby hero.

The supporting cast is excellent, and best of all is Ray Milland. One senses the actor is enjoying himself as the conniving misogynist. In one early scene, Allan throws his clothes into a suitcase as he reluctantly moves out of his boarding room, allowing Diana to have her own private space. For the shot, Milland uses a violent thrust that Asquith captures from *inside* the suitcase. This well-played bit of character development sets up the leads' ensuing "battle of the sexes" in a funny if disquieting way. What this moment also signifies is the growing difference between Ray Milland and Cary Grant—the latter would rarely be so outwardly "ungentlemanly" in a similar situation. Milland was proving himself to be a more reckless sort of character type, clearly harder to suppress or define.

The critics were sharply divided over *French without Tears*. The *Hollywood Reporter* was exuberant: "Here is a picture which flows along smoothly, is consistently amusing and even, at moments, hilarious. . . . Ray Milland's performance is equal to the best of his previous efforts, and he makes the most of every opportunity." At the other extreme, Howard Barnes in the *New York Herald Tribune* called it "torpid and mannered," but he did add, "Ray Milland is the only player who occasionally makes the comic embellishments bearable."

As *French without Tears* wrapped, Milland became concerned about the looming Nazi threat in England. Having witnessed people wearing gas masks and practicing raid drills, he insisted Mal and her mother leave for America early, promising to join them in several weeks.

After the production, Milland went to Horsham in Sussex (southeast of Wales) to spend time with his mother. He bought her and her husband a house to be closer to his sister, Olivia, who had recently married and was now Olivia Charles of Sussex. As the mother of a movie star, Elizabeth fast became a local celebrity herself and was occasionally interviewed about her son and daughter-in-law. In April 1939, she told *Picturegoer* that Mal Milland had "done a great deal to make Ray a success." Despite his mitzvah, Ray became increasingly distant from his mother.

Milland took the *Normandie* home, several months before the Brits declared war on Germany. Once comfortably rested from the overseas shoot and just before *Beau Geste* premiered in July 1939, Milland received joyous news from Mal: she was pregnant!

Back at Paramount, Milland was given a starring role in a Technicolor adventure—and another remake. *Untamed* emerged as one more attempt to pair the now-dependable box-office draw in Milland with a female newcomer, though this time not from Europe. Patricia Morison was the actor's latest partner, and once again the big studio build-up didn't work.

Shot in July of 1939 and released in July of 1940, *Untamed* was the studio's reworking of *Mantrap* (1926) starring Clara Bow, based on a serialized Sinclair Lewis novel. In this version, the studio added color in order to highlight the many scenic portions of the story. But in every other way, *Untamed* must have seemed desperately old fashioned, even in 1940.

In *Untamed*, Milland plays William, a Manhattan physician on vacation in Hudson Bay. His guide, Joe (Akim Tamiroff), saves him from a bear attack and takes him to his village, where he is nursed back to health by Joe's wife, Alverna (Morison). When Joe leaves on an expedition, the two fall in love, but the forbidden affair is disrupted by village gossip and the outbreak of a contagious disease. William braves a blizzard to get needed medicine just as Joe returns and thinks Alverna has run off with her lover. Joe tries to find and kill the couple, but he freezes to death. The following spring, William and Alverna are free to declare their love to one another.

Untamed starts with an eye-popping sequence in Manhattan. Once in Canada (actually Big Bear Valley and Cedar Lake in San Bernardino) the film becomes something of a travelogue. Akim Tamiroff's cartoonish performance tilts the story dangerously toward camp, and the sophisticated Patricia Morison is wrongly cast as the loving but impetuous child bride who falls for the visiting doctor. (The studio attempted to turn the New York–born actress into an exotic type with a Lamour-like look.) At least, though, Morison later said she enjoyed working with Milland.

Playing a nine-year-old boy in the town who contracts the virus, Darryl Hickman also liked performing with Milland but preferred spending time with either Morison or Tamiroff between takes. In an interview, Hickman described Morison as someone "almost motherly [and] very nice to me," while Milland was "very polite and very charming and very nice to work with but not interactive personally. [Milland] kept to himself [and was] a highly reserved, British-type man. . . . Akim Tamiroff [was] gruff and grumpy but . . . treated me like a grandson."

Milland did his best to make this curiosity work, but he was defeated by the heavy hand of George Archainbaud, Milland's *Return of Sophie Lang* director. Darryl Hickman added that Archainbaud was "not especially pleasant to work with . . . [H]e was a craftsman, but I didn't feel there was a lot of sensitivity in the way he directed actors." Milland's fight scene with Big Boy, the 640-pound Siberian bear, is the most exciting portion. An additional highlight that augurs Milland's horror film future is a shocking facial close-up of the dead, frost-bitten Joe, dragged into town by a dog sled (makeup expert Wally Westmore turned Akim Tamiroff into a sheet-white mutant).

Variety led the way with the unfriendly reviews: "Milland, Miss Morison and Tamiroff do a walk-through of their parts, failing to overcome deficiencies of both the material and ordinary direction."

Milland was further misused by his home studio when his bosses loaned him out to Twentieth Century-Fox for a Sonja Henie vehicle, *Everything Happens at Night*. The actor could have refused the assignment and been put on suspension (i.e. unpaid time away from the studio), but it is an Old World European tradition to "go along" without protest. Milland soon protected himself against other kinds of onerous demands, especially long working hours (sometimes from early morning to midnight), by joining the new union, the Screen Actors Guild.

The provocative-sounding *Everything Happens at Night* with its wartime theme was hardly characteristic of Sonja Henie films, all wholesome musicals with the star showing off her most prominent skill—ice skating. Production Head Darryl F. Zanuck insisted on injecting a lighter tone, but even with the dialogue additions (some by F. Scott Fitzgerald!) to the Art Arthur–Robert Harari screenplay, *Everything Happens at Night* was far more austere in its look and tone than anything Henie fans would have come to expect.

Based on a true story, *Everything Happens at Night* follows two rival reporters—American Ken Morgan (Robert Cummings) and British Geoffrey Thompson (Milland)—as they compete to snag a story about a Nobel Prize–winning doctor who stood up to the Gestapo. While staying at the same Swiss inn, Ken and Geoffrey also vie for the attention of a nurse, Louise (Henie), who is actually the daughter of the doctor (Maurice Moscovitch). At the climax, the newsmen help smuggle Louise and her father over the French border. At the end, Geoffrey is tricked into staying ashore, while a ship to America departs with Louise, her father, and Ken.

Directed by Irving Cummings in September 1939 and swiftly turned around for a holiday release in December, this hybrid war drama–musical comedy might have been much better with a different leading lady. Norway's Henie had always been limited in her on-screen abilities, and her main ice-skating sequence is imaginative but forced on the narrative in way that makes it a bizarre distraction. (The fantasy number was directed by Gregory Ratoff and set to a "Blue Danube" rumba.)

Ray Milland handles both the comic dueling with Robert Cummings and the tense, melodramatic scenes with equal aplomb. Yet, while Milland is billed second to Henie, it is third-billed Robert Cummings whose character wins her over. (Zanuck chose Cummings over Milland at the last minute, just before the finale was shot.) As with *Say It in French*, Milland is a "a man alone," even at the end of an ostensible comedy, and again separated by a ship departure.

Viewers today should be most intrigued comparing the byplay between Milland and Cummings with their more famous tension-filled "reunion" fifteen years later, *Dial M for Murder* (1954). (Interestingly, while Milland was "Americanizing" himself early in his acting career, Missouri-born Cummings started out by attempting different British dialects in order to advance in the business.)

Some of the reviews of 1939 were contemptuous, such as Frank S. Nugent's in the *New York Times*: "Dismissing its implausibilities—and using a 10-ton snow plow for the purpose—we suggest it is not good for Miss Henie, although Mr. Milland and Mr. Cummings are diligently lighthearted and we suggest that Twentieth Century-Fox summon a repairman: the refrigerator for keeping Miss Henie on ice seems finally to have collapsed of nervous exhaustion."

Milland was loaned out again, to RKO for *Irene*, yet another remake. Based on a long-running 1919 Broadway show and 1926 silent film, *Irene* was bought by Imperadio Pictures and RKO with Fred Astaire and Ginger Rogers first in mind.

This time, Cary Grant would be invoked by the casting of Billie Burke and Roland Young, both from Grant's 1937 hit, *Topper*. As one of many Anglophilic pictures made before the US entry into World War II (production starting November 1939), *Irene* top-lined the British Anna Neagle in the title role and was directed by her mentor (and future husband) Herbert Wilcox, also from England. Having Ray Milland would be a benefit to both the British and American markets, since Neagle was far better known in the United Kingdom. In the British ads, Neagle completely dominated the cover art, while in the US ads, she shared space equally with Milland. Moreover, Milland's presence would recall *Easy Living*, a similar Cinderella yarn, though that earlier film emphasized screwball over sentiment.

Alice Duer Miller updated the musty libretto, which is set in New York and follows a young Irish émigré, Irene, who gets a job as a model in a clothing boutique owned by two wealthy Long Island playboys—Don (Milland) and Bob (Alan Marshal). When Irene accidentally ruins a dress she is supposed to wear to a charity function, she substitutes it with a beautiful blue gown that belonged to her late mother. Irene becomes the hit of the party and is mistaken for an upper-crust descendant of Ireland. She is introduced as the toast of the town until a jealous model exposes her. Don stands by Irene through the turmoil and wins her in the end.

The indisputable highlight of *Irene* is the fancy party scene, which is in Technicolor while the rest of the film is in black and white. This lengthy color sequence ends with the most memorable of the songs: Neagle performs "Alice Blue Gown" while wearing the dress (cinematographer Russell Metty ingeniously mutes the background colors to accentuate the garment's tint). Earlier at the party, Neagle and Milland dance smoothly and elegantly to the melody (on the Astaire-Rogers soundstages!), and Milland exhibits a skill he never had a chance to display before or after this film. It was fun nostalgia for both stars, who had won that ballroom contest together as unknowns more than twelve years earlier in England.

Wilcox focused most of his attention on Neagle, but he also enjoyed working with Milland and wanted him to costar with Neagle in a follow-up (this didn't happen until they all reunited for a segment in the all-star *Forever and a Day*). Wilcox's direction is too restrained, but he is aided by the excellent camerawork of Metty and the adroit cast: Milland, Burke, Young, Marsha Hunt, Arthur Treacher, Ethel Griffies, and in a comic film-within-the-film parody of a newsreel, the Dandridge Sisters (including Dorothy Dandridge). As Irene's grandmother, May Robson provides the comic coup de grâce: before running off with Irene at the fade out, Don plants a kiss on Granny's lips, and the grouchy matriarch candidly concludes to herself, "Not bad!"

The *Los Angeles Times* declared *Irene* "an airy, fluffy, light-spirited entertainment" and singled out the leading man: "Much interest derives from the performance by Ray Milland as the hero. . . . He is very consistent and logical in this interpretation, which strengthens the plot." Of course, the music contributed another plus, and the film's single Oscar nomination was for its scoring (by Anthony Collins). After everything, *Irene* was a winner with audiences: with a budget of $578,000, the movie earned $1,620,000.

While quietly appreciating his accolades, Milland could not have missed the symbolism of *Irene*'s opening titles. He is portrayed as a marionette

Irene (1940), with Anna Neagle. Photo credit: RKO Radio Pictures / Photofest.

pulled by strings during the sequence (along with one in the likeness of Anna Neagle). What better visual metaphor could have been created to define the predicament of a star under contract by an all-powerful studio ordered to do things against his or her will?

As proof, Milland was loaned to Columbia Pictures (Hollywood's "Siberia") for *The Doctor Takes a Wife*, a movie more in keeping with his typical forays into romantic comedy (no singing, dancing, or skating required). What had been originally titled *As Good as Married* was shot in January and February 1940 and released in April, the same month as *French without Tears* and *Irene*.

The "Siberia" moniker derived from mogul Harry Cohn's severe cost-cutting methods and infamous temper. Regardless, Milland never complained and did a fine job with *The Doctor Takes a Wife*, which turned out to be another big moneymaker. At home, early during filming, Mal's girlfriends fêted her with a baby shower at Josephine Wayne's home (the first Mrs. John Wayne). Mal returned the favor the following year by hosting the Wayne baby's christening.

Though made at the tail-end of the screwball comedy era, *The Doctor Takes a Wife* is lively and becomes funnier as it progresses. In it, Milland is Dr. Tim Sterling, a chauvinistic medical-school professor who is tricked by a famous author, June Cameron (Loretta Young), into giving her a ride into New York City. On the trip, the two argue about gender issues. For convoluted reasons, after they arrive in town, Tim reluctantly spends the night in June's apartment, and the next day they are mistaken as married. Though they despise each other, the two keep up the bogus front of a marriage to avoid a scandal. More complications ensue before opposites attract, and Tim and June end up together.

Playing the first of his many "professor" roles, Milland shows terrific ease handling both the sharp dialogue and the slapstick. Loretta Young provides a smart sparring partner, and Reginald Gardiner and Gail Patrick rise above their stock types. In the most interesting casting, Edmund Gwenn plays Tim's father: they were both Welsh and would become the first (Milland) and second (Gwenn) actors from Wales to win Academy Awards. They reunited in 1950 for *A Woman of Distinction*, a sadly inferior film.

The reviews were especially enthusiastic about Ray Milland. Bosley Crowther of the *New York Times* even credited Milland as the primary asset to the picture: "Thanks to Mr. Milland's genteel clowning and a couple of dependable farce situations . . . the comic pace is generally maintained." Edwin Schallert of the *Los Angeles Times* wrote, "*The Doctor Takes a Wife* is an airy trifle, but airy trifles are more than acceptable when they are as diverting as this picture. . . . The dialogue is exceedingly clever, and is well put over by Ray Milland, who does some of his best work in this production."

Milland was ecstatic after *The Doctor Takes a Wife* wrapped, but it wasn't because of the lively buzz around his newest cinematic creation. In late February, he celebrated finishing the production by taking a skiing vacation in Sun Valley, Idaho. During his trip, Mal called and announced she was in labor—two weeks ahead of schedule. He quickly chartered a plane back to Los Angeles. On March 6, 1940, Mal gave birth to a baby boy at 4:29 a.m. in a Los Angeles hospital. The Millands named their six-pound, chubby-cheeked baby Daniel David Milland, and soon Ray told columnist Kay Proctor, "How could I help but have faith in the future? We ourselves can give our son everything of love and comforts. We have insured his financial security insofar as it is humanly possible by planning and saving for the tomorrow in which we live."

Professionally, too, Milland should have been pleased in 1940. Thanks to several hits and despite some misfires, he was becoming one of Paramount's most bankable stars. By this time, Milland garnered not one but two separate fan clubs, his incoming fan mail jumped from hundreds to thousands per week, and, on the lot, he was given his own office with assistants.

After acknowledging the box office and critical response to *The Doctor Takes a Wife*, Paramount reconsidered loaning out such a valuable contractee. At Fox, Darryl Zanuck wanted to borrow Milland again, this time to play a German who flirts with Nazism in *Four Sons*, but the mogul had to settle for Alan Curtis in the 1940 war drama. Paramount itself scrapped plans to send Milland back to England for more farces like *French without Tears* (one was supposed to costar Madeleine Carroll). Except for a cameo in a war-relief production, Milland would not leave his home studio anytime again until 1949.

And yet, during the making of his next picture, Ray Milland thought his career was over!

CHAPTER 4

A WAR BEGINS . . . A STAR IS BORN (1940–1943)

TODAY, *ARISE, MY LOVE* IS CONSIDERED BY MANY A LIVELY IF STRANGE MIXture of disparate genres. At the time of its release, the film was a surprise hit with audiences and fairly well received by the critics. But during production, Ray Milland told his wife, Mal, to start packing their bags! The film he was working on was so bad, he figured if it was released, it would end his career and he would have to find a different profession in England. He wasn't joking, either: during the first rough-cut screening, he left the theater to call his wife and reiterate, "Mal honey, when this picture comes out I'm finished. Sell everything we've got and we'll try to start a new life somewhere else."

Fortunately, Ray Milland was completely wrong. *Arise, My Love* furthered his upward trajectory at Paramount. Realizing his mistake, Milland acquired better representation, hiring Zeppo Marx (a.k.a. Herbert Manfred Marx), formerly part of the Marx Brothers, but since the late 1930s, a respected talent agent.

Arise, My Love was based on American flyer Harold Edward Dahl's account of his days as a POW during the Spanish Civil War and the deft way his wife personally implored dictator Francisco Franco to have him freed from prison. Out of this premise, screenwriters Billy Wilder and Charles Brackett fashioned an offbeat love story against a "real-time" war backdrop. The original plan to star Joel McCrea fell through when producer Walter Wanger refused to loan him out. Immediately, leading lady Claudette Colbert lobbied for Ray Milland, her friend and costar from 1935's *Gilded Lily*.

After production began on June 24, 1940, script changes were made throughout the shoot (which lasted until mid-August) to keep up with world events, including the Occupation of Paris and the Battle of Britain. The film was released in October 1940, more than a year away from America's entry into the war.

In other ways, the war intruded on the making of *Arise, My Love* and resulted in a personal tragedy for Ray Milland. Early during production, Milland was well aware his family members in Wales could be targeted at any time by the German Blitzkrieg; in July 1940, he learned via cable that his older sister, Olivia Charles, was killed during one such bombing raid over Sussex. Due to the extreme dangers of traveling, Milland had no choice but to mourn Olivia from afar—and channel his emotions into his work. Milland's profound loss, coupled with the news of the United Kingdom's defeat at the Battle of Dunkirk in June, prompted him to join his British Colony compatriots for an emergency meeting where war relief tasks were assigned to its most eager-to-assist members.

The "ripped-from-the-headlines" *Arise, My Love* narrative begins in the summer of 1939 when columnist Augusta "Gusto" Nash (Claudette Colbert) travels to Spain to cover the heroic story of Tom Martin (Milland), a downed flyer awaiting execution. She poses as his wife in a ploy to have him released from prison, and the two escape to Paris, where Augusta tries to write her story while Tom persistently woos her. Augusta is eventually sent to Berlin at the point Hitler invades Poland, and Tom continues to chase her. They end up on the SS *Athenia* just as the Germans torpedo the ship. After they are rescued, Augusta and Tom return to the United States to warn the country of the seriousness of the Nazi threat.

Apparently, audiences were eager to have grim current events depicted in a fanciful way as *Arise, My Love* teeters uneasily between romantic comedy and action adventure. Yet the film's single Oscar was awarded to its Best Story (by Benjamin Glazer and Hans Székely), and years later, Colbert cited *Arise, My Love* as her personal favorite of all her films. When the two stars worked together five years earlier in *The Gilded Lily*, Milland was the rejected suitor, but now Milland was promoted to costarring status, and he handled the assignment with extraordinary charisma.

CLAUDETTE COLBERT

As a licensed pilot in real life, Milland felt completely comfortable playing Tom Martin, and his teaming with Colbert was a happy association, both on and off the set. The two became even better friends, and nearly something more. In fact, director Mitchell Leisen had to use a stopwatch to make sure their kisses did not exceed the Production Code's permitted length for such clinches. However, what disturbed the Hays Office the most did not involve Colbert. As a result of a scene in a hotel bathroom, during which two pilot friends visit Tom while he takes a bath, Joseph Breen wrote to producer Arthur Hornblow Jr. that because "the camera angles are pitched in such a way to come as near as possible to the exposure of Mr. Milland's sex organs . . . this whole sequence and, more especially, the scene of Milland in the bathtub, constitute in our judgement the most shocking exhibition of consummate bad taste which we have ever seen on the motion picture screen."

Although Milland and Colbert had a follow-up, *Skylark*, it is too bad they didn't continue further as a screen couple. Colbert's knowing way with a line of dialogue provided the perfect counterpoint to Milland's cheeky insouciance. Milland would attain some of this chemistry with Paulette Goddard a little later in the decade, but for now, Milland was appearing opposite one of the most popular and highest paid stars of the day—and it was not only a great partnership but also a major boost to his stock as a leading man.

Some of the stars' best moments together include their "meet cute" firing-squad rescue—the real-life event that inspired the making of the film—and a nightclub scene with Colbert singing and humming to Milland the 1929 classic, "Dream Lover." Colbert is also stirring in her final speech, referencing the film's title (from the Bible's Song of Solomon) in relation to the fall of France and the need for Allied nations to retaliate.

Critics embraced *Arise, My Love* much in the same way audiences did and several noticed a new confidence in Milland's work. In the *Los Angeles Times*, Richard Griffith called it "a pleasant surprise" and added, "The basic timeliness of the story is sharpened to concert pitch by brilliant dialogue and fine performances by Claudette Colbert and Ray Milland, the latter achieving full stellar stature for the first time." The *Christian Science Monitor* wrote, "Ray Milland plays Tom with a new authority. . . . Claudette Colbert turns in what may likely be her best performance since *It Happened One Night*."

Another kind of war, a private one, began during production. As Milland tells it, late in the night he received a call from influential gossip columnist Hedda Hopper, "who, in arrogant and imperious fashion, told me that I was to appear on her nationally broadcast radio show. I told her that I was facing a week of night shooting and that it would be quite impossible." Milland continues: "She said, 'Listen, you limey son-of-a-bitch, nobody, but nobody refuses to go on the *Hedda Hopper Show*. You show up on Tuesday night or I'll run you out of town and don't think I can't!' I hung up on her. Stupid woman." Hopper did not run Milland out of town (he was becoming much too big a star, protected by his studio), but she laid in wait for years to seek her revenge—during the making of *Dial M for Murder* in 1953—at a vulnerable moment for the actor.

Milland stayed away from Hopper's show, but he happily performed on such radio programs as *Lux Radio Theatre*. When the *Arise, My Love* edition aired on June 8, 1942, Milland was joined by his *Doctor Takes a Wife* costar, Loretta Young, not Colbert. After World War II, *Arise, My Love* had enough nostalgic resonance to be updated for an *Academy Award Theater* thirty-minute radio recap (airing June 1, 1946), again with Milland but no Colbert.

With Milland achieving top stardom, *Lux Radio Theatre* became a regular career activity for him throughout the 1940s, and under Cecil B. DeMille's supervision, *Lux* became a highly rated staple of CBS Radio. Future MGM screenwriter-producer George Wells was the head writer of the show during the late 1930s and early 1940s and worked with Ray Milland several times, starting with Milland's debut show, an adaptation of 1938's *Alexander's Ragtime Band*. For the 1940 radio version of the Twentieth Century-Fox hit, Alice Faye (also in her *Lux* debut) repeated her role as Stella, the band singer, and Ray Milland replaced Tyrone Power as "Alexander," the band leader hero of the show. Wells's fast-paced banter and use of Irving Berlin songs made this a fun entry that Faye "remembered enjoying." For their five days of work, Milland and Faye each earned $5,000, the lucrative fee for all stars on *Lux*.

Between 1940 and 1950, Milland performed in fifteen *Lux* shows, most of them adaptations of his own movies. In an interview, George Wells explained how *Lux Radio* operated and evolved during his tenure:

> Advertising companies ran the radio business in the early days, not the networks. They bought the shows and married them to sponsors—and sponsors did the whole shows. . . . We only worked from plays [in the beginning]. . . . Later on, we worked from movie scripts. That came about from me [because of the difficulty of adapting plays as radio scripts]. . . . And then right after that, the show moved [from New York to California] . . . and then we established very close contact with the motion picture studios. . . . It became a backscratching bit: we gave them publicity, they gave us their material and their stars. . . . Most of [the stars] were very good about it; they liked it, most of them, and they recognized the problem I had. I was doing a script in an hour that they [had] spent ninety minutes to two hours doing.

While *Lux* would keep Milland busier than ever, Paramount revised his contract with an increased salary and announced some new plans for him. One intriguing idea was the movie translation of Clare Boothe Luce's *Kiss the Boys Goodbye*, opposite Mary Martin. In effect, Milland would have played a satiric facsimile of David O. Selznick—pompous filmmaker "Lloyd Lloyd"—who

I Wanted Wings (1941), with Veronica Lake

conducts an extensive search for the female lead in a major motion picture (a thinly disguised *Gone with the Wind*). Additionally, Milland would have sung a duet with Martin, "I'll Never Let a Day Pass By," but, as with Mitchell Leisen's *Midnight*, Paramount cast Don Ameche instead.

Milland's next picture, *I Wanted Wings*, focused even more intently on serious war themes than *Arise, My Love*, though both were shot and released well before America's involvement in World War II. In the tradition of other aviator-training stories, *I Wanted Wings* represented one of Hollywood's many cinematic recruiting posters during the country's peacetime draft. The unapologetically prowar endeavor was filmed between August and December 1940 and premiered in March 1941. Obviously, audiences could not get enough of this kind of comrades-in-arms portrait: the others from the major studios were equally well attended, including MGM's *Flight Command* (1940) and Warner Bros.' *Dive Bomber* (1941).

Paramount invested a lot of money and talent in *I Wanted Wings*. Starting with a $1 million budget (that went over by $262, 454.87), preproduction involved location shooting at Randolph Field and Kelly Field near San Antonio, Texas. But the original director, *Tropic Holiday*'s Theodore Reed, was replaced on September 7, 1940, because the studio felt his dailies were unsatisfactory ("a disastrous start," says author James Curtis). To Milland's relief, Mitchell Leisen was summoned to take over for the remainder of the shoot, much of which was still on location in Texas.

I Wanted Wings revolves around three young cadets who strive to overcome their various personal dilemmas in order to "earn their wings" and join the army air force. The three men are Jeff (Milland, as yet another Long Island playboy), Al (William Holden), and Tom (Wayne Morris), and they are supervised by the strict Captain Mercer (Brian Donlevy). When not training, the men are distracted by the women in their lives: Jeff meets a photographer, Carolyn (Constance Moore), and they eventually fall in love, but Jeff is also attracted to Al's former girlfriend, Sally (Veronica Lake), a nightclub singer.

Early in the production, Milland's instinct for adventure led to his nearly killing himself on location. According to Neil Doyle,

> He went up with a pilot for a test run and being an avid amateur parachutist decided to make a jump [at about seven thousand feet] before the plane landed. When the plane began to sputter the pilot advised him not to jump as they were low on gas and they needed to land quickly. After the landing, Ray told the costume man about his plan to jump and noticed how the color drained from the man's face. The parachute, the man explained, was just a costume prop!

Later In the shoot, Leisen told Milland to rush toward a burning plane for an action scene. Milland followed orders, and the fire singed off his eyelashes. Ray Milland thereafter had to wear false eyelashes!

Despite his mishaps, Milland was the only one on the set to help and support newcomer Veronica Lake, especially when Leisen would yell at her in front of the crew. Leisen, along with Constance Moore and Brian Donlevy, found Lake unprofessional, saying she arrived late to the set, didn't know her lines, and needed multiple retakes. (At least there were no reported incidents between Milland and Donlevy.)

Ironically for a movie about male heroics, *I Wanted Wings* is best remembered as the movie that launched Veronica Lake as a sex symbol. (The role was intended for Rita Hayworth, but Columbia refused to loan her out.) Apart from singing the sultry "Born to Love" ("ghosted" by Martha Mears), Lake debuts her famous "peek-a-boo-bang" hairstyle. She also has romantic interludes with both Milland and Holden and turns up in the over-the-top climax.

If some of Lake's scenes feel shoe-horned into the story, the actress adds much energy to a movie that flags at times. The training scenes are repetitive, the attempts at humor are forced, and the romance between Jeff and Carolyn is bland. Future Milland costar Paulette Goddard would have been a far better Carolyn, a character modeled after Margaret Bourke-White.

Most of the reviews were complimentary. Edwin Schallert's in the *Los Angeles Times* was typical: "The picture is the most elaborate technically so far to emerge and its human story, though indulging in hokum part of the time, has plenty of popular appeal.... Ray Milland and Holden are excellent."

Milland is especially impressive during the moments Jeff unexpectedly divulges his fears, such as when he becomes emotionally paralyzed while Al helps Tom out of a crashed plane. Milland recites one particular line (to Holden) with a conviction unusual for heroic male stars of the time: "The louder I talk, the more scared I am—that's just between you and me!"

While *I Wanted Wings* was still in production, Paramount realized it had a formidable duo in Milland and Claudette Colbert. The studio heads had purchased the play, *Skylark*, with Colbert and Melvyn Douglas in mind but changed course once they saw the box-office returns for *Arise, My Love*.

Skylark had been first serialized in novel form by Samson Raphaelson and then became a 1939 Broadway show starring Gertrude Lawrence and Donald Cook. For the movie, much of what had been risqué on the stage was considerably toned down in the screenplay by Zion Myers and Allan Scott (screenwriter of Milland's *Wise Girl*).

Director Mark Sandrich hardly possessed the famous "Lubitsch Touch" and kept the movie stagebound, but he allowed the stars to shine. More than anything else, it was Colbert and Milland who saved *Skylark* from the commonplace. (Its only Academy Award nomination was for Best Sound Recording.)

In this comedy of manners, Colbert plays Lydia Kenyon, an upper-class housewife who feels neglected by her workaholic husband, Tony (Milland), an advertising executive. During their anniversary party, Lydia makes Tony jealous by running off with a handsome divorce lawyer, Bill (Brian Aherne). Later, Tony gets fired, and Lydia demands a divorce. In a contrived ending not in the play, Tony takes a government job helping Latin American allies during war preparations, and Lydia, realizing she doesn't love Bill, joins Tony in Havana.

Off-screen, the romantic feelings between Milland and Colbert that had started on the set of *Arise, My Love* almost became a real love affair. According to Amy Fine Collins, "While they were making *Skylark* (1941), Milland, an irresistible Lothario, propositioned her. After some hesitation Colbert [who was married] finally consented to an assignation at her secretary's apartment in Westwood. 'On the way there, she said to herself, "No, I just can't do it." And she turned around and drove home,' says a Hollywood source. 'Claudette's problem, you see, was that she just could not lie. It was not in her character.'"

Rather than cultivate a reputation as "an irresistible Lothario," Milland emphasized his homebody attributes in interviews, particularly now that he was a father. To some extent, this "family-man" image was true. Early forties magazine photos of Milland doting on Danny appear genuine, and according to the *Los Angeles Times*, "Milland remained an introvert, a man who invented all kinds of excuses to avoid movie openings and exhibitor meetings." He would eventually admit, "I got out of most of those by having a relative die suddenly. . . . I honestly believe I had more relatives kick the bucket than any individual west of the Rockies."

As a way of demonstrating the convention of "putting on airs" of the era, Ray and Mal hired a nursemaid for Danny, Marie Wilson (no relation to the actress), and a Black married couple, Asa and Eleanor Surratt, as their butler and housekeeper, respectively.

After *Skylark* wrapped in April, Milland participated in the May 1941 shoot of a segment in the all-star *Forever and a Day*, but the war propaganda epic would not be seen by audiences for another two years.

When *Skylark* was released in November, crowds were treated to the reteaming of Colbert and Milland, and the reviews were complimentary. Howard Barnes in the *New York Herald Tribune* wrote perceptively: "Miss Colbert is the chief agent in holding the fragments of a random tale together, but she has stalwart assistance. Ray Milland is remarkably resourceful in making the advertising man a heel while successful, and a dashing Lochinvar when down and out." Nevertheless, *Skylark* was the last Milland-Colbert collaboration, other than the *Lux Radio* version in February 1942, for which they and Brian Aherne reprised their roles, and *Lux Radio*'s *Practically Yours* (in August 1945), with Milland replacing Fred MacMurray from the 1944 comedy feature.

Skylark's deficiencies proved there was only one Ernst Lubitsch. After the director's departure from Paramount, Mitchell Leisen became the heir apparent to the "Lubitsch Touch," designating the action-oriented *I Wanted Wings* an outlier assignment. Billy Wilder and Preston Sturges were two screenwriters under contract who never appreciated the way Leisen directed their scripts (Sturges thought he was "a bloated phony"). When they finally seized their opportunity to direct their own work, Wilder and Sturges supplanted Leisen in the eyes of the critics as closer to the spirit and artistry of Lubitsch. Wilder would soon unite with Ray Milland for two classics, but the single time Preston Sturges directed Milland was for an unbilled walk-on bit (in long shot) in his 1941 Hollywood satire, *Sullivan's Travels*, filmed during the spring that year.

The only other Milland-Sturges connection occurred nearly a year later, in March 1942, when Milland accepted the Henry Fonda part on the *Lux Radio* version of Sturges's *The Lady Eve*, costarring the 1941 movie's lead, Barbara Stanwyck. In this case, Milland was badly miscast as a naive millionaire tricked by card sharks, though he handled the fast-paced line readings well.

Executives beyond the Paramount gates took note of the back-to-back triumphs of *Arise, My Love* and *I Wanted Wings* (the latter was Paramount's biggest money maker of the year). In April 1941, while preparing *How Green Was My Valley*, Darryl F. Zanuck, the vice president in charge of production at Twentieth Century-Fox, wrote a memo to director John Ford, asking "if there is some way we can borrow Ray Milland from Paramount, [sic] I think he would be great as the preacher."

Yet a changing of the guard happened at Paramount by the time of Zanuck's request. Production head William LeBaron left to work for Zanuck at Fox in February 1941, and songwriter-turned-producer B. G. "Buddy" DeSylva was immediately installed in his place. Down the line, this corporate game of musical chairs would help Milland's career, as DeSylva would be a more enthusiastic supporter than LeBaron had ever been, but in the moment it meant DeSylva better recognized Milland's worth to the studio and quashed the loan-out.

Milland could only speculate in what ways starring in *How Green Was My Valley* might have changed his professional stature: it became a multi-Oscar winner (including Best Picture), in a story set in his homeland (South Wales), even if shot entirely in Hollywood. Ultimately, Canadian-born Walter Pidgeon became the preacher and revived his sagging career while Paramount tried to figure out how best to use Milland. He was to take over for William Holden in something called *Channel Port*, written by Leonard Lee, but that one was never made. Then Milland was announced for Edward H. Griffith's melodrama *Virginia*, which did get made but with Fred MacMurray pinch-hitting.

Briefly, Paramount considered loaning out Milland to producer Alexander Korda for *Lydia*, directed by Julian Duvivier. The United Artists' release was completed in late summer 1941—without Milland—and concerned four men (Joseph Cotten, Alan Marshal, Bob Reeves, Hans Jaray) who all love the mysterious Lydia (Merle Oberon).

PAULETTE GODDARD

By contrast, Paramount pressed Milland into much lighter fare. Though his 1942 output culminated with a comedy classic, *The Major and the Minor*, it is a testament to the force of Ray Milland's attractive if flawed leading man persona that he survived the rest of 1942 and 1943; in fact, he actually advanced his standing within Paramount and outwardly with his fan base despite appearing in four other films frankly beneath his talent: *Reap the Wild Wind*, *The Lady Has Plans*, *Are Husbands Necessary?* and *The Crystal Ball*, three of them costarring Paulette Goddard.

Milland and Goddard were first teamed in *Reap the Wild Wind*, a March 1942 release from the mercurial Cecil B. DeMille.

The Technicolor epic was based on a Thelma Strabel story, yet it is clear that its true inspiration was the cinematic behemoth of 1939, *Gone with the Wind*. In fact, Paulette Goddard not only plays a role similar to Scarlett O'Hara but makes up for having missed out on securing the coveted part (she had been the favored choice of David O. Selznick until he discovered Vivien Leigh). Scarlett's "Fiddle dee dee" line is reassigned to Louise Beavers—doing a weak imitation of Hattie McDaniel's "Mammy." Of course, even the "Wind" in the film's title evokes the earlier megahit.

Though principal photography began in 1941, technically, *Reap the Wild Wind* started while *Gone with the Wind* was still in some theaters. In 1940, a crew was sent to the Florida reefs for background location shots. Later, the studio proudly let it be known that it would be the most expensive Hollywood blockbuster since *Gone with the Wind*, although during production (from June 2 to August 30, 1941), studio heads privately fretted about the film going over its already exorbitant $1,650,000 budget.

Truthfully, there is no comparison between the quality of the two motion pictures—*Gone with the Wind*, for all its political incorrectness, is an enduring work, while *Reap the Wild Wind* is mostly tiresome and forgettable (if slightly less racist). Usually, director Cecil B. DeMille would present more tricks up his sleeve, no matter how artless, but other than an exciting climax involving a giant squid, DeMille does little with the material to make it come to life.

The screenplay by Charles Bennett, Jesse Lasky Jr., Alan Le May, and Jeanie MacPherson is set in Florida in 1840 and centers on Loxi Clairborne (Goddard), the manager of a shipwreck salvage business in competition with the ruthless King Cutler (Raymond Massey). When Loxi loses her own ship, she asks Steve Tolliver (Milland), a Charleston lawyer, for the loan of his prized vessel and makes plans for her friend Jack (John Wayne) to be its captain. Eventually, she becomes romantically torn between Jack and Steve, not

Ray Milland, Paulette Goddard, and John Wayne in *Reap the Wild Wind* (1942)

realizing Cutler has convinced Jack to sabotage Steve's ship. Cutler's orders result in the apparent demise of Loxi's cousin, Drusilla (Susan Hayward), who was believed to be on board. During a break from a courtroom trial against Cutler, Jack helps Steve find proof of Drusilla's death and dies in a battle with a giant squid. At the end of the trial, Steve kills the guilty and dangerous Cutler in order to protect the others in the courtroom. He and Loxi then travel to Charleston with plans to marry.

Reap the Wild Wind's action-packed narrative promises many thrills, yet the various episodes are bogged down by either excessive dialogue, the trial scenes in particular, or unwanted "comic" relief. Of the latter, Steve uses Loxi's dog for silly ventriloquist bits, then later punishes Loxi by way of a sexist spanking spectacle. (Costume designer Natalie Visart attached an actual mousetrap inside Goddard's hoopskirt in order for it to stay upright during the prolonged paddling.)

DeMille had never been known for his expert handling of actors, so Goddard's evident limitations are not surprising. In fact, his autocratic bullying probably inhibited many of his players. Millard later explained, "He did not know a thing about acting. He couldn't tell you the first word about how to play a scene.... He had coaches on the set, drama coaches, who would tell him what to tell us." Milland was more annoyed than intimidated by DeMille, coming a long way from his 1930 MGM screen-test encounter with the director. Milland tried his best to be stalwart, yet, on-screen, he seems to be privately laughing at the absurdity of his assignment, which would have been the best way to approach such a cartoonish enterprise.

For Milland, the most important aspect of *Reap the Wild Wind* was that he was billed above both Wayne and Goddard. Wayne had had his breakout, star-making moment in John Ford's *Stagecoach* in 1939, but Milland was actually more popular (and certainly more valuable to Paramount) at the time of this production. Initially, DeMille did not want Milland in his movie because he didn't believe he was a big enough name, so Paramount's vice president, Y. Frank Freeman, conducted a poll that proved to DeMille that Milland, indeed, was the most in-demand actor on the lot.

It is noteworthy that Milland is the true hero of the piece, with Wayne's character revealing his shady side by helping the oily villain (Massey) before redeeming himself. In one scene, Milland even knocks down Wayne with a solid punch to the face, and Milland "gets the girl" in the end, both rare sights to behold in a John Wayne film from any period. (Wayne took the blow in stride, a quite different outcome than the Clark Gable knock-out incident in 1931.)

Besting John Wayne aside, Milland was disgruntled making *Reap the Wild Wind*. He loathed wearing the tight pants of the period but was all the more incensed that—in an attempt to remodel him as a sexy dandy—the daily electrolysis treatments he suffered through to curl his hair was the reason he started losing his thick thatch at a relatively young age. "They gave me women's permanents with the electric curlers and all that," he would later complain. "After seven weeks of shooting, I found my hair coming out by the handfuls." Within a few years, he would regularly wear a toupée.

All in all, Milland thought the whole production a "horrible" ordeal. His worst experience occurred during his underwater fight with the giant squid in a huge studio tank; ironically, the sequence wound up the highlight of the movie—and another harbinger of Milland's horror-picture future. According to historian Joe Winters,

> The squid, made by prop men at a cost of $2000, had mechanical insides that were operated by electric motors. It could reach out and encircle a man with its eight and twelve-foot tentacles. The night before the scene was to be filmed, Milland had to attend a party where they served only champagne. Not only was he hung over for the morning shoot, but he got thirsty, and the water he drank immediately re-activated the effects of the champagne from the night before! ... This and a combination of "cures" from co-star John Wayne and others made for

a nightmarish afternoon. DeMille himself never caught on and stated that in all his years in Hollywood and the theatre he had never seen a finer or more perceptive day's acting than he had that day!

Photoplay Magazine must have agreed with DeMille because it bestowed Milland with its Best Performance of the Month award in May 1942. In another inadvertently humorous moment, DeMille staged a solemn but well-publicized event to donate to the war effort the rubber used to create the squid, so movie memorabilia collectors should forget about ever finding this "artifact" from the Golden Age.

Reap the Wild Wind divided critics. *Variety* cautioned, "If interest in the sea-faring vicissitudes of the principals sags in spots . . . the cause may be attributed to the manner in which the story is told, rather than any lapse in the scenic panorama or in the efforts of the players . . . [T]he pacing is uneven." For whatever reason, the *New York Times*' prickly Bosley Crowther loved it: "It is the master turned loose, with no holds barred." Audiences agreed—*Reap the Wild Wind* went on to gross $4 million in US and Canadian rentals alone. At the Oscars the following year, the film won for Best Visual Effects, yet lost in its other two categories, Art Direction and Color Cinematography. Thus, the Academy got it right: the squid stole the show!

For DeMille, his sixty-sixth motion picture happened to coincide with his thirtieth year in the industry, and the Millands dutifully attended the world premiere honoring the director on March 18, 1942, at the brand-new Paramount Theatre on Hollywood Boulevard. Privately, the actor was relieved the torture was over.

Despite their both being major assets to Paramount for many years, Milland never again worked on a DeMille epic, though a press blurb around the time of *Reap*'s release claimed Milland was considering starring in the director's *Rurales*, the story of Benito Juárez's mid-nineteenth-century rural mounted police force. That movie started preproduction (test footage still exists) but was not completed. Milland only collaborated one other time, when he reprised his role opposite Goddard in the DeMille-supervised *Lux Radio* rendering of *Reap the Wild Wind*, approximately one year after the premiere (in March 1943).

Following the *Reap* shoot, the Milland-Wayne friendship was sorely tested. There are least two accounts of what happened. According to John Wayne biographer Jean Ramer, "[Wayne's marital problems] might have blown over if Duke hadn't decided to go to Mexico City with his friends, Ward Bond, Fred MacMurray and Ray Milland to investigate buying a studio there to set up an independent film company. The deal didn't succeed. But a Mexican movie actress, Esperanza Bauer [sic] succeeded in charming Duke right out of his mind."

Michael Munn, another Wayne biographer, relates the story in a somewhat different way, not mentioning the film company idea: Milland went on vacation to Mexico with Wayne, Bo Roos, their new business manager, Fred MacMurray, and Ward Bond. Milland became jealous during the trip after he introduced Wayne to Esperanza Baur (a.k.a. "Chata"), an aquaintance, and then saw them take off together. Two more historians, Scott Eyman and Andrew Allen, separately recount the most lurid version: Milland played matchmaker, introducing Wayne to Baur, whose mother was a prostitute, and she herself was rumored to be the same. (Wayne and Baur married in 1946 and divorced in 1954.) Both Eyman and Allen assert that Milland knew Baur because she was Milland's mistress. Whatever happened, by the end of the trip, Milland and Wayne weren't on speaking terms and didn't mend fences for a while.

At the time, Milland sounded philosophical about the ending of friendships in general: "I seldom have an open break with anyone. We just sense we have nothing left to give each other and drift apart. Sometimes, after six months or a year, we are drawn together again."

Returning to the studio, Milland joined Paulette Goddard for *The Lady Has Plans*, a minor effort but, in fairness, quite a bit better than *Reap the Wild Wind*. Based on a story by Leo Birinski, *The Lady Has Plans* was undeniably influenced by *Arise, My Love*, combining the action thriller with many comic elements and featuring World War II correspondents as central characters. Claudette Colbert was even considered for the leading role opposite Milland (as was Madeleine Carroll) before Goddard was cast. Production started before the US entry into the war (from late September to late October 1941) but released afterwards, in March 1942.

In Harry Tugend's screenplay, Goddard plays Sidney Royce, a reporter in Lisbon mistaken for a Nazi spy (Margaret Hayes) who has had her back tattooed with the secret plans for a radio-controlled torpedo. Sidney's new partner, Kenneth (Milland), realizes the mixup and works with her to thwart the Nazis by drawing a fake diagram on *her* back. Their scheme to outwit the Gestapo backfires, and they are held in a dungeon. Following their escape, Sidney and Kenneth go "on the air" with a phone call from their hotel lobby and reveal the Nazi plot to the world.

The Lady Has Plans is consistently agreeable. In contrast to *Reap the Wild Wind*, Milland and Goddard form a smart twosome. Milland is especially adept with the dialogue. At one point, when first charged to seduce Sidney in order to copy the plans off her back, he exclaims to an Allied agent, "No lovemaking to a murderess for me. When I kiss a girl, I close my eyes. I always like to be able to open them up again!"

Milland enjoyed working with Paulette Goddard, and they became good friends. Much later, though, Milland made the harsh assessment: "[I] always liked working with Paulette. She was not a brilliant actress, she had no sense of timing and everything about her playing was mechanical and contrived, but nobody knew it better than she did, and she was completely honest about it. She is the most honest actress I ever knew."

Edward Norris, the actor playing Milland's sidekick, agreed with Milland about Goddard and had biting words for the director: "[Sidney Lanfield] had a reputation as a rough guy. The set was not a very happy place. He was always looking for somebody to blame for something. . . . Milland was very fine. I thought he was very smooth, easy going, knew his work, a real professional. Paulette was trying to have fun. She was a neighbor of mine and involved with Chaplin at the time. I liked her, but didn't think much of her as an actress. I thought she was listening to too many people."

The behind-the-scenes drama aside, *The Lady Has Plans* received favorable notices and was a hit with American audiences looking for a way to laugh during the grim first months of the war. The *Christian Science Monitor* called it "an amusing skit" and used a startling, modern-day phrase to describe Goddard's character: "Miss Goddard, as Sidney, represents the new feminism."

Milland's third release in 1942, in July, was somehow highly popular yet woefully unfunny. Shot between late November 1941 and early 1942, *Are Husbands Necessary?* was based on Isabel Scott Rorick's 1941 novel, *Mr. and Mrs. Cugat, the Record of a Happy Marriage*, about a wife constantly trying to improve her marriage and her husband's career. (Scott Rorick's material also formed the basis of *I Love Lucy*.) Perhaps the quick turnaround from book to film explains why the movie interpretation of the witty best-seller seems like a hodgepodge of underdeveloped ideas (four writers worked on it, including the usually skillful Tess Slesinger).

Director Norman Taurog had directed Milland in the better *We're Not Dressing* nearly a decade earlier (and then recommended Paramount sign Milland long term); with *Are Husbands Necessary?*, Taurog loses his footing, letting the disjointed screenplay dictate the action. In any case, Paramount was contented with a movie that grossed $1,050,000 (in US rentals) on a budget of $552,000.

Milland received top billing as Mr. Cugat, a bank executive, but the focus was on the leading lady. Betty Field's strong suit was playing intense young women in heavy, dramatic films, including *Kings Row*, released just one month prior to *Are Husbands Necessary?* Here, Field was completely out of her depth in a part that better suited Gracie Allen. (In fact, Burns and Allen executed the funnier *Lux Radio* condensation in February 1943). Actually, Field and Milland could have worked effectively together with different material, and that became the case when they costarred in the radio rendition of his 1944 thriller, *The Uninvited*.

As for Milland, all his Mr. Cugat can do is temper his frustrated reactions to his wife's shenanigans. Milland's best moment is a goofy, all-too-brief song and dance with a former paramour (Patricia Morison, his costar from *Untamed*); his worst moment comes during an interminable costume-party sequence where he arrives as a medieval knight whose lit cigarette falls into his armor, which causes him to flop about on the floor in an attempt to put out the fire.

The reviews were deservedly harsh. Bosley Crowther of the *New York Times* thought it "an almost pitiful endeavor" though felt Milland "holds up well."

Before starting his next movie, Paramount announced in March 1942 that Milland would be the French pirate hero of *Frenchman's Creek*, a Technicolor adaptation of Daphne du Maurier's 1941 novel. By the time shooting commenced, the 1944 romantic adventure starred Arturo de Córdova and Joan Fontaine.

At last, Milland appeared in something superior—*The Major and the Minor*. The September release went into production in mid-March, ending in early May 1942, and was another box-office winner. The difference this time was that *The Major and the Minor* gave Milland a great part in a near-great movie.

Tired of having his screenplays directed by other people, Billy Wilder pressured Paramount for a chance to direct his own. For this auspicious occasion, he updated a story from the 1920s, the Edward Childs Carpenter play *Connie Goes Home* (1923). (Childs Carpenter was the playwright of *The Bachelor Father*, one of Milland's first Hollywood films.)

Collaborating with Charles Brackett, Wilder developed a racy and topical romantic comedy about a woman, Susan Applegate, who is disillusioned with big-city life in New York and decides to return home to Iowa. Susan's hitch is that she doesn't have enough money for the trip, so she disguises herself as a twelve-year-old girl as a way to pay only half the train fare. When the conductor detects her hoax, she hides in the private compartment of Major Philip Kirby. Their instant friendship is misunderstood by Philip's fiancée, Pamela, forcing Susan (now "Su-Su") to travel to Philip's military academy to show Pamela she is only a little girl. Susan is detained at the school longer than planned and becomes the star attraction among the young cadets, while Philip denies to himself his romantic feelings for her. When Susan learns that Pamela is trying to keep Philip from getting into combat, she pulls strings to

A publicity photo for *The Major and the Minor* (1942), with Ginger Rogers

help him before leaving for her home town. En route to joining the troops, Philip stops off in Iowa and is delighted to discover Su-Su is really an adult. They rush away for a quick marriage before Philip reports for duty.

Wilder knew he needed a big star to play Susan, and he was able to entice one of the biggest, Ginger Rogers. As a freelance actress, the 1940 Oscar winner was happy to give Wilder a chance because she liked him personally and also thought the script could bring about a hit movie. (Wilder's agreement to cast Rogers's real-life mother, Lela, as her mother in the story cinched the deal.)

Predictably, Wilder and Brackett wanted Cary Grant for Philip but were unable to interest him (considering the undertones of pedophilia). Yet Wilder knew that Ray Milland was no longer thought of as a Cary Grant wannabe and had observed Milland's unique abilities in several films, including those he had cowritten. (Coincidentally, Milland and Wilder, along with Edward G. Robinson, were in the process of amassing the largest fine art collections in Hollywood.) One evening, Wilder and Milland were both in their cars at a red traffic light when Wilder shouted over to the actor, "I'm doing a picture. Would you like to be in it?" Milland said, "Sure," and Wilder soon sent him the script, which Milland recognized as exceptional. For his work, Milland was paid $46,667 (pro rata per picture), less than a third of Rogers's staggering $175,000 salary for the one movie. By 1943, Milland renegotiated his contract yet again and would earn $169,000 by the end of that year.

The casting turned out to be perfect. Rogers is at her best playing the "dual" role. Milland manages to find the delicate, precarious balance between paternal affection for "Su-Su" and his growing but suppressed sexual interest in this precocious "child." (With finesse, he doesn't allow the major to come across as foolish for not recognizing the disguise.) Wilder later stated that the film was a forerunner to *Lolita*, Vladimir Nabokov's controversial 1955 novel about a grown man's obsession with an underage but alluring youth.

Two aspects of *The Major and the Minor* are off-putting today. The scenes of the teenage cadets making overt, aggressive passes at Su-Su are meant to be funny but are actually offensive, given she is supposed to be twelve years old; and the subplot about Susan's eagerness to get Philip actively involved in the war adds a strain of propaganda that sours the last section of the story.

Nevertheless, reviewers of the day were ecstatic. Mae Tinee of the *Chicago Daily Tribune* thought it "delightful" and Ray Milland "fascinating." *Variety* called it "sparkling" and Milland "a standout," and Bosley Crowther of the *New York Times* described it as a "deliciously risqué contretemps.... Miss Rogers and Mr. Milland have played it with spirit and taste." The studio suits were the most elated, with their $928,000 investment accruing $2.5 million in US rentals alone.

In 1943, Rogers and Milland repeated their roles on *Lux Radio Theatre*, but the May 31 broadcast missed the mark without the visual humor of Rogers dressed as little Su-Su.

Milland ended 1942 with an appearance in *Star-Spangled Rhythm*, the first all-star spectacle designed to entertain both the troops overseas and everyone else on the home front. The shoot took place during summer 1942, and the December 30, 1942, premiere was followed by a general release at the beginning of 1943. Other films of this type were soon to follow in 1943 and 1944: *Thousands Cheer* at MGM, *Thank Your Lucky Stars* at Warner Bros., and *Follow the Boys* at Universal.

Star-Spangled Rhythm's comedy and musical acts are connected by a Harry Tugend storyline about a Paramount gatekeeper (Victor Moore) who poses as a mogul in order to impress his son (Eddie Bracken), a sailor on leave who falls for his father's friend (Betty Hutton) while visiting the studio. The rambunctious energy of Hutton and the slow-burn comedy of Moore keep the narrative buzzing, despite interruptions by the many guest stars (even directors Cecil B. DeMille and Preston Sturges show up).

The finale includes the bulk of the cameos—an army camp show emceed by Bob Hope, featuring such bits as Paulette Goddard, Dorothy Lamour, and

Veronica Lake spoofing their screen images in "A Sweater, a Sarong and a Peek-a-Boo Bang" and Bing Crosby wrapping up the pageantry with the patriotic "Old Glory."

Ray Milland's appearance is one of the more brazen aspects of the show-within-the show—an undercutting of his matinée-idol image—in a sketch titled "If Men Played Cards as Women Do." In this blackout routine, Milland joins Fred MacMurray, Franchot Tone, and Lynne Overman as they abandon their masculine personas and mimic so-called female attitudes during a bridge game (complimenting each other's hats and new suits, gossiping about anyone who leaves the room, and jumping up on a table when a mouse appears). Despite the blatant sexism, there is something amusing about watching these "macho" actors act "feminine," and, like the others, Milland is complaisant about the self-ribbing.

Also seen widely in early 1943 was *The Crystal Ball*, which had been shot between late July and early September 1942. The light comedy teamed Milland with Paulette Goddard again, but it lacked the modest sparkle of *The Lady Has Plans*. (At an early stage, Ginger Rogers was considered for the lead, opposite either Milland or Charles Boyer.)

Virginia Van Upp's screenplay concerns a penniless Texas beauty queen, Toni Gerard (Goddard), trying to make her way in New York. Toni becomes involved with a phony psychic, Madame Zenobia (Gladys George), while also pursuing a government lawyer, Brad Cavanaugh (Milland), who is dating a widowed socialite, Jo Ainsley (Virginia Field). The many plot strands include Toni taking the place of the psychic and using other sneaky means to snare Brad away from the snooty Jo.

Though the picture is steadily amiable, it is rarely very funny. Van Upp gives little shape to the meandering story, which wouldn't be an issue if the dialogue or situations had more humor. Like *The Lady Has Plans*, the mise-en-scène—by director Elliott Nugent—is lackluster, but at least the earlier film had a tighter, better-structured narrative.

The Crystal Ball would have been much worse with a different cast. Milland has rarely looked better, and he again matches up well with Goddard. Virginia Field plays the role of the "other woman" perfectly, and Gladys George runs off with her few scenes as the psychic.

One cast member who would soon become a star was Yvonne De Carlo, but her scenes as a secretary were deleted before the film's release. Apparently, Milland's wandering eye fell upon De Carlo, as she affirmed in her 1987 autobiography, though De Carlo says he was but one of many boyfriends in her life at the time. It is unclear how much Mal Milland was aware of her husband's indiscretions (or what he called his "peccadilloes").

Ray Milland, Daniel Milland, and Muriel Milland (1942).
Photo credit: Paramount Pictures / Photofest.

The Crystal Ball was another Milland vehicle that pleased audiences more than critics. "Paulette Goddard and Ray Milland ... are not at their happiest in an attempt at farce that doesn't quite come off," wrote Joseph Pihodna in the *New York Herald Tribune*. Still, the modestly budgeted movie grossed $1 million in domestic rentals.

Shortly after finishing *The Crystal Ball*, Milland undertook a few radio programs, starting with the premiere episode of *The Kate Smith Hour* in September 1942. Then, for some reason, he consented to play a part that reminded listeners of the old comparisons to Cary Grant. In November 1942, he and Irene Dunne teamed for the dramatic *Lux Radio To Mary, with Love*, a very similar story to George Stevens' *Penny Serenade*, the 1941 classic starring Grant and Dunne. (Later, in July 1943, Milland agreed to play an actual Grant movie role for *Screen Guild Theater*—Leo McCarey's 1942 *Once upon a Honeymoon*, with Linda Darnell filling in for Ginger Rogers.) Milland's choices were odd given that he had finally emerged from the shadow of Cary Grant.

Milland started preproduction in December 1942 on *Lady in the Dark* with Ginger Rogers. Before and during the prolonged *Lady in the Dark* shoot in early 1943, Paramount contemplated teaming him with Vera Zorina for W. Somerset Maugham's *Hour before the Dawn*, as a British pacifist who plots to kill his new bride when he discovers she is a Nazi spy. Instead, Franchot Tone and Veronica Lake were assigned the leads in the 1944 fiasco, but it is interesting that the studio would have considered Milland playing a wife murderer at this high point in his career.

Milland spent the better part of 1943 on the war effort. Previously, in August 1942, he had donated his forty-foot, high-powered speedboat to the US Navy, and like so many Hollywood leading men (e.g. Clark Gable, James Stewart, Tyrone Power), he wanted to enlist. To Milland's chagrin, his severe left-hand injuries from his *Hotel Imperial* and circular saw accidents made it impossible for him to serve. (He didn't mention to the draft board he also suffered from migraine headaches.)

Alternatively, Milland used his time raising funds for the Allies, visiting the legendary Hollywood Canteen, and entertaining troops both on the home front and overseas at USO-HVC camp shows. Since he was not really a singer or dancer, Milland performed a magic act involving chickens and goldfish! According to James Robert Parish and Don E. Stanke, "On one such early outing, a belligerent G.I. shouted out: 'Why aren't you in the Army?' Instantaneously, Ray shot back, in a tongue-in-cheek manner: 'What, with a war going on? Think I'm crazy?' This jocular yet thought-provoking reply made the rounds of military camps in the months ahead and earned Ray a special popularity with the troops." His retort notwithstanding, Milland, like Bob Hope, took chances and entertained the armed forces in combat zones.

Milland's most personally gratifying contribution to the Allied cause was in the position of civilian flight instructor, coincidentally the same job carried out by Robert Cummings, his costar from *Everything Happens at Night*. Technically titled a "civilian contract primary flight instructor," Milland was first stationed in Arizona before his visit to the Solomon Islands, a dangerous trip made one year after the Allied campaign against Japan.

During his Guadalcanal stay, when not teaching cadets to fly, he performed for the troops alongside Mary Elliott and Rosita Moreno, a Spanish actress under contract to Paramount since 1930. (Milland flaunted his Spanish-language skills in ensemble comedy skits.) Towards the end of the Solomon Islands tour, he contracted dengue fever and malaria, losing more than thirty pounds, and was forced to halt his live entertaining. When finally recovered and back in Hollywood, he continued using his fluency in Spanish on government-sponsored radio programs broadcast to Latin American countries, an assignment requested by Paramount. (Meanwhile, the studio exploited Paulette Goddard on war-bond drives as available to servicemen for "exact duplicate" kisses, like the one she gave Ray Milland in their most recent movie.)

One of the odder war stories involving Ray Milland occurred in late December 1943, when his father mailed Ray a frayed photograph of himself as a youngster. The strange part was where it was found: in a captured German dugout in Tunisia. It was a small news item, but it is very possible it helped fuel a vicious, erroneous rumor at the time that Milland was somehow involved with the Nazis.

Milland's only other 1943 picture was *Forever and a Day*, the all-star drama produced at RKO, his single loan-out assignment during his second decade with Paramount. In this case, the loan to RKO was in service to Allied support, not a punishment or money grab by his studio bosses. *Forever and a Day* was populated by "British Nationals" in a bid to show the grit and gumption of the besieged country. The production consisted of multiple stories by different writers and directors.

Actor Sir Cedric Hardwicke spearheaded the pormanteau, RKO contributed $400,000 to the budget, and all the personnel donated their time and services. The studio advertised the movie with the tag line, "78 Stars in a Great Story as Big as the Cast!" The entire $1 million gross was given to British war relief.

In and out of shooting for nearly two years (from May 1941 to January 1943), Milland's part was finished early on in two weeks' time. *Forever and a Day* depended on the availability of so many writers, directors, actors, and craftspeople simultaneously working on other projects, it was quite an accomplishment that it was ever completed.

The center of the action for all the segments was the fictitious Trimble House. The yarn begins with the 1804 purchase of the land by Admiral Trimble (C. Aubrey Smith) and tells how the admiral built the Trimble home for his family, including his wife, Lucy (Dame May Whitty), and son, William (Ray Milland, in his final film with Aubrey Smith).

In the Milland segment, William rescues Susan Trenchard (Anna Neagle) from the clutches of her diabolical guardian, Ambrose Pomfret (Claude Rains), and then proposes a marriage of convenience, which eventually turns into love. When William is called to duty in the Napoleonic Wars and is killed, the family mourns his death, and Pomfret schemes to acquire the house.

For this set piece, Milland reunited with his *Irene* costar (Neagle) and director (Herbert Wilcox) and the results were similar to their 1940 musical. There is gentle whimsy up until William's tragic end. Milland and Neagle acquit themselves well, looking restrained next to Aubrey Smith and Rains, both of whom stand out with their hammier if more memorable characterizations—especially Rains's final and deadly alcohol-infused battle with the house that was never his home. The only thing Milland did not like about his assignment was having to don tight-fitting period attire again.

The other segments that follow are uniformly jaunty with well-placed moments of pathos. In one directed by René Clair, Ida Lupino plays a maid of the house who falls for a Trimble ancestor (Brian Aherne). Alfred Hitchcock had originally intended to direct Lupino opposite Cary Grant, not Aherne, but his shooting of *Suspicion* starring Grant conflicted with the start date. The best segment, directed by Edmund Goulding, comes last: a World War I tale of the building serving as a hotel, with Merle Oberon as an employee who falls in love with an American soldier (Robert Cummings).

Forever and a Day was not only populated by Milland's friends from "The British Colony" but also featured a number of past and future costars—including Cummings. Though Milland did not work with Robert Cummings or Alfred Hitchcock on this occasion, it was a decade later that they all collaborated on Milland's triumphant comeback movie, *Dial M for Murder*.

Late in 1943, Milland became briefly involved in Paramount's effort to capitalize on the overwhelming response to its color production of Ernest Hemingway's *For Whom the Bell Tolls*, costarring Gary Cooper and Ingrid Bergman. The studio hoped to remake Hemingway's *Farewell to Arms*, a tragic wartime romance originally filmed in 1932, also with Cooper, opposite Helen Hayes. Now, Milland and Bergman were slated to costar, but David O. Selznick refused to loan Bergman out, and the plan fell apart.

While a World War II update of *A Farewell to Arms* might have been a coffer's goldmine, Paramount and Ray Milland tentatively went in a new, mostly darker direction in 1944 and 1945, leading up to what many consider Milland's greatest achievement.

CHAPTER 5

AT PARAMOUNT'S PEAK (1944–1945)

THE LOST WEEKEND, RELEASED IN 1945, CHANGED NEARLY EVERYTHING FOR Ray Milland—in particular how he would be perceived by critics, the industry, and audiences worldwide. His searing, Oscar-winning performance demonstrated a dynamic acting range, previously untapped, as it also broke with the traditional expectations of a matinée idol. What many forget today is that just one year before, in 1944, Milland was already riding high with tremendously popular movies and, at the same time, exploring the bleaker side of his screen persona.

Nineteen forty-three had *not* been a notable year for Milland's film output. His only two releases were *Forever and a Day*, in a guest appearance, and *The Crystal Ball*, a subpar comedy. Moreover, if one didn't know the inside story, it could be construed that Paramount was distancing itself from its star attraction since neither film carried the studio logo: *Forever and a Day* was distributed by RKO, and *The Crystal Ball* was produced at Paramount but distributed through United Artists.

The truth was that the studio was tremendously enthusiastic about its leading man. During this "down" year of 1943, he was shooting much better fare while working on behalf of the war effort. The front office knew one other thing, as expressed by James Robert Parish and Don E. Stanke: "Tracking the ups and downs of a star's box-office vitality cannot always be tied to rational facts or to published statistics." Parish and Stanke cite Milland and Fred MacMurray as prime examples of popular stars who "never made the charts of *Motion Picture Herald* and *Fame* as . . . the top ten money-making stars of a given year."

In 1944, Ray Milland's quartet of releases were highly profitable for Paramount. All of them showcased different facets of Milland's on-screen personality while representing a wide variety of genres: the musical superproduction, *Lady in the Dark*, the offbeat ghost story, *The Uninvited*, the earnest wartime romance, *Till We Meet Again*, and (best of all) the film noir thriller, *Ministry of Fear*.

A BANNER YEAR

First to appear was the long-delayed release of *Lady in the Dark* (lensed between December 1942 and April 1943 but not premiering until February 1944). Paramount's most expensive movie of World War II was an adaptation of Moss Hart's 1941 Broadway musical that had starred Gertrude Lawrence. As Liza Elliott, Lawrence portrayed the editor of a New York fashion magazine who undergoes psychoanalysis to better understand why she feels hopelessly indecisive. Paramount bought the show for Ginger Rogers and, given the success of *The Major and the Minor*, it made sense to the studio heads for Ray Milland to be her leading man, even though *Lady in the Dark* was much more of a "woman's picture," focusing on the female lead rather than any of the male characters.

Apart from assuming a subsidiary role, Milland had another qualm about participating in this new Ginger Rogers production. Despite its prestigious aura and the promise his advertising executive role would be "built up" from Broadway, Milland never felt completely comfortable with musicals, and while he was willing to try something new, he ended up warbling only fragments of a couple of songs, leaving all the other musical duties to Rogers (in three phantasmagorical dream sequences).

Breaking with Hollywood tradition, though, Milland was allowed to sing live on the soundstage, not in a prerecording session, and he performed more of the score, again live, when he prematurely plugged the film in early October 1943 on Gertrude Lawrence's radio show, *The Revlon Revue*, even briefly vocalizing in tandem with the great star. This stint, for which he was paid $3,000, was a euphoric experience for Milland, given that he was only a struggling hopeful at the time Lawrence was the Toast of the West End of London in the late 1920s and early 1930s. (On the air, Milland claims, perhaps jokingly, to have directed his own segment "for nothing.")

During the *Lady in the Dark* production itself, however, Milland became increasingly annoyed as Rogers, normally hard working and professional, arrived late to the set or seemed distracted and was particularly unhappy with her director, Mitchell Leisen. She complained, quite justifiably, about having to sing and dance through toxic dry ice used in one dream sequence. At another point, while shooting "The Saga of Jenny," Rogers accused Leisen of demanding she perform bumps and grinds against her will. However, when Rogers took an unannounced leave to marry her third husband, US Marine Jack Briggs, Milland thought Rogers had crossed a line, stating later, "She was physically competent and she had been wonderful for *The Major and the Minor* but this was way beyond her. And disappearing in the middle of shooting was the last straw." Milland got through the drawn-out enterprise by telling himself, "Make the best of it. This too shall pass."

In addition to the off-screen complications, *Lady in the Dark* had its share of postproduction delays. While Paramount held it back from release, producer Buddy DeSylva tinkered with or cut out several sequences. It didn't matter to most moviegoers. Though the budget became inflated at nearly $3 million, the returns were astronomical: it grossed $4.5 million in its initial US rentals.

Critics were mostly reserved in their endorsements, especially if they had seen the Broadway show. Bosley Crowther's *New York Times* remarks were typical: "[T]he authors of the screen play [sic] have chopped the original in such a way that much that was wistful and tender in it has been curiously left out." The biggest complaint was that many songs had been eliminated, above all the plaintive "My Ship." According to Leisen, DeSylva hated Weill's music and tried to excise as much of it as possible. Not surprisingly, the production was nominated for Oscars in Art Direction (Color), Cinematography (Color), and Music (Scoring of Motion Picture), though it lost in all three categories.

In retrospect, Rogers seems perfectly well cast, whether her dour demeanor was intentional or caused by incidents on the set. Ray Milland captures his pinstripe-suited character just as completely, even though Charley Johnson's churlish, competitive attitude toward his female superior represents an all-too-convincing *Mad Men* prototype. At the time, *Variety* praised him by saying, "Ray Milland gives an excellent performance."

If Charley Johnson poses a challenge to the modern viewer, Ray Milland mitigates the misogyny with his special brand of disarming wit. On one hand, his character sneeringly calls Liza "Boss Lady" multiple times and insultingly questions her sex appeal. On the other hand, Milland shows up in all Liza's dreams as a humorous gadfly in outlandish outfits. Further, during an office contretemps, he makes fun of Liza's suppressed desire for Randy Curtis (Jon Hall), the handsome movie star visiting her studio for a photo shoot; instead of a wisecrack, though, Milland's brief but teasing, ironic rendition of "Dream Lover" (*not* from *Lady in the Dark*), represents both his send up of the romantic use of the song in Leisen's *Arise, My Love* and a passive-aggressive acknowledgment that his character cares for Liza. In the end, Charley finally lowers his guard and reflectively admits to Liza and himself that he has behaved obnoxiously because he loves her.

Still, despite Milland's nuances, it is difficult to accept the concluding sequence—where Liza gives up her two other suitors in order to throw herself into the arms of Milland's natty but nasty Charley and happily bestow upon him a position equal to hers at the magazine!

The Uninvited (1944), with Ruth Hussey

Ultimately, the simplified emphasis on Freudian psychoanalysis is a less dated element in *Lady in the Dark* than this sexist denouement. Without the lavish visuals as compensation, the 1945 *Lux Radio* production with Rogers and Milland only reaffirms the wrong-headed sexual politics.

Ray Milland's fans were excited to see yet another February 1944 release, *The Uninvited*, which holds up well today, quite a bit better than *Lady in the Dark*. In fact, *The Uninvited* has become one of Milland's signature cult films, while also a box-office and critical smash in its day, albeit a "sleeper." Few Paramount executives anticipated a mere ghost story to catch on with the public or receive so many plaudits.

During preproduction, though, Milland expressed only discontent. He was angry the film lacked a ready script and that he had to work with an unknown leading lady (Gail Russell) and untested director (Lewis Allen) after there had been a failed attempt to get Alfred Hitchcock on board. Eventually, with the help of Milland's agent, Zeppo Marx, producer Charles Brackett convinced Milland to go ahead. He started shooting in mid-April 1943 and finished in mid-June, and he was pleased with the results.

Allen and Milland got along fine during the shoot—at Fort Bragg and on the backlot—and ended up working together on three more features during the rest of Milland's Paramount tenure. Likewise, despite his initial reservations about newcomer Gail Russell, Milland spent extra time with her, reading lines and calming her nerves.

In its day, the film was seen as a blend of the low-budget horror of producer Val Lewton (e.g. *The Cat People* [1942]) and Hitchcock's Gothic romance, *Rebecca* (1940). Paramount's ad campaign made the latter reference explicit, asserting *The Uninvited* was the "Most Popular Mystery Romance Since *Rebecca*."

In recent years, *The Uninvited* has been championed by such filmmakers as Steven Spielberg, Guillermo Del Toro, Martin Scorsese, and Michael Almereyda. Spielberg pays homage to it in *Poltergeist* (1982) by referencing its "mimosa" motif; Del Toro considers it one of the scariest movies of his youth; Scorsese lists it as one of the scariest movies ever; and Almereyda created a "Visual Essay" tribute for the 2013 Criterion Collection DVD and Blu-ray release, in which he specifically praises Ray Milland several times.

In Dodie Smith and Frank Partos's adaptation of Dorothy Macardle's novel, *Uneasy Freehold*, Milland and Ruth Hussey play Rick and Pam Fitzgerald, an English brother and sister who impetuously purchase a manor house on the Cornish seacoast. It turns out the mansion is haunted, and the new owners, who hear cries in the night and smell the scent of mimosa, are determined to figure out why. What they discover is that the previous owner, Commander Beech (Donald Crisp), had a daughter who died near the house from a mysterious fall off a cliff. Beech's granddaughter, Stella (Gail Russell), is alternately scared by and attracted to the house. Due to Stella's strange behavior, speaking Spanish during a séance, Beech commits her to a sanatorium run by her late mother's friend, Miss Holloway (Cornelia Otis Skinner). Rick and Pam rescue Stella, learning along the way about Stella's actual birth mother, a Spanish beauty named Carmel, and of what happened long ago among the three women that caused the spirits to be restless.

Guiding this offbeat production was first-time director Lewis Allen, a British expatriate with a prolific theater background, including the Broadway run of *French without Tears* (1937–38). Thanks immeasurably to Charles Lang's Oscar-nominated cinematography, with its chiaroscuro lighting, Allen rarely betrays a lack of skill or his theatrical roots: *The Uninvited* is highly cinematic, a mix of horror, the supernatural, and film noir.

Atmospherics aside, *The Uninvited* was unique in its day for several reasons. First, it took ghosts more seriously than other films—at least the Hollywood kind. Previously, ghost movies were geared either toward comedy (e.g. *Topper* [1937] with Cary Grant) or melodrama, where the "ghosts" are revealed to be a deception on the part of con artists (e.g. *The Smiling Ghost* [1941]). In *The Uninvited*, there was no attempt to logically explain away the apparitions.

While never mentioning World War II, as the story is set in 1937, the 1944 release resonated with wartime audiences. Historian Leslie Halliwell posits, "[T]he high death rate of World War II had brought about a new awareness of supernatural possibilities and an eagerness to wallow in them, so that a theme which five years earlier might have been regarded by most audiences as merely silly, came to attract large numbers of people wishing to be assured that death is not the end."

Another unusual aspect of the narrative is the focus on the two sibling protagonists, as opposed to a conventional romantic couple. Unlike the sadomasochistic brother and sister in the 1945 film noir *The Strange Affair of Uncle Harry*, Rick and Pam are personable and level-headed, and there is no suggestion that anything is odd about their buying a house and living together.

But cultists today have expressed their greatest interest in the coded but evident lesbian subplot. What emerges from the backstory is that Stella's mother was close to both Carmel and Miss Holloway and that Carmel was Stella's birth mother. The narrative then covertly reveals that the women's romantic triangle was the source of the jealousy that caused the series of killings. So while this embedded storyline is striking for acknowledging same-sex romantic relationships, it is also problematic in that two of the women are presented as psychologically imbalanced murderers. The clash between a progressive representation and old-fashioned stereotyping (with a "cute" coda in which Rick exorcises the house of Stella's mother's ghost) exposes a reactionary flaw to *The Uninvited*.

The performances—especially Milland's—help compensate for the mixed messaging. Despite possessing a literally darker atmosphere than *Lady in the Dark*, this film allows Milland to be a much more endearing leading man, injecting welcome comic relief into a few scenes. The final gag aside, Ray Milland is in his element as Rick, a composer suffering from writer's block who becomes enamored by the mysterious Stella and composes a melody for her, "Stella by Starlight." (His creative block prefigures the one that nearly destroys his character in *The Lost Weekend*.) Milland's languid magnetism provides the perfect counterpoint to the scary setting, allowing the skeptical viewer to identify with this worldly but slightly jaded protagonist. (During a preview screening in Inglewood, there was "wild applause for Milland's name," according to Charles Brackett.) By now, Milland was considered much more than a pretty face, but even in this film, another character refers to him as "a tall, dark man—excruciatingly handsome."

The success of *The Uninvited* led to several offshoot ventures, starting with a promotional "Shiver Opera" using Milland to introduce the "Spook Sonata," a variation on "Stella by Starlight." Later came a 1945 flop sequel,

The Unseen, directed by Lewis Allen and starring Gail Russell but missing Ray Milland and most of the original cast. A full three years after *The Uninvited*'s release, Ned Washington added lyrics to Victor Young's "Stella by Starlight," resulting in a hit song and jazz standard. Young's entire score was so influential that as late as 1997, the Moscow Symphony Orchestra rerecorded it for Marco Polo and Naxos Records.

Then there were the obligatory radio recaps (two in this case), both starring Ray Milland. In August 1944, he and Ruth Hussey reprised their roles for *Screen Guild Theater*. Betty Field, from *Are Husbands Necessary?*, replaced Gail Russell and did an effective job aurally creating the disturbed Stella, but Milland himself was more persuasive in the November 1949 *Screen Directors Playhouse* version, perhaps because Lewis Allen personally supervised this less-rushed interpretation.

In July and August of 1943, Milland worked on *Ministry of Fear* with Fritz Lang, one of the best directors of his career. In Germany during the artistically experimental Weimar period, Lang conceived some of the greatest silent epics, including *Metropolis* (1927), but once in 1930's Hollywood, having escaped the Nazi regime, Lang found himself in a factory system not amenable toward his exacting, all-encompassing approach.

As for the casting, the more laconic, one-dimensional Alan Ladd was first thought of for the lead, but Milland, with his ability to convey dread beneath an affable front, was a far superior choice to play a mentally imbalanced hero. (Ladd's zoom to stardom at Paramount, compared to Milland's lumbering climb, had as much to do with Ladd's ingratiating tough-guy persona as it did with his having superagent Sue Carrol as his wife.)

Once released in October 1944, it was easy to overlook *Ministry of Fear* given that film noir thrillers were popping up regularly in theaters. Sadly, Lang himself undervalued the film. Years after making it, Lang personally apologized to Graham Greene for his adaptation of the author's 1943 novel. But *Ministry of Fear* at least fared solidly enough with audiences and critics in 1944. *Variety* said, "Pic starts out to be a humdinger, and continues that way for the most part" and called Milland's performance "forthright."

Today, *Ministry of Fear* is considered one of Lang's best American films by many critics, including Glenn Kenny, who considers it a "quite excellent picture," and Dave Kehr, who has said it is "Lang at his finest and purest." Much credit goes to Lang's stylish mise-en-scène, but one must also recognize Ray Milland for his outstanding performance.

Seton I. Miller's screenplay retains the main ingredients of Greene's story. Milland plays Stephen Neale, a patient discharged from a sanatorium during the London Blitz. Stephen's bizarre adventures following his release should

Ministry of Fear (1944)

be enough to send him back to the asylum, but instead, he becomes an unwitting hero, protecting the British Allies against a Nazi plot.

The story evokes the Hitchcock tradition, particularly *The Thirty-Nine Steps* (1935), and the Hitchcockian "MacGuffin" that sets things in motion is nothing more complicated or less absurd than a heavily frosted cake. Stephen wins it in a carnival raffle and later realizes that between the layers exists an all-important strip of microfilm about the Allied invasion into Nazi strongholds.

Gradually, the plot convolutions become downright surrealistic, as director Michael Almeyreda suggests in his 2013 DVD "Visual Essay" about *The Uninvited*. Almeyreda adds that the "bland but uncanny" way Milland plays his roles in both films makes him the perfect film noir antihero: an ordinary but troubled man who must meet the challenge of unlikely, dangerous, or even outrageous circumstances. The story opens with Stephen nervously watching a ticking clock before being discharged from the asylum, and there is no full explanation as to why he was admitted in the first place (evidently for the mercy killing of his wife, a PCA taboo). This makes our protagonist's point of view sympathetic yet unreliable from the outset.

Thereafter, Milland's Stephen negotiates a variety of unnerving set pieces, including the ghoulish carnival sequence with the layer cake, a nightmarish séance in the dark that results in a murder (later revealed to be a staged killing), and a suspenseful climax on a rooftop with Stephen and his girlfriend, Carla (Marjorie Reynolds), outwitting the Nazi agents.

Like most Lang films, the aesthetic elements intensify the narrative. Victor Young delivers another eerie, tingling score. Henry Sharp's cinematography alternates between the expressionistic foreboding of the settings and the impressionistic point of view of Stephen Neale's distorted state of mind. In their different ways, both *The Uninvited* and *Ministry of Fear* preview the horror films Milland would make decades later.

Milland next shot *Till We Meet Again* from October to the beginning of 1944, and it was another triumph with audiences though the least remembered today of Milland's 1944 titles. Part of the collective amnesia has to do with the fact that this rarely revived film shares its name with the better-known but totally unrelated *'Til We Meet Again*, a 1940 Warner Bros. production and staple of the rotating Turner Classic Movies library.

Till We Meet Again was based on an unproduced play, *Tomorrow's Harvest*, written by Alfred Maury and purchased by Buddy DeSylva (with Ray Milland in mind) as Paramount's rejoinder to the Twentieth Century-Fox spiritually themed hit *The Song of Bernadette* (1943). Lenore Coffee was chosen to adapt the Maury play for the screen, which would have been controversial even on Broadway if it *had* been produced since it dealt with the romance between a soldier and a nun. For Hollywood, the nun's role was turned into a novice, and the "romance" was altered to be more dispassionate.

Once the screenplay was ruled acceptable by the censors, the only aspect of preproduction that caused major difficulties was the casting of the leading lady. When Paramount failed to secure Ingrid Bergman, the studio tested several of its top stars, including blonde bombshell Veronica Lake! But a noncontract player, Maureen O'Hara, was finally chosen. The beautiful and talented O'Hara might have been too mature to play a novice but was otherwise smartly cast. Regrettably, as O'Hara herself tells the story:

> On my way home from the set one evening, I started feeling extremely hot. I felt as if I was dripping with sweat all over. I checked myself and pulled up a hand covered in blood. There was quite a bit of it and I started to panic. My first thought was, Oh my God, I'm losing the baby. I rushed home and then to the hospital emergency room. The doctor gave me a choice, "Do the movie or keep the baby." There was no decision to make, so I dropped out of the picture.

O'Hara would wait another twelve years to work with Ray Milland, when she was cast in the second feature film he directed, *Lisbon* (1956). So, it was back to the drawing board for Paramount as it considered the little-known Barbara Britton. Consequently, Britton was tested and then awarded the lead, actually the more central character in the story than top-billed Milland's.

Despite Paramount's high hopes, Britton had a hard time carrying the film. According to James Robert Parish and Lennard DeCarl, "Barbara was constantly aware of how important the picture was to her future career. The combined pressure of that haunting thought, the long-working hours, and her Hollywood Canteen and other benefit work, came to a head when she was playing a scene where shots were fired into a wall next to her. Barbara fell apart and suffered a minor nervous breakdown." Later, the reviews of Britton's performance were lukewarm, and Paramount quickly lost interest in its new star.

Fortunately, neither the casting of Britton nor the censorship of the subject matter hindered the efforts of the director—Frank Borzage—to create a satisfying work. Unlike Lewis Allen, who started his Hollywood career with Milland, Borzage was nearing his "last act." In his day, the two-time Oscar winner for Best Director was known as an expert craftsman but also one of the cinema's great romanticists, turning sometimes routine or even unlikely material into rapturously intimate narratives (e.g. his 1948 cult favorite, *Moonrise*). For this reason, critic Hervé Dumont considers *Till We Meet Again* "astonishing."

Thus, *Till We Meet Again* features an improbable premise for romance. Milland plays John, an American World War II flyer who has been shot down over the French countryside during a German air raid. Sister Louise Clothilde (Britton) helps the shell-shocked hero hide from the Nazis. Major Krupp (Konstantine Shayne) suspects John is inside the convent and that he possesses top-secret information. After Louise's mother superior (Lucile Watson) is killed, Louise finds her mission to assist John a greater calling. In order to protect him, Louise pretends to be his wife and takes refuge with him in a bombed-out farmhouse. Eventually, Krupp tracks the couple down, forcing John and Louise to separate and Louise to make a beatific sacrifice.

Critical reactions of the day were mixed, and unlike *The Uninvited*, the film has not been reassessed, Hervé Dumont's article notwithstanding. The *New York Times* grumbled, "The general level of the acting is not above average. Miss Britton ... did not give depth to the role of a fearful, yet brave woman who had been torn from her lifelong seclusion and security. Mr. Milland is satisfactory but not outstanding as the aviator." What the unnamed *Times* critic missed about Milland's performance was the sensitivity he brings to his scenes with Barbara Britton, especially his soliloquy about his wife back home. Lyrical moments like these stand out in a movie about the stark realities of war, where not even religious figures are sacred to the enemy.

Before *Till We Meet Again* was released at the end of summer 1944, Ray Milland worked on the lavish comedy-drama *Kitty*, though it would take nearly two years before it was seen by the public.

In late 1944, as a complete change of pace, Billy Wilder and Charles Brackett tried again to unite Ray Milland and Ingrid Bergman, this time in a musical-comedy version of Ferenc Molnár's play, *Olympia*. When David O. Selznick informed Wilder and Brackett that Bergman would be too busy to be loaned out to Paramount, Selznick suggested Joan Fontaine instead. Eventually the Wilder-Brackett movie was made in 1948 as *The Emperor Waltz* with Fontaine and Bing Crosby.

A heavy drama titled *Behold My Wife!* was also scheduled for Milland, opposite Gail Russell (Veronica Lake was also named). But the Paramount property, dating back to 1920, was considered too old hat and ultimately abandoned. In fact, Milland was becoming so busy that his planned cameo in the all-star *Duffy's Tavern* (filmed in 1944, released in 1945) was likewise canceled.

THE LOST WEEKEND

As exceptional as Milland's work proved to be in his 1944 releases, what was about to come was even more extraordinary. *The Lost Weekend* would be his next project and probably the film for which he will always be most associated. Whether or not Milland gives his best performance in it, *The Lost Weekend* became an immediate cinematic landmark on multiple levels. But it almost didn't get out to the public at all.

Charles Jackson's 1944 best-seller about the ugly side of alcoholism, *The Lost Weekend*, was not typical material for Hollywood in the 1940s. Nevertheless, director Billy Wilder was intrigued by the book after working with Raymond Chandler on the screenplay for *Double Indemnity* (1944). Wilder saw parallels between the antihero writer in Jackson's story and the real-life alcoholic Chandler. In addition, Wilder observed Elizabeth Brackett, wife of Charles Brackett, his more frequent writing partner, was also an alcoholic.

Due to the critical and box-office sensation of *Double Indemnity*, Wilder had enough clout to persuade his reluctant bosses to buy the rights to the Jackson novel and turn it into a motion picture. Some of book's material was too provocative to be fully expressed, such as Jackson's thesis that protagonist Don Birnam drinks as a way to avoid confronting his homosexuality. Still, Wilder and Brackett were able to incorporate aspects of both the gay subtext and the alcoholic's hellish perspective into the final script.

In the movie narrative, New York writer Birnam plans a weekend in the country but, at the last minute, encourages his girlfriend, Helen, and his brother, Wick, to travel together without him. He promises he will do some writing while they are away, but they both suspect he will use his time to resume his excessive drinking. After clearing the apartment of any trace of alcohol and refusing Don money to buy liquor, Wick and Helen leave. Yet Don figures out a way to secure two bottles of alcohol and stashes them in such places as a vacuum bag and a lamp fixture. The remainder of the weekend becomes a series of unexpected blunders on his part—not remembering where he hid his liquor, stealing money from a woman's purse in a bar (and getting caught), trying to pawn his typewriter without any luck, and having an accident on a staircase that lands him in Bellevue Hospital's rehabilitation ward.

The most expositionally loaded sequences are those where Don visits a local dive (based on P. J. Clarke's) and tells his tale of woe to a gruff, unsympathetic bartender. The flashbacks include the backstory of how Don met Helen—after a matinée of Verdi's *La traviata* and its "Drinking Song." Near the end of the weekend, Helen returns from her trip and discovers Don is planning to kill himself. She tries to stop him, but it is the surly bartender's unexpected return of his hocked typewriter that reverses Don's fatal plans: he decides to write his story and hopes it will help other poor souls like himself.

Despite their working well together on *The Major and The Minor*, Ray Milland was *not* Billy Wilder's first choice for the role of Don Birnam. Initially, Wilder wanted Broadway actor José Ferrer, but Ferrer turned him down, and Buddy DeSylva wanted an established and good-looking screen star in any case. Next, Wilder thought Cary Grant would be interesting cast against type, but Grant did not want to damage his screen persona with such a downbeat role.

Encouraged by DeSylva, Wilder finally selected Ray Milland, or, as Milland tells it: "All the studio had was Alan Ladd, Eddie Bracken, Sonny Tufts and myself, although they could have borrowed practically anybody else they wanted." Milland had long been eager to alter his debonair image, but even he had some misgivings about tackling such a challenging part. Apparently, the adventurous Ray Milland had his limits. DeSylva had no such reservations and sent Milland a copy of the book with a note inside, saying, "Read it. Study it. You're going to play it!"

Still, as Paramount's most bankable star, Milland knew *The Lost Weekend* would be a major gamble, and without much understanding about alcoholism, he felt at a loss about how to express Don Birnam's inner turmoil. It was Mal Milland who helped her husband make his decision, as he later recalled.

He describes the talk they had in their home library soon after he finished reading the Jackson novel:

> "[H]ow was the book? Any good?"
> "Beautifully written," I said, "but depressing and unrelieved. Damned interesting though, only it's going to call for some pretty serious acting and I don't know whether I'm equipped for it."
> She gave me an old-fashioned look and said, "How do you know? Up until now you haven't had many opportunities to find out. You've just been coasting. To me, the story sounds very worthwhile and it will probably cause a lot of comment. Besides, it's a challenge. So stop dithering and get to work on it. Even if turns out not to be any good you will at least have learned something from it."
> "Yes, but if I'm lousy in it, I could very well be through in this racket, which would mean finis to this sybaritic life we've been leading. But for you, my nagging wife, I'll do it and I'll do my damnedest. I'm warning you, though, I'm not going to be very pleasant to live with for the next three months."
> "Were you ever?"

Milland was still not completely convinced. Thus, he made the mistake of "auditioning" in front of Mal and Mal's younger sister, Harriet, and her husband, who were guests for dinner one night. In preparation, Milland became completely drunk and then read portions of the book to his "audience." The results were comically bad ("pathetic, a shambles," says Milland), made all the more ridiculous when one of their dogs knocked Milland over at the end of his soliloquy. But at this point, or at least by the next morning, Ray Milland had already Crossed the Rubicon. He decided he was going to be Don Birnam.

Casting the supporting roles was not as involved, though the part of Helen ran into a couple of setbacks. Wilder originally wanted Katharine Hepburn, who liked the idea but was already committed to filming *Without Love* at MGM. Wilder's next choice, Jean Arthur, flatly turned it down. After nearly getting Jennifer Jones, in the end, Wilder selected Jane Wyman, despite her being under contract to Warner Bros. Easily enough, a loan-out was arranged.

During the lengthy preproduction in late summer 1944, Ray and Mal attended a few functions, most prominently David O. Selznick's banquet for the Hollywood Republicans honoring Earl Warren, the California governor elected in 1942. By this time, Milland had declared himself a Republican, and with the presidential elections looming, he threw his support behind

Thomas E. Dewey, the eventual losing Republican challenger to FDR. That night, the Millands mingled with Warren and his wife, Nina, Fred and Lillian MacMurray, Ginger Rogers and her mother, Lela, plus Preston Sturges, Jeanette MacDonald, Walt Disney, Herman Mankiewicz, Adolph Menjou, Lionel Barrymore, and many others. The event culminated with a speech by Warren and the induction of Barrymore as president of the Hollywood Republican Committee and Ginger Rogers as vice president.

Milland spent the rest of his time before filming *The Lost Weekend* studying, Method-like, the movements and expressions of alcoholics, reading about the disease at the local library, and talking to author Charles Jackson himself and several doctors who regularly treated hardcore drinkers. Once the Wilder-Brackett script was approved by the Hays Office, though only fragments were ever submitted, Paramount had to consider Wilder's then-unique idea to shoot some portions on location in New York City. Paramount was reluctant since the studio already had a "New York" backlot. Yet Wilder insisted on capturing the grit of the city and refused to back down. So on September 21, 1944, Wilder and a minicrew of twenty traveled to Manhattan. On September 27, Ray Milland left to join the *Lost Weekend* team, agreeing with Mal that she and four-year-old Daniel should remain in California. He also stayed away from the press, and for his trouble, the Hollywood Women's Press Club nominated him the least cooperative actor of 1944.

The room Milland booked in New York was at the Waldorf Astoria, which offered quite a contrast from the dreary apartment set (constructed at Paramount's New York Marathon Street studio) that would represent his character's home in the story. While waiting for the shoot to begin, and in order to look more emaciated, Milland maintained a strict diet of tea, toast, grapefruit juice, and hard-boiled eggs. He also took advantage of his time by requesting to visit Bellevue's psychiatric ward, staying over for three nights, in order to witness what actual alcoholics go through at the depths of their despair. Between the frightening sounds and nauseating smells of the dark room, Milland was not entirely braced for what he experienced—he barely lasted two of the three nights. When he finally had enough, he escaped the way his character does in the movie, but he was nearly forced back into the ward by the police until he could convince them he was not an actual patient.

Ultimately, the rough time helped him shape his portrait of Don Birnam. Never before or after did Ray Milland prepare so hard or research so much for a part, and he wasn't even sure it would make a difference. Still, there were many more challenges to come.

Starting on October 1, and for the next three weeks, Wilder, Milland, and the crew gathered to plan angles they would need to frame Birnam walking through the city streets in an alcoholic stupor. The way Wilder found to avoid onlookers was to film clandestinely, as noted by Parish and Stanke: "[T]he company went on location to New York's then dingy Third Avenue (with its elevated train) where Milland's Don Birnam, failed writer, attempts to peddle his typewriter for the money needed to purchase drink. Unshaven, and generally disreputable looking, the actor scuffed along Third Avenue [in character] while cameras and their operators, hidden in trash cans, milk trucks, and large crates, picked up his movements as he went, unrecognized, past and around native pedestrians."

Wilder's innovative strategy did not go smoothly, however, partly because of lighting and weather-related issues. There were other problems as well. When Milland was secretly filmed in front of Bellevue, a police detective tried to arrest him for appearing disorderly. Wilder intervened in time, but it wasn't the last instance bystanders interfered. During a different setup, a fan pestered Milland to the point where the actor had to admit he was Ray Milland and not only give the woman his autograph but also the promise of a Hollywood screen test—all just to get rid of her! Another, more embarrassing incident occurred when he tried but failed to avoid one of Mal's friends who happened to be walking along Third Avenue while he was looking his very worst. Sure enough, the tabloids quickly began running gossipy accounts about actor Ray Milland on a drunken spree in New York; as soon as he saw these articles, Milland got on the phone at his hotel and yelled at Paramount's publicity flacks to reveal the truth to the newspapers. Thus, the three weeks in Manhattan turned out to be almost as tortuous for everyone involved as it was for the fictional Mr. Birnam during his weekend.

Once Milland and the crew returned to Hollywood, the balance of the shoot was more orderly, even without a completely finished script. Most of the remaining scenes took place either in an accurate recreation of P. J. Clarke's saloon or Birnam's small brownstone apartment. (Of the latter scenes, editor Doane Harrison did a superb job of maintaining the continuity between the shots taken in New York and those from the California set.)

The Millands agreed to pretend to the Hollywood community that the toll of *The Lost Weekend* production was not affecting their marriage. On New Year's Eve 1944, the couple cheerfully attended the biggest party in town, Jack and Mary Benny's all-night dinner-to-breakfast gathering at the Benny mansion. Nearly every major star in Hollywood was present, even some retired ones, like Norma Shearer, the headliner of Milland's early picture *Strangers May Kiss* (1931).

But behind the scenes, Ray and Mal were experiencing the greatest strain on their marriage to date. As Milland had predicted, tackling the part of a desperate addict proved psychically and physically taxing, so much so that he and Mal decided he was indeed too hard to live with: on March 31, 1945, Ray Milland moved out of their home. (Two weeks later, there was more unexpected and depressing news when FDR died suddenly, making Harry Truman president of the United States.) Since the Milland separation took place after most of *The Lost Weekend* had been shot, with only retakes needed into early 1945, it was rumored that the couple's three-month split had really been caused by Ray's romantic interest in Margaret Banks, a star of the American Ballet Theatre. At another point during the estrangement, Ray dated twenty-year-old millionaire Gloria Vanderbilt, according to author Maura Spiegel. Though the Millands reconciled on June 28, 1945, this would not be the last time their marriage would be in trouble.

By today's standards, *The Lost Weekend* lacks some of the gut-wrenching punch it delivered in 1945. There have been so many imitations and parodies over the years, it remains potent but needs to be seen within the context of its time. Up until *The Lost Weekend*, especially post-Prohibition, there had never been a film so completely devoted to understanding the mind of an alcoholic.

Previously, alcoholism had been treated mostly as funny (the stumbling-drunk stereotype would continue for many years after the film's release), but even serious attempts at showing the ill effects of drinking were usually too detached from the alcoholic character to make viewers empathize with their behavior. Well-intentioned portrayals of this type included Fredric March in *A Star Is Born* (1937) and Van Heflin in *Johnny Eager* (1942). The closest thing to *The Lost Weekend*'s raw scrutiny came nearly two decades earlier, but not out of Hollywood: *Ten Nights in a Barroom* (1926), the independent, all-Black "race movie," featured an outstanding performance by Charles Gilpin and a comparable DTs (delirium tremens) nightmare sequence.

The Lost Weekend goes even further. Those scenes of Birnam's sweaty walk up the East Side to hock his typewriter are agonizing. Birnam's detention at Bellevue is made chilling by the shadowy photography, Frank Faylen's sadistic nurse, and the cries of the other patients. (Wilder received unprecedented access to film in the actual ward where Milland had stayed.) When Birnam trips down the flight of stairs, the fall is from a first-person perspective. (Cinematographer John F. Seitz strapped a camera to his chest to achieve the effect.). Another, more subtle photographic technique—shining harsh lights on Milland's gaunt, unshaven face—is employed in the scene where Birnam robs a liquor store during his Third Avenue odyssey. Of the many atypical Hollywood shots of Milland in the movie, perhaps the most extraordinary is the extreme close-up of Milland's eye after one of Birnam's drunken binges.

The Lost Weekend (1945)

Thus, the film diagrams the destruction of the character Don Birnam as as it simultaneously indexes the deconstruction of the movie star Ray Milland.

The supporting performances are memorable, in particular Howard da Silva's mean-spirited bartender and Doris Dowling's hooker-barfly. In addition to an uncredited bit as a fellow drunk in the Bellevue ward, Douglas Spencer was starting an important function in Ray Milland's career. Though he looked nothing like Milland, Spencer was assigned as his stand-in and would continue with that job for many years beyond their Paramount association.

Of course, it is Ray Milland who carries *The Lost Weekend*. He expresses the irritability of a man who has genuine talent but not the capacity to actualize it. Birnam's disdain for those around him, even when they are acting kindly, should make most viewers dislike him. This is certainly the case in the "meet ugly" way he introduces himself to Helen—by throwing her umbrella at her feet. But the revelation of his distress when no one is present is what attracts us to his character, at least enough to feel some compassion. One of the most moving yet pathetic moments involves the prostitute (Dowling), when Birnam swaps roles and prostitutes himself by giving her the kiss she wants in exchange for money so he can purchase more liquor. (Wilder's experience as an "escort" in his youth and Milland's theory that actors were not much different from prostitutes helped infuse this scene with extra depth and pathos.)

Charles Brackett said of the *Lost Weekend* novel, "It had more sense of horror than any horror story I have ever read." In yet another precursor to his horror period, Ray Milland's screams are downright excruciating during the infamous climax when Birnam experiences the DTs and imagines seeing a bat kill and devour a mouse on his apartment wall.

Milland excels during the quieter moments, too, such as in Birnam's attempt to lift money from the woman's purse in the fancy bar. We actually root for Don Birnam when it would normally make little sense for the audience to want a theft to succeed. This scene displays the best of Milland, Wilder, and the editing scheme of Doane Harrison.

Just as Milland finished this personally demanding and professionally chancy work, Paramount quickly cast him in two safe, low-budget comedies. Milland started *The Well Groomed Bride* on February 2, 1945, and completed it in late March, around the same time Billy Wilder asked him back to do retakes on *The Lost Weekend*, primarily to make the final scene more upbeat; and *The Trouble with Women* commenced at the end of May 1945 and finished in mid-July. Later in the year, Milland began another production, the big-budget drama *The Imperfect Lady*, shot from early September to early November 1945.

By this time, however, it was becoming clear that *The Lost Weekend* was going to have a huge impact on Milland's career, Hollywood-at-large, and popular culture in general. His other films were held back from release in order to test the effect of this most important yet risky of all ventures. The insider "buzz" ranged from blockbuster to bust on both sides of the Atlantic. Milland was profiled in *Esquire* for an October "Actor of the Month" piece, accompanied by beautiful color photos by the renowned George Hurrell (Wilder received an article of his own in the same issue); and a month after the film's November 29 release, Milland appeared on the cover of *What's On in London*, a popular arts magazine in England.

In the midst of all this exciting professional activity, Mal's mother died in Los Angeles on October 4, 1945, at age sixty-seven. She was buried next to Mal's father at Hollywood Memorial Cemetery. Elaine Grace Weber did not live to see her son-in-law's major achievement, and after the strain on their marriage earlier in the year, the Millands' nervous enthusiasm regarding *The Lost Weekend* was considerably dampened by this latest family loss.

Continuing Milland's shift into gloomy creative realms, and following President Truman's bombing of Hiroshima and Nagasaki to end the war, the studio announced plans in December 1945 for Milland to star in *The Last Man in the World*, to be scripted by James Hilton, directed by Zoltan Korda, and produced by Sol C. Siegel. This particular movie about the earth's destruction by atomic attack was not realized, yet several with the same theme were produced during the Cold War 1950s and '60s, and Milland directed and starred in his own, *Panic in Year Zero!*, in 1962. Nevertheless, it is significant that he was already being considered for all-out horror and sci-fi material in 1945.

During the wait for the public reaction to *The Lost Weekend*, several postproduction ups and downs occurred. Stanley Bear of the Allied Liquor Industries, a national trade organization, wrote to Paramount head Y. Frank Freedman about his concerns over the film's negative portrayal of consuming alcohol; Bear offered a mammoth sum of money ($5 million via gangster Frank Costello) to shelve the film forever. The Hays Office remained in the dark about the "sordid" nature of the film—until a print was finally delivered—then it, too, disapproved of showing an alcoholic's life in such stark detail. Some executives at Paramount were shuddered, others stood firm. To his credit, President Barney Balaban was quoted saying, "Once we make a picture, we don't just flush it down the toilet."

But another disaster was looming. At a Santa Barbara preview, attendees were laughing inappropriately—and many walked out. Other previews followed that induced giggling, squirming, even booing. Now, Balaban had to seriously consider pulling a film others at Paramount had never completely supported. Just in time, the filmmakers realized the cause of the audience responses: the temporary music track used during the trial-run screenings was much too jazzy and upbeat—the type to cue laughs, which were obviously not intended. Perhaps some viewers were also confused by seeing that excellent farceur, Ray Milland, in such a downbeat role. Robert Osborne later wrote, "*The Lost Weekend* received the worst preview reactions of any major motion picture that went on to survive such adverse comment."

To remedy the problem, Wilder and his team enlisted Miklos Rozsa to compose a score to mirror Don Birnam's psychological pain. Rozsa wrote a leitmotif similar to the one he had used in *Double Indemnity* and added intermittently a theremin, the electronic, quivering-sounding instrument first developed in 1920 by Leon Theremin but only used once before cinematically—again by Rozsa the same year as *The Lost Weekend*—in Alfred Hitchcock's *Spellbound*. The simple change of scoring turned the next preview audience—along with attending industry types—into a rapt crowd. A London showing went especially well. Now the film was ready for the critics.

The reviews were universally glowing. *Variety* called the film "a particularly outstanding achievement.... Ray Milland has certainly given no better performance in his career." Bosley Crowther in the *New York Times* wrote, "[It is] a shatteringly realistic and morbidly fascinating film.... Mr. Milland, in a splendid performance, catches all the ugly nature of a 'drunk,' yet reveals the inner torment and degradation of a respectable man who knows his weakness and his shame." The film's cinematographer, John F Seitz, added,

"[S]ix months ago, I considered him just the handsome leading-man type. But, in this picture, Ray has proved himself to be perhaps the most interesting subject I have ever photographed." Even Milland nemesis Hedda Hopper declared in her column, "*The Lost Weekend* tops them all. Ray Milland's portrayal is an engraved invitation for an Academy Award."

THE OSCARS AND THE AFTERMATH

Hopper was right. The overwhelming reaction to *The Lost Weekend* was noticed by the Academy of Motion Picture Arts and Sciences. For the first time in his career, Ray Milland was attached to a movie that had more than a chance at winning several Oscars in several major categories. Milland wasn't convinced of his own prospects, though, and tried to escape the hoopla by joining Mal for a ten-day fishing trip in Acapulco. Upon his return, he went right back to work at the studio. He later recounted,

> One Monday morning, the sound mixer said to me, "The sound department ran a rough cut of *Weekend* Saturday night, just checking the sound track [sic]. I wanna tell you something. You're going to be nominated for an Academy Award. You can't miss."
>
> I gave him a quizzical look and told him to stop kidding around. At that, he become the tiniest bit belligerent.
>
> "Look," he said, "I'll tell you how much I'm kidding around. I'm willing to bet on it, not that you'll be nominated, that's a cinch, but that you'll get the Award. And I'll make a bet on it right now. Ten bucks and you give me three to one, which is pretty good odds when you consider there'll be five nominees. What d'ya say?"
>
> "I'll do better than that," I said. "I'll give you fifty to one if you're right. Okay?"
>
> "You bet your ass it's okay. Your trouble is, you're afraid to think about it."

Similarly, Paramount nervously debated whether to place *The Lost Weekend* into consideration for Best Picture or Milland's other recently completed film, *Kitty*. Ultimately, the executives decided to hold back *Kitty* and give *The Lost Weekend* an all-out campaign in the press, hyperbolically labeling it "The Most Widely Acclaimed Motion Picture in the History of the Industry."

In early February, the nominations were announced, and the Millands learned the news the same way as everyone else: seeing it in the morning papers. From the beginning, Ray was a favorite in the running, yet he continued to doubt his chances of actually winning. His competition represented a mixed lot: Bing Crosby was repeating his role as Father O'Malley in *The Bells of St. Mary's*, a part for which Crosby had already won an Oscar the year before (in *Going My Way*); Gregory Peck was a fan favorite in *The Keys of the Kingdom*, but it was another priest role (like Crosby's); Cornel Wilde was new to the public impersonating Chopin in *A Song to Remember*, though critics were not so fond of the movie itself; and Gene Kelly was the biggest surprise as the sailor on leave in *Anchors Aweigh*, but since that film was a musical, Kelly seemed like a long shot. Further helping Milland's odds was the fact that *The Lost Weekend* was also nominated for Best Picture, Best Director, Best Screenplay, Best Cinematography, Best Scoring, and Best Editing.

Milland should have been encouraged by three preceding prizes. The Eleventh Annual New York Critics Circle Award honored both the film as Best Picture and Milland as Best Actor on January 20, 1946. In the same month, the National Board of Review inaugurated its first ever award season with Milland winning again. Later, on March 6, the Hollywood Foreign Press Association's Golden Globes announced the following: Ray Milland as Best Actor, Billy Wilder as Best Director, and the film as Best Picture. So, on March 7, 1946, Oscar day finally arrived, shortly after his Golden Globes win. A nervous Ray woke up that morning vowing not to attend the evening's ceremony, but Mal had other ideas: "I know that you're erratic, volatile, and the possessor or a foul temper. But I never thought you were a coward!" Then with a look as cold as a Canadian nun, she said, "You'll go to that ceremony tonight if we have to put you in a straitjacket. And I'm calling the troops right now!"

The rest of the day didn't go much better. Milland was beside himself, according to Charles Brackett: "Ray Milland came [to the office], so strung-up that his words weren't always in the right place in sentences."

On Oscar night, amid cheering fans and flashing camera bulbs, the elegantly dressed Ray and Muriel Milland were all smiles as they entered Grauman's Chinese Theatre. Inside, they took their appointed seats on the fifth row, near friends, coworkers, and competitors. The show was broadcast live on ABC Radio Network, cohosted by Bob Hope and James Stewart. The Millands waited through banal speeches, forced jokes, and Oscar-nominated songs, and to make matters even more nerve-racking, the printed program indicated that the Best Actor and Best Actress were to be announced last, *after* Best Picture, Best Screenplay, and Best Director!

The Lost Weekend lost in three categories early on. Technical awards went first: Best Editing to *National Velvet*, Best Black and White Cinematography

Academy Award night (1946), with Ingrid Bergman. Photo credit: Pictorial Press Ltd. / Alamy Stock Photo.

to *The Picture of Dorian Gray*, and Best Scoring to *Spellbound* (the *other* Rozsa film to use the theremin). Ray Milland wasn't feeling very hopeful.

Next came Best Picture, though, and *The Lost Weekend* won! The mood was suddenly upbeat around the *Lost Weekend* seating section. That major headline news was followed by Billy Wilder and Charles Brackett's win for Best Screenplay and Wilder's for Best Director. Finally, Ingrid Bergman, the recipient of the previous year's Best Actress award, took the stage to name the nominees for Best Actor. Teasingly, she asked if Mr. Milland was nervous before opening the envelope: "It's yours!," she exclaimed with glee. He was in shock and couldn't move. Mrs. Milland had to jab her husband in the rib cage to get him up and accept the award.

Since the Oscar show was broadcast only on radio (televised airings would not start until 1953), it is unclear whether Milland approached the microphone and said, "Thank you," or nothing at all. Due to the recording quality, it is almost impossible to verify what, if anything, Milland uttered, but either way, Milland's "speech" remains to date the shortest on record by a Best Actor winner. His own amusing account seems very likely: "I fell up the steps, took the Oscar in the wrong hand, and had to shake Bergman's elbow. My throat was dry and my eyes were full of tears. I couldn't say a word. I stumbled off the stage."

It is in keeping with Milland's modesty that he would not have said very much, though it is likely he genuinely did not believe he would win and never prepared a speech. So, rather than ramble on, Milland would have preferred dignified silence. Since this ceremony was the first after the end of World War II, Milland and every other recipient received a bronze statuette coated in gold plate. During the war, only plaster substitutes were used. In an odd, ultrapatriotic finale to the show, the group of winners gathered to sing "The Star-Spangled Banner," despite the fact the war had ended—in the summer of 1945—almost a year earlier.

Feeling tired yet exhilarated, Ray and Mal Milland left for the Paramount celebrations at La Rue's restaurant. On the way to an after party at Romanoff's, Ray experienced a poignant, reflective moment:

> For Best Actor Ray Milland, winning an Oscar was a fleeting moment to be savored. Riding with his wife in a limousine en route to the postceremony celebration, Milland directed the chauffeur to drive to the bridle path on Sunset Boulevard overlooking Hollywood. An MGM talent scout had brought the actor to this spot when he first arrived in Hollywood in 1930 and told him, "It all belongs to Ramon Novarro. He is the reigning romantic star at the moment, so tonight it belongs to him." Milland stood there with his Oscar, taking in the view of twinkling lights, and finally said, "Mr. Novarro, tonight they belong to me!"

Ray Milland achieved something else that night. He was the first Welsh actor to win an Oscar, something that not only he would celebrate, but so would the entire country of Wales. Alfred Reginald John Truscott-Jones had certainly come a long way from the Midlands.

Awards and fame aside, Ray Milland could feel morally virtuous as well. Alcoholics Anonymous (AA) had been in existence since 1935, but it took *The Lost Weekend* (book *and* film) to bring the concept home to many more millions of people that an alcoholic is someone who should no longer be seen as the object of pity, scorn, or comic derision but as a troubled individual afflicted with a disease that requires help, support, and professional care.

Though AA is never mentioned in the film, and the ending offers a simplistic road to recovery, *The Lost Weekend* was the first movie to give audiences a powerful sense of the anguish of alcoholism—not only for the alcoholic but for those who care about the person. Despite skepticism in some quarters that AA was rooted in religious teachings, many more people joined the organization after the movie's release, particularly returning servicemen. In a way, Milland undercut his humanistic "good works" by accepting the modern equivalent of at least $40,000 per year to appear in cigarette print ads for the next decade. Of course, he was one of many celebrities to do so, and the addictive, ill effects of tobacco were not fully known at the time.

As late as 2011, the Library of Congress's National Film Registry recognized the movie's societal impact by selecting *The Lost Weekend* as "culturally, historically, or aesthetically significant" because it is "an uncompromising look at the devastating effects of alcoholism" that "melded an expressionistic film-noir style with documentary realism to immerse viewers in the harrowing experiences of an aspiring New York writer willing to do almost anything for a drink."

The Lost Weekend was one of the first of the postwar period to be identified as a "social conscience problem film." Other topics followed—mostly in response to the troubles war veterans were experiencing trying to readjust to civilian life. *The Best Years of Our Lives* (1946) dealt with a variety of issues, including prejudice against physical disabilities; *Crossfire* and *Gentleman's Agreement* (both in 1947) broached antisemitism; and *Home of the Brave* (1949) addressed racism and posttraumatic stress disorders.

The legacy of *The Lost Weekend* should not be underestimated. Though drinking to excess as a comic device would never fully die, most future depictions of alcoholism on the big and small screen were more in line with the Wilder picture: *Smash-Up: The Story of a Woman* (1947) with Susan Hayward was considered a distaff *Lost Weekend*; in the 1954 remake of *A Star Is Born*, James Mason evinced more sympathy than Fredric March had in 1937; Robert Montgomery decided to condense *The Lost Weekend* for live television in 1955, with Montgomery himself playing Don Birnam (followed by another live TV remake starring Joe Maross in 1956); the television drama *The Days of Wine and Roses* in 1958 was so well respected that Hollywood adapted it in 1963, with Jack Lemmon replacing Cliff Robertson; like Lemmon, Dick Van Dyke changed his comedic image by portraying an alcoholic in the 1974 TV movie *The Morning After*; Mickey Rourke and Faye Dunaway temporarily revived their careers with *Barfly* in 1987; and Nicolas Cage won an Oscar for *Leaving Las Vegas* in 1995, exactly fifty years after Ray Milland's triumph.

Following *The Lost Weekend*, Ray Milland's own films often touched upon the topic. He played either an alcoholic (*Night into Morning* [1951]) or a recovering one (*Something to Live For* [1952]). Paradoxically, Ray Milland was not an alcoholic or even much of a drinker, yet, due to his convincing performances in these films, rumors persisted otherwise for years. In a typical article at the time about Milland, "Ginger Ale, Please," in the *Los Angeles Times* (April, 1948), Louis Berg wrote, "It got so he was afraid to be seen in public with a glass in his hand. He took to ordering ginger ale at cocktail parties." During the *Weekend* shoot itself, it was iced tea that Milland was drinking during those many scenes in his apartment and at the bars (he estimated he had swallowed sixteen gallons of tea by the end of filming). But concerned fans and citizens who thought Ray Milland needed help made life frustrating for the actor, frequently offering him either a drink to ease his "cravings" or some other kind of well-meant form of assistance.

Of course, parodies have abounded for years. One of the funniest and earliest riffs was performed by Ray Milland himself, so soon after *The Lost Weekend* captured multiple Oscars that the actor nearly jeopardized the film's moral message. Milland was a guest on the March 10, 1946, *Lucky Strike Program* starring Jack Benny, three days after his Oscar win. Live on air, Benny starts the show by teasing Milland for bringing his statuette with him, saying the actor won "a bronze Oscar with an icebag on its head." Shortly after, the two launch into a *Lost Weekend* spoof where they take turns playing the Don Birnam part opposite a scold-like Phil Harris (the bandleader known as a "tippler"), who chastises them both on the evils of drink. The sketch ends with Milland getting rid of the DTs by throwing his Oscar at the menagerie of phantom animals (all voiced by Mel Blanc).

Billy Wilder had the heartiest laugh of all, though, when he learned, belatedly, that the liquor industry had wanted to pay Paramount to ban the film or destroy the negative. Despite all the success Wilder achieved with *The Lost Weekend*, not to mention the money it made for his bosses, he was quoted saying, "If they would have given *me* the $5 million, *I* would have burned the negative!"

CHAPTER 6

DOWNFALL OF A HOMME FATALE
(1946–1949)

THE LOST WEEKEND BROUGHT RAY MILLAND NEW FANS AND GENUINE respect from both critics and the film industry. For the moment, throughout much of 1945 and 1946, he was on top of the world, and he knew it.

While shooting one of his next films, a Western called *California*, Milland fully realized the benefits of his Oscar win:

> [*California*] took three months to make, and in the middle of it I was notified that I had won the Grand Prix Award at the very first Cannes Film Festival. . . . Also my contract was rewritten and I became the highest salaried actor then on the lot [including Bing Crosby and Bob Hope]. There were many other emoluments and privileges. Great deference was shown in nightclubs and restaurants. The mere whisper of an endorsement brought showers of gifts, lawn mowers, a new kitchen, carloads of soap and cigarettes, etc., etc., most of which we gave away. Next [sic] England decided to hold the first Royal Command Film Performance. It was to be the first big gala after five years of war, and London was girding for it. My invitation, when it came, was most impressive, all covered with seals and ribbons.

What Ray Milland didn't mention in his list of achievements was that he became the first actor to win both the Oscar and the Cannes Grand Prix Award for the same role. He also won Best Actor plaudits from the Association of Brazilian Cinema Critics, the Motion Picture and Theatrical Critics of Cuba, and *Look* and *Redbook* magazines. He attained his peak of popularity symbolically when he observed the ritual of all major stars: on April 17, 1946, Milland imprinted his hands and feet in cement in front of Sid Grauman's Chinese Restaurant, adding the phrase with his finger, "THANKS SID FOR THE HONOUR," on the tinted square.

Yet, Paramount wasn't sure what do with its megastar. Should Milland return to his days as a leading man of romantic comedies or delve further into bleak material? The studio's answer was to hedge its bets and vary Milland's output, showcasing him in multiple guises. But the safest genre was comedy, and there remained the task of finally releasing several very different pre-Oscar farces: *Kitty*, *The Well Groomed Bride*, and *The Trouble with Women*. All three capitalized on Milland's marquee allure without trying to impress the critics, a hint that the actor reached the summit of his career, and there was no other way to go but down. Uneasy rests the crown, and so on.

As one prophetic indicator of his future descent, Milland's actual crown was in need of padding! According to the actor, the electrolysis hair treatments he tolerated for *Reap the Wild Wind* in 1941 were catching up with him. Ray Milland was now losing his black mane (primarily on top and in front) and asked his actor friends what to do. They all recommended Verita Bouvaire-Thompson, an expert toupée and wig maker rumored to be Humphrey Bogart's mistress and "Bacall's worst nightmare." Thus, Milland joined Jimmy Stewart, Gary Cooper, George Raft, Frank Sinatra, and Bogie himself as a regular Bouvaire-Thompson client.

KITTY AND THE BACKLOG

Meanwhile, Milland saw the release of *Kitty*, which had been shot way back in prehairpiece 1944, and it became an enormous moneymaker when it reached screens in January 1946. The $2 million production earned $3.5 million upon its initial release, thus justifying its extravagant cost.

In 1944, to preempt Twentieth Century-Fox's upcoming *Forever Amber*, Paramount purchased the rights to *Kitty*, Rosamond Marshall's 1943 bestseller. Set in 1783 London, the novel uses George Bernard Shaw's *Pygmalion* as an inspiration, with one major change from book to film necessary to appease the Hays Office: Kitty, as portrayed by Paulette Goddard, would have to be a pickpocket, not a prostitute.

Playing opposite Goddard in the last (and best) of their four unions, Milland is perfectly cast as Sir Hugh Marcy, the "Henry Higgins" figure. Interestingly, two decades later, Milland would play the actual Henry Higgins in a touring company version of *My Fair Lady*, the musical version of Shaw's story. But in keeping with Milland's increasingly edgy screen persona, there is something slightly seedy about Sir Marcy. Unlike Henry Higgins, Kitty's mentor is a man of only *apparent* wealth: Marcy and his aunt, Lady Susan Dowitt (Constance Collier, as a distaff, dipsomaniacal "Pickering"), are living in a mansion but strapped for cash. So their attempt to turn the Cockney "guttersnipe" Kitty into a "lady" is for their own financial gain, not to prove anything beneficial about the human condition or to win a gentleman's bet. Therefore, Sir Marcy is really nothing more than a pimp when he tries to attract the wealthy but degenerate Duke of Malmunster (Reginald Owen) to the regally transformed Kitty.

Another unexpected difference with *Pygmalion* is that Kitty has much more of a mind of her own from the start, to the point of marrying a man (Dennis Hoey) in an effort to help her new benefactors. All along, an attraction between Sir Marcy and Kitty simmers even though many more events occur, including Kitty's walking down the wedding aisle again and even giving birth(!), before Marcy and Kitty have a chance at uniting.

As with most Mitchell Leisen productions, décor was an essential ingredient. The director worked extensively with his production designers, recreating eighteenth-century England on the Paramount soundstages. Raoul Pène Du Bois devised the sets as well as the costumes, and Romanian-born artist Theodore Lukits accurately duplicated the work of Thomas Gainsborough (played by Cecil Kellaway in the story), having been personally recommended by Milland after Lukits painted a beautiful portrait of Mal in 1942.

Apart from its aesthetic virtues, *Kitty* is one of Leisen's best-directed films. The master stylist is aided by the Karl Tunberg–Darrell Ware script, which deftly balances comedy of manners and old-fashioned melodrama. The game ensemble of players includes not only Collier, Owen, and Kellaway but also Sara Allgood, Patric Knowles, and Eric Blore.

Topping them all are the stars themselves. Landing a *Life* magazine cover and billed over Milland for the only time, the Long Island–born Goddard does a highly commendable job with her Cockney accent in her early scenes and is convincing and funny as she develops into a "lady" (albeit a naughty, still thieving one). Milland was reluctant to wear tight, dandy attire again, but with shrewd touches, he captures the soul of a man with two competing interests, a craving for monetary gain versus an adoration for his "golden goose." His best moment comes during Sir Marcy's climactic argument with Kitty on the eve of her marriage, her third, to Brett Harwood (Knowles), at which point Marcy at long last admits to both his jealousy over the handsome Brett and his own love for her.

Notices of the day were unfairly tepid. In the *New York Times*, Bosley Crowther wrote Goddard is "pompous and posey," and Milland appears "blase and bored . . . [His] role as peacock and deadbeat is slightly odious, [and he] wears his costumes very handsomely, but wearily lets it go at that." *Variety* was somewhat kinder, writing, "Paulette Goddard credibly depicts

A publicity photo for *Kitty* (1945)

Kitty in the various phases of the slum girl's rise in station. Ray Milland has the more difficult task of keeping the unpleasant foppish character of Sir Hugh Marcy, Kitty's beloved, consistent and does well by it."

In recent years, *Kitty* has been better appreciated by critics but not often revived. One champion, David Melville, wrote in *Senses of Cinema* in 2005, "Although Paramount denied [Leisen] Technicolor, *Kitty* is a film whose visual splendour rivals Stanley Kubrick's *Barry Lyndon* (1975).... Yet its warmth and wit put Kubrick's rather glacial movie to shame."

A few months after *Kitty*'s release, in May of 1946, the less auspicious, modern-day comedy *The Well Groomed Bride* was neither embraced by critics nor a picture Milland wanted to make, but it became another financial winner.

Shot immediately after *The Lost Weekend*, *The Well Groomed Bride* starts with Milland as a naval officer ordered by his superior (James Gleason) to locate a magnum of champagne to use for a ship launching. With only twenty-four hours to find the bubbly, Lieutenant Dudley Briggs discovers there is only one magnum in all of San Francisco, and a young woman,

Margie Dawson (Olivia de Havilland), has just purchased it. Her goal is at odds with his: she wants to use the champagne for her upcoming nuptials. The rest of the story finds Briggs trying every trick to get the bottle away from Margie. In the course of their adventure through the city, the battling twosome fall in love.

The screenplay by Claude Binyon and Bob Russell is undeniably thin—stretching a sketch-length premise to feature-film proportions. Nevertheless, there is something refreshing about an entertainment laser focused on that which is completely inconsequential.

Binyon and Russell have the most fun with the notion of Milland playing a character desperate to possess an alcoholic beverage without ever wanting to actually drink it, and it is a credit to both stars for fully committing themselves to the project's existential nothingness. Milland, in particular, acquits himself ably as the lieutenant with a single-minded mission to buy, beg, borrow, or steal (if all else fails) the magnum of champagne that is the central "MacGuffin." Though she lacks the knowing buoyancy of either Claudette Colbert or Paulette Goddard (who had been originally cast), De Havilland matches Milland's machinations with a steely resolve reminiscent of her suffragette in Raoul Walsh's *Strawberry Blonde* (1941).

For De Havilland and her fans, *The Well Groomed Bride* might have seemed like a trifle, but it represented an important point in her career. She had been off the screen for nearly three years, having sued her home studio of Warner Bros. over the onerous dictates of the standard seven-year clause in her contract. De Havilland won her case and received offers from several studios. In addition to making *The Well Groomed Bride* for Paramount, securing top billing over Ray Milland, her other 1946 Paramount release, *To Each His Own*, earned De Havilland her first of two Academy Awards for Best Actress. Not only did Milland shoot a preview trailer heartily promoting *To Each His Own*, on the next year's Oscar night (March 13, 1947) at the Shrine Auditorium, it was a beaming Ray Milland, the previous year's male winner, who handed De Havilland the coveted statuette.

Milland became one of many stars who would later owe gratitude to De Havilland for her protracted showdown: within a few years, he found himself at odds with his Paramount bosses yet managed a graceful way to exit the studio—something that might not have been possible without the De Havilland Law (California Labor Code Section 2855), which still today gives greater artistic freedom to artists under long-term contracts.

De Havilland received glowing notices to go with her Oscar for *To Each His Own*, but she and Milland had to make do with mixed reviews for *The Well Groomed Bride*. *Variety* at least acknowledged, "Expert comedy playing by

Milland and Miss De Havilland must be credited with successfully bringing off as much mirth as as there is."

Late in 1946, in October, Milland went to CBS radio to tap more fully than ever into his wicked side in a condensed version of *The Seventh Veil*. Compton Bennett's 1945 British film had been an international hit, raising the profile of James Mason as the abusive guardian and piano instructor to an innocent orphan (Ann Todd). In the *This Is Hollywood* adaptation, Todd reprised her role and Milland replaced Mason in a forerunner to the similar parts Todd and Milland would play two years later in the film *So Evil My Love*. Milland was chillingly sadistic in this audio edition.

In November 1946, the Milland family flew to London to attend the Royal Command Performance of *The Lost Weekend*. The large crowds were eager to see Milland, which made him anxious, but he managed to appear relatively relaxed in front of the royal family. After the event, while still in London, the Millands quietly looked into finding a sibling for Daniel by visiting adoption agencies. What Ray and Mal didn't realize was that because Ray was no longer a British citizen, they were automatically ruled ineligible.

The Millands next traveled to South Wales for a vacation, and Ray was greeted as a hometown hero when he, Mal, and Danny visited Cardiff and Neath, with the mayor of the latter location giving him the key to the city. Milland then saw friends and family and stopped by the pub that served him his very first drink. While staying at the Angel Hotel in Cardiff, the family strolled over to see Ray's father, Alfred, marking the long-delayed first time Mal and Danny met the Jones patriarch. Still, the highlight of the trip for Ray was breakfast! Every morning, he devoured his beloved lava bread, or laver bread, which is not an actual bread but a puréed seaweed delicacy unavailable in the United States.

With little time left in South Wales, Ray tried to find his childhood sweetheart, Olwen, in Tongwynlais. "I don't remember much about Olwen . . . but she was pretty, all right, and I'll never forget her," he told a reporter, and Mal added, "Everybody has to have a first sweetheart, and Ray is no exception." Not remembering her last name, though, he never located Olwen.

In another somber moment, Ray was asked to lay a wreath at the Welsh National War Memorial in Alexandra Gardens in Cathays Park. The Millands then left Wales to attend the Cannes Film Festival showing of *The Lost Weekend* (retitled *Le poison*) and to pick up his Best Actor award from Georges Bidault, premiere of France. Shortly after this honor, the family returned to Hollywood.

Artistically speaking, Milland was not well served in 1947 by Paramount. While working on more promising films like *The Big Clock*, Milland saw four released that had been held back from exhibition, including a sprawling, listless Western, a mild period drama, a oddball comic romance, and an all-star musical in which he made a guest appearance. Yet, Milland was still a great "draw," and all these films did very well at the box office. Milland was keenly aware of Paramount's attempt to exploit his name: "Right after [*The Lost Weekend*] I made three of my worst pictures, one after another, because they shove you into everything they can after a hit."

Milland's consolation during this desultory year was that his salary was increased yet again. The US Treasury Department reported he earned $253,333 in 1947.

By granting the pay raise, Paramount sought to prevent any other studio from luring Milland away; yet his bosses were adamant about keeping him out of the director's chair, in contrast to MGM having allowed Robert Montgomery to helm *Lady in the Lake* in 1946. Rejecting his entreaties, Paramount reasoned Milland would lose some of his box-office luster by becoming a director. At the time, Milland expressed his desire one day to see the credit "Directed by Ray Milland." He explained, "I've always thought of directing. . . . In fact, in my own mind, I always direct every picture in which I appear. . . . I'd like to do a story of the Welsh people. We'll see. . . . And directing would mean the end of my having to look into the mirror at myself." It would take nearly another decade before Milland would get that chance, but obviously the actor was already eager to move onto other creative endeavors.

In front of the cameras, *California* was the most expensive of what Milland called his "worst pictures," receiving the royal Technicolor treatment. The Western started out as a promising vehicle in that it cast Milland as a rugged army deserter opposite Barbara Stanwyck in their only movie together. Milland would be directed for the first of four times by John Farrow, a talented craftsman.

California, Milland's first color film since *Lady in the Dark*, began preproduction in 1945, when *Lady*'s screenwriter, Albert Hackett, was announced as both writer and director, and Alan Ladd and Betty Hutton were supposed to costar. By the time cameras were ready to roll in late November 1945, the screenplay was rewritten by Frank Butler and Theodore Strauss, Farrow became the director, Milland replaced Ladd, Stanwyck replaced Hutton, and the production dragged on until the beginning of February 1946. After the shoot, Milland half jokingly told a reporter the reason he wanted to star in a Western, his first, was that "my son Danny was beginning to love John Wayne more than he did me."

Set in 1848, *California* follows two wagon-train riders, Johnny Trumbo (Milland) and Michael Fabian (Barry Fitzgerald), as they knock heads with a singer-turned-saloon owner, Lily Bishop (Stanwyck), on their California Gold Rush trek. Later, there is trouble in the form of an ex-slave trader named Pharaoh Coffin (George Coulouris), who plots to turn California into his own independent empire. Johnny tries to halt Coffin's political scheme while they fight for Lily's hand. At the climax, Lily saves Johnny's life by killing Coffin, and Johnny enlists in the army, with Lily promising to wait for him.

California showed potential, but its narrative never quite functioned as either a traditional Western or a revisionist one—more of an in-between muddle. In addition, the chemistry between Milland and Stanwyck was awkward, mostly because their characters were at odds with each almost the entire time.

Milland attributed one drawback to the editing done during the year *California* sat on the shelf before its January 1947 release: "I was quite a horseman and trick rider before I went into films, and in *California* there was a scene in which I got to do some real riding for the first time in pictures. . . . But the ride was sandwiched between two closely related scenes and was thought to be too long. It was cut. So . . . this one thing I was very proud of and could do well got the axe." At other times, Milland demonstrated he could easily handle Sheik, the Palomino that became his horse during the shoot.

The reviews were mixed. *Variety* encapsulated the most frequent complaint: "[I]f one was to probe beyond the surface, [it] is actually little different than dozens of other narratives of the war of the plains." The *Variety* critic perceptively noticed Milland's contrarian take on traditional Western heroics: "For a hero, though, he certainly gets kayoed frequently. And a knife-dueling sequence towards the end where he surgically disposes of his vis-à-vis, is almost funny."

On the strength of the names Milland and Stanwyck—and the Western genre itself—*California* was a big moneymaker for Paramount, earning $3.9 million, proving again that in this moment Milland could be popular in anything. A few years later, Milland partnered with Paramount's most touted postwar discovery, Lizabeth Scott, when he revived his role as Jonathan Trumbo for *Lux Radio Theatre* in January 1950.

Milland's next two 1947 releases were also holdovers and both costarred Teresa Wright. Yet, the attempt to turn Milland and Wright into a smart screen team was spoiled by the material with which they had to work.

First, in April 1947, came *The Imperfect Lady*. As with *Kitty*, Karl Tunberg (this time without Darrell Ware) wrote the screenplay, based on a story by Ladislas Fodor. Despite its aim to duplicate the same period-picture aura, *The Imperfect Lady* was not produced with the same care.

In *The Imperfect Lady*, Wright plays Millie, a showgirl in 1892 London, who marries a politician, Clive (Milland). One night, Millie is asked by a man, José (Anthony Quinn), to innocently keep him company for a few hours. When José is arrested for murder, Millie realizes that she alone can save José's life by testifying at the upcoming trial, yet she knows that admitting she spent the night with José could ruin Clive's career. In the end, Millie provides corroboration in court, and Clive stands by her.

Directed by Lewis Allen, *The Imperfect Lady* might have been more substantial had it not been so devoid of real drama. Every character is clearly innocent, and the patronizing ending begs the question: Would the liberal-minded Clive be as inclined to forgive his wife if something truly scandalous had happened between her and José? In part, the censors kept *The Imperfect Lady* from this more adventurous direction, but even *Kitty* was a comparatively ribald film made during the same period of PCA restrictions. One wonders if the prudish approach would have been altered if Paulette Goddard had been cast, which had been the original plan.

Variety complained about the "stunting screenplay and loose direction" but again appreciated Ray Milland: "[He] puts in his usual polished performance, overcoming a series of stilted and clichéd lines by using his native sense of humor to good effect." In any case, the box-office receipts ($1.8 million) were respectable.

A few months later, in June 1947, Milland and Wright were back on the big screen in a contemporary comedy titled *The Trouble with Women*, but the results were just as disappointing.

For this occasion, Milland reluctantly reunited with both Sidney Lanfield, the demanding director of *The Lady Has Plans*, and Brian Donlevy, his on- and off-screen nemesis from *Beau Geste*. The screenplay by Arthur Sheekman concerns a professor (Milland) who visits a midwestern college to lecture on his latest book, *The Subjugation of Women*. A local newspaper editor (Donlevy) assigns a reporter (Wright) to undermine the stuffy academic's subjugation theory by having him caught hitting a woman. The editor's maneuvers are complicated by his reporter's growing romantic interest in the male chauvinist; in turn, the professor becomes attracted to her, though he is betrothed to a strait-laced school administrator (Rose Hobart).

The reviews were deadly. Mildred Martin of the *Philadelphia Inquirer* went as far as saying, "Less firmly established players than Ray Milland, Teresa Wright and Brian Donlevy might find their careers threatened by *The Trouble with Women* ... an 'alleged comedy.'" At least *Newsweek* praised Milland for saving the picture: "Ray Milland isn't thrown by *The Trouble with Women*, but there would be a lot more trouble for the producer if Milland wasn't around."

If Paramount had any further aspirations for a Milland-Wright partnership, *The Trouble with Women* ended them, though they did work together once more, with Wright in a supporting role in *Something to Live For* (1952).

Milland wasn't quite done with *The Trouble with Women*. In December 1947, he reprised his role on a *Screen Guild Theater* radio adaptation (opposite Betty Hutton) and performed it again on radio for *Screen Directors Playhouse* (opposite Mary Jane Croft) in May 1949.

In August 1947, Milland turned up for a cameo in the all-star *Variety Girl*. Under George Marshall's direction, Mary Hatcher and Olga San Juan played young women seeking stardom while becoming mixed up with Paramount's efforts to endorse Variety Club International, an actual organization founded in 1928 to help underprivileged youth. Like *Star-Spangled Rhythm*, the film promoted nearly the full roster of Paramount stars in skits, songs, or mere walk-ons. Topping it off, a Technicolor Puppetoon sequence occurred in the midst of the otherwise black-and-white show. Milland's two appearances were brief, though he did rate fourth billing after Bing Crosby, Bob Hope, and Gary Cooper.

Early on, we see Milland answer his dressing-room phone by standing on a chair and grabbing the receiver out of a chandelier—a riff on *The Lost Weekend*. (A similar gag occurs in 1947's *My Favorite Brunette*, when Bob Hope's detective character finds a wine bottle in a chandelier and wisecracks, "Ah, Ray Milland must have been here.")

Milland later shows up in the final, carousel-themed production number, "Harmony," which, like the Puppetoons, would have benefited from Technicolor. In this elaborate closer, Milland joins Cooper, Veronica Lake, Dorothy Lamour, Barry Fitzgerald, Lizabeth Scott, and several other Paramount names. Dressed in white tie and tails, he and *I Wanted Wings* costar William Holden sing a short portion of the catchy tune before comic Cass Daley accompanies them for an off-key final note.

Another late 1947 "all-star" production, *Slick Hare*, emanated from Warner Bros.' animation unit as a spoof of Hollywood nightlife. A few non-Warner's personalities pop up as denizens of "The Mocrumbo" (modeled after the Mocambo), and the cartoon Ray Milland pays for a drink at the bar with a manual typewriter and then receives a batch of miniature typewriters instead of monetary change. The eight-minute short weakly mocks *The Lost Weekend*, but it does confirm that Milland was considered such a big star that even a rival studio wanted to use his image.

For his last delayed 1947 release, *Golden Earrings*, Milland reunited with Mitchell Leisen, the director of some of his biggest moneymakers. While the critics hated it, *Golden Earrings* was a huge hit in August that year,

Golden Earrings (1947), with Marlene Dietrich. Photo credit: Photo 12 / Alamy Stock Photo.

earning $2,950,000 in US rentals alone against a budget that was just under $1 million.

Shot in mid-1946, *Golden Earrings* was promoted as a major event: newly minted Oscar-winner Ray Milland would be uniting with the legendary Marlene Dietrich, who was returning to Paramount after a decade-long absence. In addition to highlighting the reemergence of Dietrich, the elaborate production was meant to evoke Paramount's Golden Years of the 1930s, pitched somewhere between the exoticism of Josef von Sternberg and the sophistication of Ernst Lubitsch.

Golden Earrings was based on a 1946 novel by Hungarian Jolán Földes (a.k.a. Yolande Foldes), about the unlikely romance between a British soldier, Ralph Denistoun, on the run from the Nazis, and a Romani "Gypsy," Lydia, who hides him in her caravan. The screenplay by Abraham Polansky, Frank Butler, and Helen Deutsch was written with Milland and Dietrich in mind.

Despite the movie's prestige value, Milland was not eager to be part of *Golden Earrings* from the start. According to Eleanor Broder, Leisen's secretary, Dietrich tried to seduce Milland, but he wasn't interested. From that point on, it was all-out war. As Leisen recalled,

> Ray Milland didn't want to make the picture. He didn't like Marlene; he thought he was too young to do it, so he was a real bastard at first. He calmed down a little by the end, but he and Marlene fought the

whole time. When we were shooting the scene where he first meets her as she's eating the stew, over and over, Marlene would stick a fish head into her mouth, suck the eye out, and the pull out the rest of the head. Then, after I yelled cut, she would stick her finger down her throat to make herself throw it up. This whole performance made Ray violently ill.

For his part, Milland later said, "I thought she was very overrated and she was always on the make." Another problem arose during filming: several unions banded together for a strike, leaving Paramount to insist the company stay on the lot to finish *Golden Earrings* and not cross the picket lines. Though they slept in their own dressing rooms, Milland and Dietrich were annoyed by their close proximity, now both day *and* night, which was not helped by Dietrich deciding to practice the zither (for a scene in the movie) during the late hours.

Despite their hostility on the set, Milland and Dietrich are well matched and make an engaging pair. Yes, Milland's look of disgust at Dietrich is genuine in the early goings—from the fish-eating bit and beyond—but the off-screen feuding adds a frisson to this quirky battle of the sexes (and cultures). In a modification of the racist spectacle of an Anglo actor applying "blackface," the scene where Lydia helps Ralph evade the Gestapo by darkening his skin (against his will) turns out to be amusing and far less offensive than it could have been. Of course, Dietrich was a pale-skinned European herself, so her entire performance could be considered an insult. Yet *Golden Earrings*, for the most part, is a more enlightened representation of Romani "Gypsies" than was common in Golden Age Hollywood films.

There were other virtues to the the eccentric mélange of romance, suspense, and opéra bouffe, but most of the critics pounced. Bosley Crowther in the *New York Times* called it "pointed nonsense . . . [I]t is slightly revolting—not to mention ridiculous in the extreme—to see Ray Milland pretending to be a British officer pretending to be a gypsy boy." *Variety* agreed it had an "oldhat plot" but otherwise spared the stars: "[Dietrich has] rarely been better. Milland . . . is in a tailor-made part which he acquits with vigor and finesse." Lastly, though the matter of Lydia and Ralph "living together" unmarried somehow passed the Breen censors, the Catholic Legion of Decency objected and slapped a "C" (for "Condemned") rating on the release print.

Despite all the antagonism, somehow the *Golden Earrings* stars managed to reconcile long enough to play the Garbo and John Barrymore parts for a *Theatre Guild on the Air* reworking of *Grand Hotel* in March 1948, with Dietrich as the weary Russian ballerina opposite Milland's doomed baron-cum-jewel thief. Mysteriously, no recording of this curio seems to exist.

Along with *Grand Hotel* and the bleaker *Of Human Bondage* (in October for radio's Ford Theater), there was a decidedly darker tinge to Milland's 1948 output. The minor exceptions included a walk-on bit in the comedy *Miss Tatlock's Millions* and a cameo of sorts in Paramount's *Olive Oyl for President*. The latter, a politically progressive Popeye cartoon, was seen in theaters in January 1948 (during President Truman's inauguration month) and, as with *Slick Hare*, it reaffirmed Milland's star status: in a dream sequence, he is a member of Olive Oyl's presidential cabinet, along with Bing Crosby, Alan Ladd, William Holden, and Bob Hope.

THE BIG CLOCK AND THE FILM NOIRS

Later in 1948, Milland's three features were noirish in look, mood, and theme. The first and best was *The Big Clock*, shot in spring 1947 and shown in theaters in April 1948. Though his teaming with John Farrow on *California* lacked spark, Milland got along well with the director, and now they had much better source material. His most significant undertaking since *The Lost Weekend*, *The Big Clock* was a hit with audiences and critics alike and would have an everlasting following.

Scripted by Jonathan Latimer, this classic film noir was based on Kenneth Fearing's 1946 pulp fiction novel. Obviously, Milland knew Paramount supported the idea of starring him early on: having purchased the rights before publication, the studio allowed Harcourt, Brace & Company to mention Milland would headline the upcoming movie on the cover of its 1946 printing.

The casting alone had a fascinating resonance. Here was Milland, Charles Laughton, and Maureen O'Sullivan reteaming for the first time since *Payment Deferred*, sixteen years earlier, only now Milland was the main attraction. By 1947, O'Sullivan was semiretired, raising her children (including a two-year-old named Maria, later Mia), but consented to return to the screen because Farrow, her husband, asked her. Joining her were Elsa Lanchester, Laughton's wife, and an ensemble of noir stalwarts: George Macready, Henry Morgan, Dan Tobin, and Rita Johnson, who had played Milland's nasty fiancée in *The Major and the Minor*.

In *The Big Clock*, Milland is at his most desperate *and* disarming as George Stroud, an editor for a Manhattan true-crime magazine. George is torn between taking a long-delayed vacation with this wife, Georgette (O'Sullivan), and staying after hours as commanded by his boss, Earl Janoth

(Laughton), a ruthless publisher. When Georgette angrily leaves without him, George goes on a drinking spree, accidentally meeting Janoth's mistress, Pauline York (Johnson), at one of the bars. They return to Pauline's apartment, but George leaves just before Janoth arrives. Then, sensing a man has been with Pauline, Janoth kills her and enlists his office assistant, Hagan (George Macready), to cover up the crime.

The ingenious part of the story begins when Janoth selects George to figure out the identity of the mystery man who was with Pauline in order to pin the crime on him. Since George was that man, he is essentially put in charge of hunting himself, looking as though he is taking the job seriously but simultaneously thwarting the magazine staff and the police. As the clues pile up against George, new evidence points to Janoth as the real killer.

Like many film noirs of the era, *The Big Clock* is intricately formulated and filled with wit and irony. Distinguishing itself, though, both book and movie indict Big Business, as represented by the seemingly dispassionate but actually psychotic Janoth, a great Laughton performance that ends with a spectacular fall down an elevator shaft. Specifically, Fearing had once worked for *Time* magazine's Henry Luce and wanted Janoth to be a stand-in for his former boss.

John Farrow paces the action well, and his choice to use a wide-angle lens to capture the beehive activity within the magazine offices is innovative, lending a sense of immediacy to the images (Daniel L. Fapp and John Seitz handled the camerawork). Art directors Roland Anderson, Hans Dreier, and Albert Nozaki deserve mention for their meticulous design of the Manhattan sets.

But it is Milland who shapes *The Big Clock* into a true classic. His handling of so many emotions—from suppressed anger at his boss to guilt over neglecting his family to attraction to his boss's mistress—builds to a crescendo in the tense scenes where he carefully mediates the pursuit of the "unknown" killer, protecting himself from exposure as that very person while still hoping to find the actual killer. Milland plays George Stroud as if he were Don Birnam, stuck with a family and nine-to-five job, and *The Big Clock* allows the actor to use even more subtlety than in his Oscar-winning performance.

Milland basked in many highly positive reviews for the first time in a while. Bosley Crowther led the way in the *New York Times* by calling *The Big Clock* "a seventeen-jewel entertainment guaranteed to give a good—if not perfect—time.... Ray Milland does a beautiful job of being a well-tailored smoothie and desperate hunted man at the same time."

The Big Clock has had an extended ripple effect among film noirs and spy thrillers—*Scandal Sheet* (1952), *A Dandy in Aspic* (1968), *Flawless* (2009)—and

A publicity photo for *The Big Clock* (1948)

Milland reprised his role for two different broadcasts, first for *Lux Radio* in November 1948 and then for *Screen Directors Playhouse* in July 1949. In later years, *The Big Clock* was affirmed as influential and officially remade twice, as *Police Python 357* (1976) and *No Way Out* (1987). Appreciation for the original *Big Clock* has only grown: in 2011, director Joe Dante was quoted as saying he has seen it multiple times and wished he had made it himself.

Milland continued in foreboding territory with his July 1948 release, *So Evil My Love*, in which he was cast in his most sinister role up to that time, a risky move on the part of the star and studio.

Shot from spring to summer 1947, *So Evil My Love* meant another trip abroad for the Milland family. The production brought together again Milland and director Lewis Allen, and it was shot in England, mostly at D & P Studios, located near Pinewood. By filming in Europe, Paramount was able to use financial assets frozen during the war. Thus, *So Evil My Love* would be branded a "runaway" production, something designed primarily for US audiences but made outside the country.

Milland's first British production since *French without Tears* in 1939, *So Evil My Love* was a Gothic noir thriller set in Victorian London, based on Marjorie Bowen's novel about a true incident. In the screenplay by Ronald Millar and Leonard Spigelgass, Olivia (Ann Todd), a missionary's widow, becomes mesmerized by Mark (Milland), an art forger lodging in her home. Mark promises future marriage if she would be willing to steal money and valuables from an old friend, Susan (Geraldine Fitzgerald). Later, Olivia convinces Susan to give her cruel husband (Raymond Huntley) medicine for a heart attack, but the remedy is actually poison, and Susan is eventually convicted of murder. On the eve of Mark and Olivia's trip to America, Olivia discovers that Mark has another girlfriend. Realizing she has been duped all along, Olivia seeks revenge.

Paramount's decision to turn Milland into a homme fatale was partly inspired by the success of *Gaslight* (1944), set during the same Victorian era, with Charles Boyer cast against type as an attractive yet threatening menace to his wife (Ingrid Bergman). Since *The Lost Weekend* unveiled a depraved side to Milland's persona, producer Hal Wallis reasoned it would not be a stretch for the actor to play either a killer or (more accurately) the instigator of a murder.

While *Gaslight* contains greater suspense and visual flair, *So Evil My Love* is well crafted and mildly absorbing, and Ray Milland skillfully layers his characterization. He is persuasively contemptible as a swindler and seducer, but he also draws a degree of compassion as a morose, fatally flawed person who seizes upon the shortcomings of others to compensate for his own.

The reviews were mixed, and the film lost money at the box office. *Variety* wrote, "It's not either principal's fault that the emotions are barely touched. . . . Within the scope of the story [Todd] gives a fine performance and the same goes for Ray Milland, but impression remains that the emotional scenes are phoney." Virginia Graham's review in London's *Spectator* was more positive—and insightful: "*So Evil My Love* merits unqualified praise . . . [Todd] is well matched by Mr. Ray Milland whose evil is more weak than wicked."

As shooting finished, Milland wrote an article about his experiences and commented on the remarkable efficiency of the British movie industry throughout the length of World War II. He was most impressed visiting Laurence Olivier on the huge set of *Hamlet*. He added, "I was very glad to return to London . . . [I]t gave me a chance to show my wife and Danny, my young son, my favourite haunts," and he was pleased to have them visit him on the set as well.

Before returning to the United States for what he estimated was his thirtieth round-trip from Europe, Milland took a break with Mal and Danny to visit Wales and then headed to Germany to work again with Lewis Allen and a second unit to film in parts of West Berlin for his next project, *Sealed Verdict*.

During the family's trip home on the Queen Elizabeth, Milland was surprised to find Billy Wilder and Charles Brackett aboard (they had been in Germany to start *A Foreign Affair*). In Hollywood, Milland resumed shooting *Sealed Verdict* from late 1947 to January 1948. Then, after the serious drama wrapped production, he reminded audiences of his quick wit on *Lux Radio Theatre*'s *The Perfect Marriage*, airing in April 1948. For this farce, based on a David Niven movie, Milland, the studio's "new" homme fatale was paired with Paramount's most prominent femme fatale, Lizabeth Scott, in a rare comedic role. Scott later recalled her costar as "amiable and charming."

During the same month of April in 1948, the Millands attended a major social event: Joan Crawford hosted a party at the Papillon Restaurant to welcome Noël Coward to Hollywood. Milland remembered that Coward was present during the lunch in England two decades earlier when the MGM talent scout noticed him. On this night, the Millands schmoozed with Irene Dunne, Ginger Rogers, and even Marlene Dietrich.

At the end of his busy April, the studio sent Milland to Lima, Peru, for the grand opening of the Paramount Tacna Theatre, the kind of emissary chore—despite the Oscar win—he would no longer have to perform after his next contract negotiation.

Sealed Verdict might have been Milland's most provocative film to date but was little seen when released in November 1948 and, even today, is little remembered. It is flawed but certainly deserves some recognition. In *The Jewish Image in American Film*, Lester D. Friedman writes, "[*Sealed Verdict*] was Hollywood's first attempt to confront [the] complex issue of guilt and innocence, one that inevitably involved Germany's treatment of Jews."

The initially daring venture was based on a novel by war correspondent Lionel Shapiro and became an example of a "rubble" film, a Hollywood presentation partly shot in war-torn Germany. Like Paramount's *A Foreign Affair*, RKO's *Berlin Express*, and MGM's *The Search*, *Sealed Verdict* benefited from its grim atmosphere.

In Jonathan Latimer's screenplay, Milland plays Major Robert Lawson, a military lawyer based in Germany entrusted with prosecuting a Nazi war criminal, General Otto Steigmann (John Hoyt). After the trial, a defense witness and French ex-collaborationist, Themis DeLisle (Florence Marley), privately tells Lawson the man is innocent. Lawson begins to doubt the conviction but is discouraged by his superiors to reopen the case.

Milland is convincing as the increasingly obsessive inquisitor. The supporting players are not as compelling, with the exception of John Hoyt as Steigmann. Czech-born Florence Marley barely registers. In fact, Milland's worst moment occurs when he declares his love for her character—it rings entirely false. Marley returned to Europe after one more Hollywood effort, though Milland liked working with her enough to invite her a decade later to costar in "Death Watch," one of the many TV shows he directed in the late 1950s. The only other name in the cast, Broderick Crawford, blusters his usual way through as the Major's obnoxious friend.

What is inherently problematic about *Sealed Verdict* is that putting the general's conviction in doubt obscures the larger significance of the 1945–46 Nuremberg trials—that is, the goal to expose and punish the Nazis who denied their participation or complicity in crimes against humanity. Latimer's more modest yet earnest aim to show truth and justice as important no matter the occasion is a noble gesture, yet the story's tangents and digressions turn its dense ideas into a botched drama. (Print ads of the day, with a beaming Milland selling "Camp Socks" from Camp & McInnes hosiery, were in questionable taste and diminished the solemnity of the piece.)

Consequently, *Sealed Verdict* feels much longer than its eighty-three-minute running time, though its artistic and thematic mishandling might very well have been intentional. During this fraught period, the studios were finding ways to work around or keep at arm's length the oncoming Communist witch hunts out of Washington. Lillian Ross wrote in a 1948 *New Yorker* article, "A Paramount man informed me that he had the perfect solution [to bamboozle the House Un-American Committee] . . . '*Confuse* the enemy—that's my technique. Confuse them all!' He has apparently confided his formula to Ray Milland." In the piece, Milland tries to recount the convoluted *Sealed Verdict* narrative to Ross but gets lost and ends the interview saying, "I'd like to see the Thomas Committee [i.e. HUAC] find anything in *that*."

Ultimately, the verdict on *Sealed Verdict* was negative. Richard L. Coe in *The Washington Post* called it "synthetic," saying, "Insincerity shines everywhere." *Newsweek* added, "*Sealed Verdict* is an unsmiling attempt on the part of Paramount studios to come to grips with the moral aspects of the German war-crimes trials. As such it ought to have been one of the most important films to come out of Hollywood since the war. It isn't."

Like *Sealed Verdict*, the comedy *Miss Tatlock's Millions* debuted in theaters in November 1948. This time, Milland was only called upon to play himself in an unbilled cameo, though he was briefly considered for the lead role. Principal photography ended in spring 1948.

Actually, Milland's guest shot is one of the few highlights to this frankly offensive farce about a stunt man (John Lund) who is hired to impersonate a "mentally incompetent" heir after the real heir's family sends the man away so they can inherit his fortune. Milland appears in the opening scene on a movie set where Mitchell Leisen (also unbilled) directs him to perform a stunt, the in-joke being that Milland is tough enough to do his own stunts, which he was, leaving Lund's character free to take the inside job at the Tatlock estate. In an interesting diary entry, Charles Brackett wrote, "Saw the rushes with a gag scene of [Ray] Milland playing John's role, which Billy [Wilder] did for the front office and which depressed me because in it Ray proved himself [a] so much better farceur than John."

Along with Brackett, blame for this mess goes to actor-turned-director Richard Haydn. After two more films, Haydn returned to character acting, but it irked Milland to see a little-known performer get multiple chances to direct, something Milland very much wanted to try.

Like John Lund, Milland was starting to suffer a decline within the Paramount pantheon. Milland himself was growing frustrated with the (lack of) direction of his career. He was later quoted saying, "When I used to get burned up and disgusted with pictures, I used to take a small plane up as far as I could go, cut the engine and just circle down. It was so quiet and peaceful, so perfect, you could finally get back to yourself." As long as he was under long-term contract, however, he was forbidden to take such risks.

Briefly, he was buoyed by the prospect of starring in *Alias Nick Beal*, in which he would play the Devil, an artistic risk rather than a physical one.

The studio wanted Milland to work again with John Farrow, director of his last biggest triumph, *The Big Clock*. He was given a choice: he could either costar with Betty Hutton in Farrow's gangster-themed musical comedy *Red, Hot and Blue* or enact the title role in Farrow's more ambitious, modernized Faust story *Alias Nick Beal*. Milland opted for the latter, with Victor Mature taking on Betty Hutton. Milland enjoyed his time on the set but was challenged after the production wrapped in late May 1948 by two events, one profoundly sad, the other infuriating.

At home, Milland's professional doldrums seemed a minor matter when Mal's second pregnancy ended suddenly. On June 7, 1948, Hedda Hopper reported the Millands had been expecting a second child, but that Mal Milland experienced a miscarriage.

Later that summer, in August, Ray Milland reached his limit when his bosses assigned him a film he vehemently did not want to make. Though reluctant in the past to go on suspension, Milland was willing to fight over *A Mask for Lucrezia*, a historical epic about the Borgias. Later, he explained what happened when he first received the script: "I high-tailed it to the front office and spent two hours trying to get out of it. No soap. I either had to do the [film] or be suspended for two months without pay, the time of the suspension to be added to my contract term. I took the suspension and stormed out. I could afford it."

Despite the prospect of joining forces with both a director (Mitchell Leisen) and a costar (Paulette Goddard) he admired, Milland felt entirely miscast in what would be another costume drama—this time with Milland playing the Duke of Ferrara, the duped second husband of Lucrezia, whom she targets as her one of her victims. Apart from considering the script inferior and his part wrong for him, Milland's additional reason for rejecting *A Mask for Lucrezia* was that he had recently seen a preview of Twentieth Century-Fox's *Prince of Foxes* (1949), starring Tyrone Power, and thought it had covered the same story more than adequately. The hapless John Lund stepped in as Milland's replacement.

Unlike his gut feeling that *Arise, My Love* would destroy his movie future, Milland was correct this time. The resulting film, released in 1949 as *Bride of Vengeance*, was both a financial and critical disaster for the studio. It severely hurt the careers of Leisen, Goddard, and Lund. Milland might have survived the picture, but it certainly would have been another setback at a time he was making more misses than hits. During much of his hiatus and beyond, Milland opted to appear on radio more frequently than ever, notably a *Suspense* show called *Night Cry* (on October 7, 1948), in which he plays an embittered detective who kills a suspect in a murder case. Milland was at his best with the noir material, which was later filmed by Otto Preminger as *Where the Sidewalk Ends* (1950), starring Dana Andrews.

Milland's fight against Paramount aligned with Paramount's own high-stakes legal drama. In May 1948, the Supreme Court had settled the *United States vs. Paramount* case, resulting in the landmark Paramount Consent Decree. From 1948 onward, all the major studios were forced to divest themselves of their lucrative theater chains and halt all other monopolistic practices. The ultimate effect was to give more power to smaller studios and independent companies, which, in the coming decades, was where Ray Milland often found himself working.

Despite its loss in the courts, Paramount soldiered on. In March 1949, the studio released *Alias Nick Beal*; it wasn't a great moneymaker, but it had the virtue of more sincere creativity than the colossally campy *Bride of Vengeance*.

There had already been many cinematic takes on the Faust legend, notably the recent *Devil and Daniel Webster* in 1941. Jonathan Latimer's adaptation of Mindret Lord's pulpy short story, "Dr. Joe Faust," centers around

Alias Nick Beal (1949), with Audrey Totter

an upright district attorney (Thomas Mitchell) who is approached to be nominated governor of his state and then led down the primrose path by a mysterious stranger named Beal (Milland). Despite warnings from his wife (Geraldine Wall) to stay away from Beal, the lawyer gravitates to temptation, which includes finding evidence that will destroy the career of his opponent and using the services of a prostitute-turned-political operative (Audrey Totter).

Along with Farrow and Latimer, Milland was joined by one of his *Big Clock* costars, George Macready, cast against type as a kindly priest who becomes the deus ex machina. Though *Alias Nick Beal* might be considered a film noir, it sports a contrasting aesthetic. With a story metaphysical in nature, much of the imagery hews closer to dark fantasy, with a nod to French Poetic Realism. To wit, the fog that constantly surrounds Nick Beal turns out to be burning sulfur.

The reviews for *Alias Nick Beal* were mostly approving. Edwin Schallert of the *Los Angeles Times* called it "fascinating," and the *New Republic*'s Robert Hatch singled out Milland's "gentlemanly Lucifer: his evil aura is a fine work of subtle and ironic understatement."

Milland later cited *Alias Nick Beal* as his personal favorite of all his films, along with *The Big Clock*. Darryl Hickman, who played one of the boys in the priest's mixed-race recreation club, has said that "Ray Milland remembered me from *Untamed* [a decade earlier] and he was very nice to me." According to Hickman, Milland was still reserved off set but interacted better during scenes, thanks to the director: "Farrow asked for me . . . [H]e was a very intellectual [and intuitive] man . . . an interesting director." (Hickman mentioned it was purely coincidental that he was in three Audrey Totter movies in 1949. They never shared screen time together nor got to know each other.)

Modern-day critics of *Nick Beal* have been even more enthusiastic, especially about Ray Milland. In 1986, Leslie Halliwell wrote, "When and if you look at the graph of Ray Milland's career, *Alias Nick Beal* is the point at which the line begins to fall. . . . It seems ironic now that as Beal he gives one of his most striking performances. Though used chiefly as an elegant prop, he never for a second fails to emanate hovering menace." In 2002, Charles P. Mitchell declared, "*Alias Nick Beal* is an unusually rich and rewarding picture that works on many levels. . . . Ray Milland is superb as the Devil . . . [He] manages to bring a sinister air to the most ordinary expressions or comments. His flawless performance completes one of the most convincing portrayals of the Devil in the history of the screen."

For Ray Milland in 1949, it was a noteworthy effort but another box-office disappointment. A benefit to Milland kept secret from the front office was that Farrow taught him directing techniques during the shoot and happily incorporated the actor's suggestions for certain scenes.

Alias Nick Beal turned out to be the last film under Milland's Paramount contract, which he renegotiated with the help of Zeppo Marx by the time of *Beal*'s spring premiere. In fact, after his suspension, Milland found himself in a good bargaining position since he still had a sizable public following. ("The studio began to treat me with a little more respect," he would write.) Milland's new arrangement allowed him to freelance at other studios while promising to appear in one Paramount film per year for the next three years. In exchange, Milland was willing to take a salary cut on his Paramount releases, determined on a per diem basis. For example, his participation in the upcoming *Copper Canyon* only netted him $120,000.

Still, the deal was mutually beneficial since the studio no longer considered its high-priced actor as much of an asset anymore (Paramount was already promoting younger talent, like Burt Lancaster), and Milland was disenchanted with his alma mater, feeling it had mishandled his post-Oscar years. Unfortunately, Zeppo Marx soon left the business, forcing Milland to sign with MCA, a more corporate, less personal talent agency.

As the news spread of Milland's availability, offers started to stream in. One Milland turned down was MGM's *Conspirator*, to be shot in England by Victor Saville. Despite the chance of returning to MGM, working opposite Elizabeth Taylor, and filming part of the story in Wales, Milland was not thrilled about playing a British major who secretly spies for the Soviet Union. All-American Robert Taylor took the assignment, and in 1950, *Conspirator* received poor reviews and lost money.

THE FREE AGENT

Thus, Milland's first film as a freelance actor—while still technically under contract to Paramount—was *It Happens Every Spring*, a baseball comedy produced at Twentieth Century-Fox, his first at that studio since 1939's *Everything Happens at Night*. *It Happens Every Spring* was shot between mid-December 1948 and the end of January 1949 in order to be released during the spring baseball season.

Writers Valentine Davies and Shirley W. Smith received an Oscar nomination for Best Motion Picture Story, which features Milland as a chemistry teacher named Vernon K. Simpson, who has an obsession with baseball and is engaged to the dean's daughter (Jean Peters). In a fluke, Vernon's experiment with methylethylpropylbutyl is a catastrophe, but in its wake, he discovers a way to use the substance to repel objects. Vernon applies the chemical to baseball bats and insists his losing but favorite baseball team hire him as a pitcher, able to throw balls that batters won't be able to hit. Taking a leave from school as "King Kelly," he saves the St. Louis team's season. Once his mission is completed, he returns to the school as the head of a new laboratory and reunites with his fiancée.

Perhaps with Howard Hawks in charge, some of the fantastic absurdities of *It Happens Every Spring* would have seemed funnier, but by 1949, veteran Lloyd Bacon had long since made a really lively comedy. It was also known that Bacon was a stickler for keeping his films on schedule, resulting in occasional technical errors and the waste of a great cast, including Jean Peters, a merely decorative ingénue, and the character actors, Paul Douglas, Ed Begley, Ray Collins, and Jesse Royce Landis. Debra Paget remembered having a few lines in this, her third feature, but not working directly with Ray Milland. Eight years later, they were costars in the far superior *River's Edge*.

In the mildly funny *It Happens Every Spring*, Milland waged a valiant effort in a quasi-dual role. At forty-two, Ray Milland was clearly too old to convincingly play a new pitcher on the baseball scene, but to his credit—and the hair

It Happens Every Spring (1949)

and makeup department at Fox—he appeared more youthful than he had in his last several films. Moreover, though he admitted later he was hardly a fan of the sport, Milland fully committed himself to learning baseball. He not only hired former major-leaguer Ike Danning for coaching, but on the first day of shooting, he hurt his arm from practicing his pitch and twisted his knee while sliding into first base. Yet Milland never let his injuries stop him from training, and he even made an appearance on opening day with the Los Angeles Angels. Thanks to his diligence, very little doubling was needed for the pitching scenes. He later complained, "[That picture] nearly killed me.... I not only sweated over that role, I strained every muscle in my body, and got blisters on the bottom of my feet from those spiked shoes."

The reviews of the day were generally favorable. *Boxoffice* called it a "warm and wholesome comedy," while *Variety* liked the "fast-paced and chuckly screenplay" but reserved most of its praise for Ray Milland, saying he "does a surprisingly good job in the baseball sequences, despite the role being completely different from anything he has essayed heretofore."

Years later, *It Happens Every Spring* became the first baseball movie to be shown coast to coast in prime time when NBC aired it on April 7, 1962, to high ratings. More recently, it still had its cheerleaders. In 2002, Hal Erickson called it "one of the most delightful baseball comedies ever made," and in

2006, Richard Carter included it among several "truly fine films" that defined 1949 as one of the best years of Hollywood releases.

Milland was gratified *It Happens Every Spring* grossed $1,850,000, though the family-friendly movie did nothing to challenge him artistically. On radio, at least, he gleefully returned to the dark side, playing the "Merry Widow Murderer" in a condensed *Ford Theater* adaptation of Alfred Hitchcock's classic, *Shadow of a Doubt* (airing in February 1949). As a philanthropist hiding his psychopathic instincts, Milland is slightly more explosive but otherwise just as guileful as Joseph Cotten had been in the 1943 film. Likewise, Ann Blyth does justice to Teresa Wright's part of the innocent niece who figures out the horrific truth about her beloved "Uncle Charlie."

Fulfilling his new contractual agreement with Paramount, Milland filmed *Copper Canyon* for the company from April to June 1949. He had so little regard for the film, he didn't mind that it sat on the shelf for more than a year. Milland's renegotiated terms freed him to appear on television if he so desired, and he made his debut on NBC's *Actor's Society Benefit Gala* in April, just before his *Copper Canyon* shoot in Sedona, Arizona. For this testimonial dinner, Milland wore formal attire and joined such friends as James Cagney, Gracie Allen, Fred MacMurray, Bob Hope, and host Humphrey Bogart.

With *Copper Canyon*, Milland and his *Alias Nick Beal* team, director John Farrow and writer Jonathan Latimer, were redressing the *outré* outcome of their prior movie with something tamer—a Western about gamblers and copper miners. Like Milland's last Western, *California*, also directed by Farrow, *Copper Canyon* would be in Technicolor, though on a smaller budget. To further ensure a return on its investment, Paramount paired Milland with the beautiful Hedy Lamarr, who was about to have a career upswing after her showy appearance in Cecil B. DeMille's 1949 epic, *Samson and Delilah*. As a result, *Copper Canyon* was Ray Milland's biggest moneymaker of the late 1940s and early '50s, earning $2.2 million in US rentals.

In Latimer's tangled screenplay, Milland plays Johnny Carter, a sharpshooting stage performer who is mistaken by a group of Southern copper miners as the Confederate hero Colonel Desmond. Carter assumes the function of peacemaker while romancing a duplicitous saloon owner (Lamarr).

According to Hedy Lamarr, the production was not an easy one: "We were all miscast. This was nobody's fault. But I'm not the type [to play in Westerns]. All through the picture everyone complained of hardships and I complained the most of all. Even my stand-in, Sylvia, was worn out at the end. I don't envy those Western regulars with all that action, the shooting, riding, roping and falling. I never made another." Paramount was just as unhappy with Lamarr for refusing to promote the film. (She told the studio she was "an actress, not a publicist.") While Milland said he "loathed" the movie and "hated working with Hedy Lamarr," he never explained his dislike of either.

Copper Canyon was more pro-Confederate than revisionist. Yet, the filmmakers concocted some appealing touches, especially Milland's vaudeville act, a lively and diverting opening to the story, and Milland himself nimbly displays gradations of anger beneath Johnny's genial, pacifist front.

As with *California*, audiences enjoyed *Copper Canyon* more than the critics, most of whom spared Milland. Orval Hopkins of the *Washington Post* wrote, "Ray Milland gives an easy, ingratiating performance . . . [T]hat's about all you can say for the film." But Bosley Crowther of the *New York Times* was completely disgruntled: "There is something slightly appalling about beholding Mr. Milland, a first-rate dramatic actor, engaging in saloon repartee and going through the conventional exercises of cowboy actors with horses and guns."

Given the quality of his pictures, the best part of this period for Ray Milland was personal. At the time of the June 1949 release of *It Happens Every Spring*, while Danny was regularly attending Hawthorne Elementary School, Ray and Mal Milland decided to adopt a child through an agency in New York. They became attached to a six-year-old girl named Victoria and reveled in her company for several months. On November 18, 1949, the adoption of Victoria Francesca was official. Ray Milland announced to the press, "We are very fond of the little girl. We have been very happy with her," and it is understood that "she is not to be to photographed until she is twelve years old and that her real identity will be guarded forever with the utmost secrecy."

What Ray revealed later about Victoria was that she had a thick Brooklyn accent, which he and an English governess the Millands hired helped modify over time. "Her broad A's, slurred and clipped speech, keep us in hysterics," Milland told a reporter. The real-life elocution lessons foreshadowed his portrayal of Henry Higgins in *My Fair Lady* on stage in the mid-1960s.

The lengthy adoption process took place while Milland worked on *A Woman of Distinction* with Rosalind Russell. His first outing for Columbia Pictures since *The Doctor Takes a Wife* in 1940 was shot in August 1949 and released in February 1950. The result was a tired retread of the kind of movies both stars had made before, particularly Russell, who received top billing and alternated top billing with Milland in the print ads.

The *Woman of Distinction* property had once been jointly owned by Paramount and Frank Capra Productions. Capra first envisioned it for Milland and Katharine Hepburn, an idea that didn't work out. (Capra also considered

Milland for *Riding High* but instead cast Bing Crosby in the race-track comedy.) In 1948, Columbia purchased the rights to the story as a vehicle for Jean Arthur and Cary Grant, but neither star was ever fully committed. Ultimately, with Milland still attached, Rosalind Russell accepted *A Woman of Distinction*, and in a switch on the old pattern, Cary Grant ended up playing the Milland part opposite Russell for the inevitable *Lux Radio Theatre* broadcast (in October 1950).

A Woman of Distinction cast Milland yet again as a professor (this time of astronomy) who is visiting a New England college to give a guest lecture. Once he arrives, he spars with the dean (Russell), a distinguished professional and single mother of an adopted daughter (Mary Jane Saunders). Susan's father (Edmund Gwenn) and daughter both take a liking to the visitor and do everything they can to bring the two academicians together.

Sadly, in the Charles Hoffman–Frank Tashlin screenplay, there is constant questioning about the dean's womanhood as long as she is without a man, and, reusing the *Lady in the Dark* template, the heroine inexplicably gives up her job to run off with the hero at the end of the story.

One would hope pros like Russell and Milland could rise above the material, but they are deterred by what are meant to be humorous episodes. Chief among these is a series of action sequences that further degrade Russell's character (e.g. getting drenched by a garden hose, enduring a mud splatter, having a mishap in a beauty parlor, and surviving a hot-rod drag race). In another physical bit, Russell pushes Milland into a lake, and there is something depressing about seeing an older, wiser Ray Milland forced to perform such slapstick, even when it appears a stunt double made the final plunge.

In the same vein, it is hard to embrace the usually lovable Edmund Gwenn when he plays such a patronizing part, going as far as insulting his young granddaughter to her face for being adopted. One can only imagine how dismayed Milland felt about this scene given his family's adoption of Victoria.

A Woman of Distinction's director, Edward Buzzell, was partly off stride because of his annoyance with Milland's disinterest in rehearsing. Buzzell would later say, "[Milland was] notorious for letting his stand-in rehearse in his place, then going to the script girl the next morning and asking 'What are we going to shoot today?'"

A Lucille Ball cameo—exchanging repartee with Milland—was one of the few highlights of *A Woman of Distinction*. Otherwise, the reviewers were not amused but praised the stars. The *Christian Science Monitor* wrote, "It's extremely light, largely sentimental, and frequently farcical. But Miss Russell and Mr. Milland have the touch that make the most of any material, and when the yarn grows thin they are able partially to conceal it by their efforts."

A Woman of Distinction was not a great hit with audiences, pressuring Milland to reassess his career options. He rejected Paramount's proposal for him to star in *Jack of Diamonds*, written by Jonathan Latimer and set in Midtown Manhattan's Diamond District. A new idea Milland liked better was narrating the first in a series of independently produced concert films distributed through Twentieth Century-Fox. The initial feature was to have Milland introduce such highbrow artists as Artur Rubinstein, Jascha Heifetz, and Jan Peerce. Plans fell through, though, and the solitary film, *Of Men and Music* (with no follow-up series), was narrated instead by off-screen musician Deems Taylor. At the same time, Paramount announced Milland would play the enigmatic title role in *Shane*, the studio having purchased the rights to Jack Schaefer's Western novel in November 1949. By the time *Shane* got off the ground four years later, Alan Ladd revived his own career by starring in the George Stevens's classic.

Before the weak reception to *A Woman of Distinction*, Milland was keener than ever on directing. Annoying Paramount, he went as far as participating in a February 1950 *Picturegoer* interview, "Ray Milland Hates Acting," in which he told writer Elliseva Sayers, "I'm trying to become a director. I keep asking and they keep stalling. I'm worth more to them as an actor. They remind me that under my contract I'm an actor, and there seems to be nothing I can do but try to talk them into it. It's no use getting temperamental—you get nowhere."

CHAPTER 7

SHADOWS AND LIGHT (1950–1953)

AT THE BEGINNING OF THE DECADE, NEW LEADING MEN WERE GETTING attention, and Ray Milland was starting to be overlooked. Not only was Milland still competing with the old guard, Cary Grant and David Niven, but there was also the less debonair but more exciting new guard, Marlon Brando and Montgomery Clift. The latest British imports formed an additional guard of their own—James Mason, Michael Wilding, Stewart Granger—all of whom had been in the business for years and were close to Milland's age but were thought of as a "new breed" simply because they were fresh faces to American audiences. On the horizon: Richard Burton, a rugged, Shakespearean-trained *Welsh* actor was touted to be the next big thing. Milland took all this competition in stride, even when dissatisfied with some of the work he was given or chose for himself.

Milland's next project was produced at MGM, the studio that fired him eighteen years earlier. In 1950, a regime headed by Dore Schary was about to replace the one headed by Louis B. Mayer, so Milland saw his invitation by producer Voldemar Vetluguin as a belated mea culpa for his unceremonious dismissal. The film was meant to showcase its female star, Lana Turner, but an added incentive was the paycheck: Milland would earn $175,000, a huge single fee for his services. (This was the last time he would receive such an exorbitant lump sum.)

A Life of Her Own had a troubled production well before Ray Milland entered the fray. Isobel Lennart's screenplay (based on a Rebecca West novella) charted the transformation of a small-town Kansas beauty into a New York supermodel and was prepared as a comeback for Turner. One of MGM's biggest stars, Turner had been suspended for refusing assignments since 1948 and initially rejected *A Life of Her Own* as well, but she eventually acquiesced. Once George Cukor replaced Vincente Minnelli as director, a slew of actors were considered for the role of the wealthy married man who falls for the model, including James Mason (Cukor's top choice), Howard Keel,

James Craig, George Murphy, Robert Ryan, and even Cary Grant. Finally, Dore Schary selected Wendell Corey against Cukor's wishes.

A Life of Her Own started production in late January 1950 but hit an immediate snag when Cukor fired Wendell Corey after only the first few days. According to Turner, Corey made a rude remark to her, and she held up production until he was recast. Much to Turner's relief, Ray Milland, a bigger name than Wendell Corey's, was asked to save the day.

In addition to the casting issues, *A Life of Her Own* was under constant scrutiny by the Breen office. The censors objected to several aspects of the story they considered "shocking and offensive," particularly the mature spin on the extramarital affair between Lily James and Steve Harleigh. Further complicating matters, the original ending saw Lily become a forty-five-year-old hotel maid who commits suicide, yet preview audiences reacted negatively. Thus, the revised conclusion, with an unpunished Lily realizing a newfound feeling of independence, was just as problematic for the censors. A dissatisfied Cukor helplessly watched MGM chop his 150-minute print to 108 minutes.

The postproduction cuts may explain why the film does not completely work. Scenes of Lily's all-important rise to fame appear mainly in montage sequences, while her romance with Steve seems to come out of left field, almost as if from a different movie. Another flaw is that the two megastars, despite the recasting, rarely achieve much chemistry. Otherwise, most of the film is superbly crafted, particularly the recurring series of noirish rendezvous set in a piano bar, accompanied by Bronislau Kaper's haunting theme music.

Stealing the thunder from both leads are Margaret Phillips as Steve's invalid wife and Ann Dvorak as an older model whose suicide early on gives Lily the idea to end her own life as well. (Milland was delighted to learn that Phillips happened to be born in South Wales, allowing him this one time to be married in a movie to a compatriot.) Tom Ewell, Jean Hagen, and Louis Calhern (Milland's costar from 1931's *Blonde Crazy*) all contribute memorable moments in a worthwhile picture that never quite gels.

Once *A Life of Her Own* hit theaters in September, critics were ready to attack Lana Turner's big-screen homecoming, helping it fail at the box office. Mae Tinee in the *Chicago Daily Tribune* wrote, "All of the participants are as talkative as the characters in a soap opera, and behave in much the same fashion.... Mr. Milland seems decidedly glum at all times." Kate Cameron in the *New York Daily News* called it "a trashy bit of fiction" but thought "Lana gives a good performance," while "Ray Milland is unhappily cast." At the time, François Truffaut defended the film, and in more recent years, several critics have seen its virtues, most prominently Edward R. O'Neill in his essay

"Notes on the Long Take in George Cukor's *A Life of Her Own*" (in *Cineaction*, September 1999). Still, Cukor biographer Emanuel Levy considers it a "forgettable picture ... [Cukor's] nadir of the entire decade."

Between the March wrap of *A Life of Her Own* and its necessary reshoots in April, Milland had a brief respite. He used part of the time to accept an invitation from the academy to present the Best Supporting Actress award during its annual ceremonies. On the evening of March 23, 1950, Milland, in full-dress suit, announced the winner: Mercedes McCambridge for *All the King's Men*. Milland was pleased that the winner was McCambridge since he had recently worked with her new husband, director Fletcher Markle, on a few of his more darkly adventurous radio shows—including *Of Human Bondage* and *Shadow of a Doubt*.

In face of his batch of recent mixed reviews, Milland appreciated receiving an award for himself. In April 1950, the Spanish Film Critics honored his body of work with the country's equivalent to an Oscar. The State Department arranged to have Ingrid Bergman's Best Actress statuette sent to RKO and Milland's Best Actor figurine sent to Paramount. And it was back at Paramount that Milland filmed *Something to Live For*, from May to July 1950, but the studio didn't like the results and kept it under wraps until 1952.

To escape from his career ups and downs, Milland frequented the Bel-Air Country Club, not so much for the sports but to play card games, like bridge. At home, he continued with his carpentry hobby, despite his hand injuries, in order to build Danny a playroom.

Professionally, Milland wasn't exactly idle. In 1950, *A Woman of Distinction*, *Copper Canyon*, and *A Life of Her Own* had each been setbacks in different ways, but the actor gave excellent performances in a handful of small-scale film noirs in 1951: *Night into Morning*, *Circle of Danger*, and *Close to My Heart*.

DEEP CUTS

Milland's solid streak started with the undervalued *Night into Morning*, a June 1951 release. Shot between November 27, 1950, and January 11, 1951, it was the second of Milland's two-picture deal with MGM, which was offered to him after producer Edwin H. Knopf viewed a print of *A Life of Her Own*. Milland himself was excited, saying at the time, "Here is something I can get my teeth into." *Night into Morning* ended up receiving many favorable reviews, but the studio relegated it to B-movie status, playing the second half of double bills, and it lost money. It was a clear sign that the name Ray Milland was not as commanding as it had been.

People In Love and *People We Love* were the working titles by screenwriters Karl Tunberg and Leonard Spigelgass. *Night into Morning* was more appropriate, though, for a story about a college professor who loses his family in a fire and takes to drink to forget his tragic loss. One scene required Milland's character to drive while drunk and crash into a sidewalk. Coincidentally, two days into production, on an unusually foggy day in Los Angeles, Milland was driving to MGM when he collided with another vehicle and was knocked out of his car. The police were called, but since he suffered only minor bruises, Milland brushed off the incident—and himself—and took a taxi the rest of the way to the studio.

When the film was released, some critics belabored the fact Milland was again playing an alcoholic (and another professor!), forewarning prospective audiences that *Night into Morning* was a rehash of *The Lost Weekend*. This was definitely not the case. In fact, arguably, this well-written and directed film contained an equally great performance by Milland.

Following several years as a radio and television director, Fletcher Markle was making only his second feature. Markle may not have possessed the dark comic vision of Billy Wilder, but he created a fine piece of work that might have otherwise turned out overly sentimental. Under Dore Schary's leadership, MGM emphasized "message" films and had probably intended *Night into Morning* as an example of something superficially uplifting. (The studio's tag line for the film was "When Dreams Go Smash—You Can Build a New Life!") Thankfully, Markle and the cast and crew avoided any obvious preaching, though the weak box-office returns meant the director would soon exit Hollywood and restart his career in television.

Milland deservedly earned widespread accolades. *Variety* wrote, "Milland accounts for his best work in some time, and his underplaying of what could easily have been an overdone dramatic character keys the performances of the others in the cast." More glowing praise came from Philip K. Scheuer in the *Los Angeles Times*: "Milland gives a beautiful performance under the detailed, low-keyed direction of Fletcher Markle—as, indeed, do all the players."

Milland made some long-term friendships through *Night into Morning*. After *A Life of Her Own*, this was his second picture with Jean Hagen, who played a seductive next-door neighbor when Milland's character rents a seedy hotel room to be his sad new home; that seduction scene would be reworked in a more florid way the following year in another underrated Milland noir, *The Thief*, with Rita Gam as the femme fatale. In 1952, Hagen stole the show as Lina Lamont in *Singin' in the Rain*, and a decade later, when looking for an actress to play his wife in *Panic in Year Zero!* (1962), Milland fondly remembered Hagen and cast her in the unusual sci-fi movie he was directing.

Milland also liked working with Nancy Davis, who later named *Night into Morning* her favorite among her own films. He developed a long-time friendship with both Davis and Ronald Reagan, whom Davis would marry on March 4, 1952, following Reagan's divorce from Jane Wyman, Milland's *Lost Weekend* costar.

Thanks in part to the Millands' friendship with the Reagans, Senator Joe McCarthy's witch hunts in Washington and the concurrent blacklisting in Hollywood did not affect Milland. Ronald Reagan's position as the president of the Screen Actors Guild and Nancy Reagan's continued work for SAG throughout the decade helped shield Milland from ever needing to testify in front of HUAC. Further, his naturalization as an American citizen and declaration as a proud Republican added further protection.

To his credit, Milland did not "name names" of so-called Communist sympathizers, the way so many politically conservative celebrities volunteered to do (e.g. Gary Cooper, Robert Montgomery, Walt Disney, Adolph Menjou, Robert Taylor, Louis B. Mayer, and of course, Hedda Hopper). Then again, Milland didn't do anything heroic, either. Later in the year, in mid-October 1951, he further aligned himself with pro-American conformity by broadcasting from Washington a public-service tribute to the Department of Defense during Civil Defense Week.

Circle of Danger followed *Night into Morning*, filmed during the winter of 1950 (into 1951) and seen in the United States in April 1951. In the Milland ouevre, it has the distinction of being the only production the Welsh actor made in Wales (in addition to Cornwall, Devon, and some shooting at London Film Studios in Islesworth). For many involved, it was a labor of love, and for Ray Milland, it meant a return to his homeland, on- and off-screen.

Circle of Danger united Milland for the only time with Jacques Tourneur, a French director who made an early impact in Hollywood with a series of innovative, low-budget horror films, including *Cat People* (1942) and *I Walked with a Zombie* (1943). Today, Tourneur's reputation has only grown, particularly for his ability to create atmospheric suspense. His best films to exhibit this quality are *Out of the Past* (1947), a quintessential film noir, and *Curse of the Demon* (1958), a cult horror favorite. Yet, Tourneur's output in between these classics remains obscure. RKO picked up *Circle of Danger* for a limited US release, and its "indie" status has much to do with its lack of appreciation: independent films had difficulty getting wide distribution and rarely received television airings.

Circle of Danger came about when Joan Harrison, one of the few women producers of the era, asked Philip MacDonald to adapt to the screen his unpublished novel, *White Heather*, which was based on a real-life war incident

Circle of Danger (1951), with Patricia Roc

in the United Kingdom. Joined by coproducers David E. Rose and John R. Sloan, Harrison hired Tourneur and planned from the start to shoot on location. They all wanted Ray Milland to be the American protagonist despite his Welsh background and accent.

With his entire family in tow, Milland arrived at the Windsor Colliery in Abertridwr for the filming of the Wales portion of the story. Milland greeted a group of miners, signing autographs and taking pictures with them. "They converged on me from all over and I loved it," he later said. Then the Millands visited Grandpapa Jones, the first time for little Victoria.

In *Circle of Danger*, Milland plays Clay Douglas, a deep-sea diver determined to find out why his brother was killed during a World War II commando strike when none of his comrades suffered any injuries. His quest takes him all over Great Britain before he discovers the shocking truth.

Shot in mostly dank-looking country settings, *Circle of Danger* hardly represents a typical film noir, and Tourneur's pacing isn't especially spine-tingling. Yet the film is gradually compelling, as it stealthily distills postwar uneasiness about shaky alliances, both interpersonal and sociopolitical. In its microcosmic way, *Circle of Danger* daringly lifts the veil on how human frailties are often excised from the routinely black-and-white telling of history. Symbolically, Oswald Morris's cinematography comes in different shades of gray. In an interview, Morris recalled how the Technicolor company was furious with him for muting the colors in *Moulin Rouge* (1952) and also how he liked to mitigate the contrasts between light and dark in his black-and-white films.

By extension, the actors, including Marius Goring and Patricia Roc, project layers of suppressed emotions in their performances—and Douglas's growing feeling of dread as he gathers clues is delicately conveyed by Milland. The only flaw in his work stems from the inherent casting problem: Douglas is warily greeted as a foreigner by most of the characters, yet with his accent and demeanor, he blends in much better than the type of American outsider he is supposed to be playing. Otherwise, this aberrant mystery turns out to be an unheralded gem.

Sadly, the reviews of the day were only lukewarm. *Variety* noted, "Under the calculating direction of Jacques Tourneur, the film minimizes action in favor of a series of character studies. . . . Milland does the best he can to make the quest a credible one." The *New York Times* didn't like the film, either, though the anonymous writer singled out Milland's work affirmatively: "Ray Milland, it must be said, endows the role of [sic] inquiring American with naturalness, a quality which, it might be added, may be due in part to the unadorned and often expert dialogue turned out by Philip MacDonald."

In *Phantom Lady: Hollywood Producer Joan Harrison, the Forgotten Woman behind Hitchcock* (Chicago Review Press, 2020), author Christina Lane details the care taken with the production. Perhaps the increasing interest in the work of both Harrison and Tourneur will one day put the spotlight on *Circle of Danger*, which at least deserves reappraisal.

Returning to the United States in early 1951, Milland considered a project at Twentieth Century-Fox that fell by the wayside. *Daddy Long Legs* was a 1919 silent classic for Mary Pickford and a 1931 sound hit for Janet Gaynor. A proposed color update would have cast rising Fox star Mitzi Gaynor as a young woman unaware of who is financing her way through college, while Milland would have played the wealthy benefactor who slowly falls in love with his ward. Other leading men were considered as well, including David Niven and, naturally, Cary Grant, yet Fox decided to postpone the idea until a few years later. In 1955, the studio revived it as a widescreen Fred Astaire musical with Leslie Caron playing the innocent student.

Before starting his next obligatory assignment at Paramount, Ray and Mal attended some functions, such as a big house party in 1951 given by Gary Cooper and his wife, "Rocky," in honor of Clark Gable. "The King" was still a major name at MGM twenty years after *Polly of the Circus*, one of Milland's earliest films. The presence of "The British Colony" (Niven, Greer Garson,

Ronald Colman) made the Millands feel more at ease than usual at these events. Gable himself had been an honorary member since marrying Lady Sylvia Ashley in 1949.

With little enthusiasm, Milland shot the subpar *Rhubarb* between mid-February and late March 1951, which garnered weak notices but a strong box office ($1,450,000) for Paramount's late August release.

As with his earlier baseball comedy, *It Happens Every Spring*, Milland smoothly extracted laughs from a far-fetched premise. This time, H. Allen Smith's 1945 novel was the basis, the story of a deceased baseball team owner who has willed his fortune to a stray cat named Rhubarb. The publicist for the team is designated the cat's guardian, and he slowly realizes that Rhubarb is actually a good-luck charm. Complications occur when the millionaire's daughter contests the will, and the publicist's wife discovers she is allergic to the cat, but matters are worked out for an upbeat finish.

Milland plays the p.r. man with the appropriate mix of irritation and admiration toward his mascot (though Millland himself disliked cats). He has some bright moments with Jan Sterling playing his wife, but most of the supporting cast is less interesting than usual for a standard Paramount production. The real star is Orangey, the cat who plays Rhubarb.

More regrettably, a succession of screenwriters removed the social satire that had made Allen Smith's novel a literary favorite. The author targeted everything from the inanities of the American legal system to the Western fixation with hobbies, sports in particular, to even modern sexual mores. But clearly the censors were wary of these themes, and the studio did not want to offend its audience.

Allen Smith and director Arthur Lubin objected to the changes, but Lubin didn't compensate with any guile. Milland's comic drunk scene was the kind of addition that not only "dumbed down" the book but also represented a step backward for the actor who had helped change attitudes toward such drivel with *The Lost Weekend*. A better gag had an unbilled Paul Douglas appear as himself—he was Jan Sterling's fiancé at the time—as he ridiculed *A Letter to Three Wives* (1949), his own best-loved film up to that point.

The reviews were merciful. *Variety* wrote, "The 94 minutes running time stretches the material rather thin, but there are sufficient laughs to fulfill comedy demands," and *Picturegoer* added, "[It] starts off amusingly, but overstays its welcome.... Ray Milland is good as the harassed employee in whose care the feline is left, and Jan Sterling is charming as his fiance [sic]."

In a bit of fateful irony, both Orangey and Ray Milland ended up working with director Roger Corman in separate 1963 films that were united on the same double bill: Milland in *X: The Man with the X-Ray Eyes* and Orangey in

Comedy of Terrors (directed by Jacques Tourneur and in which he is billed as Rhubarb!). In 1951, Orangey won a PATSY (Picture Animal Top Star of the Year) for his performance in *Rhubarb*. Milland's only reward was a well-earned vacation with Mal in the Bahamas in early April 1951.

Ray Milland did deserve an award for *Close to My Heart*, his November release, shot quickly over two weeks in late April 1951. Warner Bros. had announced in March that Milland would be making three pictures for the studio, and *Close to My Heart* would be the first. Now back at Warner's for the first time since his minor role in 1932's *Man Who Played God*, Milland turned in a terrific performance in another unfairly neglected feature.

Close to My Heart started life as a 1950 short story by James R. Webb called "A Baby for Midge," and Warner's originally planned to cast Dennis Morgan and Betsy Drake in what was expected to be a "domestic comedy": but once producer William Jacobs read the screenplay by Webb, Frank Davis, and director William Keighley (the latter two uncredited), the studio realized they had something much more dramatic to sell. (Briefly, *As Time Goes By* became the working title.) In the end, Warner's avoided promoting *Close to My Heart* as a comedy but misled the public in their print ads by calling it a "love-bright story," accompanied by a drawing of its stars kissing romantically.

In the somber *Close to My Heart*, a Los Angeles housewife, Midge Sheridan (Gene Tierney), desperately wants to adopt a child once she is told by her doctor that she cannot conceive her own. Midge's husband, Brad (Milland), is halfhearted but tries to support his wife. After running into red tape using an agency, Midge learns that an abandoned baby named Danny might be available to them. In his job as a newspaper reporter, Brad investigates Danny's biological background. He uses his resources to track down the birth parents and discovers the baby's father is a ruthless murderer on death row. Brad's sleuthing causes a rift in his marriage, which he attempts to repair, but his preoccupation places the adoption in jeopardy.

In its quiet way, like *Night into Morning*, *Close to My Heart* is a deeply stirring drama. Director Keighley and cinematographer Robert Burks (a favorite of Alfred Hitchcock, later to work on *Dial M for Murder*) imbue many scenes with a noir-ish feel that turns the otherwise drab, middle-class Sheridan home into a place of moodiness and mourning well before the story delves into its disturbing areas. With both protagonists manifesting signs of obsessiveness (Midge's compulsion to have a child, Brad's quest to find something disqualifying about Danny's background), *Close to My Heart* becomes a subtle indictment of the bourgeois thinking and lifestyle constructs of the time, including the expectations of married adults to have children and the pervasive "bad-seed" theory. Only the abrupt, overly cheerful ending is a mistake.

Max Steiner's uncharacteristically subdued scoring adds to the filmmakers' understated approach. Steiner's widow, Louise Steiner Elian, remembered that Steiner was proud of his work during this period, which contrasts with the composer's more typically Wagnerian sound.

Though not as ironic or Brechtian as the melodramas of Douglas Sirk, this critique of societal conventions is gently poignant, particularly in the latter scenes when both Midge and Brad come face-to-face with their own self-involved anguish. Surreptitiously, the screenplay embeds some of the cultural commentary into seemingly throwaway dialogue. Early on, for example, Brad sardonically encourages the couple's mongrel puppy to sit in a fancy new dog bed: "Hey, Chum! You're going to want to raise your standard of living. It's the American way!"

Tierney gives one of her best performances, deliberately downplaying her glamour facade. Milland is just as effective, starting off as an upbeat character who slowly sinks into his own narrow-minded despair. His climactic plea with the social worker (Fay Bainter) to adopt Danny is a heartbreaking scene, at least as good as the very similar one in *Penny Serenade* (1941), in which Cary Grant's character appeals to a social worker (Beulah Bondi) to adopt a baby he initially didn't want. Both Milland and Grant barely hold back their tears while choking up in these painfully moving moments. It is possible that by naming the baby Danny and knowing of the Millands' personal adoption woes, Webb, Davis, and Keighley backed Milland into this performative *cinéma à clef*.

Close to My Heart should have turned things around for both Milland and Tierney, who were both on career downswings, but it came too late and was seen too little. According to Tierney, "I had my best role in half a dozen years, the story of a woman who adopts a baby. The part was one that touched the chords of my own experience. I can understand the hunger to have a baby."

The critical reactions were mostly dismissive. The *Christian Science Monitor* complained, "While the situations are valid, they are not of themselves dramatic enough to make one feel *Close to My Heart* is a superior picture. The acting by Miss Tierney, Mr. Milland, and especially Miss Bainter—excels the story." Richard L. Coe in the *Washington Post* was downright contemptuous: "Stuff and nonsense; women are intelligent humans (too!) and while the problem will seem pathetic to women, the hokum in this telling of it will be no more acceptable to them that [sic] it is to a mere male."

Acknowledging their *actual* growing family at home, Ray and Mal decided to make the big move to 609 Mountain Drive in Beverly Hills, a larger house that was closer to the children's schools. The new property, built in 1951, would become home base for many years to come. Despite Ray's unsettled

Close to My Heart (1951), with Gene Tierney

place as a freelance actor, he and Mal maintained the appearance of Hollywood wealth with this purchase, and the family hired a couple, Marie and Fred Gillard, to work as servants in the new house.

Back at work, Milland's second Warner Bros. effort, *Bugles in the Afternoon*, wasn't nearly as good as *Close to My Heart* but nothing terrible either—an average Western, shot between early June and mid-July 1951 and released in March 1952.

In 1944, *Bugles in the Afternoon* had been planned for James Cagney, but by the time the studio gave the green light, in April 1951, Ray Milland had become a suitable substitute. Casting changes persisted: Hugh Marlowe replaced David Brian, and Forrest Tucker filled in for Robert Preston. With workmanlike director Roy Rowland in charge, the entire company traveled to Utah to shoot in various parts of the state. Like Milland's other two Westerns, Technicolor was employed.

The story starts with Milland as Kern Shafter, a member of the US Cavalry in 1876, who is demoted after striking a fellow officer in a fight over a woman. History repeats itself when Shafter reenlists as a private in the Dakota territories, only to find the man he had hit, Captain Edward Garnett (Marlowe), is now his superior—and they are both interested in the same beautiful woman, Josephine Russell (Helena Carter). Garnett sends Shafter on dangerous missions, and though Shafter is injured, both Josephine and the division's major witness first-hand Garnett's vindictive streak and realize Shafter is a heroic soldier after all.

Milland had no special affinity for this project, but once on location, he was found to be both professional and caring. Costar Helena Carter remembered, "Ray Milland was a jovial man and evidently a compassionate one, as he was instrumental in the casting of Gertrude Michael. She'd been his leading lady many years before [in *The Return of Sophie Lang* (1936)] and had fallen on hard times [due to alcoholism]. He saw that she got a good supporting role in the film [as a sympathetic saloon owner]. Nice as he was, it was difficult for me to play opposite him as he never made eye contact in any of our scenes together." As for his his loyalty, Milland invited Gertrude Michael to join him at the *Bugles* world premiere in Salt Lake City on February 28, 1952.

The reviews were mostly negative. In the *Chicago Daily Tribune*, Mae Tinee said "it all boils down to the same old story, dragged out a bit too long." The *New York Times* called it a "rickety and transparent effort" and paid Milland a back-handed compliment: "Mr. Milland manages a lithe performance that is in admirable contrast to his appearance." In truth, Milland had been gradually gaining weight since at least 1949, and in this particular film, for some reason, his face looked slightly darker than usual. He did not look his best.

Milland could take qualified comfort in the box-office returns. Earning $1.5 million in North America alone, *Bugles in the Afternoon* was a hit for the studio, though Westerns generally did good business. Since Milland's name was nearly the same small size on the advertisements as those of his costars, and his face was barely recognizable in the artwork, it is unclear how much Ray Milland, and not the genre itself, drew in the crowds.

DEEPER CUTS

Following the tremendous response by the critics and public to George Stevens's *A Place in the Sun* in the summer of 1951, Paramount felt ready to release the director's long-withheld *Something to Live For* in the spring of 1952. The studio's fear that the film would not play well was very real, and the delay did not help, but it was too big a movie to shelve without any release at all. Using deceptive poster art of Milland passionately kissing Joan Fontaine, Paramount tried to sell the movie as a torrid romance. (One ad even warned potential viewers in glaring red letters that it was "Not Suitable for Children.") Looking past the studio trickery, Milland told the press, "I think this is the best movie I've done since *Lost Weekend*."

Virtually forgotten today even among those who admire George Stevens, *Something to Live For* does not deserve such anonymity. It is a flawed work but still an exceptional movie.

As his follow-up to *I Remember Mama* (1948), Stevens decided on an intimate chamber piece. Recalling the inventive films of the 1930s that raised Stevens's profile in the first place (e.g. *Alice Adams* [1935], *Swing Time*, [1936]), *Something to Live For* tackles a "social problem" with more insight and less preaching than most of its type. As with *The Lost Weekend*, it is alcoholism that is the central theme—but the drama around it (an unrequited love story) is touching as well.

Paramount executives were initially excited to have a film starring three Oscar winners, Milland, Joan Fontaine, and Teresa Wright, regardless of the subject matter. Reversing expectations, Ray Milland was not the alcoholic this time but rather a recovering addict who helps the main protagonist—an actress on the skids (Fontaine). Dwight Taylor's screenplay was loosely based on the life of his mother, stage legend Laurette Taylor. First named *Mr. and Miss Anonymous* as a reference to Alcoholic's Anonymous (AA), the title was changed to the more melodramatic *Something to Live For*.

The stand-in for Laurette Taylor is Jenny Carey (Fontaine), a talented thespian whose career has suffered from her benders. One night, an AA member, Alan Miller (Milland), is tipped off that Jenny is on a drinking binge in her hotel room. He helps her get sober, and from there, Alan, who is married to Edna (Teresa Wright) and has two young children, takes a special interest in Jenny and her plight. At home, Alan's marriage is tested when Edna suspects he is having an affair with Jenny. Eventually, with Alan's assistance, Jenny gains enough confidence to resume her career and not depend on alcohol. Alan and Edna graciously attend the opening night of her latest show.

The central deficiency of *Something to Live For* is the way Dwight Taylor jumps into Jennie's sorry situation without giving her a backstory and then ends the movie with a simple, clean finish. It is as though some material never made it to the screen.

Apart from this structural drawback, there is much that is worthwhile. All the performances are engrossing, and Milland perfectly depicts a man torn between his family and a woman he cares for and wants to help. He also captures the essence of someone who only seems to have slayed his own demons but is still vulnerable himself. Regarding the latter, Milland is able to convey considerable feeling wordlessly during a scene in a crowded Manhattan bar as he fights his impulses to buy a drink while watching other patrons enjoy theirs. Fontaine and Wright are also affecting in their roles, though it is Milland who stands out best.

Chief among the aesthetic virtues is Victor Young's plaintive, beautiful score, one of his best. George Barnes's cinematography evokes the spirit of film noir, with many unusual angles mirroring Jenny's state of mind. The editors, William Hornbeck and Tom McAdoo, skillfully link these memorable shots, sometimes with artful dissolves. While missing the grit and irony of Wilder's *Lost Weekend*, *Something to Live For* makes up for this loss with an almost dream-like quality and pervasive sense of desolation.

Joan Fontaine was dissatisfied with the film, which she later described as "dull." Even though Stevens had been her early mentor, she felt the director was overly experimental with his technique and less concerned about his actors. She would write,

> Ray Milland and I often did takes that lasted nine or ten minutes at a time. I had to play half of one scene in my nightgown, go off-camera, completely dress, and reappear while the camera was still running.... As both Ray and I always made it a practice of seeing our rushes after work each night, we filed into the projection room at Paramount when this scene was processed. After two-and-a-half hours, we stumbled out into the dark, bleary-eyed, never again to return to the rushes during that film. One hour had been spent looking at takes of the scene through lace curtain.

But Fontaine had nothing but admiration for her costar, as she would later relate:

> Ray Milland, during the shooting, showed me a sensitive, unselfish side of him which I will always appreciate. One morning on the set just before the first take, I confessed to him that I was wrung dry from the previous day's shooting, that the final close-up we were about to make would be almost impossible since I hadn't a tear left.
> "What makes you cry in a scene, Joan?" inquired the handsome Welshman.
> "When I've exhausted the impact of the actual situation, then perhaps thinking of my mother dying, or myself dying ... and when that no longer works, I recite The Lord's Prayer."
> As the take was about to begin, from behind the camera I heard Ray's whisper, "Our Father, who art...." My tears gushed forth in gratitude. It was a one-take print.

Both Milland and Fontaine had photographic memories, enabling them to recall their lines with minimal effort, and they shared another bond outside

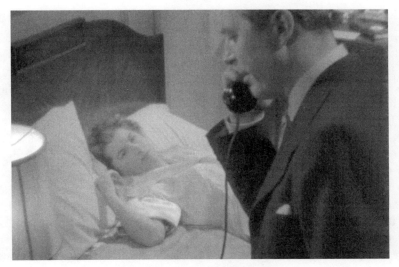

Something to Live For (1952), with Joan Fontaine

of work: both were licensed pilots and loved flying their own planes whenever possible. By costarring with Fontaine in this film, Milland became perhaps the only leading man in Hollywood to work with Fontaine, her sister Olivia, and their mother, Lilian Fontaine, all in separate films. (Lilian Fontaine had played Don Birnam's prospective mother-in-law in a standout scene in *The Lost Weekend*, and she was also in *The Imperfect Lady*.)

Reviewers were divided over *Something to Live For*. Some agreed with Fontaine and the studio that the film was a failure; others praised the effort. Otis L. Guernsey of the *New York Herald Tribune* was entirely negative: "*Something to Live For* does not touch life, it merely rambles on about it." *Variety* was mostly positive: "George Stevens' production and direction put the dramatic devices together with his usual meticulous touch. . . ."

Through the years, only a few critics have rediscovered this little-seen production. Dave Kehr was one, writing in 2012 that this "overlooked" Stevens work is "remarkably experimental," comparing the opening sequence to a Jean Cocteau movie, and adding, "Like Douglas Sirk's *All That Heaven Allows* [1955] or Nicholas Ray's *Bigger Than Life* [1956], the film is one of many '50s melodramas that express discontent with the era's nuclear family conformism: Milland is drawn to Fontaine because she shares his sense of isolation and entrapment, something his strong, cheerful wife (a marvelous Teresa Wright) will never understand."

Following some of the responses to his recent pictures, Milland's preference for radio over film work inspired him to turn his latest broadcast,

Safari, a May 1952 pilot for Hollywood Star Playhouse, into a regular series about a hunter and his intrepid exploits. In the end, only one episode, "The Adventure of the Bull Elephant," ever aired.

In front of the cameras again, Milland's next two films were thoroughly dissimilar. The black-and-white indie, *The Thief*, was shot first, from mid-May to mid-June 1952, followed by the color adventure, *Jamaica Run*.

In the late 1940s, independent producer Harry Popkin wanted Milland to star in Frederick Stephani's *The Roving Diplomat* but would have had to use the Paramount banner—a deal breaker. Although the arrangement fell through, three years later, with his revised contract, Milland was available to freelance.

By 1952, Popkin was still eager to work with Milland, but now it was to produce *The Thief*, a Cold War spy thriller, using United Artists as his distributor. Popkin hired writer-director Russell Rouse and writer Clarence Greene, who together recently scored with a daringly antiracist B thriller, *The Well* (1951). Rouse and Greene wrote *The Thief* with a unique storytelling device: no dialogue would be used!

Milland and company traveled to New York in May to film in various landmark locations, including the Empire State Building, Central Park, the Lincoln Tunnel, the Roseland Ballroom, Sardi's Restaurant, Park Avenue, and Times Square. The cast and crew also took a brief trip to Washington, DC, for scenes set in the Library of Congress and Georgetown.

The cinematographer, Sam Leavitt, deserves much of the credit for combining film noir with stark neorealism. Author Ronald Haver has described Leavitt as "a facile, proficient technician; his work on low-budget films gave him an ability to light sets in the shortest time possible, and he was a fast, no-nonsense cameraman. He was unpretentious, loved his work, and was eager to please his director."

In the Rouse-Greene screenplay, Milland plays Dr. Allan Fields, an American nuclear physicist working at Washington's Atomic Energy Commission but secretly selling vital information to Communist agents. When a fellow spy picks up the confiscated microfilm Fields has left for him, the spy is hit by a car, and an FBI inquiry starts. Fields senses his world closing in as the American agents are now on his path—all the way to New York City, where his latest assignment becomes perilous. To carry out his orders, Fields reluctantly kills an FBI operative and then suffers a nervous breakdown. This last act leads him to decide whether to escape by ship to Cairo, populated with fellow lowlifes, or to surrender himself to the authorities, accepting almost certain execution.

United Artists' main selling point revolved around the wordless screenplay. The tag line in the advertising poster read, "The Only Motion Picture of It's Kind... Not a Word Is Spoken!" For a short time, this technique seems contrived, but once the story takes shape, the lack of dialogue becomes more natural, allowing the ambient sounds to stand out. The climax is especially powerful when Fields experiences his emotional collapse in his dreary Manhattan brownstone and starts crying uncontrollably. Milland told United Press International during shooting, "This is the most exciting thing I have done. That dialogue is quite a crutch for an actor. You come to rely on it.... When you have nothing to say, you really have to be on your toes and keep thinking all the time. That's all right with me. It's quite a challenge."

Since the filmmakers' approach confers ambiguity to what is transpiring, *The Thief* rises well above the average anti-Communist movie of the era (e.g. *I Was a Communist for the F.B.I.* [1951]). Our protagonist's conflict represents something beyond his feelings about his spying (his motivations are never explained) and more of a philosophical comment on the lone individual caught in the death grip between two opposing and oppressive forces.

Milland does a remarkable job in a very difficult role. Robbed of his distinct and dulcet-sounding tones, Milland uses his face and body to convey his thoughts. About this performance, Milland filmographer Jim McKay wisely observed,

> Silence is Golden, enabling Milland to fully showcase his ability to express a hard-hitting range of visual emotions as his character slips deeper into despair with each passing scene—without a doubt, a *tour de force*. Unshaven, with beads of sweat on his brow, Milland convincingly gets under your skin as he sheds tears for killing the FBI agent, nightmares playing on his sanity much like the darkness that consumes him in *The Lost Weekend*.... Self-loathing personified, Milland, framed by a street neon light, immerses himself in the drama, his body language and angst-ridden profile in unison as his guilt-ridden scientist leaves his mark with half-finished cigarettes and glasses emptied of whisky.

Two of the most striking set pieces include the FBI agent's chase after Fields, which ends with Fields stomping the man until he falls to his death from the engineering room of the Empire State Building. The violence is gritty, realistic, and depressing, nothing like the fights Milland had choreographed for him on the Paramount soundstages. Just as memorable is the scene of flirtation in the run-down brownstone between Fields and the woman next door (Rita Gam, in her film debut). Gam's sexy but sleazy entreaties alienate the already isolated scientist, a sign of how far this once respected scientist has fallen in his ability to connect to fellow human

The Thief (1952)

beings. (In an earlier scene, Fields angrily smashes an honorary award he had once received.)

For a such a small-scale movie, *The Thief* presents excellent work from its entire team: Leavitt's expressionistic cinematography, Herschel Burke Gilbert's edgy score (which was nominated for an Oscar), Chester W. Schaeffer's precise editing, and the supporting performances—from Gam's unnamed, mirage-like femme fatale to Martin Gabel's disquietingly smooth espionage contact (Mr. Bleek!).

Best of all is Milland, who received a Golden Globe nomination in 1952, as did the film. Milland lost to Gary Cooper (for *High Noon*), but at least he could revel in some glowing reviews. A.W. Weiler of the *New York Times* was awed: "Russell Rouse, who also directed, has gotten a sensitive and towering performance from Ray Milland in the title role." *Variety*'s reviewer was almost as impressed: "Milland does a fine job of projecting the scientist's nervousness, fears and inward revulsion against his traitorous deeds. In the last half of the film, he is particularly outstanding, especially in the emotional breakdown that comes after he has killed a man." In many ways, this mental collapse is one of the bravest moments from a male actor of his generation, surpassing his own DTs nightmare sequence in *The Lost Weekend*. Milland reveals so much of his inner self in a way that is hard to imagine any other matinée-idol type dare try at the time.

For whatever reason, director-writer Rouse never again created anything as superior as *The Thief* and is better remembered today as the helmer of the laughably bad drama *The Oscar* (1966). For Milland, as a preview of things soon to come (i.e. *Dial M for Murder*), he portrayed a homicidal husband (opposite Edna Best) on radio in Agatha Christie's *Love from a Stranger*. The *Screen Guild Players* broadcast was heard in mid-October 1952.

Milland's final Paramount film was *Jamaica Run*, shot in fall 1952 and released in June 1953. Though in Technicolor and an action-adventure, the production was really a glorified programmer with a weaker than usual supporting cast, relying mainly on Milland to carry a conventional story. In so many ways, it was a marked letdown from his just-completed triumph with *The Thief*.

Milland didn't want to make *Jamaica Run* at all, but Paramount insisted on his participation in exchange for shooting *The Thief* first. Arlene Dahl, his costar in *Jamaica Run*, and her husband at the time, Fernando Lamas, were friends with Ray and Mal Milland, but she couldn't help noticing, "He was cold. He was unhappy. He wasn't really there." In an interview, Dahl continued, "He was professional, but there was no rapport because he was distant . . . and very unhappy about doing the film and sulking during the whole filming."

Based on Max Murray's 1950 novel, *The Neat Little Corpse*, as adapted and directed by Lewis R. Foster, the story involves a navy skipper, Pat (Milland), who tries to help a former girlfriend, Ena (Dahl), when she and her family are threatened with eviction from their Jamaica estate by a ruthless land developer, William (Patric Knowles). A murder mystery and court trial follow.

If audiences found *Jamaica Run* familiar, it is because several elements were taken from Milland's *Reap the Wild Wind*, including the exotic color locations (though all shot on the backlot), the deep-sea diving scenes, and the trial climax. Actually, the film was no better or worse than DeMille's epic, only less spectacular. (One misses the giant squid.) *Jamaica Run*, a minor moneymaker, did not receive the usual expert craftsmanship of most of Milland's former Paramount titles. It represented a waning exit from the company he had joined—and made a lot of money for—two decades earlier.

Mae Tinee gave Ray Milland a curious compliment in her *Chicago Daily Tribune* review: "Thanks to able performances by such old-timers as Ray Milland, Wendell Corey, and Caroll McComas, there are bits of humor here and there, and Miss Dahl never looked lovelier, but the script is both weak and involved." Thus, Ray Milland was officially labeled an "old-timer" and found himself completely on his own, without a clear sense of what to do next.

Jamaica Run's producers, William H. Pine and William C. Thomas, announced in October 1952 that Milland would direct for the first time, a Western called *Run for Cover*, but nothing came of it. At the end of November, Ray and Mal made a date night out of an invitation to attend the star-studded premiere of *Bwana Devil*, the first major 3-D film of the decade, a few months before *Jamaica Run*'s far less stupendous debut. And Paramount made it clear to the world that Milland was on the losing end of his battle with the company: a lobby card created from a *Jamaica Run* fight scene showed him looking bloody, haggard, and disheveled.

As a sign of Milland's gloomy mindset, for the first and only time, he accepted a screen role once originated by Cary Grant. The frivolous *Let's Do It Again*, shot toward the end of 1952 and released in June of 1953 (concurrent with *Jamaica Run*), was a color remake of *The Awful Truth* (1937), one of the movies that helped propel Grant to major stardom after he left Paramount. Columbia's attempt to reboot the film with Milland and Jane Wyman did not result in anything as memorable, but it was mildly enjoyable in its own right.

Actually, Alan Richman's 1922 play about a divorced couple trying to make each other jealous of their new paramours had been filmed twice before the Grant-Irene Dunne classic: a 1925 silent and a 1929 talkie. Richard Sale and Mary Loos' screenplay added a show business background, with the husband now a songwriter named Gary and the wife a retired actress named Constance. In addition to Wyman, Milland reunited with Alexander Hall, director of *The Doctor Takes a Wife* (1940), and they all tried too hard to give the proceedings an air of conviviality.

Anyone who saw the advertising art for *Let's Do It Again* in 1953 would have realized that fortunes had changed considerably since Milland last starred with Jane Wyman eight years earlier in *The Lost Weekend*. Wyman won her own Oscar for *Johnny Belinda* in 1948 and became a major box-office attraction. The *Let's Do It Again* posters featured a large picture of Wyman in a mock-striptease number she performs at the climax of the film, while the drawing of second-billed Milland was smaller and barely noticeable. (Obviously, it was Wyman, not her costar, who turned the film into a success, grossing $1.25 million.)

Columbia's one other shrewd bit of publicity was to have the stars appear together on NBC's first live telecast of the Academy Awards on March 19, 1953, a few months ahead of the *Let's Do It Again* premiere. Milland was not inclined to help out Harry Cohn or the film, which he ended up disliking, but he was willing to appear on the show when he learned his old friend, Mitchell Leisen, would be directing it (Leisen was having difficulty getting feature film work at the time). Wyman and Milland (in white tie and tails) tried to appear sober and dignified announcing the nominees for various Best Short Subjects, not the most prestigious of awards, and handing an Oscar to Mr. Walt Disney, the winner of the two-reeler, *Water Birds*.

In *Let's Do It Again*, Milland and Wyman are meant to look foolish on purpose. For example, Gary is caught in her bathrobe in one scene. Fortunately, there is a balance to the battle-of-the-sexes routines, and neither star is forced into the kind of embarrassing, mean-spirited slapstick that ruined *A Woman of Distinction*. Among the songs by Ned Washington and Lester Lee, only Wyman's ridiculous "Call of the Wild" striptease stands out (a dance designed "to separate the men from the boys," her character declares in a husky register). Perhaps for cost-cutting reasons, the very show for which Milland's Gary is writing songs is never represented. Adequately dubbed by Paul Frees, Milland sings these compositions, though he is upstaged by off-screen recordings of Dick Haymes covering the same tunes.

Soured by so many remakes from the studios in the 1950s, most reviewers whined. *Variety* called it "rather superficial, resulting in a lightweight offering that strains hard to amuse.... Hall's direction lets [Milland] interpret his role with a cloying coyness that's very unbecoming." Milland himself was the harshest critic. In his autobiography, he called *Let's Do It Again* "a fizzle of the worst kind, for which I still haven't been paid, and rightly so." Nevertheless, he praised his costar, saying Wyman was a "versatile artist" and "wonderfully cooperative."

In 1953, Universal announced Milland was set to reteam with a different costar he liked, Paulette Goddard, for yet another remake of a 1930s screwball classic—*My Man Godfrey*—but the idea was scuttled. Later, in 1957, David Niven and June Allyson filled in for William Powell and Carole Lombard in the widescreen and color facsimile.

For Ray Milland, the response toward his last two films alone suggested he needed to move in an entirely new direction, which he did in unanticipated fashion.

CHAPTER 8

"FOR HIS SIN": GRACE AND TELEVISION (1953–1955)

WITHOUT A HOME STUDIO, MILLAND HAD THE BENEFIT OF PICKING AND choosing properties of any kind. More than ever before, he could take chances on a variety of parts and even mediums. For the first time, with the encouragement of his agency, MCA, Milland decided that television might be a good fit for his talents. And while some major studios were still forbidding contracted stars from appearing on the small screen, Milland no longer had the constraint of a mogul telling him what to do.

In early 1952, MCA's first attempt to bring its new client to the small screen was as a guest star on a proposed anthology series, *America's Finest*. For the pilot episode, "Those We Love," Milland and Joan Crawford would have played a couple whose marriage is threatened by a seductive woman. Though the teaming with Crawford was promising, Revue Productions canceled the series before it started.

Later in the year, MCA and Revue convinced Milland to produce and star in his own show at a salary of $5,000 per week. As he bluntly put it, "I went into television because my agent talked me into it. . . . Anyway, I was tired of making a lot of bad movies." Despite playing darker characters since *The Lost Weekend*, Milland was sold on the situation-comedy genre and the guise of an absent-minded professor.

MEET MR. McNUTLEY

Meet Mr. McNutley was announced in December 1952, to be shot at Revue Studios and aired on Thursday evenings in the prized CBS primetime slot, 8:00 to 8:30 p.m. (EST). In addition, a radio transmission with different storylines would air one hour later on the same night, though this practice stopped at the end of the first season. General Electric agreed to be the sponsor, and the opening titles introduced Milland and Phyllis Avery (as his wife) promoting GE household appliances. The second season title sequence was far more whimsical: accompanied by the Gershwin tune "'S Wonderful," a cartoon Ray Milland with oversized head was seen rushing through Escher-esque school hallways.

Meet Mr. McNutley was hardly the first television show featuring a movie personality, but it was the first to showcase a major male movie star, let alone former matinée idol or Oscar winner. Lucille Ball's *I Love Lucy* defined for the era sitcoms about modern marriages, and the innovations by Ball, Desi Arnaz, and cinematographer Karl Freund revolutionized the genre by using celluloid, not video, and a three-camera setup that enabled close-ups and a "cleaner" look. *I Love Lucy* could be filmed before a live audience and edited later for airings. Up to this point, most sitcoms were staged and performed live before audiences on the East Coast and in the Midwest, then shown in kinescope form on the West Coast.

As producer, Ray Milland decided *Meet Mr. McNutley* should also be filmed and aired later but *not* filmed in front of a live audience, in part because many of the episodes (each costing $30,000) required actual exteriors, something unusual at the time. Milland and coproducer Charles Barton chose to experiment with Charles Douglass's then-novel "laugh-track" invention. Milland had met Barton as a fellow actor on the set of *Beau Geste* in 1939; knowing of Barton's specialization in comedy, Milland asked him to help kick off his series by producing and directing a handful of episodes during the first season, including the pilot. In most other ways, there were similarities to contemporary sitcoms, from stories about spousal conflicts to the stylistic fusion of slapstick humor and verbal sparring.

Milland's approach might have been too imitative, but at the beginning, *Mr. McNutley* was a ratings hit. This was all the more impressive since the program was pitted against NBC's high-rated game show *You Bet Your Life*, hosted by Groucho Marx. The premise of *Mr. McNutley* was simple enough: Milland played Ray McNutley, an English professor at a women's college, Lynnhaven, who, at home, enjoyed the company of his free-spirited wife, Peggy (Phyllis Avery). Barton recommended to Milland that Joe Connelly and Bob Mosher write the episodes. The team had just penned many of the scripts for the *Amos 'n' Andy* TV series (directed by Barton), and they would later become best remembered for producing and writing *Leave It to Beaver* in the late 1950s. (The house exteriors are identical for *Meet Mr. McNutley* and *Leave It to Beaver*.)

Milland handpicked his cast. Blonde, petite Phyllis Avery had an extensive background in theater but was virtually unknown to the mass public. As the bumbling next-door neighbor, Gordon Jones was a more familiar face, but most of his film roles since the 1930s were small and uncredited. Minerva Urecal, as the professor's vinegary foil, the dean of the fictional school, had a similar track record of unbilled parts for the last two decades, including two with Ray Milland, *Skylark* and *California*.

Most of the shooting took place in the spring of 1953, and the first episode aired on September 17, 1953. The ratings and reviews were propitious, as Larry Wolters's headline indicated in the *Chicago Daily Tribune*: "Ray Milland's TV Bow Looks Like Big Hit: Debuts as Mr. McNutley." This pilot, "Meet Mr. McNutley," finds our hero falling into a duck pond on a hunting trip. The similar third episode (airing October 1, 1953) was considered one of the best of the season: in "Babes in the Woods," Mr. McNutley becomes a reluctant scoutmaster who gets lost in the woods and then caught in a bear trap. The ratings maintained themselves for a while but started to fall off just as the characters were developing and the professor became less absent-minded and more tethered to Ray Milland's public persona as a wise, bookish family man. The eventual dearth of pure belly laughs, so in favor with *I Love Lucy*, accelerated the decline of the show's mass appeal.

Among the later season 1 highlights were "The Egg and Ray" (airing March 4, 1954) and "The Tree" (on March 11, 1954). In the former, with its title playing off of Claudette Colbert's 1947 *Egg and I* movie, Mr. McNutley acquires a parakeet that lays an egg but refuses to hatch it. The professor goes to great lengths to find ways to hatch the egg himself! In the latter episode, the McNutleys buy a shade tree but run into all kinds of small-town government bureaucracy and neighborly hostility over their benign purchase.

In 2020, author Gillian Kelly speculated about other reasons *Meet Mr. McNutley* ultimately failed with the public. Kelly focused primarily on the way Milland exhibited himself in "real life," particularly in print ads as a family man, in contrast to the happy but childless couple on the show:

> [In a print] advertisement for a television set from Magnavox, the "real" Milland [appears] relaxed as he sits at home with his wife and children, the domestic setting more familiar to viewers and presenting the Millands as like [sic] any other family watching television together, therefore portraying them as ordinary and relatable.... The Millands are a cultured family with varied interests and do not spend all their time watching television but come together to watch as a shared experience: a healthy image to project.... While Milland and his son are

Meet Mr. McNutley (1953), with Phyllis Avery

dressed in dark blazers and pale dress trousers, his wife and daughter both wear light blue dresses, the walls are white and the carpet beige making the rich mahogany unit draw the eye to the centre of the page and where the advertisers want us to look. This advertisement not only sells consumers the product, but also the idyllic family life we may share with The Millands if we buy this particular television set. Perhaps if this had been the type of family *Meet Mr. McNutley* had used the show would have run much longer.

To the critics who didn't like the show, Milland defensively and self-effacingly said midway through the run "I've been in 70 pictures and 60 of them were stinkers. If 60 bad pictures can't kill you, what can?"

While Milland kept busy producing and starring in *Mr. McNutley* and its alternative radio edition, he was not completely forgotten in the film world. For starters, he was on a long list of leading men being considered to play fading alcoholic movie star Norman Maine in Warner Bros.' musical remake of *A Star Is Born*, produced by Sid Luft and starring Luft's wife, Judy Garland in her movie comeback. Director George Cukor most eagerly wanted Cary Grant to play Maine, but Grant refused, once again fearing he would tarnish his image playing such a troubled character. But it is highly likely Milland would have jumped at the chance. In a way, he was becoming a Norman Maine figure in real life, minus the alcohol. In any case, James Mason was finally chosen.

Therefore, by the time he completed his first season of *Mr. McNutley* in the summer of 1953, Milland was still available to filmmakers and eager to have a comeback of his own in features. Following the lackluster *Bugles in the Afternoon*, *Jamaica Run*, and *Let's Do It Again*, Milland's rescue came in the form of Alfred Hitchcock and *Dial M for Murder*, the third and last movie of his Warner Bros. deal and his first triumph in a number of years.

DIAL M FOR MURDER

In *Dial M for Murder*, Robert Cummings' Mark tells Ray Milland's Tony that he writes "for television—for my sin." This throwaway comic line actually resonates on several levels. Nearly all the principals involved in *Dial M for Murder* were "sinners" (or about to be) vis-à-vis cinema's rival medium. Ray Milland was on a break from his television show during production, while both Robert Cummings and Alfred Hitchcock were soon to launch their own long-running series, both in 1955, and leading lady Grace Kelly had been a fixture on live television drama from 1948 to 1954 in 35 productions. The little-known but more significant irony is that *Dial M for Murder* did not start life as a play, as many assumed, but as a 1952 *television* movie in the United Kingdom.

The elitist disdain for television ("the vast wasteland"), suggested by the "for my sin" line, would not subside for many decades, but Hitchcock was already poking fun at this attitude within his own film, with 3-D designed to lure viewers away from their "free" television sets. (It was a gimmick to many but one that TV could not duplicate.) In a less fortunate bit of irony, *Dial M for Murder* was barely seen in 3-D because the so-called fad passed its peak by the time of release, so only regular "flat" prints were distributed.

For Ray Milland, his list of sins didn't stop with starring in a TV sitcom. Apparently, he also committed a biblical sin: adultery. True, it wasn't the first time, but it was his most publicly exposed time. According to multiple sources, he had an affair with Grace Kelly, which was judged harshly in the tabloid press, muting his otherwise well-received big-screen return. By most accounts, Milland fell deeply in love with Grace Kelly, so his "dalliance" was hardly a minor matter to him. But since it threatened his marriage and both of their careers, he and Kelly ended it. This interlude, though a short chapter in their lives temporally and chronologically, was a profound one—at least for Ray Milland, his own real-life Brief Encounter.

Before Grace Kelly entered his world, the pairing of Ray Milland and Alfred Hitchcock was somehow both inevitable and fortuitous. Not only did it result in a superior film, but it also resurrected the careers of both artists. Hitchcock struck a chord with *Strangers on a Train* in 1951 but otherwise had been in a slump for several years. His achievements since *Rope* in 1948 were experimental in nature but not well regarded or major hits (they have since become beloved in many quarters), and he was trying to finish his Warner Bros. contract with something more commercial. Frederick Knott's play, *Dial M for Murder*, proved to be the answer. Following the 1952 TV presentation, it had been a hit on the West End, then Broadway (the latter from 1952 to 1954, with Maurice Evans in the lead).

Hitchcock asked Knott to write the screenplay, which centers around a seemingly happy London couple, Tony and Margot Wendice (Milland and Kelly), who are keeping secrets from one another: Margot is trying to break off her love affair with American hack TV writer Mark Halliday (Cummings); Tony, a former tennis champ, is fearful his wife is going to leave him and bribes an old school acquaintance, the shady Charles Swann (Anthony Dawson), to kill Margot so he can inherit her small fortune. However, Tony's meticulous plan falls apart when put into action: Swann attempts to carry out the murder, but Margot kills Swann in self-defense. Tony, who was dining on the town with Mark during Margot's ordeal, quickly revamps his scheme by planting clues that lead the investigator, Chief Inspector Hubbard (John Williams), to believe Margot deliberately murdered Swann because he was supposedly blackmailing her about the affair. Just before the innocent Margot is executed for her crime, Hubbard figures out that Tony was behind the dastardly plot.

Hitchcock's original conception was to cast Cary Grant as Tony, Deborah Kerr as Margot, and William Holden as Mark. Grant made sense to Hitchcock since they had formed a bond while working on two previous pictures (*Suspicion* [1941], and *Notorious* [1946]). Though Grant was apparently willing to take on such a dark role this time, it was Warner Bros. that was nervous about having him seen as a malevolent type. Kerr and Holden turned down Hitchcock simply because they were unavailable. So Hitchcock had to restrategize and look elsewhere.

Whether or not Hitchcock remembered meeting Ray Milland at Elstree Studios in 1929, it is safe to say he was well aware of Milland's capabilities long before he decided to offer him *Dial M for Murder*. After production, Hitchcock was quoted saying, "Milland did everything he was told and then made it better. . . . He made a great movie for Billy Wilder and very good movie for me."

Moreover, Milland and Hitchcock shared a circuitous history. In 1943, producer Charles Brackett tried to secure Hitchcock's services for *The Uninvited*, and the director offered preproduction advice before he was forced to bow out. Milland played an actual Hitchcock villain for the first time on the 1949 radio version of *Shadow of a Doubt*. He was then the only choice of Joan Harrison, Hitchcock's assistant-turned-producer, for *Circle of Danger* in 1951, and that same year he played the flawed, tennis-playing hero, Guy, in the *Lux Radio* version of Hitchcock's *Strangers on a Train*.

If one accepts John Russell Taylor's theory that *Dial M for Murder* represents a sequel of sorts to *Strangers on a Train*, it is all the more appropriate that Milland continued in the "same" part. As Russell Taylor writes, "[I]t is curious, to say the least, that the murderous husband is an ex-tennis pro who has married well—as it might be, Guy from *Strangers on a Train* a few years on—and that he does plan his murder precisely by blackmailing someone totally unconnected to it, as though he has, after all, learned a thing or two from Bruno [the psychopathic antagonist of *Strangers*]."

Most importantly to Hitchcock, Milland did not mind taking risks with his screen image. He had already played sinister roles, such as in *So Evil My Love*, but he also maintained his place as a practitioner of Hollywood farce. *Dial M for Murder*, despite its central murder plot, required a light touch from all its players. Ray Milland could negotiate both genres exceedingly well, even if this was the most radical intertwining of the crime thriller and the drawing-room comedy of any Milland movie. When Hitchcock picked Robert Cummings for the other male lead, he was reuniting the two men from fourteen years earlier in *Everything Happens at Night*, a comparatively lightweight mix of genres, and extending their farcical rivalry over a blonde heroine. Of course, this new blonde heroine was not Sonja Henie. Hitchcock chose rising star Grace Kelly, who quickly became known as the quintessential "Hitchcock Blonde," cool and beautiful on the outside, smoldering with sexuality on the inside. (According to Kelly, she, Hitchcock, and Milland enjoyed telling off-color jokes between takes.)

In addition, by using Robert Cummings, Hitchcock revised Cummings's role in Douglas Sirk's *Sleep, My Love* (1948), where his hero thwarted husband Don Ameche's plan to "gaslight" wife Claudette Colbert into an insane asylum and, thus, inherit her wealth. Cummings was earnest in both films but showed his well-known flair for comedy in *Dial M for Murder*, not at all present in the Sirk production. Likewise, Ameche's depiction of the evil, manipulative husband contrasted with Milland's. As Bernard F. Dick writes, "Admittedly, the part [in *Sleep, My Love*] did not allow Ameche to flesh out the character. Ray Milland faced a similar problem in *Dial M for Murder* (1954), but he at least made the husband fascinating by being alternately suave and insidious. Ameche simply lowered his voice and went on autopilot, as if he realized that, given third billing, his role was only a catalyst in the Claudette-Cummings reaction."

Milland banked a few episodes for the second season of his sitcom before he started work on *Dial M for Murder*. Then, apart from some London-street stock shots, the Warner's backlot production began in early August 1953 and ended on September 25. This was an impressively short schedule given the difficulties of the 3-D process, such as moving the extraordinarily bulky stereoscopic camera around the apartment set and the fact that Hitchcock, the cast, and much of the crew were all newcomers to 3-D. The movie was also rapidly produced when one considers Hitchcock spent an entire week shooting the infamous, sexually charged murder scene, which ends with Margot killing Swann with sewing shears. Along with the limited number of shooting days, the bottom line was helped by Milland receiving $125,000 for his services—a comedown from only a few years ago and about $75,000 less than Cary Grant's standard asking price. Robert Cummings earned a mere $25,000.

Though rarely seen in 3-D, the very fact that Hitchcock employed the technique in the first place—as dictated by Jack Warner—has contributed to *Dial M for Murder*'s reputation as a minor work by the "Master of Suspense." For more enlightened critics and viewers, 3-D should represent a cinematic tool, no different than color, sound, or widescreen. (Note, too, the more favorable critical reactions today to the widespread use of 3-D.) Another factor in the disregard for the film flows from Hitchcock himself. His lack of enthusiasm is evident in several interviews, including his famous book-length discussion with François Truffaut, *Hitchcock/Truffaut*, conducted in 1962. ("There isn't very much we can say about that one, is there?," asks Hitchcock.) Yet, it is worth debating whether any artist is his or her own best, most perceptive critic. In fact, Hitchcock's true feelings about the film are truly hard to know. Robert Cummings reflected in the 1980s, "Hitch dismisses [*Dial M*] these days but he was like a kid in a candy store with all the effects."

Ultimately, the fact that *Dial M* is based on a play somehow has prejudiced cinephiles, many of whom do not seem to realize how Hitchcock subtly critiques the theatricality. At the time of its May 1954 release, *Monthly Film Bulletin* simply labeled it "A neat piece of filmed theater," and *Variety* concurred: "*Dial M* remains more of a filmed play than a motion picture."

Since 1954, a growing number of discerning viewers have countered the negative sentiments. François Truffaut himself defied Hitchcock during their 1960s exchange: "This is one of the pictures I see over and over again. I enjoy it more every time I see it." In 1983, Geoff Brown wrote in the *Times*, "*Dial M for Murder* is remarkable for the subtle, even beautiful, use of

Dial M for Murder (1954), with Anthony Dawson

Robert Cummings, Ray Milland, and Grace Kelly

three-dimensional imagery. While Knott's characters weave their complicated web of infidelity, blackmail and deceit, Hitchcock's camera pursues the actors around armchairs, table lamps, desks and doorways in long, sinuous takes. We seem to be witnessing a half-abstract ballet of objects, people, decor and space, and the effect is hypnotic."

Addressing the stage origins in her 2013 essay, "Alfred Hitchcock Presents *Dial M for Murder*," Ina Rae Hark remarks frequently about "Hitchcock preserving the play's theatricality yet turning it on its head." One of Rae Hark's examples is the memorable scene where Tony instructs Swann in the way to stage the apartment break-in and murder:

Rightly described as a director or stage manager of the action by reviewers, Tony is equally a stand-in for the playwright, explicating the play's premise in minute detail before blocking the proposed murder for Swann while the camera gives a bird's eye view of the geography of the flat in which it will take place. There is no higher praise of Hitchcock's direction and Ray Milland's performance than to note that they make this massive "info dump" mesmerizing.

As Rae Hark suggests, there are many self-reflexive moments where Hitchcock's use of complex camera angles and abrupt editing provide the real break from the proscenium arch, in contrast to conventional stage-to-screen efforts "opening up" plays with (p)added exterior scenes.

When *Dial M for Murder* was revived in the early 1980s, a handful of theaters presented it in the original 3-D format, and critics were overwhelmed by the immersive experience. Leading the way, Andrew Sarris wrote about a March 1980 screening in New York:

> [It] blew my mind. . . . Hitchcock's inspired mise-en-scene for the 3-D process requires unusual alertness on the part of the viewer to perceive the connections and implications on a screen suddenly endowed with a new vision of the universe. What up to now has seemed a relatively conventional exercise in crime and detection is magically recreated into a metaphysical speculation on the vast gulf between people even when they seem to be interacting, and on the strange ways in which objects come to possess people's minds and shape their lives.

While Ray Milland was not mentioned enough in any of the reviews of 1954 (or many since), at least he could take comfort in the fact he was top-billed in a well-regarded moneymaker from one of the great directors. Still, for all the renewed fame Milland received at the time, there was that bittersweet, ultimately distressing side to his participation. It was at the beginning of the shoot that he fell for his costar.

GRACE KELLY

Ray Milland was genuinely smitten and, while Grace Kelly had recently ended a romance with Jean-Pierre Aumont, she seemed to be just as enamored by Milland as he her. The age difference (she was twenty-three, he was forty-six) didn't get in the way of their trysts, but gossip did. It should be at least mentioned here that two well-known writers have cast doubt over whether a sexual affair really took place. In *High Society: The Life of Grace Kelly*, Donald Spoto's 2009 Kelly biography, Spoto takes a contrarian view of Kelly as a seductress of her leading men, and he tends not to believe most of the stories since they are based on hearsay. About the Milland affair, he writes, "The rumor that Grace very nearly destroyed the Milland marriage is based on the sexist notion that a beautiful young woman can easily reduce a man to nerveless idiocy." In "Hollywood Royalty: Two Sides of Grace Kelly," Anthony Lane's 2010 *New Yorker* review of the Spoto book, Lane is skeptical in his own way about the stories of Kelly's supposed predation, including the Milland seduction. A true cynic would also have to consider the p.r. credo that scandals connected to a movie often result in greater box-office returns (and Hitchcock himself was an expert at using creative methods to sell his work). In this case, though, enough named sources have asserted that a romance of some kind occurred.

Lizanne Kelly, Grace's sister, described how she saw the relationship evolve: "All the men fell in love with Grace on *Dial M*. . . . They were around her in scores—Tony Dawson . . . and Frederick Knott . . . really fell for her." Lizanne continued, saying Grace was especially flattered by the attention Milland gave her as he was a childhood idol of hers, and he would make regular visits to her apartment at the Chateau Marmont. In little time, the old-fashioned courting turned into a full-fledged romance, and neither party made any attempt to conceal their affection. Lizanne Kelly was surprised at Milland's candor, recalling, "I flew back from Hollywood on the same plane with him and we had a long talk. He told me he really was very much in love with her." One source directly from the set, costar Robert Cummings, later said, "I'm not being catty here, but I seemed be the only one who did not have an affair with Grace Kelly. Certainly, Hitch immediately fell for her, and Ray Milland pursued her mightily."

Robert Lacey, another Kelly biographer, described his subject's behavior as reckless, ignoring the warnings of family and friends about her openness. Yet the older, married Milland wasn't any more circumspect. According to Lacey, "When Joe Hyams went to interview [Milland] for the *New York Herald Tribune* that autumn [after the production ended but before the film's release], the star answered the door dressed in nothing but a towel, and the journalist got the clear impression that Milland was not alone. 'Grace appeared after a time,' remembers Hyams. 'She was dressed, but she had had time to dress. She was cool as a cucumber. She was very patrician.'" *Dial M*'s assistant director, Mel Dellar, added, "My wife and I saw them out having dinner a couple of times, and late in the evening, after we finished filming, they'd go to some little place and have a few drinks."

While the affair progressed—and Milland rented an apartment to be closer to Kelly—Mal Milland was in London, by chance the location of the film's setting recreated on the Warner Bros. soundstages. Eventually, Mal Milland returned home and caught wind of the talk about her husband's extramarital activities. Whether or not she could tell her husband was truly in love, she first wanted to determine if an actual liaison was taking place. According to yet another Kelly biographer, James Spada, "[Mal] feared it was true, but there was no proof. Several weeks after her suspicions were first aroused, her fears were validated. A close friend of the Millands, who requested anonymity, recalls . . . '[Ray] was going on a trip, and he had just left the house. Mal's sister Harriet was there, and Mal poured her heart out to her about her suspicions. Harriet got in her car, followed Jack [Ray] to the airport, and sure enough, there was Jack with Grace, going off on a tryst somewhere."

Once she had confirmation, Mal and her friends supposedly leaked information to various gossip columnists, notably Hedda Hopper, with the aim of publicly shaming the twosome. Using not-so-veiled innuendo, Hopper was exacting revenge for Milland's hanging up on her in 1940 and the subsequent years he snubbed interviews and avoided her radio show. Louella Parsons took a softer tone, writing, "I am sorry to have to print this, but the whole town is discussing it . . . and Mal does not deny that there is trouble." In September 1953, Sidney Skolsky reported in the *New York Post* about "handholding" between the two. Soon enough, the notorious tabloid magazine, *Confidential*, the *National Enquirer* of its day, printed that Ray Milland and Grace Kelly were lovers.

Understandably, it was the first mention in *Confidential* in 1953 that most alarmed Kelly's mother and father, who together flew from Philadelphia to Hollywood to convince their daughter to stop her affair with Ray Milland. Using the argument that she was putting her budding career in jeopardy, Jack and Margaret Kelly's talk forced Grace to seriously consider ending what had been a rapturous several weeks. Simultaneously, at the Milland home, Mal severely chastised Ray, according to studio publicist Andy Hervey: "You go ahead and get a divorce and marry Grace Kelly. . . . That's okay with me, because all the property is in my name," Mal added before he left the house on October 20 to stay at his apartment for about a month. (Blanche "Skip" Hathaway, Henry Hathaway's wife and a friend of Mal Milland, says it was Mal who ordered Ray out of the house.) As a way to escape the holier-than-thou judgments around her, Kelly accepted friend Rita Gam's offer to room together at Gam's apartment. It was only a coincidence that Gam was Milland's costar in *The Thief* the previous year. Not wanting more bad publicity himself and still feeling devotion to his wife of more than two decades, a chastened Ray returned to the family fold on November 17, 1953.

The gossip surrounding Milland and Kelly influenced what would have and should have been a significant career resurgence for a star who had slowly fallen out of favor since his Oscar-winning performance in *The Lost Weekend* nearly a decade earlier. Even more damaging was the fact that both he and Grace Kelly were emotionally wounded by the breakup and the way it came about. Hardly sounding like the future princess of Monaco, Kelly was quoted complaining, "At times I think I actually hate Hollywood." Milland directed his bitterness toward Hedda Hopper, saying of her, "She was venomous, vicious, a pathological liar, and quite stupid." But the otherwise chivalrous actor refused to ever talk about Grace Kelly, and never once mentioned her name in his 1974 memoirs.

According to Judith Balaban Quine, daughter of Milland's former Paramount boss, Barney Balaban, Mal Milland did not completely forget about Grace Kelly. Balaban Quine wrote in her own autobiography, "In that era I was told by a Hollywood hostess that Mal Milland . . . did not wish to be seated at the same dinner party table with me because she heard that Grace and I were friends." Balaban Quine also noted when she mentioned Ray Milland's name during a lunch date with Grace Kelly, Kelly's only comment was, "It was a bad mistake." And yet author Nigel Cawthorne says Kelly was still pining for Milland after she had started a new affair with William Holden, her 1954 leading man in both *The Bridges at Toko-Ri* and *The Country Girl*.

Somehow, a similar type of scandal didn't hurt Gary Cooper, Milland's *Beau Geste* costar, who had a well-publicized extramarital affair with Patricia Neal in 1949. Whereas Milland compounded his own problems by choosing decidedly unheroic roles, Cooper never strayed from his stalwart screen image. Thus, audiences were more willing to forgive America's "Sergeant York," while designating newcomer Patricia Neal as a homewrecker. The gossip columnists couldn't let the Kelly-Milland affair go, either. More than a year later, well after the romance was over, *Confidential* unleashed an even nastier article, "The Grass Isn't Greener in Gracie Kelly's Backyard!" In this November 1954 issue, Audrey Minor wrote, "Neither Bill Holden nor Ray Milland would take Grace's 'No' for an answer. Hollywood was baffled because both runaways had better stacked mamas at home."

Milland might have reversed much of the negative publicity very quickly had he had the foresight to accept an extraordinary offer. In 1954, according to Milland, the composing team of Alan Jay Lerner and Frederick Loewe,

The Milland family (1953): Ray, Muriel, Daniel, and Victoria.
Photo credit: Keystone Press / Alamy Stock Photo.

along with their backers, courted Milland about making his Broadway debut in their new musical adaptation of George Bernard Shaw's *Pygmalion*. Milland dismissed out of hand becoming a singing Henry Higgins, telling the *My Fair Lady* creators, "I hadn't the time and didn't want to and that it was the most asinine thing I ever heard of." During the same period, Lerner and Loewe tried to bring Deanna Durbin out of retirement to play Eliza Doolittle but were similarly rebuffed. (Had the Milland-Durbin teaming taken place, it would have meant a *Three Smart Girls* reunion two decades in the making.) Ultimately, Rex Harrison and Julie Andrews played the respective parts in the Tony Award–winning 1956 classic, with Harrison erasing the collective memories of his own extramarital scandals. Milland ended up in a 1960's touring company revival, obviously no longer thinking that musicalizing Shaw was such a mistake after all.

Undaunted by his bad press, Milland braved live television as the mystery guest on the game show *What's My Line?*, broadcast on Halloween night, 1954. Without any particular project to promote, his appearance turned out to be very brief, and he earned a mere $500, the standard payment for mystery guests. Following a cordial round of applause as he signed his name on a blackboard before sitting down, Milland tried to fool the blind-folded panel by speaking in Spanish, but he didn't get any further than the first of the four panelists, Fred Allen. The acerbic Allen identified Milland after only a few questions, and the dignified actor looked almost embarrassed when his sitcom was mentioned. After the other regulars, Dorothy Kilgallen, Arlene Francis, and Bennett Cerf, doffed their blindfolds, the banter offhandedly referenced *The Lost Weekend* and *Dial M for Murder*. Milland then rose up, shook hands with everyone, and left the stage.

Around the same time as his TV guest shot, Milland tried one other way to tamp down the hullabaloo. In a 1954 essay titled "The World Is My Mistress" for *Screenland*, a movie magazine, Milland rhapsodized philosophically:

> Like you and you—like everyone, I, too, have searched for something most of my life. Today I have found it. Today I am a peaceful man. I even like my *kind* of self better than I have ever liked myself before. Why? Because I am no longer afraid of the world. People who were born sensitive and shy will especially understand this admission. I have learned how to live with myself. Therein lies [my] salvation. I'm afraid each individual has to seek out his own solution. We are what we are *because*—People think and feel because of luck, fate, background, breeding, environment. There is still a reason why each of us fits into his own particular pattern. And because of this reason, we are loved or loathed. . . . Nostalgia can be the most harrowing experience of all.

In seeming contradiction to his *Screenland* article sentiments, at some point after *Dial M*'s release, Milland apparently instigated an abusive incident, far worse than any aspect of the Grace Kelly affair. Though it did not receive any coverage in the 1950s, the story was cited by Ned Wynn in Wynn's 1990 autobiography, *We Will Always Live in Beverly Hills*. It involved both Ray and Danny Milland, but by 1990, both had died and could not respond to or refute any part of the allegations. If Wynn's recollections were accurate, it represented a black mark on Ray Milland's character—one that could partly explain the problems his son would have as he grew older.

According to Wynn, the son of Keenan Wynn and Eve Abbott, Danny Milland was a friend and contemporary. Sometime during the midfifties, when both were teenagers, Ned Wynn witnessed Ray assault Danny:

> One day at Danny Milland's house, his father, Ray Milland, had burst into the room and started smacking Danny around for no apparent reason. Danny was very big. Taller and heavier than his father, he

could doubtless have broken Ray Milland in two. He pleaded with his father to stop, apologizing for whatever his father was angry about and covering his face while Ray, with his closed fists, hit him again and again in the face and screamed at him, "You goddamn little fucker who do you think you are!" I remember clearly the sound of the older man's fists on his son's face. The thick, blunt, dead noise it made, not like a slap at all.

If one accepts Wynn's account, there is no excuse for Ray Milland's behavior, no matter what frustrations he was experiencing, including the exposure of his affair or its repercussions on his career.

Regarding Milland's career, it is a shame he didn't work with Hitchcock again. One could easily see him as the James Mason doppelgänger-villain opposing Cary Grant in *North by Northwest* (1959). Interestingly, a single source suggested a *Dial M* Milland-Hitchcock follow-up was in the works. In the 1955 edition of *The Film Show Annual*, a British publication, a large color photo of Milland was accompanied by a caption that promoted *Dial M for Murder* and ended with "Ray's next: *To Catch a Thief*." This announcement had a germ of truth to it, at least for a short while, but because of the Grace Kelly fallout, it would have been impossible for Ray Milland to costar again with Kelly. So, instead, Hitchcock's *To Catch a Thief* (1955) became the single coupling between Kelly and Cary Grant.

Hitchcock never worked with Milland on another feature film, but he did not neglect him, either. In 1958, Hitchcock hired Milland to direct one episode and star in another of his short-lived TV series, *Suspicion*. In 1963, he asked Milland to star in an episode of *The Alfred Hitchcock Hour*. Part of Hitchcock's continued interest in Milland was a recognition of his talent, but the director was also paying back a favor. One day on the set of *Dial M*, Milland introduced him to a visiting former Paramount colleague, Herbert Coleman, who almost immediately dropped everything to become Hitchcock's assistant director, creative consultant, and sometime producer for much of the remainder of the director's career.

When *Dial M for Murder* was released in 1954, the Milland-Kelly affair had been over for many months, but the residue of the gossip hurt Milland's future much more than Kelly's. Whereas she had a string of successes in 1954, including *The Country Girl*, for which she won a Best Actress Oscar, he had no other release during the year and was only seen by audiences on his foundering sitcom.

THE RAY MILLAND SHOW

So, without any offers in the spring or summer of 1954, Milland focused on retooling *Meet Mr. McNutley*. To attract more viewers for the second season, starting in the fall, Milland renamed the series *The Ray Milland Show*. He further toned down the slapstick, changed his character from an English professor to a drama instructor, now at a coed university called Comstock, and slightly altered his character's name: McNutley became the more "dignified" McNulty.

Milland called an old Paramount friend, Harry Tugend, to get season 2 off the ground. Tugend had not only delivered a clever script for *The Lady Has Plans* in 1942, he, as a producer, had helped Milland behind the scenes through the *Golden Earrings* ordeal. Now as a coproducer of Milland's sitcom, he was responsible for hiring new writers Jules Bricken and Rick Vollaerts to create more mundane domestic situations that gradually get out of hand. Phyllis Avery was still Milland's wife, Peggy, but he had some different support, particularly Lloyd Corrigan replacing Minerva Urecal as the school dean. CBS generously kept the show at the 8:00 to 8:30 p.m. Thursday time slot, and General Electric remained the primary sponsor.

The reviews for the second season were favorable. In *Billboard*, Bob Spielman wrote, "[F]or practical purposes, Milland has stepped into a new series. . . . The change, in general, is far better, with Producer Harry Tugend giving the picture an excellent production and throwing out the slapstick in favor of material more suitable for Mr. Milland." *Broadcasting* magazine gave comparable praise: "[T]he sophistication and polish now accorded the series . . . [suits] Mr. Milland's particular brand of comedy . . . [and] the fairly easy-to-believe situations . . . are resolved with wit, charm and, surprisingly enough, sympathy."

The best change in season 2 was the more topical pop-culture nature of the humor. The very first episode, "The Professor Meets the Author" (airing September 16, 1954), found Mr. McNulty forced to produce a very bad play by a wealthy donor to the school (Hans Conreid). At one point, as the professor is dialing the phone, he turns to Peggy and mock-maniacally utters, "Dial 'B' for Blackmail!" "Sabrina Comes to Town" aired the night after the September 22 world premiere of Billy Wilder's Paramount comedy, *Sabrina*. "A Star Is Born" (on November 4) made more than one comic allusion to the very movie Milland did not land and that had recently premiered in late September. "Jury Duty" (on March 3, 1955) riffed on the live TV play *Twelve Angry Men*, which had aired in September 1954, with Ray McNulty as the one holdout against the rest of the jury—including Peggy!

But *The Ray Milland Show* did not move in the ratings. In fact, the more sophisticated approach kept viewers away. For the final episodes of season 2, Milland corralled guest stars in a last-ditch effort to keep the series alive. In "Green Thumb" (on April 14, 1955), Jack Haley played a has-been actor looking for a comeback, and in "The Molehouse Collection" (April 28, 1955), Miriam Hopkins was a famous actress donating her estate papers to the college as the faculty frets about its possibly salacious content. One of the best episodes of the season, "Christmas Story" (on December 23, 1954), was purposefully without laughs, a sensitively handled drama about an angry and embittered orphan (Beverly Washburn) who stays with the McNultys during the holidays. The acting is excellent, particularly by Washburn in a very challenging part. The former child actress wrote in 2023 that she "loved working with Ray Milland. . . . He was truly a dear man."

Yet, no matter the amount of tinkering, *The Ray Milland Show* failed to recapture the public's initial enthusiasm. Ruefully, after seventy-seven episodes, Milland and the network mutually agreed to end his venture into situation comedy. Rightly or wrongly, Hollywood and Milland himself deemed it failure.

Meanwhile, Paramount disrespected its recently departed star by rereleasing *Reap the Wild Wind* in November 1954, with both Milland and Paulette Goddard now billed below the more popular John Wayne and Susan Hayward. Milland's former studio had already made fun of his acclaimed squid encounter from the same movie by using the footage as a Bob Hope sight gag in *The Road to Bali* in 1952.

By the end of 1954, Milland understood he needed a new career course, and since he had always desired to work behind the camera, he focused his attention on an arrangement to direct for Republic Pictures, the small-scale studio. By the beginning of 1955, he had an agreement with studio head Herbert J. Yates and was preparing to shoot his first feature, a Western called *A Man Alone*.

THE GIRL IN THE RED VELVET SWING

In the spring of 1955, during production of *A Man Alone*, Milland received an offer from writer Charles Brackett, his old Paramount colleague, now a producer at Twentieth Century-Fox and president of the Academy of Motion Picture Arts and Sciences. Milland would be the top-billed lead in a prestigious production, part of a two-picture deal, though it was a film that not-so-subtly capitalized on his extramarital scandal. Basing their screenplay

A publicity photo for *The Girl in the Red Velvet Swing* (1955), with Joan Collins

on a 1953 Charles Samuels novel, Brackett and Walter Reisch wrote *The Girl in the Red Velvet Swing* as a turn-of-the-century New York period piece about the infamous affair between the distinguished but married architect Stanford White and the much younger model-turned-showgirl Evelyn Nesbit. In the course of the biopic, only loosely based on the facts, one of Nesbit's other lovers (and eventual husband), the obsessively jealous Harry Thaw, kills White.

So by accepting the part of Stanford White, Milland—consciously or not—was seeking a sort of public penance, though he must have savored the notion of edging out friendly rival Robert Montgomery during casting considerations. The American Nesbit would be played by British-born Joan Collins, then a Hollywood newcomer (replacing Marilyn Monroe, who went on suspension rather than enact another "lady of the chorus"), and Thaw would be portrayed by Farley Granger, the actor who was the original Guy in *Strangers on a Train* in 1951, the role Milland reprised on radio that same year.

Shot during the summer of 1955 and released in October, *The Girl in the Red Velvet Swing* was in color and Cinemascope, Milland's first in the widescreen format. It was directed by Richard Fleischer, who had an excellent track record at RKO helming low-budget black-and-white film noirs (particularly his breakthrough, *The Narrow Margin* [1952]). But now at a different studio, without his usual crew, and working in the relatively new aspect ratio, Fleischer was out of his depth with this unfamiliar genre.

The Girl in the Red Velvet Swing boasted a sizable budget ($1.7 million) and lavish production values but was not promising to be a classic. In fact, despite the sensational topic and the studio's p.r. hype, *The Girl* lost money, earning only $1.3 million domestically. Fleischer was partly hampered by the fact that much of the "affair" was to be depicted in a chaste, dull way with little physical contact. Unconvincingly, Nesbit is seen as a pure innocent, possibly because the real Evelyn Nesbit was still alive and had to grant permission for the project to proceed while also insisting on "supervisory" payment. The story was shown somewhat more realistically—but not any more artistically—in *Ragtime*, a 1981 Paramount release directed by Milos Forman and starring Elizabeth McGovern as Nesbit, Robert Joy as Thaw, and novelist Norman Mailer(!) as White.

In his memoirs, Farley Granger had fond memories about the movie and Ray Milland:

> I had very little to do with Ray Milland in the movie except shoot him in the face three times at point-blank range. I wish we had had some scenes together. He was a very good actor as well as very much a gentleman. I would have enjoyed the chance to work with him.... I've never seen *The Girl in the Red Velvet Swing*, so I have no idea how good or bad it is. However, up there with *Strangers on a Train*, it was one of my more enjoyable filmmaking experiences in Hollywood.... Richard Fleischer didn't deviate from his shooting schedule, and all the actors liked one another and working together.

For Milland, playing an older married man in love with a young, rising star-beauty hit close to home, but the actor, always a professional, did a superb job; he is easily the best thing about the movie, which suffers all the more after his character is murdered and, therefore, absent. The critics of the day didn't warm to the film, and Milland's melancholic, heartfelt performance has never been fully appreciated. The closest he received in 1955 to good notices came from Bosley Crowther of the *New York Times*: "Ray Milland's genteel performance of the architect-clubman White . . .

models precisely the masculine elegance and nobility to complement this [soap opera] dream."

Frankly, Milland was more concerned about the reception for *A Man Alone*, which was released less than three weeks after *The Girl in the Red Velvet Swing* in October 1955 (the same month he appeared plugging both films on NBC's *Colgate Comedy Hour*). Would his directorial debut fail or succeed? Either way, the movie's title, *A Man Alone*, was appropriate given how he was feeling about his personal and professional status at the time.

CHAPTER 9

THE COLD WAR AUTEUR (1955–1963)

IN THE 1950 ARTICLE, "RAY MILLAND HATES ACTING," MILLAND REFLECTED, "[O]ne of the reasons why I want to become a director is that I see ways of improving the movies I work in. I see the picture as a whole—not just my own part—and want to have a share in its making. I'd like to design the shots, too, and rehearse other scenes besides my own, because I know how they should be done. . . . I've never liked being an actor. I've hated it. I've always wanted to be a director. I've a feeling for the whole story, the complete picture."

There were several premature announcements throughout the early 1950s. In 1951, Milland himself told the press he wanted to adapt his short story "Room for Doubt," imagining Hitler having secretly escaped to America, as the first film he would direct. In December 1952, the *Hollywood Reporter* declared, "Ray Milland Making Debut as Director," which stated his plan to make *Stranger in Munich* in Germany in spring 1953. Apparently, Milland even went to scout locations in January 1953. Ultimately, nothing came of this thriller about the Cold War stand-off between the Western and Eastern Bloc Nations.

By 1954, Milland was more eager than ever to direct. In the mid-1950s, it had become fashionable for actors to want to get behind the camera, but the major studios were still resistant to this trend for its top stars. Thus, John Ireland and Edmond O'Brien (both with the help of codirectors) made their debuts for independent companies, and Ida Lupino already started her own in 1948.

Since Milland was no longer attached to any studio, he needed to strike a deal on his own, too. His best chance was to approach a company with less prestige than one of the majors, such as José Ferrer did with Universal-International for his directorial debut, *The Shrike*, or to go completely independent, as was the case with former costar Charles Laughton and *Night of the Hunter*, distributed by United Artists. Milland, Ferrer, and Laughton all saw their first films as director released in 1955.

Following Ferrer's example of using a smaller studio as home base, in August 1954, Milland telephoned Herbert Yates, the head of Republic Pictures, a minor-league outfit but one that occasionally backed bolder efforts, including Orson Welles's *Macbeth* (1948), John Ford's *The Quiet Man* (1952), and Nicholas Ray's *Johnny Guitar* (1954). The downside to working at Republic was that no matter what arrangement he made, Milland would never attain substantial budgets nor be surrounded by top-flight talent. Instead of Technicolor and Cinemascope, Yates could only provide the cheaper Trucolor and Naturama, respectively. There was a poison pill as well: Yates insisted Milland star in whatever he chose to direct, guaranteeing box-office appeal. In exchange, Milland secured a percentage of the profits, and at the time, he credited MCA for sealing the deal.

DIRECTED BY R. MILLAND

A Man Alone was a curious choice for a first feature since Milland's Westerns to date, though pleasing to the masses, had not been his most artistically rewarding efforts. Nonetheless, Republic had always specialized in Westerns, and *A Man Alone* turned out very well, quite a bit better than *California*, *Copper Canyon*, or *Bugles in the Afternoon*.

In an interview with *Variety* during preproduction, Milland commented on his new position: "It isn't easy for one actor to sit in judgment on another performer. . . . I wonder how many friends I'll lose before I complete the picture. One thing is certain, I'll interview at least a dozen actors for each speaking part." Unfortunately, Milland's first choice for leading lady, Joan Evans, had to turn him down due to pregnancy, but his second choice, Mary Murphy, was more than up to the challenge.

Based on Mort Briskin's original story, "The Gunman," and scripted by John Tucker Battle, *A Man Alone* began production in March 1955, first in the sand dunes near St. George, Utah, then later (in April) in Los Angeles for the interior scenes.

A Man Alone is about Wes Steele (Milland), a gunslinger traveling through the Arizona desert where he happens upon the dead passengers of a stagecoach robbery. When Wes reaches what he calls "a rotten town with a lot of rotten people in it," he plans to report the crime but ends up the chief suspect. In order to elude a posse gathering to lynch him, Wes takes refuge in a house that turns out to be the residence of the town's sheriff, Gil Corrigan (Ward Bond). Since the sheriff is bed-ridden, Wes only needs to negotiate his hiding out with the man's daughter, Nadine (Murphy). Eventually, Nadine comes around to believe in Wes's innocence, while Wes learns that the culprit behind the stagecoach massacre is the head of the mob trying to kill him—an esteemed town leader (Raymond Burr). With the help of Nadine and her father, Wes exposes the man and is at last welcomed into the town.

Other than the upbeat ending, *A Man Alone* provides an example of the cynicism that permeated the revisionist Western genre of the 1950s, starting with Anthony Mann's films starring James Stewart (e.g. *The Man from Laramie* [1955]). Milland's antihero was not a new concept, and his hunted gunslinger resembles Milland's misunderstood victim of circumstance in *The Big Clock*. Yet Steele's fundamental sang froid brutality is signaled early on when he shoots his own beloved horse after it falls down a sand trap and breaks its leg. During these early scenes, Milland as director is at his best, with special mention going to Lionel Lindon as his cinematographer. (Milland requested Lindon, who had worked on *Alias Nick Beal*, *Rhubarb*, and *Jamaica Run*.)

Milland and Lindon masterfully capture the desolate desert landscape in widescreen, particularly during the opening dust storm. Considering the more experienced Richard Fleischer's struggle with the new aspect ratio on *The Girl in the Red Velvet Swing* the same year, it is impressive that Milland commands the shape of the screen in his directorial debut (billed as *R. Milland* in the opening credits). Milland's choice to barely speak during the first thirty minutes is equally shrewd. Not only does this develop his character through actions and gestures, but it builds tension until he finally exchanges terse words with his frightened but headstrong captive (well played by Mary Murphy).

Other revisions to the genre are welcome touches, most prominently in the casting. The uber-masculine Ward Bond, a Milland friend but also a John Ford stock company member and notorious Red-baiter, is sidelined to his sickbed most of the time. Raymond Burr, known for playing villains up until his *Perry Mason* run, is disguised as a respected town big shot. Murphy, the young heroine of *The Wild One* in 1953, is far spunkier than she had been in the Brando classic. Her best moment comes when she angrily shoots at the lynch mob (including Lee Van Cleef) that approaches her house to kill Milland's injured protagonist. The choice to dye Murphy's attractive dark hair blonde marks one of the few errors on director Milland's part (a possibly inadvertent homage to—or *Vertigo*-esque hangover from—the Grace Kelly affair).

When *A Man Alone* was released in October 1955, the reviews were good enough (along with a healthy box office) to ensure Milland a deal with Yates to direct one film a year over the next four years. The *Hollywood Reporter* was particularly enthusiastic: "This is a very superior western picture with

A Man Alone (1955)

a warm and appealing love story and an element of suspense maintained in a thoroughly modern manner. . . . Milland is excellent [and] shows great promise" as a director.

Before Milland's next directing project, British producers John and James Woolf announced in April 1955 that they were about to sign the actor to play another kind of despicable character—a promoter who rapes his ward, a deaf-mute teenager, in *The Story of Esther Costello*. For unclear reasons, the film didn't get started for another year, by which point the property had changed hands several times, and Rossano Brazzi was cast as the promoter.

Lisbon would be Milland's second theatrical release as star and director, though it became a much more complicated production than *A Man Alone*.

Originally, Martin Rackin's short story had been developed by Paramount in 1953 for Joan Crawford. When Crawford rejected the script, Paramount sold the property to Republic. Yates handed it to Milland, who was initially enthusiastic about directing (again, as R. *Milland*) and producing as well (as *R. A. Milland*). A crime-adventure tale, again in Trucolor and Naturama, *Lisbon* would be Hollywood's first picture photographed entirely in Portugal. In August 1955, Milland flew to the country to scout locations.

Yet trouble occurred before the December 1955 shooting even commenced: Yates told Milland he could not cast Mary Murphy this time as his leading lady. Milland admired Murphy and thought she would be perfectly capable of playing a femme fatale, but Yates wanted a more established "name" and requested the services of Maureen O'Hara. On location, Milland was further disappointed to discover he could only rely on outmoded equipment and an untrained crew; he had to personally settle a small strike by some of the local workers; and he had enormous difficulty finding expensive-looking furniture for the film's lavish main set.

Halfway through making *Lisbon*, Milland became downright outraged when he learned that Yates had arranged the filming as a tax write-off to visit his European in-laws. (His wife, Vera Hruba Ralston, was a star at Republic.) Thus, *Lisbon* was another "runaway" production—and, thanks to Yates, one that mirrored the mercenary attitudes of the characters in its story. From then on, Milland thought of Yates as "a mean, ornery, tobacco-chewing little runt."

As with *A Man Alone*, the screenplay was furnished by John Tucker Battle; in it, *Lisbon* possesses both noirish ingredients and a passing resemblance to Howard Hawks's *To Have and Have Not* (1944) with a Cold War gloss. Milland plays Robert John Evans, a Bogart-like boat captain for hire who gets mixed up with several shady characters. His newest assignment is to rescue an American industrialist, Lloyd Merrill (Percy Marmont), caught behind the Iron Curtain. Merrill's wife, Sylvia (O'Hara), pays a huge sum to the wealthy, mysterious Aristides Mavros (Claude Rains), who enlists Robert's services, but both have ulterior motives: Sylvia hopes her husband will not survive his return so that she can inherit his fortune, while Aristides plans to have Robert killed so he will not have to pay his fee. To assure the latter, Aristides sends his assistant, Serafim (Francis Lederer), to join Robert on the boat ride into enemy territory. But Robert figures out the subterfuge, kills Serafim, and returns Sylvia's husband to her unharmed (much to her displeasure!). The police then arrest Aristides, and Robert asks Maria (Yvonne Furneaux), Aristides's young secretary, to join him on future adventures.

Despite its promising elements, *Lisbon* turned out to be only mildly entertaining. Portugal is an attractive setting as recorded by cinematographer Jack Marta, though we rarely see vivid or expressionistic shots. The best and most mordant one comes early, when Claude Rains's villain exhibits his ruthlessness by attracting humming birds to his window in order to smash them with a tennis racket and serve them to his cat for breakfast. Otherwise, Milland seems tired as our antihero and, as director, he gives little to either O'Hara or Furneaux to do, other than wear some beautiful clothes. At least O'Hara enjoyed herself and later wrote, "I got to play the villain, and Bette Davis was right—bitches *are* fun to play."

Milland worked overtime selling his latest movie. He purchased the Portuguese song, "Lisbon Antigua," with the hope it would become a hit, which it did prior to the August 1956 release. In the film, it is performed by Anita

Guerreiro in a Fado café. Milland also narrated the trailer and eagerly spoke to the press about *Lisbon*.

But for all Milland's efforts, reviewers were indifferent about his sophomore outing. The *Hollywood Reporter* was typical: "[I]ts story of international intrigue ... never quite gets off the ground dramatically and does not generate nearly enough of the interest that such a story merits." Many years later, the *Boston Globe*'s Jay Carr was somewhat more benevolent: "Milland is amiable, and *Lisbon* is more travelogue than thriller, but it's a diverting example of '50s kitsch that reaches its apogee when Rains' sadism is established in the opening shot."

Lisbon was not a success. It was becoming clear that the Milland-Yates relationship was already fraying and that Milland's deal with Republic was not destined to last. Before *Lisbon*'s August premiere, the studio announced Milland's next project would be *Stockade*, a Civil War story about a Union soldier captured by the Confederate army, and one of movie's new faces was to be sixteen-year-old Danny Milland. Robert Blees and Franklin Coen wrote the screenplay, but the drama was never made. Too many financial losses forced Yates to cease all productions in 1958, by which time his contract with Ray Milland was prematurely terminated.

Milland had no choice but to return to acting for hire. In early 1956, he appeared in an episode of *Screen Directors Playhouse* for Hal Roach Studios, sponsored by Eastman Kodak. NBC's selling angle for the series was as much about showcasing the work of major Hollywood directors as it was the stars of the half-hour shows. John Ford, Frank Borzage, Ida Lupino, Leo McCarey, and other well-known auteurs contributed episodes, yet the series only lasted one season.

Fred Zinnemann's "Markheim," which aired in April 1956, was Milland's first television production since the demise of his sitcom. For Roach, Zinnemann was a real catch and one of the most in-demand directors during the 1950s, following his Best Director Oscar for *From Here to Eternity* in 1953. Truthfully, Zinnemann was not the greatest stylist, but "Markheim" brought out something different than his usual literal approach, turning much of the show into one of the best of the series.

"Markheim" was based on an 1884 short story by Robert Louis Stevenson, the same coauthor of Milland's 1937 epic, *Ebb Tide*, but a tale closer in spirit to the horror genre toward which Milland was already leaning. In fact, during Milland's voice-over introduction, he mentions that "Markheim" bears a resemblance to "The Strange Case of Dr. Jekyll and Mr. Hyde," which Louis Stevenson wrote one year later (in 1885).

Set in the mid-1880s, the simple yet creepy fable was scripted by John McGreevey and Paul Osborn, the latter having worked on the 1941 MGM version of *Dr. Jekyll and Mr. Hyde*. It involves a man named Markheim (Milland) who, when caught stealing from a London gift shop on Christmas Day, stabs the proprietor to death. Then, just as Markheim finds the keys to open the shop safe, a stranger (Rod Steiger) appears and starts questioning him. Their tense exchange continues until Markheim decides to surrender to the authorities.

The first half of "Markheim" is truly a brilliant set piece—like Camus' *The Stranger* in miniature. Milland is at his finest here as a man whose outward air of elegance masks his criminal and homicidal tendencies. What follows after the murder is an visual tour de force on the part of Zinnemann, inspired by Louis Stevenson's poetic descriptions. The collage of ticking shop clocks that haunt Markheim, shot at canted angles, becomes an expansive version of the opening asylum scene in Lang's *Ministry of Fear*. As in *So Evil My Love* and *Dial M for Murder*, Milland transforms his unsympathetic character into one that is complex yet comprehensible. This is especially the case as he is badgered by the stranger, whom we eventually gather is Markheim's own conscience in human form.

Sadly, it is during this second half when the interplay between the two characters bogs down into a talky debate, leading to a moralistic conclusion that might have come straight out of the Crime Does Not Pay series of shorts MGM produced in the 1930s and '40s, some of which were directed by the then up-and-coming Zinnemann. Rod Steiger tones down his usual histrionics but is a jarring, much-too-modern choice as Milland's antagonistic doppelgänger.

Milland was eager to return to directing, even if for television, so Ronald Reagan came to the rescue. *General Electric Theater*, airing on CBS and hosted by Reagan, presented an opportunity in early 1956, with the first of six episodes he would oversee through 1958. Shot at Revue Studios, the TV division of Republic Studios, "That's the Man!" started things off, airing in April 1956. The story by Melville Davisson Post concerned an innocent man (Milland) and the trouble he finds after picking up the wrong purse at a party. Richard Collins's script didn't develop the idea enough, but Milland was happy to return to the director's chair and to costar again with Nancy Davis Reagan.

In the late summer of 1956, Milland got a chance to direct a half-hour show for *Ford Television Theatre*, airing on ABC: "Catch at Straws" featured Milland in a role similar to the one in his upcoming theatrical release, *Three Brave Men*.

"Catch at Straws" casts Milland as a district attorney defending a Korean War hero and POW (Kerwin Mathews) who has been accused of treason. In the style of a truncated *Perry Mason* episode, Milland's attorney investigates the matter, interviewing the man's parents, old friends, and girlfriend (Virginia Gibson). The conclusion is predictable.

Like the forthcoming *Three Brave Men*, "Catch at Straws" concerns itself with the unfair treatment of service members and the use of the justice system to remedy the problem. Milland's direction is prosaic, yet the *Hollywood Reporter* thought the teleplay "absorbing" and that "Milland doubled in brass nicely as the star and director."

ACTOR FOR HIRE

Milland followed *Lisbon* and his three TV stints with the second picture of his Twentieth Century-Fox pact—purely as an actor. Based on a true story, *Three Brave Men* held some promise as a pop-cultural corrective to the blacklist and a critique of antisemitism, a daring idea that engrossed Milland. In fact, his very last *Lux Radio* program had been *Gentleman's Agreement*, which aired in March 1955, with Milland in the role of a magazine writer who experiences prejudice by pretending to be Jewish. (In 1947, Gregory Peck starred in the film version.) Contrarily, the results of *Three Brave Men* were highly compromised and not very brave.

Starting with good intentions, producer Herbert Bayard Swope and writer-director Philip Dunne became interested in the story of Abraham Chasanow following a series of 1955 Pulitzer Prize-winning articles by Anthony Lewis in the *Washington Daily News*. Chasanow, a Jewish Maryland resident, had been wrongly discharged as an employee of the US Navy in 1953 when he was accused of being a security threat because of supposed past Communist ties. A court trial ensued, and Chasanow was cleared and reinstated.

Dunne and Bayard Swope announced their production in March 1956 as *The Chasanow Story*, but after many script rewrites, it was changed to *Three Brave Men*. Now the name of the central character would be Bernard "Bernie" Goldsmith, and the new screenplay gratuitously saluted the armed forces by adding the assistant secretary of the navy, along with Goldsmith and his lawyer, as one of the "three brave men"—for allowing Goldsmith to be cleared of the Communist charge.

In exchange for cooperation by the navy, Dunne was forced to shift his emphasis to widespread, erroneous gossip as the primary reason behind Goldman's plight and to add dialogue to the trial scenes in order to soften the navy's approach to interrogating Goldsmith.

From the beginning, Swope and Dunne wanted Ernest Borgnine, an Italian American fresh off his Oscar win for *Marty* (1955), to play Goldsmith, a Jewish American. Initially, they sought Alan Ladd to play his lawyer, but Ladd was unavailable, leaving Ray Milland free to play defense attorney Joe DiMarco. With a moderate budget of $1 million, production took place on the Fox soundstages in September and October 1956, and the finished film was released in December. Given the changes along the way, Milland was not pleased with the results.

What is most ineffectual about *Three Brave Men* is the way it reaffirms and upholds the demonization of Communism during this era. That antisemitism is shown to exist at all is as brave as *Three Brave Men* gets. According to historian Lester D. Friedman, the movie at least "shows how extremism in the defense of patriotism is indeed a vice." For Ray Milland, his advocate is emotionally cooler than his army prosecutor in *Sealed Verdict*, and, in a complete change, there is no background to his private life, let alone love interest.

The critics pounced on the weaknesses of *Three Brave Men*. In the *New York Times*, Bosley Crowther observed, "[I]n this plainly pussyfooting picture ... the obvious point of the real-life drama is avoided and an imaginary target is devised." Milland, who walks through his part, escaped the barbs but only because he was barely mentioned at all in most of the reviews, top billing notwithstanding.

At this stage, the Millands were less social than they had been in prior decades, but they still attended functions when it involved friends. In the case of John Wayne, the rift that occurred in the early 1940s was fully healed by the time Wayne invited Ray and Mal to his daughter Toni's wedding to Donald La Cava in October 1956.

With his Republic deal practically kaput, Milland continued on the big screen with a couple of releases, both directed by others. The first and far more interesting of the two was *The River's Edge*, premiering in April 1957. Twentieth Century-Fox distributed this return to the Western, a modern-day one, with Milland playing a seductive psychopath!

The River's Edge, completed between early November to mid-December 1956, was one of the last films directed by Allan Dwan, a veteran who started in 1913. Just before *The River's Edge*, Dwan made the cult film noir *Slightly Scarlet* (1956), and both were independently produced by the adventurous Benedict Bogeaus.

Like *Slightly Scarlet*, *The River's Edge* is in color but noir-inflected; even today it remains underrated and a very early example of an "Acid Western." Harold Jacob Smith and James Leicester's screenplay incorporates the kind of tension and paranoia common in Cold War Westerns.

The River's Edge centers around a thief, Nardo Denning (Milland), who comes to New Mexico to beguile his former girlfriend, Meg (Debra Paget), an ex-con trying to make a new life for herself with her rancher husband, Ben (Anthony Quinn). Denning seeks to find safe harbor in Mexico with a stolen million-dollar bounty he carries in a bag. He cajoles the bored Meg and forces Ben at gunpoint to be his guides as the three travel over the Mexican border. Once Meg realizes Denning is a ruthless killer, she switches her allegiance back to Ben. The three attempt to survive the rest of the trip, despite the injuries they suffer and the nagging threat that any one of them might kill or be killed.

The denouement is an elaborate rewrite of the ironic endings of two noir classics, *Too Late for Tears* (1949) and *The Killing* (1955), both with innumerable dollar bills haphazardly flung all over their unlucky protagonists. The difference in *The River's Edge* is that in widescreen and garish color, the spectacle of capitalism's most tangible symbol tossed to the wind signifies an extraordinary visual moment, capped by Nardo Denning's literal and figurative fall from grace, assuming he ever had any grace.

Similar to Milland's direction of *A Man Alone*, Dwan and cinematographer Harold Lipstein adopt Cinemascope not to convey vistas but to show the characters alone and isolated in wide shots. Thus, the noir element of alienation is powerful and omnipresent. In keeping with the genre, there is also irony in the choice of music, such as when Denning seduces Meg while the romantic World War II song, "You'll Never Know (How Much I Love You)," plays in the background.

Best of all are the performances. In an interview, Paget credited Dwan with transforming her from kittenish ingenue to tough, sullen leading lady: "[He was] a very good director . . . a very nice man, very kind, very knowledgeable . . . [but] he wouldn't let any of the actresses wear earrings! I always thought that so odd . . . It was something about how it distracted from when they did those big close-ups." Anthony Quinn underplays his scenes, which makes a huge difference from the kind of overwrought work Quinn was lauded for in the 1950s.

Milland is particularly mesmerizing in *The River's Edge*. As a seemingly laid-back charmer in light-colored suits, Denning initially masks his greedy, deranged nature—the ultimate homme fatale. His cold-blooded killings are startling for their directness and all the more "modern" by the presence of visible blood—something the Production Code was still frowning upon in the late 1950s. Happily for his fans, Milland looked handsomer and more youthful than he had in his last several films, easily making the younger Meg's renewed attraction to him understandable. Debra Paget remembered herself as "very shy" (too shy to mention to Milland her family's ancestral connection to British royalty) and Milland as "very polite, very reserved but very nice and gentlemanly." (Paget also recalled this first of several movies she made in Mexico as "a wonderful" experience, taking her mother along as a chaperone.)

The River's Edge has a few flaws, such as Debra Paget's makeup being too perfect for all the physical and mental *sturm und drang* Meg endures; also, the title song by Bobby Troup and Louis Forbes is quite laughable.

Still, critics of the day were overly dismissive. From *Variety*: "Mild rating for the melodramatics comes from deliberate pacing and not too credible plotting. Story is grim and the violence bloodthirsty." The *New York Times* reviewer was blunter, calling the "threadbare, unconvincing little melodrama . . . junk."

Some critics in recent years have rediscovered *The River's Edge*, including Dave Kehr, making up for the original trashing by the *New York Times*: [It is] "very hip. . . . Dwan has discovered a sort of alienating abstraction that at times suggests Michelangelo Antonioni." Richard Brody, in a 2012 *New Yorker* piece, concurred: "Director Allan Dwan fills the sunbaked landscape with an acrid haze of moods and a suffocating tangle of emotions, which he conjures with sharp, stark images of stifled frenzy . . . [I]n a few slashing brushstrokes, Dwan captures the ecstatic horror of life on the edge."

Despite the indifferent 1957 reception, producer Benedict Bogeaus was so pleased with *The River's Edge* that he wanted to enlist Milland in a follow-up, *White Shadows of the South Seas*, a modified *Love Is a Many-Splendored Thing* (1955). The color and CinemaScope interracial love story would have costarred Shirley Yamaguchi, but the production never happened.

Before starting his next feature, Milland found time to direct two more episodes for *General Electric Theater*. First came "Never Turn Back," airing January 1957, about two shoplifters (Milland and Eleanore Tanin) who are attracted to one another during their first heist together. Milland's return to a "thief" role, complicated by a romantic entanglement, offered a worthy dramatic vehicle for actor Milland, nicely handled by director Milland, and a companion piece to *The River's Edge*. Around the same time, he considered returning to serial television with a half-hour comedy-drama called *The Congressman*, to be produced for ABC, which was announced in February 1957 but went nowhere.

Still early in the year, Milland starred in and directed "The Girl in the Grass" for *Schlitz Playhouse*, airing March 1957, on CBS. Though the story came from Margery Sharp and was adapted by Dwight Taylor (the screenwriter of Milland's *Something to Live For*), by this late date, Milland seemed to be picking at the Grace Kelly scandal scab by playing a husband who feels neglected by his wife (Fay Baker) and begins a flirtation with a young woman in a park (Carolyn Jones).

Milland shot in early spring the *General Electric Theater* show, "Angel of Wrath," airing in May 1957, with Milland as a Broadway star who is alarmed to find out his investment in a publishing firm is supporting a scandal sheet. His argument with the publisher turns into a fight, which ends in the publisher's death. As director, Milland is well assisted by cinematographer John L. Russell of *Alfred Hitchcock Presents*, who would work with Milland again on his 1959 detective show, *Markham*, just before photographing *Psycho* in 1960.

Milland then accepted an offer from England to appear in the feature, *High Flight*, the flip side of the coin to *The River's Edge*, both in story and tone. Whereas *The River's Edge* explored pessimistic themes in a current-day Western landscape, *High Flight* paid tribute to the Royal Air Force through purely romanticized imperialism.

For Milland, *High Flight* represented a nostalgic throwback to his air force trilogy, *Wings over Honolulu*, *Men with Wings*, and *I Wanted Wings*. In what seems like a remake of the last of these three, Milland is the tough, disliked commander Brian Donlevy essayed in 1941, with a batch of fresh faces filling in for Milland, William Holden, and Wayne Morris. Apart from revisiting the genre, Milland felt gratified assuming on-screen the flight instructor position he had occupied in real life during World War II.

The biggest differences from *I Wanted Wings* are obvious: the story is set in postwar England, romantic interests are minimized, and unfortunately, the craftsmanship compares poorly, though it does have the benefit of color and Cinemascope during the flying sequences.

Coproducers Albert R. Broccoli (later of James Bond fame) and Irving Allen knew that the *High Flight* subject matter would be a profit maker and that Milland still had a following in England. The film was shot—from early April to mid-June of 1957—at RAF Cranwell in Lincolnshire and RAF Leuchars in Fife, Scotland. Oddly, only UK audiences saw the film in color, presumably to save costs in duplicating prints for the US market.

John Gilling, later an expert in horror and sci-fi (e.g. *The Night Caller* [1965]), was assigned to *High Flight*, yet a full forty minutes of the eighty-nine-minute running time are devoted to flying scenes, the best parts of the movie, and much of this footage was culled from the 1956 Farnborough Airshow, which had nothing to do with Gilling.

In the story by Ken Hughes, Joseph Landon, and Gilling himself, Milland's Wing Commander Rudge trains the new cadets, including the privileged and temperamental Tony Winchester (Kenneth Haigh). Matters boil to the surface when Winchester accuses Rudge of having been responsible for his father's death years earlier during a World War II flight exercise. Eventually, through hard work and a display of bravery on a flight near East Germany, Tony earns the respect of Rudge, and they achieve a rapprochement.

Milland is more than adequate as a strict mentor with a heart. His past "indiscretion" is not fully explained, but it obviously haunts him. What weakens *High Flight* is that the tale of the cadets is often interrupted by forced comic interludes, such as when Tony's friend (Anthony Newley) builds a flying saucer, or drone prototype, that goes haywire and invades the home of the airbase's bishop during a tea party.

Most reviews relayed mild approval, such as *Variety*'s rundown: "[It is a] surprisingly gentle and uneventful affair. . . . Milland gives a highly competent and authoritative performance."

In the midst of the *High Flight* production, Milland's MCA agents sent out a press release stating he would be returning to the London stage for the first time since 1930. The May 1957 announcement promised Milland would come back in the fall (coinciding with *High Flight*'s release) to star in James M. Barrie's *The Admirable Crichton*, the play on which his 1934 *We're Not Dressing* was based. Whether or not this idea was in serious consideration, Milland never did the show, preferring to continue directing instead.

THE SAFECRACKER AND THE GE SHOWS

Wanting to return to moviemaking but no longer associated with Republic, Milland sought out another company. He found a temporary home at MGM's British studios in Borehamwood for *The Safecracker*, but as usual he was asked to star in the film in exchange for getting the opportunity to direct. Helping with the new project was David E. Rose, the coproducer of *Circle of Danger*, using the independent Coronado Productions banner that had been started in 1950.

With renewed excitement over directing a feature again, Milland stayed in England after *High Flight* wrapped in June 1957, securing permission from RAF Abingdon to use the flyers' training tower for a scene in his new movie. Before the shoot started, he took a short trip to Wales to see his family, and it ended up the last time he saw his father alive. Milland then worked with his mostly British cast and crew on a tight budget ($471,000), impressively completing the whole production two days early under an already short schedule. The only mishap occurred when he hurt his back dropping from the training tower during an action scene.

The Safecracker (1958) lobby card, with Jeanette Sterke

Based on the true account of a British safecracker who spied on the Germans during World War II, the original title, *The Tale of Willie Gordon*, was wisely changed to *The Safecracker*. Bruce Thomas and Rhys Davies, the lauded Welsh author, provided the dramatized story, and Paul Monash wrote the screenplay.

Working in widescreen but in black and white, Milland directs with more authority than ever while also giving a multilayered performance. He plays a safecracker who has been sentenced to ten years in prison but allowed an early parole if he promises to use his skills as part of a secret mission for the Allied cause. The part is perfect for Milland to be both a devious criminal and a reluctant recruit. His mission in occupied Belgium is about survival, not patriotism—that is, eliminating the eight years left on his sentence if he comes through. This leads the downbeat drama to an extended serio-comic sequence where Milland (at age fifty) endures the rigors of basic training alongside men half his age. Milland's tired, forlorn facial expressions say it all, enabling his character to become endearing to the viewer.

For these all-too-human reasons and because Milland's Colley Dawson lives with his elderly mother (Barbara Everest), then later falls for a Dutch underground fighter (Jeanette Sterke), we slowly come around to rooting for this otherwise selfish criminal. During the tense climax, Dawson slips into a German chateau to steal from a safe a top-secret list of Axis spies working in England. His subsequent demise is indeed both unexpected and tragic: he stays too long in the mansion in order to pick up one more valuable trinket he sees on a shelf, at which point he is shot to death.

The Safecracker found favor with some critics, including Margaret Hinxman in *Picturegoer Parade*, who wrote, "[D]irector-actor Milland has produced a rare and diverting piece of entertainment for the screen ... [T]here's a pearl of a performance by Jeannette Sterke ... [B]est of all Milland has given himself a wryly human role that puts him back in the top rank of actors."

Jeanette Michell (formerly Jeanette Sterke) remembered that "the film was made with no problems," and Milland as a director and fellow actor was "kind and charming."

The Safecracker eked out a small profit for MGM but was not well marketed by the studio. Needing special handling, it was dumped onto the bottom half of a double bill in the United States with *Underwater Warrior*, conjoined by the silly tag line, "Undersea Perils and Undercover Thrills!" The accompanying poster art, a cartoon drawing of Milland opening a safe, suggested the movie was more of a comedy than a wartime thriller. When David E. Rose announced that he and Milland would follow-up *The Safecracker*, nothing came of it.

In the midst of praising the film and Ray Milland, the *Hollywood Reporter's* review somewhat brutally explained *The Safecracker's* minimal impact: "[I]t has only Ray Milland's name to sell it and as such it may not prove a strong attraction." At least Milland could relish the fact he made a very good movie.

In recent years, more writers have reassessed *The Safecracker*: in 2002, historian David Thomson called it "brilliant," and in 2022, *Films of the Golden Age* editor Bob King remarked, "In *The Safecracker* (1958), Ray Milland has become a criminal because the exquisitely beautiful things he loves are always separated from him by barriers designed to defeat him. Milland plays his middle-aged thief as someone still held in thrall, despite the fact that over the years he has become wary and tired. It is Milland's magic as an actor that makes this sad little film something that can be watched with pleasure."

Returning to the United States, Milland worked on the first of two *GE* shows he directed without a required appearance (the second show came in late 1958). Tallulah Bankhead was the star of "Eyes of a Stranger," filmed in the fall and aired on December 8, 1957. Jameson Brewer's original story opens with a socialite (Bankhead) in denial about going blind and sparring with the doctor (Richard Denning) determined to help her. Though the first half seems like a *Reader's Digest* version of *Dark Victory* (1939), the second half, including the eye-replacement surgery and twist ending, previews a horror premise more fully explored in later films, like *The Eye* (*Gin gwai* [2002]), not to mention Milland's own *X: The Man with the X-Ray Eyes* (1963).

While putting together the *GE* shows all year, Milland started thinking about producing, directing, and starring in a new TV series in 1957. He announced *No Holds Barred* in October as "dealing with controversial subjects currently considered taboo on tv," but the show was not picked up by any of the networks. Around the same time, all three TV networks were starting to regularly air old Hollywood movies in prime time. This proved to be both a blessing and a curse for Ray Milland. He was suddenly getting much more attention for his earlier work, but he was also competing against his younger self whenever he appeared in anything new.

The Safecracker's weak marketing campaign and box-office returns were further signs that his professional future was uncertain. With motion-picture offers starting to fade, Milland turned more than ever to television. Following *The Safecracker* in 1958, it would be another four years before Milland appeared in a theatrical release and another twelve before he was back at a major studio. Needing to get away, he and Mal went to Cannes for a short holiday in early 1958.

Soon after *The Safecracker*'s unceremonious premiere, Milland was hired by Alfred Hitchcock to work on two episodes of *Suspicion*, Hitchcock's hour-long NBC anthology series. Milland agreed to act in one show and direct another, both shot in spring and aired in June 1958. First, Leigh Brackett's novel, *An Eye for an Eye*, retitled "Eye for Eye," would lead to a fully realized TV series produced by and starring Milland as a private detective named Markham.

In this unofficial *Markham* pilot, directed by Jules Bricken, Markham becomes embroiled in a domestic situation when a friend (MacDonald Carey) asks him to help rescue his kidnapped wife. Cinematographer Ray Rennahan is most responsible for the TV noir look of "Eye for Eye," which is surprising given that all his past associations with Milland were on Technicolor features (*Ebb Tide*, *Her Jungle Love*, *Lady in the Dark*, *California*). The Markham character was clearly written with Milland in mind, as scenarists Jameson Brewer and John Kneubuhl embedded dialogue that exemplify his increasingly remote screen persona.

Strictly as a director, Milland joined forces again with Rennahan for "Death Watch," the second *Suspicion* show, an excellent, tightly plotted *policier* from the sibling writing team of John and Ward Hawkins. Milland steadily builds tension in the story of a home tutor (Janice Rule) who is the only eyewitness to a mob execution and must be given round-the-clock police protection before she testifies at trial.

"Death Watch" resembles the storyline in Phil Karson's feature *Tight Spot* (1955) and demonstrates how adroit Milland could be as a director when *not* appearing before the camera. Most notably, he draws excellent performances from his cast, especially Rule and Edmond O'Brien as the lead detective.

With less enthusiasm, Milland directed the *GE Theater* episode "The World's Greatest Quarterback," which aired in October 1958. In the teleplay by Thomas Nord Riley, Ernie Kovacs plays a former football hero who returns to his hometown, hiding the fact he is now a broke used-car salesman. He and his estranged wife, a bank president (Audrey Totter), battle over whether to sell a Picasso painting in their joint possession.

While Milland did not like to direct and act at the same time, he would have been far preferable to the miscast Kovacs playing the down-and-out ex-partner, who is also an ex-drinker (paging *The Lost Weekend*) and an ex-athlete trying to get money through his wife (paging *Dial M for Murder*). Milland's friend and *Alias Nick Beal* costar, Totter, does her best to leaven the sentiment of the piece. .

Milland's final *GE Theater* entry was much better: "Battle for a Soul," which aired in November 1958. This time Milland is a man imprisoned for stealing jewels who insists he never committed the crime. His plan to avenge those who betrayed him (including a character played by his 1940 *Irene* costar, Alan Marshal) is quintessential Milland material. Lionel Lindon again photographed and Elmer Bernstein provided the score.

At the beginning of August 1958, shortly after completing his latest *GE* show, Milland was hit with profoundly sad news: his sister, Beryl, now Beryl Akehurst, called to tell him their father had died (at the age of eighty-two). The Milland family traveled to Beryl's home in Horsham, where Alfred Jones had been living in his final days. The Millands reunited with Ray's many relatives for the funeral, stayed a week, then returned to California. Subsequently, Danny Milland interrupted his burgeoning acting career with military service. His joining the Army continued the family tradition established by his now late grandfather.

After a period of deep mourning, Ray Milland tried to keep busy both behind and in front of the TV cameras. First, during the fall, he directed and starred in an episode of *Alcoa-Goodyear Theatre* for a February 1959 airing on NBC. "A London Affair" finds Milland as Binyon, a gentleman on a trip to London who becomes strangely attracted to a mysterious pickpocket (Gia

Scala). The unexpected conclusion is touching and tragic, a skillful blend of mystery, romance, and despair, no doubt infused by Milland's tremendous feeling of loss.

In early 1959, Ray Milland seriously considered retirement. He was more disillusioned than ever about Hollywood and his place in it. He also knew that—if necessary—he could afford to quit the business, given his fair amount of savings, fine art investments, and the residuals he was earning from his sitcom reruns. For a few months, he puttered about until he was urged by his new MCA agent, Gene Corman, into producing and starring in a new TV series. As Milland put it later, "I was thinking about retiring and did, for six months. All my wife could think of was how to get me back to work. I'm a nervous guy and I've got to keep myself occupied."

MARKHAM

Milland jumped back into the TV-series game by producing and starring in *Markham*. Strikingly different from *The Ray Milland Show*, *Markham* was the brainchild of Leigh Brackett, author of the detective novel that had launched things a year earlier with the stand-alone *Suspicion* episode. To help, Milland hired Warren Duff, best known for producing the 1947 film noir classic *Out of the Past* (whose main character happened to be named Markham!), and Joseph Sistrom, an executive he knew from his Paramount days. Apart from some actual location shooting in New York, *Markham* was mostly photographed in Hollywood at Revue Studios, the same soundstages for *Alfred Hitchcock Presents*.

Markham is definitive TV noir, an edgier variation on *Perry Mason*. Not only is the protagonist a jaded lawyer turned private eye, the Markham character's voice-over narration is straight out of classic pulp fiction. The black-and-white cinematography takes advantage of the various exotic locales, but Markham's headquarters is glamorous Sutton Place within gritty Manhattan, and nearly all the episodes contain at least a few scenes set in darkly-lit rooms. Most of all, Milland's mere presence lends a film noir ambiance.

Milland could not have asked for a better time slot from CBS: the show aired immediately after *Gunsmoke* on Saturday nights. Yet, for various reasons, *Markham* didn't catch on. By the second season, it was moved to Thursday night at 9:30 p.m. (EST). Altogether, fifty-nine episodes were shot and aired.

The premiere episode, "A Princely Sum," debuted on May 2, 1959, and, as promised in the publicity, the story took the viewer from Cairo to Washington, where our detective hero is investigating a friend's death. Artistically,

Markham (1959)

this was an average episode, directed by Richard Bartlett, perhaps not the best one to kick off a new show. *Variety* called the premiere "mediocre," saying that "the first script, as an intro to the series, gave the viewer little to look forward to."

For later episodes, Milland brought in his directors and other colleagues from his feature film days. "The Father" benefited from the direction of Robert Florey (*Hotel Imperial* [1939]), who, with Lionel Lindon, Milland's frequent cinematographer, mined the story of a father who kills his son's girlfriend for all its twisted worth. Florey and *The Big Clock*'s screenwriter, Jonathan Latimer, created the intriguing "Vendetta in Venice," with Paula Raymond in a dual role.

Florey's "Incident in Bel Air" featured Phillip Terry, who had played Don Birnam's brother in *The Lost Weekend* (1945), here cast as a police lieutenant trying to help Markham figure out which of two sexy sisters is a killer. "The Marble Face," directed by Bretaigne Windust, featured John Hoyt, the convicted Nazi in *Sealed Verdict* (1948).

It was a sound and generous idea at first to assemble old friends to comprise his cast and crew (some who needed work), but as a fatigued star and producer, Milland eventually realized he needed someone overall in charge who could better shape the stories and not shoot over budget. He called on Mitchell Leisen, who was now working exclusively in television. "We brought Mitch in on a trial basis for one show" remembered Milland later.

"[A]nd he did so well, we kept him for the rest of the season. He stayed on schedule and under budget . . . [and he] could make the tackiest sets look lavish just by the way he lit them. . . ." In fact, it was Leisen who directed one of the best episodes in the series, "A Cry from the Penthouse," during which an unknown sadist traps Markham on a freezing-cold apartment balcony.

In his position, Milland also used *Markham* to promote stars-in-the-making. In the first season, Gena Rowlands was the femme fatale in "The Altar," written by Stirling Silliphant; and future Oscar winner Louise Fletcher (*One Flew over the Cuckoo's Nest* [1975]) played a kidnapped heiress in "Strange Visitor," directed by Florey. Fletcher remembered "being excited to work with [Milland]. He was a big star in my time. . . . He was the perfect gentleman and very sweet and generous. . . . He didn't have any of the scary mannerisms of big stars one encountered back in the day. He made me feel I belonged right there where I was."

Despite *Markham*'s high points, Milland couldn't do too much about its drawbacks. The first season sponsor required an unfortunate link to *The Lost Weekend*: Milland himself hawks Schlitz beer during the commercial breaks, happily pouring a glass. In its day, this bit of product plugging must have looked inappropriately humorous or simply unseemly.

More evidently, *Markham* was competing with other detective shows, including writer-director Blake Edwards's cutting-edge *Peter Gunn* (1958–1961). Both *Markham* and *Peter Gunn* were half an hour in length, but *Markham* needed more time to develop its stories since each episode introduced entirely new characters, whereas *Peter Gunn* had a cast of regulars. The promise of exotic locations as part of the show's prepublicity was a mistake, too, since so many episodes were clearly shot on Hollywood backlots. One more style element worked against *Markham*: Juan García Esquivel's theme music was forgettable compared to Henry Mancini's iconic jazz score for *Peter Gunn*.

As a way to boost the ratings for *Markham*, Milland consented to be a panelist on *What's My Line?*, airing in November 1959 on CBS. The cross-promotional appearance enabled a plug of his series at the top of the broadcast. In dinner jacket and bow tie, Milland looked relaxed and in decent shape but was in a lowkey mood, not making a single witty remark. Rightfully, the spotlight was on the offbeat jobholders and mystery guest Harry Belafonte.

What's My Line? was a reputable gig, yet it would be hard for Milland not to notice he was getting flat fees for TV work while Cary Grant was starring in two big-screen blockbusters in December 1959, *North by Northwest* and *Operation Petticoat*. For the latter, Grant arranged to receive 75 percent of the profits from Universal Studios, amounting to a $3 million take-home haul. (In the 1940s, Milland and Grant's prominence and payments were far more commensurate.) To make matters more irritating, Grant looked much younger than his actual age of fifty-five, and Milland looked quite a bit older than his age of fifty-two. Outwardly, Milland used self-deprecation mixed with annoyance when it came to his appearance. "If you're counting my eyebrows, I can help you. There are two," he snapped at one reporter.

Meanwhile, Milland could see the writing on the wall for the series, but his spirits were lifted somewhat by a belated Hollywood honor. In early 1960, the Hollywood Walk of Fame, sponsored by the Hollywood Chamber of Commerce, chose to induct Ray Milland. This tradition, attended by his family and friends on February 8, meant two Hollywood Boulevard tiles were engraved with his name, star-shaped icons and listings of his achievements, one for motion pictures (at 1621 Vine Street) and the other for television (at 1634 Vine Street).

Before the actual cancellation of *Markham*, Milland gave a candid interview to *The Hartford Courant* in April 1960, saying he planned "to suspend his career and go back to college when the show ends." Milland added grumpily, "'I don't want to worry about looking just right any more . . . [I dislike] pulling myself up in the morning, going through makeup and standing under a hot sun or hot lights." When the show finally ended, he and Mal went to Europe, where he once again contemplated retirement. "My time is past," he said wistfully.

CROSSROADS

It was a glum period for Milland, learning of the deaths of fellow movie idols, costars, and friends (many of them suddenly and at relatively young ages)—Tyrone Power and Ronald Colman in 1958; Errol Flynn and Edmund Gwenn in 1959; Clark Gable, Ward Bond, Margaret Sullavan, and Douglas Spencer (Milland's regular stand-in) in 1960; and (later) Gary Cooper, Gail Russell, and Marion Davies in 1961.

At this point, the Millands began vacationing on the French Riviera, which became their annual sojourn for many years to come. In little time, the restlessness bug bit again. During a stay in England, Milland attempted to direct a theatrical feature on his own. He enlisted Barré Lyndon (real name: Alfred Edgar) to write the screenplay for *Shadow of a Lady*, to be independently produced by Bernard Luber and Barre Shlaes. Milland would have starred in the picture, but the deal never came together.

Later in 1960, the Millands returned to the United States, and Ray took a break from more artistic endeavors by showing off his golfing skills, albeit with a seven-hole handicap. On an episode of *Celebrity Golf*, he pitted himself against the show's host, professional Sam Sneed. The total nine-hole game at the Lakeside Country Club in North Hollywood was shot in 1960 but didn't air until April 9, 1961.

With so many plans going awry over the last several years, Milland briefly considered an ill-advised return to the sitcom genre. Milland had gotten to know Mark Goodson and Bill Todman from his *What's My Line?* appearances, and early in 1961, with backing from the Goodson-Todman Production Company, he developed a series pilot called *Count Your Chickens*, replete with a familiar *Egg and I* (or *Green Acres*) premise about an urban executive who moves his family to the country to run a farm. By 1962, Goodson and Todman started scaling back their West Coast productions and dropped *Count Your Chickens*.

Milland was given another rare opportunity to direct without acting when producer Hubbell Robinson contacted him in March 1961 to film an episode of the Boris Karloff anthology series *Thriller*, airing on NBC in April. In a sense, Milland was taking his first real plunge into the horror genre by selecting "Yours Truly, Jack the Ripper," a 1943 short story by Robert Bloch.

For *Thriller*, Barré Lyndon updated Bloch's work by having a time-and-space-traveling Jack the Ripper appear in present-day London and commit a murder. Scotland Yard detective Sir Guy Williams (John Williams) and his assistant, Dr. John Carmody (Donald Woods), are on the case.

With a short, made-for-television schedule and relatively meager budget, Milland directed the tale with as much flourish as possible. He and art director Loyd S. Papez (who had worked on *Markham*) staged many scenes in fog-enshrouded streets and back alleys, bestowing a more cinematic look than most of the other episodes in the *Thriller* series.

As usual, Milland worked well with his actors, especially John Williams, his "nemesis" from *Dial M for Murder* but here as a much more somber and perplexed inspector. Boris Karloff only introduced and closed the show. It is a credit to Milland, Lyndon, and the entire *Thriller* production that the ending was not only a jolt but one that implicitly critiqued authority figures and offered no comfort to the audience.

Dick Powell hired Milland to direct an episode of his *Dick Powell Theatre* in late 1961 titled "Open Season." It aired after Christmas day in most markets, a counterholiday programming move.

"Open Season" is an average entry in the anthology series, which rotated actors, writers, and directors. Elizabeth Wilson's story takes place in Texas, near Mexico, where Devery Shay (Dorothy Malone) plans on getting a quick divorce across the border but is hounded by both her husband (Paul

Richards) and a mobster (Thomas Gomez) to stay married so that she cannot testify against her spouse in an upcoming trial.

"Open Season" is a talkier and less intricate variation on Milland's "Death Watch," and Milland's direction is fair, not outstanding. The episode would have benefited from location shooting but the majority of the scenes take place on interior sets at Republic Studios, a depressingly familiar place for Milland. Cinematographer George E. Diskant had photographed *The Narrow Margin* and other excellent film noirs but demonstrates little of his artistry here.

Milland's lone big-screen movie of this period was a super-spectacular but one in which he was neither seen nor given screen credit. In Nicholas Ray's *King of Kings* (1961), produced by MGM, Milland plays Satan, lending only his voice for a single sequence. However, the casting of Milland had a resonance both within the film and beyond. (Milland's costar in *The Thief*, Rita Gam, appears as Herodias in this telling of Christ's story.)

Milland had already played the Devil—in human form—in *Alias Nick Beal*, a dozen years earlier. Now an unseen Satan, Milland relies entirely on his famously mellifluous voice, a clever touch on the part of Nick Ray. As an orator, Milland refuses to compete with Orson Welles, who is likewise unseen and unbilled as both the narrator and the voice of God; Welles's booming voice contrasts with Satan's deliberately seductive entreaties during Jesus's forty-day-forty-night desert fast (well enacted by Jeffrey Hunter). Milland is used too little, but his evocative vignette is a highlight of this undervalued biblical epic.

While Ray Milland was struggling to get back on the big screen, his son—recently discharged from the army—received some hopeful news. In October 1961, just as *King of Kings* premiered, a new company, Artists & Production Associates (APA), announced it signed twenty-one-year-old, six-foot-four-inch-tall Danny to a term contract. The heads of APA were among the biggest movie names of the early 1960s: Jack Lemmon, Blake Edwards, Richard Quine, and Max Arnow.

For a little while, Danny Milland's career prospects looked bright, but Ray Milland's own return to theatrical films would have to wait another year. Toward the end of 1961, he was invited by Fred Astaire and Astaire's *Alcoa Theatre* producer, Eric Ambler, the spy-thriller author, to star in "Pattern of Guilt." This TV noir episode was directed by Bernard Girard at Revue Studios, using some of the same team from *Alfred Hitchcock Presents* and *The Alfred Hitchcock Hour*. Astaire acted strictly as host.

The story and teleplay by Helen Nielsen concerns a reporter (Milland) following a detective (Myron McCormick) on a serial murder case while experiencing his own financial and marital dilemmas. The reporter is too poor to make a settlement with his ex-wife (Lucy Prentis) and wants out of his marriage to his greedy new bride (Joanna Moore). His idea is to stage the murder of his current wife and pin the blame on the serial killer.

Milland excels in this role, the Everyman caught in a perilous situation just beyond his capabilities of solving. As in *Dial M for Murder*, Milland conveys a range of emotions with seemingly little effort—his mixed feelings about his wife and ex-wife, his desperation to find an answer to his problem, and his inability to carry out the murder, followed by an impulsive desire to kill.

Just as Danny was celebrating his APA deal, Danny's friend Ned Wynn turned twenty-one, and his parents threw him an all-star birthday party. Ray and Mal Milland attended, along with some of his past costars: Lana Turner, Rosalind Russell, and Martha Raye, plus a little-known actor named Aaron Spelling. (In the 1970s and '80s, Spelling would become a high-profile TV producer and would work frequently with Ray Milland.)

THE DEEPEST CUTS

Suddenly, Milland found himself in demand again for features when independent producer-director Roger Corman bypassed casting Vincent Price for the third and latest of his popular series of Edgar Allan Poe adaptations. Corman offered the lead role in *Premature Burial* to Milland in the fall of 1961. It was Corman's thirty-fifth film in his first seven years of moviemaking, but his ingenuity was seemingly endless, as this unfairly neglected film attests.

Actually, Milland's casting was more complicated than merely Corman changing course. Corman was ready to leave his home at American International Pictures (AIP) for a newly formed production company under the Pathé banner. As he remembers, "I was planning to hire Vincent again, but AIP, aware of my intentions, locked Vincent into an exclusive contract. I went with Ray Milland [who happened to be a client of Corman's brother, Gene, through MCA], the best available actor for the part—a sophisticated, debonair native Welshman who still had a cultured trace of a 'mid-Atlantic' accent."

But in a devious move, in order to control Corman and his new Poe film, AIP's executives, Samuel Z. Arkoff and James H. Nicholson, secretly managed to buy a stake in the new Pathé production company. Corman was dismayed when—after the fact—he learned this takeover was a fait accompli; he went ahead with the production anyway, even if it meant working for his old bosses. At least Milland remained in the starring role, and Corman still made the movie he wanted.

The choice of Milland was fortuitous for both the project and Milland himself. Vincent Price provided the right declamatory technique for his debauched characters in *The House of Usher* (1960) and *The Pit and the Pendulum* (1961), but he was not nearly as well suited to play Poe's haunted antihero in *Premature Burial*. What Milland could and did bring to the role was his sense of world weariness and dread of the unknown beneath a veneer of Old-World class and privilege. These were not deeper levels Price usually projected.

As a loose adaptation of Poe's 1844 short story, screenwriters Charles Beaumont and Ray Russell dwelled on characterization over narrative, which is the main reason why *Premature Burial* has rarely received enthusiastic reviews or has been considered one of the more entertaining Poe-inspired films. Yet, as a study in psychological terror, Corman and his crew created the perfect atmosphere for Milland's portrayal.

Set in Victorian England, Poe's story concerns Sir Guy Carrell, an aristocrat who has been gripped by a fear of being buried alive ever since believing his father suffered this fate years earlier. Despite his torment, Sir Guy marries the young, beautiful Emily (Hazel Court) and brings her father (Alan Napier) to live with them in his mansion. Following the wedding, Sir Guy builds a tomb with many escape hatches in case he is ever buried alive. A concerned Emily then issues an ultimatum: either Sir Guy destroys his crypt, or she leaves him. Sir Guy tries to exorcise his fears by digging up his father's coffin, but his "therapy" backfires, making Emily believe he has had a heart attack. Sir Guy awakens to realize both she and her father have been plotting against him in order to seize his estate. He kills her and her father, after which Sir Guy is killed by his long-suffering sister (Heather Angel).

Unlike Poe's original story, which ends happily, with the unnamed protagonist recovering from his phobia, Sir Guy's death seems gratuitous and against the grain of the revenge melodrama. The ambiguity of his devoted sister killing him is not a failing of the story or the film—merely a surprise that leads to a melancholic and tragic conclusion scattered with corpses and regrets.

Corman does a skillful job of casting, with occasional nods to Milland's life and work. Hazel Court establishes Emily's love for her older husband quite convincingly—up until her unmasking. (The May-December relationship again revived the essence of the Grace Kelly affair.) Court had already costarred with Milland in a 1959 *Markham* episode, "Double Negative," and she valued working with him, later recalling, "[He] was charming. We talked a lot about poetry. Of course, his background was Welsh. So the Welsh loved poetry. And he wrote a lot of poetry, too."

Alan Napier had supported Milland two decades earlier, in both *The Uninvited* and *Ministry of Fear*, and Heather Angel's appearance (her last in any film) served as another touch of nostalgic deference. She had played the heroine to his leading man in *Bulldog Drummond Escapes* (1937), and it was Milland who recommended her to Corman.

But Corman's coup was his casting of Milland himself. Few actors could portray the deep-seated turmoil of a cataleptic better than the actor who specialized in being secretive in stories as different as *The Lost Weekend* and *Dial M for Murder*. There is something distancing as usual with Milland, but, gradually, his inner torture becomes commiserative. The actor's finest scene is a lengthy one in the crypt, where he proudly demonstrates to his new bride and their doctor friend (Richard Ney) his detailed escape plans in case he ever is buried alive. Milland's soliloquy is comparable to his twenty-three-minute scene explaining the intricate murder scheme to his hired "friend" in *Dial M for Murder*.

On a typically tight budget for a Corman film, at only $450,000, the director and production designer, Daniel Haller, created the look of a more sumptuous, big-budget feature. Only a few sets (filled with dry-ice "fog") were actually built to depict Victorian England. Corman's stylized approach was not only a cost-saving measure but appropriately expressionistic. As the director later wrote, "I felt Poe films, being psychological horror film stories, represented the unconscious mind, and I should shoot them in an artificial environment, because the unconscious mind didn't see realities."

Corman's best cinematic touches are keyed to Milland's performance, particularly during Guy's hallucinatory nightmare sequence, accompanied by a chilling version of the film's leitmotif, the nineteenth-century Irish anthem "Molly Malone." With Floyd Crosby, the Oscar-winning cinematographer (and father of musician David Crosby), Corman shoots this section with tints and filters and at distorted angles. Equally arresting, as part of Emily's attempt to scare Sir Guy, maggots are seen crawling in a poisoned cup, but these shots were cut by British censors before *Premature Burial* could be released in the United Kingdom.

The reviews of the day overlooked the film's many virtues and were not kind. *Variety* wrote, "Roger Corman seems to have run thin in imagination on this third trip to the same literary well... [with a screenplay] short on the kind of plot surprises which create suspense and interest." Milland didn't fare much better. *Monthly Film Bulletin* dismissed his work as "stolid," and John L. Scott in the *Los Angeles Times* put the nail in the coffin: "Milland gives it a good honest try, but seems a bit too sincere and heavy-handed about the ghoulish business." While it did not bring in the same grosses as the previous

Panic in Year Zero! (1962), with Mary Mitchel, Frankie Avalon, Ray Milland, and Jean Hagen

AIP Poe films, *Premature Burial* earned a respectable $1.25 million in its first three months, and for what it is worth, it won a Golden Laurel "Sleeper of the Year" Award in 1962.

After *Premature Burial*, Milland took some needed time off, but AIP lured him back to work with the promise of directing what would become his fourth feature. He was intrigued by the material, this time more overtly Cold War in theme than any of his previous directorial efforts—an end-of-the-world nuclear holocaust scenario.

The Jay Simms story was scripted by Simms and John Morton and first titled *Survival*, then *The End of the World*, before producers Samuel Arkoff and James Nicholson renamed it *Panic in Year Zero!* Milland was given a paltry budget of $225,000 and only a few weeks to shoot in black and white, starting in late February 1962. Just before production, he was quoted saying, "I play a father in the film and I quickly adopt the attitude that to survive you have to revert almost to animal instinct and cunning. . . . And by God, I really feel that way."

Milland had overall control of the production, including the casting of former costar Jean Hagen as his wife in the story (in her final film). However, Arkoff and Nicholson insisted on having vocalist Frankie Avalon play his son in order to attract a young audience.

The story begins with the Baldwin family taking a weekend trip and realizing a nuclear bomb has been dropped on Los Angeles. They continue onto a campsite, picking up ammunition and supplies along the way. At their destination, the family hides in a cave to escape the radiation, but the Baldwins' daughter (Mary Mitchel) is captured and raped by two delinquent teens at a nearby farmhouse. Father (Milland) and son (Avalon) take revenge by killing the hoodlums. A third thug attempts a surprise attack, and the son is hurt in the melee. While the Baldwins are looking for a doctor, they hear on the radio that a ceasefire has occurred between nations, and the region is now safe from nuclear warfare.

Panic in Year Zero! demonstrates how fully assured Milland had become as a director and—with the help of his crew—highly resourceful. The spare, stark images may have been a result of his bare-bones budget, but his approach thoroughly complements the cautionary dystopian theme. Apart from the nearly absurd ending, what distinguishes *Panic* from most other end-of-the-world movies is the way it suggests so much but shows so little. Milland's minute focus on one family creates a microscopic pre-Cuban Missile Crisis dynamic, allowing the viewer to imagine the bomb's impact on the wider population.

Milland was not eager having Frankie Avalon play his son, but as director he subverts our expectations by changing the image of the clean-cut singing heartthrob into one of a cold-blooded killer. In a similar vein, as he promised in preproduction interviews, Milland turns his heroic patriarch into a surly survivalist, reduced to a near-primal state.

Panic in Year Zero! was well received in its day. The *Hollywood Reporter* called it "a good, sound melodrama . . . Ray Milland's direction . . . is exceptionally good." *Box Office* called it a "timely and suspenseful 'It Could Happen Here' drama."

In early February 1962, while just starting the film, Milland promoted the movie on NBC's *Here's Hollywood* interview program. Later, in July, AIP paired *Panic in Year Zero!* with the company's multistory horror film, *Tales of Terror*, mainly to drive-in theaters, but the producers realized they had a big moneymaker in its own right and rereleased *Panic in Year Zero!* in 1965 using one of its original working titles, *The End of the World*.

Panic's surface Cold War themes and apparent endorsement of gunplay led critic Raymond Durgnat to reject Milland as a "right-wing director," but since the 1960s, the film has grown in stature. In 2005, Michael Atkinson in the *Village Voice* wrote, "This forgotten, saber-toothed 1962 AIP cheapie might be the most expressive on-the-ground nightmare of the Cold War era, providing a template not only for countless social-breakdown genre flicks (most particularly, Michael Haneke's *Time of the Wolf*) but also for authentic crisis . . . [T]he movie is nevertheless an anxious, detail-rich essay on moral collapse." Welsh novelist David Llewellyn was quoted in 2015 saying that *Panic in Year Zero!* is one of Milland's many films that "are genuine classics that have stood the test of time" and "a film that certainly needs more attention. It feels so much ahead of its time." And in 2017, N. B. Fredericton, seeing its influence on *Night of the Living Dead* (1968) and the future glut of zombie movies, called *Panic in Year Zero!*, "*The Walking Dead* of 1962."

Following the *Panic* shoot, Milland escorted his seventeen-year-old daughter, now calling herself Vicki, to the April 1962 Oscar ceremonies in Santa Monica. Afterwards, Vicki returned to New York, where she was attending Bennett College in Millbrook, studying childhood education—her mother's college major.

Things were going less well for Danny Milland, now twenty-two. He was briefly enrolled in geology courses at UCLA before dropping out, and he had not progressed very far with his acting career. Most distressingly, a mystery surrounding a missing young woman seemed to involve Danny.

After enrolling at the University of Madrid in the fall, Danny was offered a minor role in the musical-comedy feature *Escala en Hi-Fi* (a.k.a. *Scale in Hi-Fi*), to be shot close to the campus. Shortly thereafter, a disturbing article ran in the *New York Post* on November 4, 1962. The gist of it was that eighteen-year-old Leslie Ruth Jensen from Lakewood, California, told her family she was eloping with Danny Milland, first stopping in New York to get married, then traveling to Spain. But after she left the West Coast, she was never heard from again. Ray Milland confirmed to authorities he had met Danny in Los Angeles and saw him off on his flight to New York (from where he flew to Spain) but said he was alone. It appears the mystery surrounding Leslie Ruth Jensen's whereabouts has never been solved.

By early 1963, Danny was back in the United States and secured a small part on an episode of *Wagon Train*, with Suzanne Pleshette as the guest star. The *Wagon Train* episode aired in October 1963, the same month *Escala en Hi-Fi* premiered in Spain, never reaching the US. Together, they would constitute the last credits in the short acting career of Danny Milland.

Meanwhile, Ray continued with AIP and Roger Corman, starring in *X: The Man with the X-Ray Eyes*. The only problem with working with Corman was that the director had limited funds for his cast and crew, Milland included, who was paid a fraction of the amount he used to get in his Paramount heyday. To supplement his earnings, he reluctantly moonlighted as the host of syndicated *Death Valley Days* reruns. With the long-running Western TV show retitled *Trails West*, Milland continued off and on with this light emcee chore for about a year, after which Rory Calhoun took over.

X: The Man with the X-Ray Eyes was not greeted as a comeback for Ray Milland the way *Dial M for Murder* had been earlier or *Love Story* would be later. Yet, this sci-fi- horror picture looms large retrospectively in Milland's career. Somewhat like the prejudice against 3-D diminishing the prestige of *Dial M*, the exploitation gimmick of *X: The Man with the X-Ray Eyes* that enticed audiences in 1963—the teasing if unrealized promise of seeing nudity—forever branded the work disreputable no matter how hard it is to dismiss.

As only one of the many films Corman directed during this period, including the Poe adaptations, *X* (its working title) stands out as a stunningly original work. Corman himself devised the scenario about a scientist who experiments with expanding the range of human vision, tragically using himself as his test subject. Robert Dillon and Ray Russell scripted Corman's story, and the central role was conceived with Milland in mind.

Shot in three weeks in March 1963 on a budget of under $300,000, *X: The Man with the X-Ray Eyes* involves Dr. James Xavier, an ambitious research scientist who develops eye drops he believes will allow humans to see into the ultraviolet and x-ray spectrums. He experiments on himself against the warnings of friend and colleague Dr. Diane Fairfax (Diana Van der Vlis). At first, Dr. Xavier finds amazing results as he is able to see through clothing and other objects. Yet, as time passes, the doctor realizes he cannot control the degree of his visual strength, which finally allows him to see only texture and light. After he accidentally kills a fellow scientist (Harold J. Stone), Dr. Xavier goes on the lam and hides out in a Las Vegas carnival, where he performs as part of a mind-reading act. Finally, chased by the police, he leaves Vegas, driving wildly through the desert, where he happens upon a tent revival. Seeking guidance and redemption, he takes the biblical word of the evangelist literally: "If thine eye offends thee ... pluck it out!"

Working with many of the same crew members from *Premature Burial* and *Panic in Year Zero!*, Milland found himself more at home than ever with cutting-edge material. Neither hero nor villain, Milland was playing the ultimate tragic antihero, a determined, well-meaning individual whose all-consuming hamartia destroys him ("I'm closing in on the Gods," he tells a friend early on). The horrific, abrupt, and unresolved open ending, where Dr. Xavier tries too late to save himself by actually plucking his eyes out, is an allusion to the preacher's biblical passage as well as the Oedipus myth (with X evoking Rex). Ultimately, *X: The Man with the X-Ray Eyes* questions the twentieth-century secular obsession regarding science as a religion. It is hard to imagine any other actor of Milland's ilk performing such a profound, sad, and disturbing final scene.

Aesthetically, Corman augments the narrative and Milland's performance with touches both impressionistic and expressionistic, beyond *Premature Burial* or any of the director's other films. Of course, the lure for most viewers at the time, especially the younger set, was the promotional prospect of seeing through clothes, in the manner of our protagonist. Corman cheats here because of censorship rules. (We see bodies dancing at a party through the doctor's eyes, but the nudity stops short of the erogenous zones.) In any case, Corman dispenses with this humorous gambit rather quickly, highlighted by Milland's hilariously stiff attempt at the Twist, before moving onto the more frightening aspects of the story. Ultimately, Dr. Xavier's increasingly distorted vision has the visual effect of an avant garde mise-en-scène, fully realized by cinematographer Floyd Crosby in the mad-dash car-ride climax.

In other ways as well, Corman and Milland create self-reflexivity about the nature of commercial cinema's seductive appeal. Milland's wearing dark sunglasses, ostensibly for Dr. Xavier to protect his eyes and hide from the authorities, slyly comments on Ray Milland as "Movie Star," most pointedly when his character becomes the featured attraction at the carnival. Here, he is cheered and whistled at, first as a mind reader and then as a faith healer, both money-making schemes by the loathsome carnival barker (Don Rickles) who stands in for the "mogul" in Corman's entertainment industry allegory. At the end of the Vegas casino sequence, Dr. Xavier tosses his winnings at a crowd that dives for the dollar bills, a shorthand visualization of Milland's rejection of the Powers That Be he catered to most of his career as well as a reference back to the climax of *The River's Edge* and a distant echo of the anarchic automat scene from *Easy Living*.

Corman's pop-culture references in the carnival sequence include such classics as *He Who Gets Slapped* (1924) and *Nightmare Alley* (1947). The director's use of the idiosyncratic Diana Van der Vlis as the doctor's potential but thwarted love interest adds an off-key element to even the most traditional horror tropes (the hand-wringing, pearl-clutching girlfriend), and the casting of "insult comic" Rickles as the doctor's exploitative boss at the carnival is inspired. Nearly a decade later, during a *Tonight Show* appearance in 1972, Milland unfairly dismissed *X: The Man with the X-Ray Eyes* but had nothing but praise for Rickles as an actor. (Rickles acknowledged Milland's gesture by inviting him back on the *Tonight Show* in 1974, when the comic was guest-hosting for a week.)

Despite its drive-in theater status, *X: The Man with the X-Ray Eyes* received mixed but creditable attention from critics, as did another AIP feature on the same double bill, Francis Ford Coppola's *Dementia 13*, both of which have since become cult classics. *Variety* had a flat response: "Director Roger Corman keeps this moving and Ray Milland is competent as the doomed man." Vincent Canby of the *New York Times* was much more laudatory, writing, "Alertly directed and produced ... it shapes up as a modern parable about a dedicated doctor done in by humanity after he tampers with the unknown ... [T]he concept is original and the tone is thoughtful. So, most persuasively, is Mr. Milland."

X: The Man with the X-Ray Eyes (1963)

X: The Man with the X-Ray Eyes premiered in September and, later in 1963, took top honors at the Trieste Science Fiction Film Festival. Along with *Panic in Year Zero!*, it made Ray Milland "cool" to a younger generation but bewildered his older fans.

For Ray Milland's prospects, a planned return to Paramount for a big-budget feature was an encouraging sign, announced to the press in spring 1963, but negotiations fell through. He was to be part of the all-star ensemble (along with Alan Ladd, Robert Cummings, and Audrey Totter) in *The Carpetbaggers*, a sprawling Hollywood saga set in the 1930s based on Harold Robbins's best-seller, which itself was a thinly veiled Howard Hughes biography. When released in 1964, the movie made a fortune but was critically panned.

In lieu of the movie guest spot, Milland welcomed Alfred Hitchcock's invitation to star in the premiere episode of the *Alfred Hitchcock Hour*'s second season, which was shot at Universal Studios and aired in late September 1963 on CBS.

The program titled "A Home Away from Home" was an original work by Robert Bloch, casting Milland as a patient pretending to be the director of a mental sanatorium. In Bloch's teleplay, the suspense develops when the real director's niece (Claire Griswold) arrives for a visit. She does not know what her uncle looks like or that he has been killed by his "substitute" (Milland), a psychopath who has locked up the rest of the professional staff and replaced them with patients.

Milland was reuniting with Joan Harrison, who had produced *Circle of Danger* in 1951, a few years before she became the producer of the *Alfred*

Hitchcock Presents half-hour series. (In 1962, the show expanded to the hour-long format and lasted until 1965.) Hitchcock assigned Herschel Daugherty to direct "A Home Away from Home," and Daugherty does a solid job, if not up to Hitchcock's own standard. The best aspects of the episode are Bloch's dialogue, Bernard Herrmann's score, and the performances by Milland and company.

In essence, Bloch creates a dramatization of Thomas Szasz's controversial 1961 book, *The Myth of Mental Illness: Foundations of a Theory of Personal Conduct*. The blurring of lines between doctors and patients reinforces the show's mission to question whether psychiatry can really "cure" mental illness or if mental illness is real thing at all, an inquiring tenet of former psychoanalyst Szasz's then-radical thesis.

The fact that Ray Milland's character was once a practicing doctor but now a patient pretending to be a doctor also references *The Cabinet of Dr. Caligari* (1919), a German expressionist classic. In the original *Caligari*, the head of an insane asylum is psychopathic himself, turning his patients into killers via hypnosis. Thus, *Caligari*, "A Home Away from Home," and, to an extent, Hitchcock's *Spellbound* (1945) depict the pop-culture concept of "the patients running the asylum." Milland's Dr. Fenwick advocates letting "the mentally ill be set free," and Bloch adds some humorous touches, such as when Fenwick's "nurse" (Virginia Gregg) greets the innocent niece by saying, "The others [on the staff] are just *crazy* to meet you!" (Off screen, Gregg had been one of the voices of "Mother" in *Psycho*.)

Milland's character vacillates between the humane—playing the warm, welcoming doctor—and the monstrous—strangling the actual head of the institute. His performance is pitch perfect as a charmer who easily convinces the "normal" outside world of his professional standing while hiding his own psychopathology. Critic Jack Edmund Nolan goes as far as to consider this Milland's "best role in any medium."

But once again, a sexual scandal disrupted Milland's work on a Hitchcock project. Prior to the shooting of the show, Milland became tangentially embroiled in the very public divorce between the Duke and Duchess of Argyll. In order to prove his wife's infidelity in the British courts, the duke produced a list of the duchess' eighty-eight supposed lovers through the years. Ray Milland appeared on the list, though it was never determined when or if any tryst took place.

In 1963, Milland accepted the task of hosting two shows. The first was *Hollywood Come Home*, a candid documentary about the changes to the industry since the postwar years and the reason behind its decreased output of titles. Milland narrated the syndicated program, which made use of some behind-the-scenes footage, including Joan Crawford and Bette Davis on the set of *Whatever Happened to Baby Jane?*, and remarks by Darryl F. Zanuck, Otto Preminger, Mervyn LeRoy, and others.

Next came a *DuPont Show of the Week*, a TV Western titled "The Silver Burro," which aired in November. Scripted by Bill Deming and Allan Sloane and directed by William Corrigan, "The Silver Burro" tells the supposedly true 1885 story of an Idaho prospector (Carroll O'Connor) who enlists help in finding his lost burro, which is finally discovered sitting atop a huge silver mine. The miner's attempt to cut his search party out of the booty leads to a nasty legal battle.

The morality tale was simplistic, and Ray Milland's role as a present-day, on-screen narrator was undemanding (similar to his *Trails West* duties). Soon after this forgettable show and one more feature film, he backed himself into a whole new venture: performing in the theater.

CHAPTER 10

ENTR'ACTE (1964–1970)

RAY MILLAND'S ENTRY INTO TV AND MOVIE HORROR DURING THE EARLY 1960S afforded him a new, younger fan base, but he was still seen by most audiences as an aging star from an earlier period, the incrementally fading Golden Age of Hollywood. Milland kept busy, but the mid- to late sixties turned out to be the least productive, least satisfying period of his professional life.

THE CONFESSION

Before reluctantly embarking on a career in the theater over the next few years, Milland made one more feature that unwittingly highlighted his diminished stature as a star. *The Confession* came about when Ginger Rogers and her actor-turned-producer husband, William Marshall, sought his services to reunite with Rogers one last time for an independent production shot in Jamaica. The town of Bog Walk was to be the location of the couple's new movie-studio enterprise and the site meant to double for the Italian village of the film's story.

On paper, *The Confession* reads like a winner, particularly with its talented cast and crew. Apart from Rogers and Milland, the players included character actors from the old days, specifically Walter Abel and Cecil Kellaway, plus newcomers Barbara Eden, Elliott Gould (in his debut), and Michael Ansara (married to Eden at the time). Producer Marshall asked Allan Scott to write the original screenplay (years earlier he had penned several Rogers's hits—and *Wise Girl* and *Skylark* for Milland). *The Confession* turned out to be Scott's last film, and his participation allowed the appealing Pippa Scott, his daughter, to snag a supporting role.

Marshall first requested Victor Stoloff to direct, but Stoloff's best work had been in documentaries, not comedies or genre films, and his immediate discomfort led to Marshall replacing him with William Dieterle, who had guided Ginger Rogers through *I'll Be Seeing You* in 1944. Along with Scott, *The Confession* became the swansong for Dieterle and Robert Bronner, the cinematographer of many A pictures for MGM in the 1950s.

Despite everything, during the April-through-May '64 shoot, there were early signs the movie was doomed. Marshall's inexperience as a producer became apparent, starting with his need to change directors, then his last-minute scramble for additional funding. While naively expecting the government of Jamaica to share the costs for William Marshall Productions, he received the bulk of the financing from Leo Lewis, a St. Louis entrepreneur with no ties to the industry. As a result, Marshall was forced to bring aboard Kay Lewis, Leo Lewis's spouse and another neophyte producer. When the power generators needed to light interiors proved inadequate, Marshall and Lewis were stumped, unable to fix them; instead, they ordered the indoor scenes rescripted on the spot for exterior settings. Of more concern to the cast and crew throughout the shoot, Marshall was frequently drunk—at least according to Harold J. Kennedy, a producer who later wrote a scathing article about his chaotic working experience with Marshall and Rogers.

Elliott Gould, at twenty-five, was totally unfamiliar with moviemaking and recalls his first day as a disaster:

> Well, what I remember was that [in] my first shot . . . my character was supposed to be drunk, and there were a lot of people there. I'd been a child performer in song and dance as well as a chorus boy, but I knew nothing about being in movies or the craft of movie acting. So I started breathing heavily, really hyperventilating, acting drunk and threatening Ray Milland . . . and somebody behind the director yelled, "Cut!" It was an elderly man who was the sound man, and he walked up to the director and pointed at me and said, "He's breathing too loud! The shot's been ruined!" And I thought, "If I can't even breathe right, how am I ever going to learn to act?"

Allan Scott's screenplay turned out to be a pastiche of several genres—romantic comedy, religious parody, and caper film. In *The Confession*, multiple storylines merge to tell how a prostitute, Pia (Barbara Eden), discovers she is pregnant and decides to pray to a statue of St. Joseph for guidance, not realizing the icon happens to be hiding a cache of gold bullion. Ray Milland plays Mario, a thief hired to find the gold, who ends up falling for the brothel's Madame Rinaldi (Ginger Rogers), and aiding Pia by "answering" her as the voice of St. Joseph whenever she prays to the statue.

Fortunately, Milland and Rogers sparred nicely (on camera), making Scott's dialogue seem funnier than it was. Two decades after *The Major and the Minor* and *Lady in the Dark*, the stars were able to exhibit their skills at retro battle-of-the-sexes charisma. Their scenes without each other may have been less effective, but both appeared right for their roles, a mix of seediness and old-style glamour. Rogers and Milland's final scene together found the two laughing and waving to the camera, as if to say how the whole movie was a goof but also to bid farewell to their fans.

Predictably, troubles followed *The Confession* after its completion. "Among other things," Rogers later remembered, "the financial backers tried to confiscate the rushes before they were shipped back to the states." Marshall and Rogers entered litigation that did not resolve the matter. *The Confession* received scanty distribution and quickly disappeared following a rash of scathing reviews. The following year (1965), Marshall resold the movie as *Seven Different Ways*, using Golden Eagle as its distributor, and again it was ignored by the public. Later again, Rogers reflected, "I never in the world would have agreed to [appear in *The Confession*] had the producer not been my husband."

Finally, despite Rogers divorcing him in 1969, Marshall made one last attempt at recouping their losses in 1971 by renaming the movie a third time—as *Quick, Let's Get Married*. At this point, Marshall was capitalizing on Ray Milland's renewed recognition from *Love Story* (1970), Eden's popularity from her run on the *I Dream of Jeannie* TV series (1965–1970), and Gould's triumvirate of sudden fame: his Oscar-nominated portrayal in *Bob & Carol & Ted & Alice* (1969); his darkly comic blockbuster, *M*A*S*H* (1970); and his appearance on the cover of *Time* magazine (also in 1970). *Quick, Let's Get Married* played only smaller cities and was a flop for the third time, marking the pathetic end of the Rogers-Marshall production company.

During the *Confession* filming, Kay Lewis approached Milland about directing a romantic comedy called *Brown Eye, Pic-a-Pie*, and he warily signed on, but the start date in Jamaica was stalled by "construction difficulties." A new location, Greece, was contemplated, but that didn't pan out, either. To keep interest going, Lewis announced little-known Austrian actor Carl Schell, a *Confession* supporting player, would be the star. By the time Lewis thought she secured a spot in London to shoot, Milland bowed out. In 1966, the movie was revamped as a thriller and shot in Yugoslavia with a new cast and crew.

CHAPTER 10

MY FAIR LADY AND *HOSTILE WITNESS*

In 1964, with great uncertainty around his future movie career, Milland transitioned into a different creative medium—the theater. Initially, he was not thrilled with the idea of performing on stage at all, so he rejected a last-minute plea by the Kenley Players in Ohio to replace Brian Aherne in a road company tour of *My Fair Lady*. Shortly after his absolute refusal, he accepted the same offer under odd circumstances—as if out of a *Lost Weekend* parody sketch. According to Milland, "Fonda, Stewart and MacMurray were over for dinner—you know how it is, guys get together in the kitchen at two a.m. and get loaded." Gail Rock of the *New York Times* continued Milland's story: "The next morning Mrs. Milland told her husband that she was pleased he had agreed to do *My Fair Lady*. He had no idea to what she was referring. 'You were all four on the phone last night and you agreed to replacing Brian Aherne, who had begun the tour,' Mal explained."

Founded by John Kenley in Ohio in 1940, the Kenley Players were a major attraction for bus-and-truck tours of hit Broadway shows starring either erstwhile movie stars or up-and-coming personalities (Barbara Eden would be a headliner in 1967). In his quick reversal, Milland convinced himself it would be a fun change of pace to not only appear on stage for the first time since *The Woman in Room 13* in 1930 but to try his hand at a full-fledged singing role.

Milland worked out an arrangement with the Kenley brothers, John and Frank, to appear at the Packard Music Hall in Warren, Ohio, and the four-thousand-capacity Veterans Memorial Auditorium in Columbus during the summer months of 1964, starting in June. Before traveling to the midwest and while still in LA, Milland hosted a CBS special, "The Music from Hollywood" on *The International Hour*, airing in mid-May. His primary duty on the show was to introduce a series of performances by musicians and vocalists at the Hollywood Bowl. Soon enough, though, Milland himself would be on a stage singing.

Fresh from his difficult shoot in Jamaica, Milland had little time to rehearse or even memorize his lines. He had never seen *My Fair Lady*, yet he received his copy of the play eight days before opening night. The show's musical director, George Mumford, remembered: "[H]e tackled a tremendous script for his debut in a musical. Two weeks rehearsal were hardly enough for even an expert of the legit stage. You've got to admire his courage."

Fortunately, Milland was well received as Henry Higgins, the part originated on Broadway by Rex Harrison in 1956 but first envisioned by its creators (Alan Jay Lerner and Frederick Loewe) for Milland, according to Milland. Capitalizing on Warner Bros.' much-anticipated movie-version release

My Fair Lady (1964) theater program

in October 1964, also starring Harrison, the Kenley production was well attended, with a record 2,650 patrons on opening night, turning away 250!

The arrogant, misogynistic Higgins was the perfect fit for Milland, and hearing him talk-sing the score was an added bonus. Playing opposite him was the little-known Marilyn Taylor Savage as Eliza Doolittle, the cockney flower seller who is transformed (as part of a bet) into "an upper-class lady" by the Edwardian professor of phonetics, Higgins. David Nillo directed the pared-down reworking of Broadway's then-record breaker (at 2,717 performances over its six years).

Apparently, no audio recording exists, but Milland was critically praised for his handling of such classics as "The Rain in Spain," "Why Can't a Woman Be More like a Man?," and "I've Grown Accustomed to Her Face." Glenn C. Pullen poked a little fun at Milland as a singer in his *Plain Dealer* review: "Although the star cannot sing any better than this reviewer can, he recites the lyrics with witty, rapid-fire impact in mockery." Milland later told Gail

Rock in his *New York Times'* interview: "[W]e got good notices, even from Claudia Cassidy, the toughest critic in Chicago. Some of my friends called and accused me of sleeping with her." For the next twenty weeks, following his Ohio dates, he toured the East Coast (Upstate New York, Massachusetts, Connecticut, and Rhode Island), usually to full houses.

Despite delighting fans and getting positive reviews, Milland later admitted to his distaste for the theater: "To me, the stage is sheer hell. I do it to see if I can lick it. The boredom is incredible—night after night, the same people saying the same words. Some actors act by numbers, you know; they will always pick up the pencil as they say a certain word or light a cigarette on another line. Some nights when I got bored, I would move the pencil, and they would complain to the stagehands. They couldn't function if the pencil wasn't in the same place every night. God, can you imagine?" By coincidence, during the very same period (summer 1964), another once-popular movie actor of the 1940s and friend of the Millands, Zachary Scott, began his own well-received *My Fair Lady* tour through several East Coast theaters. The biggest difference between Milland and Scott, who had both played their share of cads on-screen but rarely ever sang, was in their attitude. According to Ronald L. Davis, Scott's biographer, "[T]he star told interviewers that he'd always preferred working in the theater to doing movies and television."

Due to his busy touring schedule, Milland was unable to celebrate Danny's marriage to new girlfriend Cleo Janet Fannan, a twenty-four-year-old (four months younger than Danny) who was born in LA but grew up in Honolulu. In September 1964, Danny and Cleo Janet wed in a simple ceremony in Los Angeles. By 1965, however, Danny's celebratory mood was severely dampened. He still had some hopes for his acting career, but the gigs kept falling through. To earn an income, he became a salesman in an LA men's clothing store. Across the country, Vicki Milland graduated from Millbrook in 1965, soon to become a grade-school teacher—which included a semester in France early on.

Once his *My Fair Lady* tour ended, Ray Milland only received a limited number of invitations for acting engagements, but one stood out. During a respite in London, Milland was offered by a producer a chance to star on Broadway. Thus, he continued working on the stage with a brand-new play, *Hostile Witness*. Later, it led to a movie comeback when the play was adapted into a film—not only starring Milland but also directed by him.

The British courtroom mystery was written by Jack Roffey, much in the manner of Frederick Knott or Anthony Schaffer. The original 1964 West End production had lasted more than a full year and starred Michael Denison in the leading role. For Broadway, though, producers Jay Julien and Andre

Goulston wanted a bigger name. They reached out to Milland, who agreed to be cast as Simon Crawford, a barrister with a solid track record and a tough-as-nails reputation.

In Roffey's story, Simon arrives home one day to find his daughter has been killed in a hit-and-run collision. Devastated, he promises retribution. Soon after, his neighbor and friend, a judge, is slain, and Simon is the chief suspect of a revenge-murder plot. He is prevented from trying the case in court and grudgingly assigns his young assistant, Sheila Larkin, to prepare his defense and solve the mystery. The play alternates chiefly between scenes at Simon's home and those at the Old Bailey.

Reginald Denham, who had previously directed *Dial M for Murder* on Broadway, worked with Milland and company for nearly three months before the opening. During rehearsals, in late November 1965, Milland took a night off to be the mystery guest again on *What's My Line?* in an effort to promote his forthcoming Broadway debut. Looking professorial in glasses and a dark suit, Milland fielded questions from the blindfolded panel—Arlene Francis, Tony Randall, Bennett Cerf, and Helen Gurley Brown—but Cerf quickly guessed his identity. Up to that point, the most amusing exchange occurred when Francis asked him, "Are you a popular motion picture actor?," and Milland retorted with gloomy self-deprecation, "Not anymore!"

A few nights later, Milland made his first visit to *The Tonight Show* starring Johnny Carson, at a time when it was based in New York City. His appearance was meant to publicize *Hostile Witness*, but when he told a *Jungle Princess* anecdote about losing control of his bladder during a swimming scene with Dorothy Lamour, the FCC took notice and warned Carson not to let "the industry degenerate into indecency." It would be several years before Milland was asked back on the famous talk show.

Starting on February 17, 1966, the Broadway version of *Hostile Witness* made its bow and lasted a solid seven months at the Music Box Theatre. After the exciting opening night, Milland was visited backstage by many movie-colony friends and well-wishers, including Joan Fontaine, Joan Bennett, and Gloria Swanson.

Most of the next day's reviews were highly complimentary. William Glover wrote in the Associate Press, "Milland gives an urbane, sharply etched portrayal that avoids those pitfalls of stereotype frequent in such parts."

Hostile Witness kept Milland busy through most of 1966 and some of 1967. He did find time, however, to appear on a few more television specials. On March 6, 1966, while still on Broadway, he performed a scene on *The Ed Sullivan Show* opposite his nightly costar, Melville Cooper. In June, he took part in the short-lived game show *The Face Is Familiar*, along with fellow guest star Florence Henderson and host Jack Whitaker. Also in June, as a new member of the Broadway community, he was given the honor of presenting an award at the twentieth annual Tony Awards (*Hostile Witness* itself was not nominated). One fellow presenter was former costar Maureen O'Sullivan. The cohosts of the evening were impresario George Abbott and another motion picture costar, his most recent, Ginger Rogers.

Milland agreed to take *Hostile Witness* on tour in late 1966. He started out at the Auditorium in Denver, Colorado, in September, then the Huntington Hartford Theatre in Los Angeles at the end of the year, and finishing at the Coconut Grove Playhouse in Miami in February 1967. Wherever the show went, the production and Milland's reviews were flattering. Cecil Smith of the *Los Angeles Times* thought the California edition "absorbing, completely satisfactory, and a wholly successful thriller."

Milland was in LA during his tour around the time of Danny's first serious brush with the law, but he was unable to intervene. Danny and his wife, Cleo Janet, were arrested in December 1966 for possession of heroin. During sentencing, they also pleaded guilty to forging prescriptions as a way to access drugs. Both were sent to a California state institution for treatment as addicts. In a January 1967 TV appearance on the syndicated *Mike Douglas Show*, Ray continued promoting *Hostile Witness* and did his best to avoid discussing the upsetting family news.

In March, Milland went abroad with an extended run of *Hostile Witness* in Australia, which packed the houses but, for some reason, received negative notices. During his extensive and wearying tour, Milland was alone most of the time. At a West End swing in England, he was feeling especially lonely. His moodiness resulted from several things: he had just turned sixty, his relationship with Danny was more strained than ever, and he couldn't help noticing Cary Grant had entered a comfortable retirement. Milland felt he was at a professional and personal low point, and if world events were on his mind as well, the escalating, highly televised Vietnam War was deeply troubling.

An incident in 1967, related by Farley Granger, illustrates how Milland came across to his fellow actors at the time. Granger was in London to star in a TV movie of *Laura* with George Sanders. During a lunch break at an Italian restaurant on Kings Road, Sanders pointed out to Granger that Milland was sitting by himself in a corner booth and would probably appreciate a greeting. Granger had not seen Milland since they costarred more than a decade earlier in *The Girl in the Red Velvet Swing:* "I went over to say hello, and he seemed quite touched." Granger thought highly of Sanders for proposing the act of kindness.

Still in London, Ray Milland's distaste for the theater and desire to return to moviemaking inspired him to find financial backing and transform *Hostile Witness* into a big-screen thriller.

RETURNING TO FILM

Ever since his Republic deal fell through in the late 1950s, Milland knew the task of mounting a movie on his own wasn't going to be easy. He called on his old friend David E. Rose, the coproducer of *Circle of Danger* and *The Safecracker*, to help raise funds—attaining $700,000 in total. Milland announced in March 1967 his intentions to lens *Hostile Witness* in England, with Edward Small and United Artists handling his distribution. As with all of Milland's previous directorial features, he promised to act as well, and he was able to engage the popular young British actress Sylvia Syms to play Simon's headstrong assistant (Angela Thornton had done it on Broadway). Despite the fact that Jack Roffey had never written for the screen before, Milland wanted the playwright to pen the script. *Hostile Witness* was then shot at Shepperton Studios in August 1967 over a five-week period. Mal joined her husband midway through filming, setting up house in a small rental flat on Upper Grosvenor Street near the American Embassy. Milland brought the production in a week early and under budget, creating what would turn out to be the last work of any kind he would ever direct.

Artistically, *Hostile Witness* is a cut above most courtroom dramas. Milland builds the suspense at a steady pace, leading to a climax that is unexpected, and he deserves considerable credit for removing much of theatrical flavor of the piece.

As an actor, Milland does another fine job as a cocky man in a high position who becomes embittered by tragedy. (The opening reel is not unlike that of *Night into Morning*, in which his character endures the death of his family in an accident.) Milland's Simon does not take to drink, but he does become more irascible than ever, prompting the film's best scene, when his exasperated but determined junior partner (Syms) quits his defense case because of his rude behavior. Syms and Milland play well against each other throughout the story.

Around the time of shooting, Milland received another offer to appear on stage—in a musical version of Oscar Wilde's only novel, *The Picture of Dorian Gray*, as adapted by Constance Cox with songs by Christopher Matthew and Jerry Wayne. Milland would have portrayed Lord Henry Wotton, another seductive Lucifer type. However, nothing ever came of this curious project.

Then, for unclear reasons, United Artists held up exhibiting *Hostile Witness* (and then getting only limited play at first in 1969).

Once he finished the movie, Milland became professionally inactive in 1967, spending much of the time traveling back and forth from Europe to Los Angeles. Milland kept himself busy by writing several short stories, publishing some of them under pseudonyms, many in the *Orange County Illustrated* magazine. (By the end of his life he had a total of twenty-four in print.) He was especially proud when one of them earned the Southern California Press Club Award. In late September 1967, Milland was seen plugging *Hostile Witness* on a BBC-TV talk show called *Dee Time*, hosted by Simon Dee, despite the fact the movie had no definite release date.

Nineteen sixty-eight wasn't much more productive. While back in the states and still expecting *Hostile Witness* to open, Milland made a late August appearance on another prime-time celebrity game show, the first incarnation of *The Hollywood Squares* (on NBC). In typically contrarian fashion, and letting out some of his current frustrations, Milland chose to rant rather than banter, shocking the host, Peter Marshall, and his fellow panelists, Kaye Ballard, Wally Cox, Arthur Godfrey, June Lockhart, Abbe Dalton, Arte Johnson, and Paul Lynde. His impromptu diatribe against "dirty movies" came from left field (actually, right field) and was poorly received in what turned out to be his first and last appearance on the live broadcast. Milland's prudish statements dovetailed with his open support of Richard Nixon, who was cynically running to be a moral "law-and-order" president.

Milland did *not* make a cameo in *Red Roses for the Fuehrer* (a.k.a. *Code Name, Red Roses*) despite the credit he is given by two reliable sources: James Robert Parish and Don E. Stanke's book *The Debonairs* and the film journal *Film Dope*. Director Fernando Di Leo's 1968 World War II espionage epic—and celebration of the Italian underground—starred James Daly, Pier Angeli, and Peter Van Eyck. It is possible that the various authors mistook Michael Wilding for Ray Milland, with the former making a guest appearance but Milland having nothing to do with the project.

Instead, during this time, Milland was sought by producer E. Jack Neuman and producer-director Jerry Thorpe to play a part in a TV movie called *The Protectors*, to be shot in the fall of '68 in snowy Denver, Colorado. Neuman, later known for developing the crime show *Police Story*, wrote the somewhat convoluted tale of a police chief (top-billed Van Johnson) on the trail of both a physically ailing assassin (John Saxon) and his blasé syndicate boss (Fritz Weaver). Second-billed Milland plays a businessman serving on a board who requests the syndicate's assassin to kill an executive (Robert Middleton) when the fellow board member refuses to help Milland's character out of a financial bind. (Obviously, the billing order had more to with name recognition than screen time—Milland is on-screen no longer than any of the other actors.)

Thorpe's direction was standard for TV movies of the era, yet the material itself was considered too provocative by the three major networks. Thus, Universal Studios bought *The Protectors* and released it to theaters in August 1970 as *Company of Killers*. Much to Milland's annoyance in 1968, he had two films sitting on the shelf—this TV movie and *Hostile Witness*.

Only the cast makes *Company of Killers* at all worth seeing today. Johnson is properly earnest in the forgettable role of the police sergeant. Milland, though, gets to enact yet another self-absorbed "killer-by-proxy" character as well as a man caught between his wife (Diana Lynn) and his mistress (Marian Collier). His expressions, both troubled and troubling, which he tries to hide from both women, are pure Milland. In a 2013 review, Peter Hanson singled out Milland's "usual blend of reptilian charm and sweaty anxiety" as a highlight.

Given Milland's distant relationship with Daniel, one can only imagine what he was thinking when, in one early scene, his character complains about his "worthless son." Milland also experienced a somber reunion with Diana Lynn, playing his estranged wife in a few brief scenes. The fact that Milland's *Major and the Minor* costar made her last acting appearance here is sad enough, but it is also tragic to know that one year after the movie hit theaters, in 1971, Lynn died of a stroke at age forty-five.

Jack Marta, the cinematographer for *Lisbon*, was a reassuring presence for Milland on the set, although Marta overlit some of the scenes. Most contemporary reviewers ignored *Company of Killers* when it briefly made it into theaters. More recent reviewers have not been much more favorable: Rose Thompson of the *Radio Times Guide to Films* stated in 2000, "[T]his police drama aims to deliver gritty realism in its depiction of the way cops work, but [it] eventually falls back on clichés."

A busier Milland ended the decade in 1969 with more brief appearances on television, the delayed release of *Hostile Witness*, two final stage productions, and another full-length TV movie.

His assorted 1969 television spots included *The Jackie Gleason Show* in April, shot in Miami Beach with Art Carney, Frank Sinatra Jr., and Victor Borge, and *The Merv Griffin Show* on two occasions, in May with Dave Brubeck and Rocky Graziano (as a guest announcer) and June with Betsy Palmer, Marcia Wallace, and Graziano again.

At long last, in 1969, *Hostile Witness* was shown in several countries but did not return very much on its investment. Oddly, it wasn't until 1970 that

Hostile Witness (1968 film), with Ewan Roberts

the film made its debut in the United Kingdom, its most target-rich region. Perhaps UA saw Milland as more of a draw that year following the tremendous response to *Love Story*, but *Hostile Witness* still lost money.

During the spring and summer of 1969, Milland returned to the stage and headed the cast of the bittersweet musical *Take Me Along*. He was now on the dinner-theater circuit, specifically the Meadowbrook Theatre in Cedar Grove, New Jersey, nowhere near Broadway. This type of theater experience meant that the audience ingested food during the show and danced afterward. For Ray Milland, it represented a low ebb playing in such a venue.

Still, *Take Me Along* had become a staple among touring companies since its long-running 1959 Broadway debut and gave Milland a chance to dance as well as sing, using the full range of his voice, not the talk-singing of *My Fair Lady*.

The Joseph Stein–Robert Russell book was based on Eugene O'Neill's *Ah, Wilderness!*, with music and lyrics by Bob Merrill. Milland played Nat Miller, the patriarch of a large family in 1910 Connecticut, trying to keep up with changing times. On Broadway, Walter Pidgeon played Nat Miller, yet the showier supporting role of Sid Miller, Nat's alcoholic brother-in-law, became the headliner and was played by top-billed Jackie Gleason (who won a Tony Award for it). Deliberately, Milland chose not to play the alcoholic, and as the only "name" in the 1969 revival, he received top billing and performed the show-stopping title song (a duet with Coley Worth as Uncle Sid). Stuart Bishop directed the quaint production, which received mostly positive reviews. After eight weeks, Ray Milland had enough of dinner theater and gladly accepted a major role in a TV movie.

ABC purchased Paul Gallico's 1964 novel, *The Hand of Mary Constable*, and announced in July 1969 that director Walter Grauman had signed Milland, Gene Tierney, and Don Murray to star. Gallico adapted his own work with the help of Luther Davis and retitled it *Daughter of the Mind*. Placing Milland back into something akin to the horror genre, the production took place in the fall on the Twentieth Century-Fox backlot. The December 9, 1969 broadcast received half-hearted reviews, but the show has acquired a minor cult following through the years.

Gallico's story centers around a Nobel Prize–winning cybernetic scientist, Dr. Samuel Constable (Milland), who claims to have seen his dead daughter, Mary (Pamelyn Ferdin), alive. While his invalid wife, Lenore (Tierney), doubts her husband, an ESP expert, Dr. Alex Lauder (Murray), decides to investigate. Lauder and Constable conduct experiments to figure out how Mary could possibly be living, but they are dogged by Detective Wiener (Ed Asner), who suspects there is a plot behind the apparition.

In retrospect, *Daughter of the Mind* comes across like a pilot for *The Sixth Sense*, a 1972 TV series in which Gary Collins played a role very similar to Dr. Lauder. Within the Milland canon, the film evokes *The Uninvited*, except that the story ends up debunking the supernatural conceit.

It is primarily Ray Milland who raises the quality of *Daughter of the Mind*. His early scenes of desperately trying to connect with his deceased young daughter are both eerie and poignant. Milland continues to cleverly balance his haunted character's desire to believe in the supernatural and his scientist's penchant for skepticism and truth. One can see Milland enjoying himself with former supporting players like George Macready, Virginia Christine, and old friend John Carradine, but these moments are brief.

A much bigger disappointment is Milland's reunion with Gene Tierney, eighteen years after *Close to My Heart*. What should have been touching is merely strained. The wheelchair-bound Tierney looks uncomfortable, and she is hindered by playing a one-dimensional, unsympathetic character at constant odds with her husband's newfound faith in the afterlife. Following many years of emotional turmoil, Tierney's first-ever TV movie was also her penultimate professional work. Tierney wrote in her memoirs, "I played the crippled wife of Ray Milland.... That appearance was to be my last before the cameras, not entirely by choice, but certainly without complaint."

While on the Fox lot finishing *Daughter of the Mind*, Milland made two cameos on *Bracken's World*, an NBC series about the movie industry. First came an episode called "Don't You Cry for Susannah" (with an *All About Eve*–style storyline), shot by fellow actor-turned-director Paul Henried and featuring series regulars Eleanor Parker and Dennis Cole. Peter Haskell was the show's protagonist, a producer-director working at the fictional Century Studios, headed by the unseen production chief, John Bracken. It aired in October 1969.

Created, produced, and developed by former MGM screenwriter Dorothy Kingsley, *Bracken's World* represented an insider's look at Hollywood and was popular enough to last two seasons, Milland appeared for a second time during the first season, in "Focus on a Gun," shot in late 1969 and shown in January 1970. It told a *Mulholland Drive*-type story about one of the studio starlets (Laraine Stephens) falling for a gangster (Joe Don Baker) while competing for a role.

Milland's guest appearance occurs when he meets up on the lot with Peter Haskell's character. The hotshot producer tells the actor that their next project together will have "no names," to which Milland (wearing his makeup bib!) jovially replies, "That's the way they do it today. No names. But if they are any good, they'll get a name, then they won't be able to get a job—they'll have to become producers!" With their caustic honesty, the lines sound as if they were ad-libbed by Milland himself.

In joyous family news, Victoria Milland married Edmund Lowell Graham in 1969 in Los Angeles. Graham, a North Carolina native, had had a career in the US Air Force before becoming a lawyer. Sadly, around the time of the wedding, Danny Milland and Cleo Janet quietly divorced.

In late fall 1969, Milland signed onto *The Front Page*, another stage production. The Ben Hecht-Charles MacArthur classic was first seen on Broadway in 1928 and then filmed multiple times. In a sense, Milland was back to playing a Cary Grant role since one of the film adaptations, *His Girl Friday* (1940), starred Grant. The play's is about a news editor (Milland) trying all kinds of underhanded ways to prevent his best reporter (Allen Jenkins) from leaving the newsroom and marrying an appealing young woman (Olive Deering).

Milland and Jenkins were obviously too old for their roles. (Jenkins had appeared in the 1928 Broadway original!) At least Milland was a good choice to play a devious manipulator (for laughs this time). Directed by Harold J. Kennedy, the East Coast tour ended in December at the Parker Playhouse in Fort Lauderdale, Florida.

Just before starting his *Front Page* run, Milland received an unexpected phone call that led to a major career renewal. His stock was revitalized enormously by his next endeavor, a movie so popular it remains critic proof even today, though some critics then and since have regarded it as a kind of horror—the worst kind—a sappy love story called *Love Story*!

LOVE STORY

Ray Milland appears on-screen in *Love Story* for slightly under 10 (out of 101) minutes. Yet *Love Story* brought Ray Milland back from relative obscurity. It was his biggest financial success in many years, including anything he had done in film, television, radio, or the theater as far back as 1954's *Dial M for Murder*—and it was his first major studio release since 1958's *The Safecracker*.

Moreover, Ray Milland was returning to Paramount for the first time in sixteen years, a changed studio since Gulf and Western, the American conglomerate, bought the company in 1966. Director Arthur Hiller further explains, "When we did *Love Story*, Paramount was going under. They wanted to back out of the production but [Paramount production head] Robert Evans got in there and he fought for it. Finally I had to literally swear I would not go over two million dollars." (In another sign of Hollywood in transition, *Love Story* would become the first Ray Milland movie with a rating from the Motion Picture Association of America, the PCA having officially ended in 1968. *Love Story* would receive the now-defunct GP, meaning all ages admitted but parental guidance suggested.)

Milland's involvement transpired in an unforeseeable way. The call he received as he was starting *The Front Page* came from Howard Minsky, a Paramount executive he hadn't heard from in two decades. Minsky offered Milland the part of the hero's cantankerous father ("sans peruke") and had already worked out a plan with the *Front Page* producers as to how he could do both productions at the same time—with lots of complicated commuting involved. Milland received a script within an hour of the conversation; he was moved by what he read, and then he shared it with Mal. She was also touched and urged her husband to do it, "if it isn't going to be too rough . . . I've got a feeling about it." (Mal was concerned about her husband's enacting the subplot's contentious father-son relationship with its parallels to the Ray-Danny discord.) Sealing the deal, Milland met with Erich Segal, the author who came up with *Love Story*, and was very impressed with him.

Robert Evans tapped Segal, a Brooklyn-born academic, to develop the screenplay. Only much later, when production was underway, did Evans have the shrewd idea to commission Segal to turn the screenplay into a book (a rare reversal at the time). Segal's short novel, released on Valentine's Day in 1970, several months ahead of the film's Christmas premiere, was a runaway best-seller that built up enormous publicity for the picture despite some harsh literary reviews.

The modernized Romeo-and-Juliet story concerns two students from different backgrounds who fall in love: Harvard's wealthy Oliver Barrett IV

(Ryan O'Neal), scion of New England's Oliver Barrett III (Ray Milland), and Radcliffe's working-class Jennifer Cavilleri (Ali MacGraw), who is attending the Ivy League Boston school on a scholarship and is the daughter of a Rhode Island bakery owner (John Marley). At first, the only conflict in the young lovers' idyll emerges when Oliver's father objects to his son's involvement with someone beneath his station. Oliver renounces his father's snobbery and asks Jenny to live with him off-campus. Later, however, Oliver and Jenny receive tragic news: Jenny has terminal cancer. With little time left to live, Jenny decides to enjoy her time with Oliver as long as possible. After her death, Oliver rejects his father's overtures to reconcile.

Never getting to revisit the old Paramount soundstages, Milland traveled to Boston in mid-November 1969 for some of his scenes. He returned to *The Front Page* and then flew to New York in early December for additional scenes. While waiting in Manhattan to restart *Love Story*, Milland reappeared on the *Mike Douglas Show* for a December 11 episode with Kay Thompson and the Chambers Brothers. Next, he shot his key moments as Oliver Barrett within a stately home in Long Island (doubling for Boston) and then met up with his *Front Page* company in Florida for his final performances.

Despite the downbeat aspects of the *Love Story* narrative, Ali MacGraw, who was Robert Evans's wife at the time, describes the production as a busy but fun experience for everyone:

> I loved working with [Ryan O'Neal]; he was sexy and sensitive, surly and funny, all things, all the time. He and Arthur Hiller made all of us laugh from morning to night, and like *Goodbye, Columbus* before it, *Love Story* gave me the mistaken feeling that making a film was a sweet ensemble experience. From the first time that Ryan and Arthur and I met to rehearse in an apartment overlooking Central Park in New York, I felt that I was part of something special. I think we all did.

Arthur Hiller's best television efforts (the 1959 "Morning of the Bride" episode of *Alfred Hitchcock Presents*) or films (*The Americanization of Emily* [1964], *The Out-of-Towners* [1970]) largely depended on the quality of his material. In the case of *Love Story*, one can tell Hiller is struggling to find ways of giving some distinction to Segal's elemental screenplay and turgid dialogue. If Hiller fails much of the time, he at least tries valiantly to generate genuine pathos. Jenny's final walk with Oliver is shot by cinematographer Richard Kratina in a single take from a slowly rising crane that captures the characters in a blinding white field of snow; this artistic touch isolates the young lovers within the cold, hostile world in a dramatic manner.

Love Story (1970), with Ryan O'Neal

Once he was finished with his *Love Story* and *Front Page* shuttling, Milland would have to wait nearly a year before Paramount delivered the film to the public. In the interim, Ray and Mal were delighted to see old friend John Wayne, at sixty-two, win a Best Actor award at the April Oscar ceremony, twenty-five years after Ray's triumph. They sent the humorous cable, "Congratulations from both of us. What took you so long?," to which Wayne replied via cable, "You asked me what took so long? There was some drunken bum on a lost weekend ahead of me!"

In late May 1970, Vicki made a rare public appearance on a daytime TV show, Art Linkletter's *Life with Linkletter*. Along with Rosemarie Stack (Mrs. Robert Stack) and Maggie McNellis, Victoria modeled outfits made of wrinkle-proof material created by one Lord Charles Spencer Churchill.

Still not knowing how much *Love Story* would impact his career, Milland hesitantly agreed to a short stint in another stage production during the summer of 1970. *Critic's Choice* was a 1960 comedy by Ira Levin that had a brief stay on Broadway starring Henry Fonda and Georgann Johnson, with Otto Preminger directing. The 1963 movie starred Bob Hope and Lucille Ball, but it was not a hit, either. Still, Milland gamely portrayed a theater critic whose wife (Jeanette Leahy) decides to write a play, forcing her husband into the uncomfortable position of reviewing it.

The *Critic's Choice* run lasted from June 9 to the 21st at the Little Theatre on the Square in Sullivan, Illinois, under the direction of J. Michael Bloom. During this stint, Milland considered some ambitious future plans in the theater. He announced he would portray Death in *Death Takes a Holiday* and adapt two novels into plays, Thornton Wilder's *Bridge of San Luis Rey* and

Graham Greene's *Ministry of Fear*. But in the end, *Critic's Choice* turned out to be Milland's last stage performance.

Still waiting for *Love Story*'s effect on the public, Milland supplied solid support on a television program titled *The Name of the Game*. His episode, "A Love to Remember," was shot in the summer of 1970 and aired in late September on NBC. As the most expensive series in TV history up the that point (costing $400,000 per ninety-minute episode), the well-produced mystery featured a teleplay by Dick Nelson about the series' magazine publishing hero (Gene Barry) encountering a woman (Lee Grant) at his college reunion, only to learn that the student by her name had died twenty-five years earlier!

Directed on the Universal lot by Nicholas Colasanto (best remembered today for playing Coach on *Cheers*), "A Love to Remember" cast Milland as the disturbed woman's wealthy, ascot-attired uncle who thwarts her classmate's efforts to find out the truth. One other brief Milland appearance before *Love Story*'s premiere was not seen in the United States: in late November, he surprised his former Paramount colleague, Bob Hope, by showing up as one of several guests paying tribute on the British edition of *This Is Your Life*.

Milland's theater and TV outings were thoroughly overshadowed when, finally, *Love Story* made its much-awaited bow in December 1970, exemplifying the era in a way that much better movies simply didn't. Despite his efforts during filming to bring some classiness to the enterprise, director Arthur Hiller couldn't escape the accusations of humorless sentimentality. In particular, there was nothing Hiller could ever do with the movie's most famous catchphrase, "Love means never having to say you're sorry," first delivered by Jenny to Oliver and then at the conclusion by Oliver to his father. Parodies abounded regarding the line, most notably when Barbra Streisand utters it to Ryan O'Neal at the end of *What's Up, Doc?* (1972), to which he replies, "That's the dumbest thing I've ever heard!" In an indirect link to Milland's horror-movie future, an ad campaign for *The Abominable Dr. Phibes* (1971) used the slogan "Love Means Never Having to Say You're Ugly!" Other send-ups of the movie itself included a 1971 *Carol Burnett Show* episode with Milton Frome in the Milland role.

Ray Milland easily stole the acting honors, even though O'Neal, MacGraw, and John Marley all received Oscar nominations (as did Hiller, Segal, and composer Francis Lai, with Lai the only winner, for Best Original Score). Milland's initial appearance would have been somewhat shocking to his fans: he looked older than his sixty-three years, in part because, for the first time on-screen, the actor showed up without his toupée. If nothing else, he should have scored a few points for brave honesty, but his *Something to Live*

For costar, Joan Fontaine, was aghast, saying, "One of the reasons I stopped making pictures is so nobody could do to me what they did to poor Ray Milland in *Love Story*. He looked half-dead. No toupèe [sic] and those big closeups. His face looked like the craters of the moon."

Milland essays the film's villain, representing Old World pomposity, the type of role he would play many times in the future. In 1970, younger viewers would have seen Oliver Barrett III as a symbol of what is wrong with the world—that is, the bad side of the Generation Gap. Yet, as the story progresses, and despite his limited number of scenes, Milland's character becomes increasingly empathetic, possibly upending Segal's intentions. In a confrontation where Oliver demands money from his father but does not disclose that it is to help the gravely ill Jenny, Milland displays a range of emotions with the subtlest facial expressions—disgust, anger, compassion, confusion—before he writes the cheque. By his final scene, in his awkward attempt to make peace with his distraught son, he is barely able to speak his lines (including "I'm sorry"), a highly effective way to present a fragile side to the tough Old Man (and possibly divide audience loyalties). If millions of people were moved by the end of *Love Story*, it is more than likely some of the mass emotion had as much to do with the father-son conflict as it did the dying heroine.

Love Story was a box-office smash, from its December opening weekend onward. The $2.2 million production was the biggest hit of 1970, saving Paramount from bankruptcy and earning over $50 million in its initial run. As of the early seventies, *Love Story* became the fourth highest grosser of all time. The three bigger earners were *The Godfather*, *Gone with the Wind*, and *The Sound of Music*. In 1972, when *Love Story* first aired on ABC-TV, it became the highest-rated movie or show to date. By February 2020, when a limited fiftieth-anniversary rerelease arrived in theaters, the accumulative gross shot up to an astounding $136.4 million.

A real surprise to Paramount in 1970 was that a number of legit reviews were quite supportive. Charles Champlin in the *Los Angeles Times* wrote, "[T]he plot-line has been honored many times.... It's the telling that matters: the surfaces and the textures and the charm of the actors. And it is hard to see how these quantities could have been significantly improved upon in *Love Story*."

More predictably, other critics disliked the film, bracing for what would quickly become a pop-culture phenomenon. Vincent Canby in the *New York Times* wrote, "I can't remember any movie of such comparable high-style kitsch since Leo McCarey's *Love Affair* (1939) and his 1957 remake, *An Affair to Remember*. The only really depressing thing about *Love Story* is the thought of all the terrible imitations that will inevitably follow it." Molly Haskell called it "synthetic," and Gary Arnold of the *Washington Post* was even more direct: "I found this one of the most thoroughly resistible sentimental movies I've ever seen. There is scarcely a character or situation or line in the story that rings true, that suggests real simplicity or generosity of feeling, a sentiment or emotion honestly experienced and expressed."

As for Ray Milland, *Love Story* was purely beneficial. He personally liked the movie, at least he said he did, and hoped it would start a trend away from the more violent and sexually explicit fare of the day. He embraced the furore surrounding the movie, accepting his invitation to *The Tonight Show* in May 1971 to chat with Johnny Carson about *Love Story*, with NBC conveniently forgetting about the FCC incident in 1965 that had been keeping him off the show. Later, in August 1971, he and Mal flew to London for the first Royal Command Performance of one of his movies since *The Lost Weekend*. On the night of the royal *Love Story* screening, Milland, in white tie and tails, was interviewed by Thames Television journalist Michael Parkinson; he stated that the film was "very, very modern and in some spots, a little too modern . . . but it stresses the three things I think are most important: love, respect and sentiment." When asked about his own part, he said with more characteristic candor, "I play a very rich, rather decent, normal . . . louse of a father."

By the start of the new decade, Ray Milland was reborn as a louse, at least as far as his on-screen persona was concerned. During the remaining years of his life, he worked steadily, almost as often as he had during his salad days, reproducing increasingly disconsolate or malicious variations of Oliver Barrett III.

CHAPTER 11

BABYLON REVISITED (1971–1977)

WITH *LOVE STORY*, RAY MILLAND RETURNED TO THE BIG SCREEN, REVIVED HIS career, and made himself in demand again—even if few of his subsequent productions were as consequential or profitable.

Milland was realistic about his current place in the business: his days as a leading man were over. In typically forthright fashion, he told an interviewer, "Do what you can with what you've got. I know actors from my generation who sit at home and cry 'Why don't they send me any scripts?' I tell them, 'Because you still think of yourself as a leading man. You're 68, not 28. Face it.'" Consequently, he decided not to wear his toupée in public.

The downside of this period is that Ray Milland was seen by and large as attaching himself to inferior material. One could blame Roland Leif, Milland's new agent during the 1970s and '80s, but in the end, Milland always decided for himself. In fact, one day when talking to former *Dial M for Murder* costar Anthony Dawson, he explained his new four-part criteria for choosing projects: "How big is the part, what's my billing, where do we shoot it, and how much do I get paid?" Later repeated in print, Milland's comment was brutally honest but not very helpful toward changing anyone's mind about the quality of the work.

His next several years were immersed in travel from one location to another, ready to appear before the cameras—with little time for very much else. Mal often accompanied Ray on these exotic shoots, treating them like paid vacations. Producer John Houseman once posited a somewhat converse view of Ray Milland: "[He] was a man who was afraid to say no. He needed work and was always afraid that his career was over after a picture was over. He should have been tougher, but he was such a pleasant man that he never pushed it."

If for no other reason, Milland had to toil away at his craft in order to maintain his Beverly Hills home and new housing purchases in the South of France and Marbella, Spain. Having learned a few things over the years,

Milland verified he would be paid upfront in this new world of international filmmaking with its slippery financing: "I always managed to have my salary deposited in an American bank *before* I started a picture." Helping, too, William Morrow and Company would soon offer Milland a generous advance for his autobiography. The publishers were inspired by David Niven's well-received, best-selling memoir, *The Moon's a Balloon*, from G. P. Putnam's Sons in 1972, and hoped for similar results from a Milland tell-all.

THE PROFESSIONAL GUEST STAR

Looking back at Milland's seventies output, one can find worthwhile creations and even a few unpolished gems; at the same time, the harsh criticism was occasionally justified. It is downright depressing to see Milland in a some of these efforts, particularly the international coproductions seemingly shot on the fly. (A repeatedly used subplot about evil attempts to manipulate the stock market make one movie seem like the next.) A factor beyond Milland or anyone's control was that the demise of the Golden Age factory system resulted in the loss of consistent quality; agents and then lawyers became far greater power brokers than any moguls, and, for all their faults, those older heads of studios had a knack for moviemaking that the younger breed of "suits" did not. Finally, for good or for bad, the New Hollywood also promoted sex and violence in a far more graphic way than ever before, and both elements found their way into Milland's films.

Generally speaking, Milland transcended the shoddiness, and even the worst of these projects paid deference to Milland by referencing aspects of the actor's large, impressive canon. In at least one way the homages to Milland's past dovetailed with the changes in Hollywood's present. Packaged deals meant clientele from the same talent agency were repeatedly linked. Therefore, with Milland represented by MCA, his costars of yore—if MCA habitué—were frequently "sold" along with him.

First, *River of Gold* would serve to complete Milland's "sunken-treasure" trilogy (after *Reap the Wild Wind* and *Jamaica Run*). The ABC-TV movie promoted Milland as the top-credited cast member, yet he only appeared in a supporting role. He and Mal traveled to Acapulco during the winter for the Aaron Spelling production, which aired in early March 1971 to relatively high ratings.

This aquatic *Treasure of the Sierra Madre* starts as two friends (Roger Davis, Dack Rambo) dive for riches off the Mexican coast and run afoul of a wealthier, much greedier treasure hunter (Milland). Later, in nearby Acapulco, the friends meet a mystery woman (Suzanne Pleshette) who offers to help find an underwater cache.

Despite the homages to *Sierra Madre* (the guys' boat is dubbed *The Fred C. Dobbs*), there exists little of the punch of that John Huston classic since the protagonists are basically two nice slackers. The most creative contribution from screenwriter Salvatore C. Puedes and director David Friedkin is the unexpected halfway-point demise of second-billed Pleshette.

Otherwise, *River of Gold* is a slightly confusing caper in a picturesque setting (the original plans were to shoot in Greece). Milland's gruff performance would become typical going forward, though his character's name, *Evelyn Rose*, amusingly undercuts his macho toughness. Milland's best moment within his three scenes occurs while attending the funeral for Pleshette's character, reading his sentimental lines with palpable sarcasm: "Very touching, a final farewell, tragic business, I've been upset all day." Nevertheless, Kevin Thomas in the *Los Angeles Times* concluded *River of Gold* "looked as though people lost interest half way through."

Milland's next guest-star appearance occurred during the third season of the *Night Gallery*. "The Hand of Borgus Weems" episode was completed at the old Universal lot early in 1971 and aired on NBC in September.

Based on a short story by George Langelaan, "Borgus Weems" is a spin on the old tale of a man's hand that seems to be controlled by a preternatural force. In this variation, George Maharis plays Peter, a San Francisco resident whose hand is intent upon killing people. Rather than commit a crime, Peter begs a prominent surgeon, Dr. Ravadon (Milland), for an amputation. Peter and Ravadon soon realize the hand belonged to the late Borgus Weems and had a reason for seeking revenge on a series of people.

Donning a grey toupée, Milland gives a lowkey performance as the surgeon, ceding the spotlight to Maharis. In its way, the piece presaged the more significant if deranged Milland-transplant movie the following year, *The Thing with Two Heads*. Don Page in the *Los Angeles Times* tried to be funny by labeling "Borgus Weems" "heavyhanded."

Starting in early 1971, thanks to his *Love Story* comeback, Milland was suddenly in demand on the late-night talk-show circuit, including four appearances on *The Tonight Show* between 1971 and 1972. Interviewed by Johnny Carson, Milland was a welcome and witty raconteur about Hollywood in the old days, and he basked in the adulation.

During the summer of 1971, Milland was overjoyed to learn that Vicki was pregnant with her first child. Shortly after, with nothing immediately lined up and being ever restless, Milland was wooed back to the stage. Joan Fontaine asked him to play her husband in *Relatively Speaking*, Alan Ayckbourne's

Ray Milland next to Shirley Bassey, greeting Princess Margaret at the royal film premiere of *Love Story* in 1971. Photo credit: Keystone Press / Alamy Stock Photo.

marital farce about "the swinging sixties." During rehearsals, out of nowhere, the two friends clashed over billing and dialogue changes, leading Milland to drop out before the scheduled June 29 opening at California's New Arlington Park Theatre. Ian Martin became his last-minute replacement, and with this incident, Milland said his decisive final goodbye to the boards.

Back on television in early August 1971, he participated in a daytime Canadian talk show called *Mantrap*, produced by Dick Clark, during which women celebrities peppered a male guest with questions. In Milland's case, the female panelists—Stefanie Powers, Pamela Mason, and Sue Lyon—and host Alan Hamel brought up such topics as abortion, welfare, organized religion, and public education. Perhaps remembering his *Hollywood Squares* debacle, Milland tried hard to avoid causing controversy. The payday was modest, but the commute was easy: he and Mal took the northbound shuttle from Los Angeles to the Vancouver studios. They followed the broadcast with a brief vacation.

During the late summer, Milland worked on the first official episode of the long-running series *Columbo*; this mainstay of the Sunday night *NBC Mystery Movie* anthology starred Peter Falk as an outwardly sloppy but covertly canny Los Angeles homicide detective.

In October 1971, TV audiences could catch Milland in "Death Lends a Hand," which inaugurated the formula of having a white-collar culprit be identified from the start and Columbo slowly cornering the killer into a confession. Robert Culp was the guest star, and Pat Crowley, his victim, a woman who has had an extramarital affair yet rebuffs a blackmail attempt by Culp's character. "Special-guest-star" Milland (without toupée) played Crowley's older husband, a man haunted by her loss. The creators of *Columbo*, Richard Levinson and William Link, wrote this episode and won an Emmy Award for their work.

Director Bernard L. Kowalski guides "Death Lends a Hand" acceptably, and it is well photographed by Russell Metty (who had first worked with Ray Milland on *Irene* more than three decades earlier). While it is fun to watch the Falk-Culp cat-and-mouse routine, it is Milland who steals the show, providing a welcome gravitas not usually associated with *Columbo*. Despite the husband's wealthy status, the actor's sad and moody expressions linger sympathetically in the mind.

Immediately after *Columbo*, Milland collaborated again with director Kowalski on a full-length TV movie, *Black Noon*, which was shot in a desert area north of Los Angeles. Though tediously paced for a seventy-four-minute story, *Black Noon* has attracted a devoted following over the years. The unusual combination of horror and the Western gives *Black Noon* distinction, and the denouement is quite jolting.

Andrew J. Fenady produced *Black Noon* on a low budget and wrote the original teleplay about a preacher and his wife (Roy Thinnes and Lynn Loring) forced to stop in a small western town in the late 1800s. As mysterious accidents, illnesses, and even deaths occur, the preacher finds his services are needed, but his wife feels trapped.

Milland plays the chief town elder, ostensibly a kindly fellow minister. The shock ending shows how the benign but peculiar residents, led by Milland's Caleb Hobbs, are actually devil worshippers determined to kill religious figures. Gloria Grahame, the former film noir femme fatale, and Henry Silva, a veteran villain, are underused. On the other hand, Ray Milland registers strongly in his return to the theme of satanism (decades after *Alias Nick Beal*).

At the time of the CBS airing in November 1971, *Variety* called *Black Noon*, "Spooky, hokey escapism." More recently, Gloria Grahame biographer Robert J. Lentz praised both Milland and the movie in general: "Ray

Milland is terrific as Caleb.... And of all the horror projects in which Gloria participated in the latter stages of her career, this is the classiest and most evocative."

Milland took a short break from horror with *Embassy* (a.k.a. *Target: Embassy*), which necessitated his traveling to Beirut in September 1971, just prior to the Lebanese Civil War. The British-financed production was seen in a few countries before its hasty US premiere in Milwaukee in December 1972.

Embassy uneasily blends Cold War intrigue with blaxploitation. In William Fairchild's screenplay, Richard Roundtree plays a CIA officer at the US embassy in Lebanon facing two crises at once: an ailing Russian defector (Max von Sydow) demands refuge just before a KGB agent (Chuck Connors) disguised as a US Air Force officer arrives to kill him.

Fourth-billed Ray Milland plays the dignified yet wily embassy ambassador, and he dominates the first quarter of the story, the best section, as the troubles begin at the embassy (the American Life Insurance building doubled for the interiors). Milland delivers his lines with customary panache, including his off-color bon mot: "A good diplomat should be able to juggle four balls in the air without losing his own!"

On a more serious note, Roundtree plays a professional African American agent in a dapper suit, not a common sight for audiences of the day. Sadly, both he and Milland's Ugly American character are supporting the very Western imperialism the Lebanese crowds are protesting outside.

The name cast is backed by an ace team—Mel Ferrer as producer; director Gordon Hessler, a horror specialist; and most promisingly, legendary French cinematographer Raoul Coutard. Yet, for whatever reasons, *Embassy* looks second-rate, its ugly mise-en-scène rife with technical errors.

So *Embassy* came and went and has been forgotten. Milland's next two films, both revisitations to horror, now with blaxploitation inflections, would grow in stature through the years and earn much larger cult attention than the throwaway *Embassy*.

FROGS AND THE THING WITH TWO HEADS

Milland agreed to a two-picture deal with AIP, starting with *Frogs*, filmed in November 1971 and arriving in theaters in March 1972. Part of a cycle of "eco-horror" in the early seventies, *Frogs* gave the nuclearized animal subgenre of the 1950s (e.g. *Them!* [1954]) a politically liberal facelift. More personally, knowing Ray Milland would be their star, screenwriters Robert Hutchison and Robert Blees acknowledged the actor's Celtic roots via the

Liamhigyn Y Dwr, a mythical, carnivorous frog-like bat-lizard hybrid found in ponds, lakes, and swamps.

In the Hutchison-Blees story, Milland plays the wealthy owner of a Southern plantation. A visiting ecologist (Sam Elliott) deduces that the wheelchair-bound man has been responsible for dumping pesticides in the water surrounding his island mansion. At the same time that the angry tycoon presides over his birthday party, the pollutants ignite a vengeful streak within the local creatures, including the alligators, snakes, and, of course, frogs. After several party guests are killed by the animals, the survivors leave the island while the patriarch stays in his manor, where he gets his just deserts—then becomes dessert.

Though not particularly frightening, *Frogs* holds one's interest, in part for its progressive viewpoint. Milland had already entered the curmudgeon phase of his career, and he does not disappoint as a short-tempered, controlling "master of the house" who refuses to acknowledge the sociopolitical changes impacting his realm. Apart from the animal revenge, the sexual revolution is just under the surface as well. One scene that would challenge any Old World view shows a wealthy Black house guest (Judy Pace), half of an interracial couple, flirting with the Black maid (Mae Mercer), thus confronting and collapsing class, race, and same-sex issues.

In what was her first feature film, Joan Van Ark remembered, "[T]he shoot was difficult in part because of the swampy Florida location [Eden Gardens State Park] and due to the difficulty in staging the animal attacks." Van Ark had mainly positive things to say about Ray Milland, who played her grandfather: "[Even though] he was a little distant and kept to himself . . . I felt moved in our final scene together through the way he looked straight ahead, not at me, and I looked at him. It was a genuine and heartfelt deep moment, which I felt on the set and made me well-up seeing it again recently. I saw something kind and even sensitive in his eyes, despite the fact he was playing a domineering character . . . the villain of the piece."

Many reviews were scornful, but *Variety* liked it: "Cast is generally first class and Milland's presence, though comparatively brief, is always commanding." Van Ark also related that her neighbor, director Quentin Tarantino, told her how much he admired the movie.

As usual, Milland was his own harshest critic, saying, "I just did that [awful] film in a hurry, so I could get out of town for Thanksgiving." Uncomfortable with the location's swarm of insects and director George McCowan's tendency to get drunk, Milland, in a rare unprofessional move, departed just before the shoot wrapped, leaving his body double to finish the grisly final scene. Nevertheless, Milland honored his AIP contract and appeared

Frogs (1972), with Sam Elliott and Joan Van Ark

next in *The Thing with Two Heads*, a combination of horror, sci-fi, satire, and blaxploitation—the very definition of a cult movie.

Before starting *The Thing with Two Heads* and on the day *Frogs* opened in major cities (March 10, 1972), Milland was elated to learn that Vicki gave birth to her first son, Travis Cameron Graham, making Ray Milland a grandfather at age sixty-five.

The following month, Milland guest starred on NBC's *Bob Hope Special*, which aired April 10, 1972, Oscar night that year, paying satiric tribute to the award show.

Milland was joined by two other Academy Award winners, Shirley Jones and Ingrid Bergman, the actress who had handed Milland his statuette on Oscar night in 1946. Milland appears in a spoof of *The Lost Weekend*, with his struggling writer now a "girl-aholic," suffering from an inexorable attraction to women. Hope appears as the Girl-aholics Anonymous representative who tries to help the addict using "aversion therapy." The politically incorrect shtick isn't too funny, but Milland participates with good-natured self-deprecation, especially given his extramarital history. A better sketch matches Hope against Bergman as married Oscar contenders trying to sabotage each other's big night. It might have been more fun to see Milland with Bergman in this segment, but the two never meet on the show.

At last, it was time for the most notorious movie in which he would ever appear. In 1971, AIP had a modest hit with *The Incredible Two-Headed Transplant*, but *The Thing with Two Heads* would be more outrageous, despite its similar premise. James Gordon White cowrote both films, and one of his writing partners, Lee Frost, directed as well, primarily in the Los Angeles area. In an amazingly fast turnaround, it was shot in June 1972 and premiered in July 1972.

If Milland had reservations about starring in this particular movie, he didn't reveal them to the press, and by all accounts, he was his usual professional if reserved self on set. Once again, he plays a wealthy, wheelchair-bound racist, this time a transplant surgeon who resents the fact that the newest member on his staff is a Black man, Dr. Fred Williams (Don Marshall). When Milland's Dr. Kirshner learns he has terminal cancer, he instructs his assistant, Desmond (Roger Perry), to find a healthy body on which to graft his head in order to stay alive. The only person Desmond can find is a Black death-row inmate, Jack Moss (Roosevelt "Rosey" Grier). Though the operation succeeds, both Moss and Kirshner are disgusted to discover they are sharing the same body. From there, Moss forces Williams to help him escape from the hospital in order to find his wife, Lila (Chelsea Brown), and have her help him prove he is an innocent man. Moss also demands Williams sever Kirshner's head from his body.

After the release of *The Thing with Two Heads*, older audience members started wondering how the one-time Oscar winner could be associated with this kind of movie. For those who hadn't been observing Milland's professional trajectory, it was a reasonable question, but this movie was hardly his career nadir, as some would have had it. If one evaluates *The Thing with Two Heads* for its sheer entertainment value, it is an immensely satisfying credit on his résumé, what writer Nate Patrin calls "[*The*] *Defiant Ones* Gone Batshit"!

Beyond the conceptual craziness, there are many moments to enjoy along the way, most prominently the sight of ex-football player Rosey Grier wearing a latex head of Milland on his broad shoulder in several long shots and Milland returning the favor on a couple of occasions by wearing a Grier bust. Whether or not the technical absurdities are meant to be so noticeable, they lend themselves to the more satiric aspects, such as when Lila (Brown) first sees her husband with his extra head and exclaims, "Honey, I was wondering . . . do you have two of anything else?" Milland is equally funny growling horrendously racist lines like, "What are we having for dessert, watermelon?" In the surrealist ending, Kirshner's head is left on a surgical table crying out for a body, while the three other main characters—Dr. Williams, Moss, and Lila—ride off into the night singing the gospel-inspired, "Oh Happy Day!"

Laughs aside, a message of Black empowerment drives the film, starting with the opening tension between the two doctors and Don Marshall's character telling Milland's, "[Y]ou're a bigot. A bigot of the highest caliber. And because of that, you have underestimated me and my intelligence."

Yes, AIP sold the film with such taglines as "They transplanted a WHITE BIGOT'S HEAD onto a SOUL BROTHER'S BODY!," but there exists a serious undercurrent addressing racism. Don Marshall's performance bestows much of this moral grace.

A few reviewers were remarkably pleased with *Two Heads*. *Variety* said it was "slickly imaginative" and had "excellent special effects," while Kevin Thomas of the *Los Angeles Times* was on target about what seemed to be the film's intentions: "[It is] every bit as preposterous as it sounds. It is also utterly hilarious, and any picture that can point up the absurdity and cruelty of racial prejudice with such incessant laughter deserves respect. Indeed, this American International release is a well-calculated, competently made exploitation picture that offers lots of fun."

Obviously, Ray Milland didn't benefit career-wise from his participation, yet he was sanguine about the matter. He told a reporter in October 1972, "I saw old *Two Heads* with an audience the other night, and you know something—the damned thing's entertaining! The audience was eating it up. Even I was going along for the ride."

THE BAD FATHER FIGURE

Later in the year, Milland could be seen on two detective shows, both airing in October. First came *Cool Million*, a series incorporated into the *NBC Wednesday Night Mystery Movie* rotation but yanked after five episodes.

Milland returned to Canada, near Niagara Falls, for the episode, "Hunt for a Lonely Girl." He plays a self-made millionaire who is falsely accused of murdering a business rival. Enter Jefferson Keyes (James Farentino), a "burned" spy who now works as a private detective for only wealthy clients that can meet his "cool-million" fee. Beyond the opening sequence with Milland, the neo-noir is all Farentino's.

Leaving behind the dismal *Cool Million*, Milland returned to the Universal lot for his second *Columbo* episode. In "The Greenhouse Jungle," he plays the guest-star villain trapped by the tenacious but unassuming detective played by Peter Falk. Milland's ascot-attired horticulturalist plots with his nephew (Bradford Dillman) to fake the nephew's kidnapping and use the incident to blackmail his other relatives. The uncle then shakes up the scheme by killing his nephew so he can hoard all the ransom money for himself.

Written by Jonathan Latimer, Milland's *Big Clock* and *Alias Nick Beal* screenwriter, "The Greenhouse Jungle" contains more story intricacy than "Death Lends a Hand," but it isn't quite as good. One would expect Milland's character to be razor sharp in his exchanges with Columbo, yet his exasperated reactions to the detective from the very start reduce Milland to portraying an obvious culprit. The other cast members are not even up to the show's usual standard, such as Bob Dishy's officious detective sidekick.

Two horror features and a sci-fi adventure comprised Milland's 1973 output.

He was pleased to finally return to the old Paramount lot to shoot the PG-rated *Terror in the Wax Museum* from mid-October to November 1972. It was touching and nostalgic for him to see the landmark Bronson Gate at the entrance. Fittingly, Milland's costar from 1934's *We're Not Dressing*, Bing Crosby (now strictly in producer guise with Andrew J. Fenady), packaged this homage to old-fashioned British horror and completed it in sixteen days on a tidy budget of approximately $400,000.

Though the Fenady-Jameson Brewer screenplay was original, the writers were clearly inspired by the lineage of *The Mystery of the Wax Museum* (1933) and *House of Wax* (1953). In *Terror in the Wax Museum*, Milland is a frustrated assistant working at a wax museum in late nineteenth-century London. When the owner (John Carradine) is killed, Milland's character becomes a suspect—along with the relatives and others who are seeking financial control.

Milland gets top billing and a solid role. He is at his best when taking over as docent from his deceased boss, exhibiting a wicked delight in describing to the tour groups how each famous victim in wax was killed.

For his fans, *Terror in the Wax Museum* becomes a virtual index of Milland references with several "reunions": Broderick Crawford from *Sealed Verdict* exchanges a brief scowl with Milland; Patric Knowles, the villain of *Jamaica Run* and Milland's youthful romantic rival in *Kitty*, is now a rival for the museum premises; and Elsa Lanchester, who posed a mild, comical threat in *The Big Clock*, is a fierce competitor here, again for monetary gain. Perhaps the funniest "cameo" and in-joke comes in the form of the wax figure of Lucrezia Borgia, as depicted in *Bride of Vengeance*, the 1949 film Milland refused to do. Other teasing, subtle touches include a *Lost Weekend* reference to Milland's character having a night of drinking he can't remember and a character saying of him, "He'd once been an actor!"

Though not as suspenseful as Milland's own Jack the Ripper *Thrille*r episode a decade earlier, *Terror in the Wax Museum* is one of Milland's more enjoyable productions of the 1970s.

In 1972, during a rare trip to Hollywood, Frankie Howerd, the British music-hall-comic-turned-movie-actor, visited Milland and pitched the idea of starring together in *The House in Nightmare Park*, an original parody of

British haunted house thrillers set during the same Victorian era as *Terror in the Wax Museum*. Milland, who had always liked Howerd's work, contentedly agreed, quickly completed *Wax Museum*, and traveled to England's Pinewood Studios for the November-through-December '72 shoot.

Milland might have been better off not taking the trip, though, for *The House in Nightmare Park* is exclusively a Howerd vehicle, and while the comedian was popular in Great Britain, his eccentric brand of humor never translated outside the United Kingdom. In fact, the US release was delayed by four years, when it was alternately retitled *Crazy House* and *Night of the Laughing Dead* and used comparisons to Mel Brooks' *Young Frankenstein* (1974) in its ad campaign in order to lure reluctant viewers. One tag line was funnier than any of the jokes in the picture: "Don't See It Alone—Bring the Children!"

The story and screenplay by Clive Exton and Terry Nation features Howerd as a 1907 entertainer who inherits a large estate, wherein his relatives await his homecoming. One of those family members is the man's uncle (second-billed Milland), who becomes a murder suspect when, one-by-one, the guests in the mansion are murdered, apparently to scare the trouper away from his newly acquired property. Howerd then assumes the role of a bumbling Clouseau-type inspector and tries to identify the killer.

There are a few inspired moments along the way, mainly the disturbing final image and, earlier, a spooky "Dance of the Dolls" sequence with the house guests (including Milland!) singing and dancing as life-sized marionettes. But most of the story lacks chills, and the jokes about Hammer horror, *Gunga Din*, and even *Beau Geste* are lost because director Peter Sykes allows Howerd to run roughshod with his tiresome mugging.

Howerd claimed *Nightmare Park* was his personal favorite of all his films, and Milland maintained loyalty to his friend by later appearing (alongside Richard Burton) on a 1976 British *This Is Your Life* tribute to Howerd.

Just before traveling to England, Milland learned of the death of Mitchell Leisen, which didn't come by surprise (his friend had been suffering from heart disease) but helped explain Milland's lack of exuberance making *Nightmare Park*. He came back to California in time to see Vicki modeling clothes on television again when a December 1972 *Merv Griffin Show* featured Joan Fontaine introducing daughters of movie stars in *au courant* fashions—Christina Quinn, Anthony Quinn's daughter, Francisca Hilton, Zsa Zsa Gabor's daughter, Debbie Dozier, Fontaine's own daughter, and several others.

In early 1973, as America was starting to reel from Richard Nixon's Watergate scandal, Milland took his next trip to Capetown, South Africa, for yet another dud, the sci-fi adventure *The Big Game*, released in the spring. In it, Milland plays a scientist who has invented a mind-control radar intended to help foster world peace. The action begins when two mercenaries (Stephen Boyd, Cameron Mitchell) bring the device on a boat to Australia for testing. They are pitted against a political group, "The Organization," trying to steal the instrument for nefarious purposes.

During production, he could tell *The Big Game* "smelled of disaster." With his scientist-in-glasses guise and peculiar invention, Milland evokes *X: The Man with the X-Ray Eyes*, minus the depth or any display of ambivalence over his potentially dangerous mechanism. He literally phones in his performance as his character is often on the telephone, though his indifference towards his son's fate, when kidnapped by the terrorists, is in keeping with Milland's mien following *Love Story*.

A very sad piece of casting is that of an uncredited Anthony Dawson, briefly seen as one of the team members managing the secret shipment. Two decades earlier, he was the memorable patsy to Milland's villain in *Dial M for Murder*, but here the two actors do not reunite for even a moment. On a more depressing note, *The Big Game* was the first of three pictures Milland lensed in South Africa (doubling for Australia here), at the time under Apartheid, a white, minority-ruled regime.

Some better thrillers occupied Milland's time before their 1974 release dates. During the same stretch, Milland finished his memoirs for William Morrow and Company, provocatively calling it *Wide-Eyed in Babylon*.

Conveniently, Milland was able to stay in South Africa to film his few scenes for *Gold* in early 1973. The coproduction between South Africa and the United Kingdom was a bigger-budgeted affair than most of Milland's current efforts, costing $2 million.

Gold focuses on a mining engineer (Roger Moore) who is high-pressured by his manager (Bradford Dillman, Milland's "Greenhouse Jungle" costar) to take a position that he does not realize will enable a group of international investors (including John Gielgud as one) to manipulate the company's stock. Their plan is to create an underground disaster by having a mine "accidentally" flooded. Further complicating the situation is that the manager's wife (Susannah York) and the engineer fall in love. Milland plays York's grandfather and owner of the mine.

Gold resembles a seventies'-era James Bond film in part because so many Bond crew members were involved, from star Roger Moore to director Peter Hunt to editor John Glen. Adding to the high-grade production, Elmer Bernstein provided the score, and one of the songs, "Wherever Loves Takes Me" by Bernstein and Don Black, was nominated for a Best Song Oscar.

Ray Milland does not dominate the story, but he does run away with his few scenes. As the crusty, cigar-smoking mine owner—unaware of his grandson-in-law's scheme with the London stockbrokers—Milland delivers his lines with declarative wit, even when the dialogue is not necessarily that funny. After getting bad news about the mine during a party scene, he asserts, "I'm much too old to stand around here drinking!," another one of his late career's endless *Lost Weekend* references.

Despite the controversy of shooting in South Africa, many critics approved of *Gold*, which was a moneymaker in September 1974. *Variety* pegged it as "an exciting motion picture" with "terrifying underground sequences."

The Student Connection, shot in 1974 in Montpellier and Toulon, allowed Milland the convenience of making a movie near the family's new villa in the South of France.

The Giallo-infused picture is considerably better than one would expect from its unfortunate, porno-styled title. Milland expertly plays both headmaster and doctor at an all-boys' school in France. In an early scene, one of his young students sees him murdering the man he had hired (Charley Bravo) to kill the husband of his mistress (Sylva Koscina). But deviating from old film noirs like *The Window* (1949), neither the murderer (Milland) nor the viewer knows which youngster is the witness. The rest of the intricately plotted narrative moves along parallel tracks, as the police try to figure out who executed the husband, then the assassin, and the headmaster attempts to ferret out and kill the child that saw him commit the latter murder.

The Student Connection, a Spanish-Italian coproduction, suffers from the postdubbing of most of the cast, Milland excluded. Otherwise, it is neatly directed and cowritten by Rafael Romero Marchent and photographed in widescreen by Godofredo Pacheco in a toned-down style compared to other Giallo films, such as Dario Argento or Mario Bava's garish and gory work during this time.

For Milland, the best aspect of *The Student Connection* (and the main reason for his accepting the project) is that it gives the actor a complex lead role. He plays a murderer by proxy again, having hired a professional to do his dirty work. In the end, when his character believes that it is his mistress's son (Fernando E. Romero) who was the witness, he cannot bring himself to execute this particular boy and, thus, commits suicide by hanging, a melancholy climax, followed by one more unforeseen story curveball.

The Student Connection received a limited showing in the United States, premiering in Lafayette, Indiana, in 1975. When it was later released on VHS, it was retitled *Witness to Murder* but still mostly ignored.

Milland returned to California and softened his evildoer routine for *Escape to Witch Mountain*, his first and only Walt Disney production. Lensed in spring 1974 at several California locations and released in March 1975, *Witch*

Escape to Witch Mountain (1975), with Donald Pleasence

Mountain marked an attempt by the Disney company to tackle less lighthearted material after the 1966 death of its founder, Walt Disney.

Based on a 1968 Alexander Key novel, *Escape to Witch Mountain* centers around two orphaned children (Kim Richards, Ike Eisenmann) who are adopted by a millionaire (second-billed Milland) who learns from his assistant (Donald Pleasence) that he could exploit the youngsters' extrasensory powers for his own greedy purposes—namely, manipulating the stock market. Ultimately, the wealthy man's scheme is prevented when the children escape from his mansion and join an embittered widower (top-billed Eddie Albert), who helps them find their home.

As in *The Student Connection*, Milland's character, Alexander Bolt, seeks to hurt or kill children, and as before, he fails. More than any other cranky, egotistical figure of the many he personified, Milland's Bolt most physically resembles Charles Foster Kane, *Citizen Kane*'s version of William Randolph Hearst, the tycoon who had been part of Milland's life in the 1930s. In fact, Bolt's home is called Xanthus, a play on Xanadu, the Kane replica of San Simeon.

In the Disney tradition, *Escape to Witch Mountain* updates the folkloric tropes of children's fairy tales, like *Hansel and Gretel*. This revamping, combined with the sci-fi elements that confer superpowers to the children's survival abilities, best explains why the movie was an immediate favorite among young audiences in its day and ever since. The reviews, though, were excessively unfriendly. The *New York Times*' Vincent Canby wrote, "*Escape to Witch Mountain* is a Walt Disney production for children who will watch absolutely anything that moves." Critics aside, profitable sequels and remakes have emerged over many years, turning the original into a de facto classic.

If one is to give credence to a "blind item" from cyberspace, then an appalling revelation about Danny Milland was alleged in 2018 regarding *Witch Mountain*. On the *Crazy Days and Nights* blog (crazydaysandnights.net), the anonymous host, an entertainment lawyer, tells the story of a former child star (likely Kim Richards) being repeatedly raped by the son of a former A-list Oscar winner (likely Danny Milland, who apparently visited the *Witch Mountain* locations). According to the reporting, it is unclear if either Ray or Kim Richards's mother knew about the incidents, but the anonymous author of another website (foxella.com) republished the full story and outright names Kim Richards and Danny Milland. It is hard to trust unverified sources with such explosive accusations, but it does appear at the very least Danny Milland was deeply troubled at this point in his life.

At age thirty-four, in 1974, Danny proposed marriage to Jacqueline May. But the forty-one-year-old May was reluctant to take the plunge with Danny, saying at the time, "Being a movie star's son does have its problems, believe it or not, and it does make it difficult for him to lead a normal life." According to May, Danny was receiving only one hundred dollars per month from his father, and she added, "He lives in a terrible place in West Hollywood where they play cards all day long. He eats in hamburger joints. It's sad. After the opulence he grew up with, it's hard for him to keep his head straight in depressing surroundings." Later, Danny and Jacqueline May got engaged but never married.

While feeling helpless about his son's plight, Milland next played an updated Nick Beal in *The Dead Don't Die*, a TV movie written by Robert Bloch and shot on the Universal soundstages in late 1974. It aired on NBC in January 1975 to mild reviews and ratings.

"Special-guest-star" Milland is a tough but seemingly helpful dance-hall operator in 1930's Chicago. His assistance to top-billed George Hamilton's sailor on leave is suspicious from the start. He offers to help the distraught young man find the real killer of his brother's wife after his brother is convicted and executed for the crime. Yet, once the sailor uncovers a possible voodoo connection to his brother and sister-in-law's deaths, he finds himself among an "army of the dead" in a netherworld ruled by Milland's character.

Like director Curtis Harrington's feature films, *The Dead Don't Die* is more creepy than terrifying. With cinematographer James Crabe, Harrington does an able job of fusing film noir and horror. Better yet, the frequent use of Robert Prince's dance-hall organ music lends an unnerving atmosphere to many scenes. Milland admirably restrains himself up until his character's true nature is exposed at the climax. The rest of the cast is not put to good use: notably Joan Blondell, playing a shopkeeper, shows little of her usual gusto and never shares the frame with Milland, her 1931 *Blonde Crazy* costar.

MEMOIRS

Finally, *Wide-Eyed in Babylon* reached book stores in September 1974 with some fanfare and mostly flattering reviews. Milland was lightly chastised for his many omissions, most conspicuously *Dial M for Murder*. Since that movie had brought about a marital scandal, it was a topic he didn't care to revisit. His loving dedication to Mal Milland at the beginning of the book said everything about his priorities.

Wide-Eyed is basically a collection of anecdotes, wittily told but not always in chronological order. Candid as it is, the book uses some questionable, even offensive language, which has become more problematic through the years. However, most book critics of the day were won over by Milland's storytelling abilities. *Kirkus Reviews* wrote, "As incisively outspoken and wryly humorous as it is intensely personal. . . . Wickedly readable." A less enthusiastic *Variety* reviewer felt, "Milland writes a quite literary grade prose . . . [and] has the virtue of humor. A nice irony runs through his narrative."

While on a book tour around the country, Milland consented to several interviews. In one, he remarked about contemporary movies: "I have a particular opinion about them and it's not very high, but I find some of the actors interesting. Charles Bronson, for instance." (Bronson hardly symbolized a new face, but Milland was in good company with his selection: while visiting the set of the actor's *St. Ives* in 1975, the great Swedish director Ingmar Bergman declared that Bronson was "scandalously underestimated.")

Milland finished his tour in Neath, then England, in 1975. In between visiting his old friends and relatives, he stopped by the Junior Gnoll School of his youth. During his February stay in Wales, he was interviewed about his book and career on a BBC radio show called *Nine-Five on Monday*. In London in April, he appeared on two high-toned television talk shows. First came *Film '75*, on which host Barry Norman lobbed softball questions to Milland about how it felt to win his Oscar and why he abandoned his toupée for *Love Story* ("Because I hated wearing it!," the actor snapped back). About two weeks later, on *The Book Programme*, host Robert Robertson and a panel of reporters queried Milland with more hard-hitting questions. Then the book peddling was pretty much over, but Milland was seriously considering writing another book, a fiction novel, and becoming a full-time author.

AT HOME AND ABROAD

Following his p.r. junket and return to the United States, Milland took on more of the same kind of movie and TV fare. He was committed now to performing full time, saying, "Funny thing, I never liked acting.... It always embarrassed me. But I like working. I've retired twice, and always had to come back because I got so darn bored. So now I pick the parts I figure I can get some enjoyment out of.... The day you start to retire is the time you start to die."

In early 1975, *Columbo* producers Richard Levinson and William Link invited Milland to join their newest NBC mystery, *Ellery Queen*, this time as a character embodying wealth without evil.

Ellery Queen started as a series of novels by Frederic Dannay and Manfred Bennington Lee about a mystery writer and his detective father working together on baffling cases. "Too Many Suspects," the debut episode (in March 1975), gave Milland a sizable part. Set in 1947 Manhattan, the story begins with the murder of a young fashion designer, the mistress of a financier (Milland). Ellery Queen (Jim Hutton) helps his father (David Wayne) figure out whodunit.

Milland looks weary, and his character becomes increasingly less vital to the story, but the writers integrate references to his canon and personal life. This latter element comes in the form of Milland playing a man in love with a younger woman again, but also with his wife. And his character's inability to remember what bar he visited on the night of the murder, due to an alcoholic blackout, is yet another homage to *The Lost Weekend*.

Directed by David Greene, "Too Many Suspects" maintains a well-disguised mystery over a ninety-eight-minute running time, and unlike the anachronistic hairstyles and costumes, Elmer Bernstein's score evokes the late forties era. The most creative moment has nothing to do with a plot revelation: it is just before the climax when Ellery turns to the viewer, breaking the fourth wall, and asks in direct address if *you* have figured out the mystery yet!

Still in early 1975, Milland traveled from Hollywood to Canada for what would be his most obscure project, an episode of a short-lived TV series, *From Sea to Shining Sea*, which aired in syndication in April 1975. Mysteriously, Milland's appearance, though top-billed, is not mentioned in most of his filmographies.

In 1974, John and Helen Secondari developed the idea of teaching North American history lessons through a format that jumped from one era to another. But *From Sea to Shining Sea* did not last very long and was jinxed from the start. Part of its very first episode, when aired in New York City in

September 1974, was missing its sound—and then roundly panned! Robert Culp, as the time-traveling John Freeborn, left the series immediately and was replaced by David Huffman. John Secondari himself did not live to see the subsequent episodes—he died in February 1975.

Lawrence Doheny directed the third installment, "The Unwanted," with guest-star Milland playing a stern judge who presides over an immigration case. Set in 1888, J. P. Miller's story boils down to prejudice against Irish settlers who want jobs but are wrongly accused of taking employment away from "real" Americans. Freeborn supports the transporter on trial (Richard Boone), while Judge Kinner (Milland) is disdainful of the whole matter.

Despite his top billing, Milland only appears during the courtroom climax, looking sour and unusually jowly behind the bench. Unlike the ill-fated first episode, "The Unwanted" received high marks, even from the *New York Times*' John J. O'Connor: "It's a true story, dramatized effectively on appropriate locations. And the production has a strong cast of performers . . . [and] an intelligent and nicely constructed script."

Milland ended 1975 with his own *This Is Your Life* British ITV episode, shot on October 15 and aired on November 19 (though never seen in the United States). While Ray and Mal were visiting England that fall, producer Jack Crawshaw and host Eamonn Andrews secretly planned for his family to make appearances; tributes and testimonials from past costars were harder to arrange, so most were pretaped. Milland seemed genuinely surprised by the amiable "ambush" outside the Thames Television Studios. His willing cooperation with the program started with a quip: "If I'd known this was happening, I'd have worn a hairpiece!"

Andrews then escorted Milland inside Thames to have brief visits with his family and friends, including Mal, Danny, Victoria, her husband, Edmund Lowell, and grandson Travis; coming from Wales, his nephews and sisters, Beryl and Enid, greeted their famous relative. He was most caught off guard seeing Estelle Brody, the actress who had helped him get his start in the industry in the late 1920s, and there were testimonials from Bob Hope, Dorothy Lamour, and Frankie Howerd. The only past costar to embrace Milland in person was Jan Sterling (from *Rhubarb*).

RICH MAN, POOR MAN

Nineteen seventy-six was a busier year, with Milland in an acclaimed TV miniseries, two TV movies, and three feature films, including one—for the first time in a long time—from a major "name" director.

The miniseries, *Rich Man, Poor Man*, started things off, having been shot late in 1975. The first of the twelve "chapters" aired February 1, 1976, on ABC. Milland did not appear in all of the chapters, but he dominated five, starting with chapters 3 and 4, both airing on February 2. His wealthy, self-important patriarch was par for the course during this period, but the show's enormous appeal across the country (and later worldwide) presented Milland in a vehicle considered high quality and significant; as one of the industry's earliest TV miniseries, it earned him his first and only Emmy nomination—for Outstanding Continuing Performance by a Supporting Actor in a Drama Series. Needless to say, he was both surprised and gratified.

Actually, like *Roots*, another highly-rated ABC miniseries the following year, *Rich Man, Poor Man* lacked aesthetic appeal, but together they popularized the miniseries concept. The presence of many stars supporting the lesser-known lead players provided insurance for ABC, protecting its $6 million investment. Milland was pleased to be part of the ensemble and to be photographed by Russell Metty for the third time.

Based on the 1969 novel by Irwin Shaw, Dean Riesner's teleplay tracks the divergent course of two brothers from the German American Jordache family, starting in 1945 and ending in the mid-1960s. Rudy (Peter Strauss) becomes a well-educated "master of the universe" in business, while Tom (Nick Nolte) rebels at the world and takes menial jobs before turning to boxing.

As a fraternal melodrama, the brothers' stories are compulsively watchable in the best "soap-opera" tradition, as codirected by David Greene and Boris Sagal. "Poor man" Nolte gives a star-making performance, but it is the "rich man" Strauss who carries the greater narrative load. His character's biggest conflict manifests itself while he is working for the wealthy Duncan Calderwood (Milland), who comes to expect his protégé to marry his gawky daughter (Kim Darby); yet Rudy is in love with his long-time girlfriend, the beautiful Julie (Susan Blakely).

With his hair-color changes and eventual baldness charting the passage of time, Milland is as smooth as ever as the entrepreneur-capitalist. One standout moment in chapter 3 finds him luring Rudy into accepting a job with his company. Milland conjures his "Nick Beal" persona here. His best scene, however, comes during his final appearance, in chapter 6, as he lashes out at Rudy, falsely accusing him of seducing his daughter, while *simultaneously* trying to entice him with money and another promotion if he will take her off his hands!

Milland does not share many scenes with the impressive array of other guest stars, but he is a key member, along with such past coplayers as Gloria Grahame (*Black Noon*), George Maharis (*Night Gallery*), Van Johnson (*Company of Killers*), Kim Darby (*Cool Million*), and Ed Asner (*Daughter of the Mind*). In fact, Asner won an Emmy for Outstanding Lead Actor for a Single Performance in a TV Series for his portrayal of the Jordache patriarch. Unfortunately, Milland lost his Supporting Actor bid to Anthony Zerbe for ABC's *Harry O*.

Most reviewers approved of the show, which became the second highest rated of the 1976-through-1977 season (after *All in the Family*) and garnered a total of twenty-three Emmy nominations. The tremendous reception prompted ABC to immediately greenlight a sequel, *Rich Man, Poor Man Book II*, airing between September 1976 and March 1977. Milland made a brief cameo in the first episode only.

NOSTALGIA

Milland then followed his TV triumph with a trip to England for another 1975 shoot. *Aces High* was released in Europe in 1976. Its American debut was on HBO in 1980, not in the theaters.

For *Aces High*, director Jack Gold and screenwriter Howard Barker combined an updated version of R. C. Sherriff's 1928 play, *Journey's End*, with Cecil Lewis's memoir, *Sagittarius Rising*, both personal reflections on World War I, specifically the all-male camaraderie of British units.

From the start, Milland was attracted to the project's nostalgic evocation of both his former aviation dramas and his experiences as a licensed pilot. He takes a backseat to the younger actors (like Malcolm McDowell), only appearing in two scenes, both of which implicitly criticize military hierarchy. Milland, Trevor Howard, and Richard Johnson lend deliberately pompous authority to their roles as top brass, physically and emotionally removed from the fight against the Germans. Their detachment is chilling as they send their underlings to near-certain death.

Other than Milland's scenes, what should have been a sharp condemnation of warfare turns out to be a mostly standard-issue war movie. Even the excitement of the aerial fights is greatly diminished by the use of rear projection. Janet Maslin's 1979 *New York Times* review was mostly negative: "*Aces High* is nothing worse than a well-cast, well-mounted war movie without any particular spark. At its worst, it is merely listless."

Towards the end of 1975, Milland was delighted to take part in his most prestigious opportunity in years. Based on the unfinished 1941 F. Scott Fitzgerald novel, *The Last Tycoon* became the final film directed by Elia Kazan. It also happened to offer Milland another return to Paramount and was the most substantially budgeted (at $5.5 million) of his latter-day pictures. On a personal note, the story concerned studio politics at MGM in the 1930s, something Milland knew about all too well.

Photographed in October 1975, *The Last Tycoon* started out as Sam Spiegel's labor of love, but the legendary producer of *The African Queen* (1951) and *Lawrence of Arabia* (1962) didn't realize how much labor would be needed to get the Fitzgerald text onto the big screen. Previously, there had been TV adaptations, but Spiegel was determined to gather the best talent to create a germane version for post-Golden Age Hollywood.

Like many Ray Milland movies of the 1970s and '80s, *The Last Tycoon* promoted an all-star cast. In this case, the gallery of "names" was present as much to sell the property to the public as to evoke an earlier era of filmmaking, namely, MGM under the auspices of production head Irving Thalberg (renamed Monroe Stahr by Fitzgerald). Fortunately for Spiegel, this type of irony-tinged movie nostalgia was in vogue: *The Day of the Locust* (1975), *Hearts of the West* (1975), *The Wild Party* (1975), *A Matter of Time* (1976), and so on.

Spiegel's angle was to have a movie that mirrored the open-ended nature of Fitzgerald's incomplete last work; to adapt the book, he hired Harold Pinter, the British writer of enigmatic, elliptical narratives. In the ostensibly simple story, the young executive of International World Films, Stahr, slowly alienates everyone around him—his "minions," his boss, a union head, and the only woman he truly loves.

Well before Milland joined the production, it was already plagued with troubles. Peter Bogdanovich and Al Pacino turned down Spiegel's offer to direct and star, respectively. Later, second-choice director Mike Nichols quit over the casting of Robert De Niro as Stahr, so Spiegel replaced Nichols with Elia Kazan. It had been many years since Kazan had a hit, but his name maintained its artistic cachet, along with political controversy (for having "named names" during the 1950s HUAC Red Scare). Once filming got underway, problems persisted: newcomer Theresa Russell alleged Spiegel made unwanted sexual advances.

In the film, Ray Milland was cast as Mort Fleishacker, the New York lawyer for studio boss Pat Brady (Robert Mitchum), a thinly veiled Louis B. Mayer. Spiegel's choice of Milland was self-reflexive on two counts: for having worked for Louis B. Mayer and the fact that *The Lost Weekend*'s Don Birnam stated his favorite author was F. Scott Fitzgerald, at least in Charles Jackson's novel. (In the Wilder movie, a Fitzgerald novel can be glimpsed on Birnam's bookcase.) Milland and Mitchum spend most of their screen time together, and it is refreshing to see these two old pros enact a bond of understated corporate arrogance. It is possible that Milland, Mitchum, Pinter, and Kazan were all taunting Spiegel under his nose as this very type

The Last Tycoon (1976), with Robert Mitchum and Robert De Niro.
Photo credit: Album / Alamy Stock Photo.

of unpleasant executive. Milland shares little or no time with previous costars like John Carradine (as a studio tour guide), Donald Pleasence (miscast as Fitzgerald), or Peter Strauss (as a screenwriter).

But in 1976, the results disappointed critics and audiences almost as much as Spiegel himself. He was quoted as saying, "The greatest young actor in America today is Robert De Niro, the greatest living director is Elia Kazan, and I may be the greatest producer of all time. How the hell could we make such a bad fucking movie?" A typical review at the time came from Ruth Batchelor of the *Los Angeles Free Press*: "I hope for the sake of Fitzgerald's memory, *The Last Tycoon* will be the last effort to cinematize the author." The box-office returns were similarly miserable: $1.8 million. And it was only nominated for an Oscar for Best Art Direction, then lost even that. *Village Voice* critic Andrew Sarris was one of its few defenders, calling it "an accomplished film . . . eminently worth supporting if we are to preserve a literate cinema."

In an unfortunate footnote to his *Last Tycoon* experience, Milland was accused by costar Tony Curtis of antisemitism. Curtis did not share any scenes with Milland (who happened to be playing a Jewish character), but

Curtis later related in his autobiography that he overheard Milland in a group discussion say something about "the usurpers who were trying to get into Hollywood." It appears Curtis never confronted Milland about his assumptions, but he felt confident publishing them in 2008, more than two decades after Milland's death. While it is possible Milland made such a comment, it is also possible that Curtis's motives were impure: he suggests how he had been romantically involved with Grace Kelly in the 1950s and how he thought Milland was jealous of his looks on the *Tycoon* set!

The Last Tycoon could have provided Ray Milland with a bitterly graceful exit from the business, the ultimate iconoclastic move. By denouncing through his craft the very industry that alternately nurtured and rejected him through the years, Milland said more in a way with his truncated performance than the whole of his memoirs of two years earlier. Yet the commercial and critical disinterest in *The Last Tycoon* kept an ever-more-cynical Milland soldiering on with a slew of movies and television shows of variable quality, and assured, sadly by acquiescence, there would be many more twisted Tycoons to come. Neither Stahr nor Spiegel was the last of their kind, but Spiegel, like Kazan, would never make another movie.

Milland headed next to Switzerland for *The Swiss Conspiracy*, a routine action adventure financed by American and West German investors, which did not reach US theaters until September 1977. Apart from a few expletives, director Jack Arnold's feature could have been another TV movie. Norman Klenman's screenplay tells how a US Justice Department officer (David Janssen) tries to help a Zurich banker (Milland) figure out who is blackmailing five of his wealthiest clients.

Despite many fist fights, gun fights, and car chases, there is a flat quality to *The Swiss Conspiracy*. Inexplicably, the natural beauty of Zurich and Geneva is only visible on rare occasions (for example, in an amazing final widescreen shot), and Klaus Doldinger's musical theme rates as one of the most generic-sounding action scores of the era. Milland (without toupée) tried to infuse some life into his crotchety banker character, but by wearing tinted glasses in his scenes, he rarely had the chance to use his facial expressions.

Milland returned to Hollywood (specifically déclassé Burbank) to rejoin David Janssen for *Mayday at 40,000 Feet!*, the most unintentionally hilarious of all Milland's late career projects. Clearly influenced by *Airport* (1970) and its laughable sequel, *Airport 1975* (1974), *Mayday* anticipated the *parodie par excellence, Airplane!* (1980).

Producer and cowriter Andrew Fenady (of *Black Noon* and *Terror in the Wax Museum*) asked Milland to participate and gave him the most substantive of the guest spots in a TV movie about a commercial flight disrupted by a crazed killer. The psychopath is an extradited prisoner (Marjoe Gortner) who shoots the pilot (Janssen) and a fellow passenger after destroying part of the hydraulic oil lines. The rest of the action shifts to Milland's irritable and alcoholic doctor forcing himself to help the wounded while the first officer (Christopher George) attempts a precarious landing.

In *Mayday*, Milland crudely parodies his seventies screen persona—a tour de force of irascibility. From the first moment we see him in the airport, his ill-tempered character demands to know where he can find the nearest bar, and on the plane, he shouts to the flight attendants, "How long does it take to get a drink around here!?" His embittered state changes gradually during the second half of the story as he is reluctantly pressed into duty. By the end, having saved the wounded pilot and passenger, his faith in humankind is restored (very unconvincingly!).

It is unclear whether director Robert Butler meant for *Mayday* to be quite so silly. The CBS movie aired in November and was released by Warner Bros. in different countries in 1977 as a theatrical feature.

At this point, Milland didn't mind appearing in nonsensical material and followed *Mayday at 40,000 Feet!* with the similarly foolish *Look What's Happened to Rosemary's Baby*. This ABC sequel to 1968's *Rosemary's Baby* was influenced as much by the success of *The Exorcist* (1973) as it was the Roman Polanski classic, based on Ira Levin's novel.

Anthony Wilson's teleplay begins with Rosemary (Patty Duke, subbing for Mia Farrow) kidnapping her "son of Satan," Adrian, from the devil's coven headed by Mr. and Mrs. Castevet (Milland and Ruth Gordon). Once Rosemary is killed, "the tribe" members attempt to recapture and reindoctrinate the adult Adrian (Stephen McHattie). They are successful when they send a seemingly innocent nurse (Donna Mills) to seduce Adrian.

Between Wilson's writing and the direction of Sam O'Steen (editor of the Polanski film), *Look What's Happened to Rosemary's Baby* vacillates between a straight sequel and out-and-out spoof. The funniest lines are uttered by Milland and Gordon as the bickering Castevets. At one point, during a Hollywood visit, Mrs. Castevet carps, "Will you lay off all this killing talk? We're only out here for a couple of days and we were going to meet Charlton Heston!"

Ray Milland seems to relish his latest devil worshipping, happily crashing his old Paramount stomping grounds in a couple of backlot scenes. Tina Louise, who plays Adrian's aunt, shares one of the film's wilder moments with Milland (the coven transforming Adrian into the antichrist), but being in a group tableau, she didn't recall working specifically with Milland. Still, she remembered that she thought "he was a remarkable actor," particularly admiring *The Lost Weekend*.

Some of the others in the all-star cast are less effective. Broderick Crawford appears briefly as a sheriff and spends no time with Milland, while George Maharis, as Adrian's father, is perfunctory five years after Milland's *Night Gallery* episode and a year after *Rich Man, Poor Man*.

Its Halloween weekend airing assured high ratings, and *Look What's Happened to Rosemary's Baby* continued to do well in syndicated reruns.

Milland's 1977 releases included two miniseries and four "foreign" coproductions, some much more interesting than others.

HIGHS AND LOWS

During the summer of 1976, Milland flew to Bucharest to film his few scenes for *Oil*, a Romanian-Italian feature. Milland's participation was meant to strengthen the international box office in a cast comprised mostly of Romanian actors. The other Hollywood names, Stuart Whitman and Woody Strode, didn't help the film receive much play in the United States.

In Ioan Grigorescu's screenplay, Milland plays "The Boss" (a.k.a. Mr. Stewart), an American oilfield baron stationed in the Sahara Desert. He initiates the action when he realizes he can manipulate stock-market oil prices by arranging to destroy his own oilfield. Though he enlists an American specialist (Whitman) to help his Romanian crew cap an oil rig, the others on the team turn out to be saboteurs who undermine the rescue effort.

More remote than ever, Milland is literally isolated in his scenes, all set in a spacious, ornately designed office. The rest of the story takes place primarily on the oil field, with the bursting oil derrick and roaring fire as a repeating central image. Occasionally, director Mircea Drăgan turns *Oil* into something visually impressive, but too much of the time, it is a dreary, overlong action movie. Given the Arab oil embargo and rising gas prices in the United States at the time, *Oil* could have garnered a following, but it was poorly distributed.

Milland was pleased to return to England—and take his customary detour to see friends and family in Wales—when he signed onto *The Uncanny*. His latest horror picture, directed by Denis Héroux in November and December 1976, was first released in Canada in August 1977. Though a British-Canadian coproduction with a $1.1 million budget, most of *The Uncanny* was shot in Québec (Montreal and Senneville). It was only because top-billed Peter Cushing didn't like to travel that his scenes with Milland were done at Pinewood Studios in the United Kingdom.

Coming late in the British horror-anthology cycle, *The Uncanny* tells three separate accounts of feline revenge. In the framing device, Cushing is an author who visits the estate of a publisher (Milland) to convince him not only to consider his latest work (the three cat tales) but to believe that these furry pets are supernatural creatures ready to take over the world. As the writer nervously tells the stories, the publisher scoffs at his paranoid conclusions. Every episode climaxes with angry cats killing the villains, and the stand-off between author and publisher is resolved at the end.

As with *Frogs*, Milland was back in avenging-animal territory, even though Milland is not one of the animal haters this time, and the progressive politics are muted at best. Of this kind of horror subgenre, *The Uncanny* lacks both the scares and campy laughs one would expect, and it is disheartening to learn that some cats were mistreated during filming, causing cinematographer Harry Waxman to threaten to quit.

After poor showings in Canada and the United Kingdom (where it originally received an X rating), Rank Film Distributors never bothered with an official American theatrical release. Thus, there were few contemporary reviews, and the more recent commentary hasn't been favorable: Matt Brunson's View from the Couch observes, "It's always fun watching Cushing, Milland and [Donald] Pleasence in practically anything, but their presence isn't enough to elevate this humdrum horror outing."

Milland was relieved to return home at the end of 1976, where he worked on *Seventh Avenue*, NBC's three-part imitation of *Rich Man, Poor Man*. He filmed his few scenes on the Universal backlot, not Manhattan, where the story was set. This latest all-star miniseries revolved around a working-class laborer (Steven Keats) who rises to the top of New York's cutthroat garment center. It aired throughout February 1977, but like Milland's other three-part miniseries later that year, *Testimony of Two Men*, it was eclipsed in ratings, reviews, and Emmy wins by ABC's eight-part *Roots*, which had found an enormous audience in January 1977.

Seventh Avenue was based on Norman Bogner's 1967 novel, with its title referencing the primary location of Manhattan's fashion district. Our overly ambitious protagonist emerges from the struggling émigré Blackman family on the Lower East Side, and his actions trigger the inevitable tales of greed, lust, and revenge. Codirected by Richard Irving and Russ Marberry, *Seventh Avenue* juggles many storylines, punctuated by a *What Makes Sammy Run?* spirit to the career path of Jay Blackman (Keats).

The guest stars that populate this world include Ray Milland and Gloria Grahame, both from *Rich Man, Poor Man* and *Black Noon*. Of the group making appearances, Milland and Grahame best exemplify the 1930s through 1950s time period. Grahame plays a building superintendent who secretly works for the mob, and Milland (in part 2) is Douglas Fredericks, the slick competitor to the antihero Jay. In an unusual reversal, the younger man is not only greedy but devious while Milland's tough businessman is outmatched and defeated by his rival. Though seen too briefly, Milland meaningfully conveys the emotions of an undermined authority figure. Another personality from the story's era, Eli Wallach, impresses as a desperate man who kills himself on a cutting machine.

John Leonard expressed a mixed reaction in his *New York Times* review: "[T]here is a certain vulgar energy about the first hour . . . [and] some gritty detail about the dress business, warehousing, wholesaling, showrooms, loan sharks and price fixes . . . [but then] the plot sags and pace plods."

Filmed at the beginning of the year and aired in May 1977, *Testimony of Two Men* has been rightfully forgotten, though it holds the dubious distinction as the first syndicated miniseries, part of something then called Operation Prime Time (OPT).

Testimony of Two Men started out as a *Gone with the Wind* corrective, the portrait of Union soldiers returning to their families following the Civil War, specifically in Pennsylvania. Since it aired after the highly rated first TV showings of *Gone with the Wind* in 1976 (on HBO, then NBC), *Testimony* capitalized on the renewed interest in all things related to the war. Yet none of the characters are as memorable as those written by Margaret Mitchell. Like Taylor Caldwell's 1968 novel on which it is based, the story centers around the lives, loves, and scandals of three former soldiers, Dr. Martin Eton (Steve Forrest), Dr. Jonathan Ferrier (David Birney), and Ferrier's less responsible younger brother (David Huffman).

Ray Milland plays Jonas Witherby, the vicious owner of a gunpowder factory who marries a prostitute (Devon Ericson), from whom he embezzles money. Witherby later helps a powerful senator (J. D. Cannon) bring down Dr. Ferrier before Witherby is killed (his munitions plant explodes while he is in it). Despite looking withdrawn and sporting an ugly brown toupée in his early scenes, Milland nicely underplays his corrupt character. Producer Jack Laird surrounds Milland with a large ensemble: Ralph Bellamy, Joan Van Ark, Dan Dailey, Cameron Mitchell, Margaret O'Brien, William Shatner, and Inga Swenson. Too bad codirectors Leo Penn and Larry Yust are of little help making the starchy Hollywood production feel at all raw or "real."

John J. O'Connor's *New York Times* review spared nothing in its contempt: "[S]omeone at M.C.A. Universal doesn't seem to understand that a bestselling novel and what the publicity calls an all-star cast do not, in themselves, guarantee quality. Other ingredients such as adequate preparation and rehearsal, technical care and artistic imagination are also required."

The Pyjama Girl Case (1977)

In February 1977, Milland traveled to Australia for something different. In the Spanish- and Italian-financed production *The Pyjama Girl Case*, Milland was the star, not a guest star, and this murder mystery was far more lurid than anything he had ever been part of before. The story was based on a real-life Australian cold case from 1934, updated to the 1970s. (A short 2006 American documentary titled *The Pyjama Girl Mystery: A True Story of Murder, Obsession and Lies* used excerpts from Milland's film.)

The 1977 release (seen in most regions in 1978) is as baffling as the case itself. A strange mishmash of police procedural (with a few noir touches), romantic melodrama and soft-porn Giallo, *The Pyjama Girl Case* could have been a superior film but is marred by some unfortunate aesthetic choices and the usual terrible postdubbing.

The narrative itself, cowritten by Flavio Mogherini (the film's director) and Rafael Sánchez Campoy, follows two separate routes. One is about a retired detective (Milland) figuring out who killed a young woman on a beach and then burned her body to disguise her identity. The other storyline, a possible red herring, shows how the young victim's similar-looking friend (Dalila Di Lazzaro) has many suitors in her life but is unhappy with all of them.

The artistic touches vary wildly. Mogherini's Neorealist background as an art director for Rossellini and Pasolini is a likely factor regarding the more striking imagery, yet there are many routine shots, too. The score, all credited to Riz Ortolani, ranges from a melodic, bittersweet leitmotif to annoying synthesizer passages. Two songs sung by Amanda Lear, cowritten by Lear and Ortoloni, with Lear's hypnotically low, Germanically masculine tone, add an unusual gender-bending factor to a movie that too often focuses on women's nudity from the point of view of lascivious men.

Milland's performance is both characteristic and its own mystery. His detective is a Columbo type, wearing a rumpled beige raincoat and out-of-place ascot. Apart from not appearing as elegantly attired as usual, Milland looks much older than his actual age, the result mostly of constant traveling. Liberated from his plutocratic persona, Milland consented to be a cantankerous gadfly who swears a lot (he says "shit" at one early point) and even ridicules a sleazy suspect by using a vulgar hand gesture to indicate he caught the man masturbating.

Milland retains his witty sense of humor but with greater misanthropy than ever. His character's disdain for humankind is best illustrated by his eye rolling and sour expressions, yet images of the detective alone—on a beach searching for clues and in a museum near a grotesque exhibition of the nude corpse—are sad and disquieting.

Of the reviews of the day, few found much to recommend but some recent reassessments have recognized *The Pyjama Girl Case* as a worthy cult item. Ben Martyn wrote in 2018, "[It] has an inconsistent tone and limited emotional impact.... But it's a cleverly constructed film with valuable political undertones." Andrew F. Peirce added in 2019, "It feels unique in the world of horror, outwardly rejecting acts of violence and making us consider our desire to see death and torture, forcing us to realise that these narratives can come from a place of truth."

In the United States in the spring, Milland slowed down for the rest of the year. In March 1977, Grace Kelly returned briefly to the forefront when he was approached by the BBC to be interviewed for the documentary, *Once upon a Time... Is Now Grace Kelly*, narrated by Kelly, which aired in the US on NBC at the end of year. But if he hadn't mentioned Kelly in his memoirs, Milland certainly wasn't going to be asked questions about her for a film. Instead, he signed an agreement allowing his name and likeness be used, while others, like Alfred Hitchcock, Jimmy Stewart, and William Holden fully participated as "talking heads." Soon after, he was overjoyed on April 22, 1977, when Vicki gave birth to her second child, Alexander Gregson Graham.

Workwise, Milland returned to familiar terrain—Mexico—in August 1977 for *Survival Run*. Interweaving action adventure, road picture, and youth melodrama, *Survival Run* (a.k.a. *Spree*) was released in Europe in spring 1979 and in the US in February 1980. The budget of $850,000 was sizable for what would have been considered an "exploitation" picture (it received an R rating due to its nudity and violence).

Milland endured a difficult time in Baja California, Mexico. Apart from the extreme heat, a flash flood one day destroyed some of the equipment. Furthermore, the delays cost Milland the chance to attend the September

11 prime time Emmy Awards ceremony in Pasadena, during which he was up for his *Rich Man, Poor Man* award.

In the film, cowritten by *Survival Run*'s director, Larry Spiegel, second-billed Milland appears strikingly all in white as "The Professor," the leader of a gang of seedy prospectors in the Mexican desert. When a bunch of teenagers on vacation crash their van and happen upon the mercenaries, they are welcomed initially. However, after one of the Professor's hired hands rapes one of the girls, the rest of the men turn on the other youngsters, and a deadly engagement ensues.

Milland easily walks off with the picture, turning his low-key nihilism into something almost attractive (one of the teenage girls actually flirts with him). The Professor's persistent contempt for his factotums ends with a darkly amusing moment when he gladly bids "adieu" to one who falls to his death. It is this very indifference to life and the welfare of others that connects (or should connect) Ray Milland to cynical younger generations, despite the fact his character is out to kill the members of that very group. Misunderstanding Milland's all-powerful, near-mythic presence, *Variety* commented cattily, "There are also several intriguing highlights, most notably how the villainous Milland manages to keep his pearly white suit spotless after what has had to have been an extremely messy trek through the desert."

Milland's final 1977 production, *Slavers*, continued his prominent guest-star status as another heinous villain. Late in the year, Milland returned to Africa, this time Zimbabwe (then called Rhodesia), for what became another arduous shoot.

Benefiting from the massive interest in the slave-trade era following the airing of the miniseries *Roots*, *Slavers* tried to distinguish itself by declaring in prepublicity how much more accurate this tale would be told. For the US release, the West German production received an R rating, though like *Survival Run*, the US cut was tamer and less brutal than the original.

Directed, produced and co-written by German-born Jürgen Goslar, *Slavers* is set in the post-Civil War period when slave trading was considered less "essential." Fighting over the last of the shipments from Africa to America, an alcoholic Scottish trader (top-billed Trevor Howard) tries to steal back his slaves from the ruthless Arab, Hassan (Milland). Later in the story, they square off against each other and another trader (Cameron Mitchell), leading to many deaths and only one surviving trader.

Slavers represented a definite low point for Ray Milland. The film is repulsively violent in its supposed attempt to be more "realistic" than *Roots*. To wit, Milland's character blithely shoots slaves in the head for sport. Further, it was a mistake for Milland—far greater than in *Golden Earrings* thirty years earlier—to darken his face and pretend to be of another race, even if he looked younger and more handsome than he did in other recent endeavors. Despite having a generous $2.5 million budget, the movie drags along and has little artistic merit, though Milland and Howard display a certain amount of glee being evil.

One night, back at their hotel, Milland discussed with Howard how they ended up in such a lousy production. Milland later confessed in an interview,

> I made this awful film called *Slavers* . . . and Trevor Howard was in it, who I always thought was a marvelous actor . . . and after about a week into the picture, I said to him, "Look, Trevor, just why are you making this picture which we all know is going to be awful?" And he said, "I was wondering why you're doing it." Neither of us could figure out what each other was doing in it, and thankfully I don't think the film's ever been shown.

On top of the abhorrent nature of what is on the screen, the production itself was struck by disaster when thirty-nine crew members on a ferry were thrown overboard during a storm, leaving thirty-four who were rescued but five who died. A police investigation developed, as did considerable tension on the set. One also gets the queasy feeling that both the animals and many of the African extras were not treated well in this supposedly valiant effort to expose the cruel nature of slave traders.

After this true career nadir, Milland continued with his "professional guest star" appearances in films and television. Soon enough, though, the Milland family itself would be rocked by tragedy, and Ray's health would deteriorate.

CHAPTER 12

THE LONG VOYAGE HOME (1977–1986)

EITHER BY FATE, COINCIDENCE, OR HIS OWN CHOICE OF MATERIAL, SEVERAL of Milland's latter-day projects had nautical themes, harkening back to both his youthful fascination with water and his days as a preadolescent sailor. The fact that he literally ended up in the ocean (where his ashes were scattered) became a telling and bittersweet end for this lifelong adventurer.

As a younger man, Milland starred in such films as *Ebb Tide* and *Reap the Wild Wind*. After *Love Story*, there were just as many stories with ships, oceans, or seaside motifs—from *River of Gold*'s competitive sea hunt to *From Sea to Shining Sea*'s perilous immigrant voyage to *The Slavers*' excruciating barge expeditions.

In the fall of 1977, Milland joined another all-star cast for *Cruise into Terror*, an ABC-TV movie that aired in early February 1978. This curious cross between *The Love Boat* and a horror movie about an ocean trip that becomes deadly was coproduced by Aaron Spelling, the force behind *The Love Boat*, a TV show on which Milland would also soon appear. If nothing else, *Cruise into Terror* provided Milland an agreeable vacation to the Channel Islands off the California coast.

FROM *CRUISE INTO TERROR* TO *THE LOVE BOAT*

The Michael Braverman teleplay *Cruise into Terror* brings together a group of travelers on a pleasure outing around the Gulf of Mexico. What the vacationers do not count on is that a sunken Egyptian tomb, brought on board during the cruise, contains the son of Satan. *Cruise into Terror* flounders for nearly an hour before the satanic forces either start killing the passengers or have them turn on each other. This last half hour is over the top in the manner of *Mayday at 40,000 Feet!*

Playing an archaeologist, Milland is accompanied by Hugh O'Brian as the reliable captain, Stella Stevens as a promiscuous divorcée, John Forsythe and Lee Meriwether as a reverend and his unhappy wife, and the real-life married Georges, Christopher and Lynda Day, both from *Mayday at 40,000 Feet!*, as another troubled couple.

Cruise into Terror appropriates from *Jaws* (1975), with shark point-of-view shots and John Williams-like musical riffs by Gerald Fried. Cinematographer Archie Dalzell, who had once worked with Milland on a *Markham* episode, does an unremarkable job here, and Bruce Kessler's direction leaves much to be desired.

Naturally, Milland's character, Dr. Isiah Bakkun, is more interested in the sarcophagus than his fellow passengers, and the egghead scientist is typically ill-tempered, such as when he growls a choice epigram at the overwrought reverend (Forsythe): "More crimes and cruelties have been perpetrated in the name of God than any other source!" One only wishes Ray Milland had greater screen time than some of the other actors.

Towards the end of the year, Milland traveled to Montreal for an R-rated theatrical film cofinanced by French and Canadian backers and distributed by Roger Corman. *Blackout*, a "ripped-from-the-headlines" thriller about the actual 1977 New York City blackout, contained the now familiar all-star cast and multiple storylines.

Along with Milland, June Allyson and Jean-Pierre Aumont were the biggest names in a fictionalized story about four escaped convicts who use the twenty-five-hour power outage as an opportunity to sadistically loot, rape, and murder the tenants of a high-rise apartment building. (Though they share no scenes together, both Milland and Jean-Pierre Aumont happened to have been boyfriends to Grace Kelly in the same year, 1953.)

As the building's owner, Milland plays one of the wealthier tenants menaced by the vandals. Before there is any blackout or terror, his Richard Stafford is already in a foul mood: he snaps at his wife—with the tone of Don Birnam demanding a drink—"Catherine, there is no ice!" Later, he complains bitterly about the "fat cats" who are responsible for the blackout, a subtle bit of political commentary.

The Milland character's toughness extends to standing up to the villains, gun in hand, once they break into his apartment; he is the only character who stares down these miscreants, daring them to shoot him first. By contrast, the top-billed hero of the piece (Jim Mitchum as a police officer) flinches at times or proves ineffectual. Aware of Milland as an aesthete, the filmmakers

Blackout (1978)

create the best, most ghoulish moment by having Richard make the visibly agonizing choice between saving his precious art collection or allowing the hoodlums to kill him and his wife.

Blackout is a middling thriller but at least more artistically consistent than some of Milland's other latter-day films. One of the few contemporary reviews of the time, from *Variety*, was favorable, calling it "a refreshing and sturdy pic . . . [with] excellent performances by June Allyson and Ray Milland."

If Milland felt at all forgotten by his older fans, he was told a funny story in 1978 by old friend Ronald Reagan that cheered him up. At the time, according to congressman John Linder (R-Ga.), "A fellow inched up to [Reagan, who was visiting Manhattan] and wanted to say hello, and Governor Reagan said hello. The gentleman said, may I have your autograph, Mr. Milland? And Reagan kindly wrote 'Ray Milland,' and walked on. And [advisor Michael Deaver] said, why didn't you tell him who you were? He said, I know who I am. He wanted to meet Ray Milland."

In Los Angeles early in 1978, Milland agreed to a guest shot on the lightweight *Hardy Boys/Nancy Drew Mysteries*. This Sunday night show was based on a series of young-adult books about teen sleuths, all created decades earlier by Edward Stratemeyer with the help of ghostwriters. The episodic TV edition ran for three seasons (1977–1979) with Shaun Cassidy and Parker Stevenson as the Hardy Boys and Janet Julian as Nancy Drew (for much of the run).

The two-part "Voodoo Doll" episode, broadcast in February 1978 on ABC, finds the Hardy Boys on vacation in New Orleans at Mardi Gras. During their stay, they meet an elderly professor of "the black arts" (Milland) who seems to hold valuable knowledge about a woman who has disappeared.

"The Voodoo Doll" gave Milland a few mildly engaging moments and permitted him to side-step the show's most embarrassing padding: the witless banter between the Hardy Boys, the kid-friendly magic acts that make *Escape to Witch Mountain* look sophisticated, and a risible lounge act from an out-of-place Bobby Troup.

Staying in Hollywood for an ABC presentation with greater weight, Milland immediately began work on the premiere episode of *Battlestar Galactica*, the network's take on the supremely profitable outer space epic *Star Wars* (1977). Actually, *Battlestar* was designed as another miniseries but given a large enough budget to become a full-fledged series.

The three-hour pilot, "Saga of a Star World," costing a then-record-setting $8 million, was shot on the Universal lot and aired in September 1978. The premise is established right away: multiple colonies of humans are engaged in a thousand-years war against a race of robots called Cylons. Milland portrays Sire Uri, a corrupt human leader who hoards food and supplies for the upper echelon of his society. Sire Uri even tricks his populace into believing the Cylons are no longer a danger, which allows the cybernetic race to launch a sneak attack.

Special-guest-star Milland's malevolent commander was a fanciful, futuristic version of the type of character he had been depicting for the last several years. The actor was joined by some show business veterans—Lew Ayres, Wilfred Hyde-White, and Lorne Greene, the last of whom continued with the series. The actual stars were Dirk Benedict and Richard Hatch, both playing viper pilots in search of refuge on planet earth and pitted against Milland's villain.

The September 17, 1978 premiere enjoyed high ratings, but the series itself was buried by the rival networks' sly counterprogramming. It was canceled by 1979, after twenty-one episodes. In an attempt to capitalize on the initial interest, Universal had the pilot reedited as a feature film distributed in November 1978.

Critics noted *Battlestar Galactica* lacked the cinematic style of *Star Wars*, despite its expensive sets and special effects. When the feature compilation appeared, the *Hollywood Reporter* put it bluntly: "Richard A. Colla directed, and Robert L. Kimble led the team of editors faced with the impossible task of carving a masterpiece out of a monstrosity. What they got is a monumental turkey—and just in time for Thanksgiving."

Milland had no interest in continuing with the *Battlestar* series and was happy to accept an offer in spring 1978 to return to making major motion pictures.

In 1977, Erich Segal published a sequel to *Love Story* titled *Oliver's Story* and sold it to Paramount. The studio then asked Milland to help recapture the magic of the original. Milland joined Ryan O'Neal in reexploring their father-son conflict, now following the death of Ali MacGraw's young bride. Shot mostly in Massachusetts, with key scenes set near Cambridge's Charles River, *Oliver's Story* differed in some significant ways from *Love Story*. Obviously, Jenny (MacGraw) was gone, but so were most of the supporting cast members.

On the other side of the camera, David V. Picker replaced Robert Evans as *Love Story*'s producer. John Korty, a talented documentarian, took the reins from director Arthur Hiller, then wrote the screenplay and collaborated on the score with Lee Holdridge and the returning Francis Lai.

The narrative shows how Jenny's death causes Oliver to blunt his grieving by busying himself in law firm work. Oliver's concerned family and lawyer colleagues encourage him to "move on" with his life. After therapy, he meets a divorced heiress (Candice Bergen) whom he comes to care for but never loves. Later, another woman (Nicola Pagett) signals a more upbeat future for Oliver. Significantly, too, he has an honest and moving reconciliation with his father.

The $6 million production stretched over a few months in spring and summer 1978, and the poor test-screening responses resulted in an equally prolonged postproduction. Much of the last third of the movie was removed (involving the romance between Oliver and Nicola Pagett's character).

The PG-rated film premiered in time for the Christmas season but was a bust at the box office and disparaged by critics. Janet Maslin of the *New York Times* called it "stodgy through and through." One of the few sympathetic reviews came from *Variety*, calling it "sensitive," and adding, "The most moving segments come, ironically, not out of the O'Neal-Bergen encounters, but from a few brief scenes between O'Neal and Ray Milland, who encores as his wealthy banker father. It is a tribute to both performances and Korty's direction that this most basic of conflicts is resolved here in a genuinely satisfying manner." But nothing quite worked to sell the film, certainly not its abysmal catchphrase, "It takes someone very special to help you forget someone very special."

Milland returned to Hollywood in the summer of 1978 to participate in *Fantasy Island*, a series produced by Aaron Spelling. It was not a nautical show but like much of *Oliver's Story*'s location shoot, one surrounded by water. The hit program was in its second season and would last until 1984, using the formula of having guest stars play characters longing to live out their wildest dreams, all masterminded by the Pacific Island host, Mr. Roarke (Ricardo Montalban).

Milland's "The Nightmare" was appropriately the most chilling of the three separate stories aired in the November 1978 episode. Written by Robert Heverly and directed on the Warner Bros.' backlot by George McCowan (*Frogs*), "The Nightmare" stars Pamela Franklin as a newlywed suffering from a recurring nightmare involving clowns, childhood toys, and a dangerous fire. Her fantasy-wish is to understand the meaning behind her sleep disturbances. Ray Milland plays Franklin's father, not a guest looking for a fantasy but one looking to *stop* a fantasy, ostensibly out of concern for his daughter's safety. His son-in-law is played by Brett Halsey, who had appeared with Milland in *Columbo*'s "Death Lends a Hand" in 1971.

The genuinely frightening nightmare sequence is the highlight of this unusually downbeat episode, though the "happy" conclusion of the mystery leaves unanswered questions. At least as a whole, the "Nightmare" story is far more interesting than the other two on the show—one involving a former drag racer (Paul Sand), the other about a big-game hunter (Darren McGavin).

Milland was off to South Africa again for *Game for Vultures*, yet another European-funded action adventure with a delayed US release. Shot in October and November of 1978 in Pretoria and Johannesburg (both doubling for Rhodesia), then later London, *Game for Vultures* was distributed by Columbia Pictures throughout Europe, Africa, and other continents in 1979 but did not get into American theaters until 1980.

In part, the lukewarm international critical reaction and lack of audience enthusiasm caused this film about the Rhodesian Bush War to be held back from US exhibition. By the time of the US release, the war was over. It was also the case that the politics of the movie were suspect during a time of growing world-wide unease about Apartheid.

The subplots created by Phillip Baird, based on a 1975 novel by Michael Hartmann, center around a South African arms dealer (Richard Harris) who is enticed by a money baron (Milland) to smuggle German-manufactured helicopters into Rhodesia, violating an international arms-embargo decree. When a South African freedom fighter (Richard Roundtree) learns the black-market deal will hurt his people, he and his guerrilla warriors plot to sabotage the transfer of the helicopters. A final showdown between the arms dealer and the freedom fighter stops the transaction, though the war rages on.

There is not a great deal to like about *Game for Vultures*, from its politically incorrect attempt to rationalize white minority rule to its lack of any finesse from director James Fargo. As cast member Joan Collins recalled, the film was "forgettable . . . with a script so full of complications that none of us understood it all." Collins, incidentally, was "reuniting" with Ray Milland a quarter of a century after *The Girl in the Red Velvet Swing*, yet they were given no joint scenes together. Milland was also reuniting with Richard Roundtree seven years after *Embassy*, and they were given one tense but short scene.

As with almost all Milland films, there are a few bright spots. The three scenes between Milland and Harris (of the erstwhile British "Angry Young Men" era) mark a kinship in acting styles. Both men are fully convincing yet somehow able to wink at the viewer with an acerbic but knowing attitude toward the substandard material they've been handed.

Milland is granted something else: a degree of character development over the course of his few scenes. He is again a greedy corporate type, with only a modicum of concern about the collateral damage of his actions. Yet, at the point his smuggling deal falls through, he becomes physically ill, leading to the film's one outstanding sequence: riding home during the night in an old-fashioned carriage, he points a gun to his head; at the moment he shoots, the viewer is left to wonder whether he has gained any sense of empathy or is simply unable to face the consequences of being caught.

At the start of 1979, Milland okayed the script for *The Darker Side of Terror*, a New Age *Frankenstein* tale. It was shot early in the year and aired in April 1979 on CBS.

As with *X: The Man with the X-Ray Eyes* and *The Thing with Two Heads*, Milland was cast as a scientist who defies the authorities, this time by experimenting with cloning, again tempting fate by playing God. Milland was joined by two other excellent actors, Robert Forster and Adrienne Barbeau.

The story by John Herman Shaner and Al Ramrus concerns a college research scientist (Forster) who is skeptical of his mentor's (Milland) claim that he is able to clone human beings. When the older professor finds a way to steal his colleague's DNA and clone him, his protégé realizes the benefits of "embryonic engineering." What neither scientist counts on is that the ectogen (Forster) develops murderous impulses due to a metabolic dysfunction. Another unexpected result of this hazardous endeavor is that the younger scientist's affection-starved wife (Barbeau) finds the clone preferable to her husband!

The sci-fi updating of not only *Frankenstein* but also *Dr. Jekyll and Mr. Hyde* and *Invasion of the Body Snatchers* is more predictable than one would hope, too rarely touching upon the ethics associated with the topical cloning debate. Still, there are some truly disturbing moments, especially the ending, which caps a titanic struggle between the younger scientist and his own clone.

The Darker Side of Terror is elevated by its leads. In particular, third-billed Ray Milland mixes command with apprehension in his few scenes, whether grousing about his school superiors' attitudes against his illegal experiments

("I will not be shackled by timid men!") or, in a memorable plot turn, fatally mistaking his former student for the clone he helped create. The *Hollywood Reporter* called it "an intelligently spawned tale ... made in a thoughtful and ingenious manner. ... [David] Sheiner [as a crafty colleague] and Milland etch their contributions effectively."

Before moving on to his next project, *Cave In!*, Milland learned that John Wayne was dying of stomach cancer. Wayne took a gallant final bow at the April 9, 1979 Academy Awards ceremony and died just two months later, on June 11, at age seventy-two. Ray and Mal attended the funeral in Newport Beach, and not too much later, Milland would receive his own cancer diagnosis.

Cave In! was shot in 1979 but shelved by NBC until a 1983 broadcast. During a downturn in his "disaster-movie" career, producer Irwin Allen (*The Poseidon Adventure* [1972], *The Towering Inferno* [1974]) shifted to television and used the Warner Bros. backlot for this entire production.

Norman Katkov's teleplay, directed by George Fenady (*Terror in the Wax Museum*), concerns a group of tourists in a national park who are forced to bond together in order to escape a cave-in. Fourth-billed Ray Milland plays another shrewd, manipulative professor, this time one who is especially mean to his daughter (Sheila Larken). The others in the cast are not top-tier stars: Dennis Cole, Susan Sullivan, Julie Sommars, and Leslie Nielsen. The *Hollywood Reporter* wasn't nearly as generous as it had been with *The Darker Side of Terror*, calling *Cave-In!* "a prime candidate thus far for *le terrible television* hall of fame."

In a biographical footnote, water finds a way into *Cave-In!* Milland's character has a phobia of water, just as the actor had as a child; yet, in order to survive and reach terra firma, he is forced to traverse a series of rocks surrounded by boiling water. Milland's successive TV ventures also took him back to the water, albeit in a less dramatic mode.

Late in 1979, Milland embarked on *The Love Boat*—literally. For more typical episodes, guest stars joined the weekly cast on the Twentieth Century-Fox soundstage ship replica while stock ocean footage was inserted between the multiple storylines. But in the two-part "Alaskan Wedding Cruise," actual filming took place aboard the *Pacific Princess* (a.k.a. the MS *Pacific* cruise liner), with a stop at the Glacier Bay National Park and Preserve.

At this point in his life, Milland relished the opportunity to film at sea, and that became an inducement to his involvement in producer Aaron Spelling's show. During its nine seasons, *The Love Boat*'s mix of new television personalities, Golden Age stars, and cast regulars playing crew members

The Love Boat (1979)

made the ABC Saturday night show a high-rated favorite among viewers but a mediocrity to critics.

In the "Peter and Alicia" portion of the "Alaska" episode, which aired in September 1979, Milland plays Peter Bradbury, the groom's (Mark Harmon) wealthy father, who tries to conceal his ailing health from the family he deserted years earlier. Alicia is played by Eleanor Parker, Peter's ex-wife, who is concealing a secret of her own: she is on the verge of bankruptcy.

It is apparent that both writer Ray Jessel and director Roger Duchowny knew their Milland iconography. Before we see his character, he is described as "the Black Sheep of the family," and his noirish entrance, wearing a dark suit and fedora, is set against the bustling, colorful docked ship backdrop. Referencing *The Lost Weekend*, his ex-wife accuses him of betraying his family by his drinking habits, to which he assures her he has been "on the wagon" for many years. Milland's scenes of strained reconciliation with his son (Harmon) replicates his *Love Story* conflict. Lastly, the script throws in a reference to his character having become a professor, a part he had played multiple times.

Typically, the *The Love Boat* appearances by the Golden Age couples evoke a romantic spirit, so it is in keeping with Milland's contrarian persona that his character is more pitted against than paired off with Eleanor Parker's. Yet one bit of nostalgia that doesn't quite work was the choice of Parker herself.

Instead of any number of available costars from his heyday that might have been cast, Parker is one with whom Milland never worked.

Back from his *Love Boat* trip, Milland agreed to star in what sounded like another low-budget horror film. As it turned out, *The Attic* was something unique.

THE ATTIC

A few years after producing *Frogs*, George Edwards joined Tony Crechales to write *The Attic*, about the tortured relationship between a single woman and her disabled father, and Edwards planned to direct for the first time. They were able to attract two high profile names: Carrie Snodgress as the woman, Louise, and Ray Milland as her father, Wendell.

The story focuses on Louise's doomed attempts to break free from her oppressive life catering to the abusive Wendell. Feeling responsible for the injury that left him bound to a wheelchair, Louise devotes herself to her father, despite his mean, ungrateful attitude. When she is fired from her job at a bookstore, Louise realizes she is more dependent upon her father's money than ever. Although she manages to suppress her impulses to kill Wendell, an incident occurs that exposes the grim reality behind so much of her suffering.

The Attic cast and crew traveled to Wichita, Kansas, in September 1979 for the location shoot. The production ran into difficulties when, according to cinematographer Gary Graver, Edwards did not always show up, leaving Graver to take over as director. Whatever happened to Edwards, *The Attic* became his sole directorial credit. The fate of *The Attic* itself was also a sorry one: it was held up for distribution by a full year until the Atlantic Releasing Corporation finally took a chance on it in 1980.

The delayed and ultimately poor distribution of the film is understandable given its defiance of genre expectations: it is the peculiar nature of it that transforms *The Attic* into a worthwhile piece. Most of the story is a deliberately paced, Altmanesque character study with only hints of horror around its frayed edges, an oddball mixture of Roman Polanski's *Repulsion* (1965) and Grant Wood's *American Gothic* (1930). Once the truth is revealed in the final reels, it turns the comically macabre narrative into something both upsetting and melancholic.

Best known for her Oscar-nominated turn in *Diary of a Mad Housewife* (1970), Snodgress deserves the most credit for giving the drama a touching, haunting feel. And while it may seem at first that Ray Milland is doing his usual angry-old-man act, the actor skillfully suggests a deep-seated inner hate or trauma of his own, prompting his character's sudden bursts of malicious fury. Milland was pleased to have a sizable part with genuine depth for a change. And he somehow mitigates Wendell's awfulness with absurdist humor—namely, his bathtub scene, in which he wears a bizarre-looking plastic bathing cap while playing with a rubber ducky and perusing *Reader's Digest* (quite a far cry from his beefcake bathing scenes in *The Jungle Princess* or the *Arise, My Love* bathtub interlude that outraged the censors).

The Attic was not widely seen and only received a few reviews, all of which were negative. In the *Boston Globe*, Michael Blowen called it "a trunkful of stale ideas and couple of old relics . . . a dusty, dirty little film that fogs the distant memories of two fine performers." Without any defenders, the picture disappeared quickly, yet if ever a film deserved a revival and cult following, it would be *The Attic*.

In early 1980, *The Love Boat*'s executive producer, Aaron Spelling, asked Milland to guest star on *Charlie's Angels*, another one of Spelling's hit shows airing on ABC. In its fourth season, the series followed three women (Jaclyn Smith, Cheryl Ladd, Shelley Hack) who solve crimes when summoned by their unseen boss, Charlie (voiced by John Forsythe). Though B. W. Sandefur wrote a two-part episode, "One Love . . . Two Angels," Milland appeared only in the first hour, which aired in May 1980.

Milland plays Oliver Barrows, another millionaire curmudgeon (one character even calls him a curmudgeon). The wealthy hotelier has a long-lost daughter and enlists a young attorney (Patrick Duffy) to find her. The lawyer's trail leads to Kelly (Smith), and much of part one of the show involves the awkward reunion between father and possible daughter. But an executive at the company (Robert Reed) kills Oliver as part of a scheme to steal Oliver's fortune. Without Milland's presence, part 2 is completely humdrum.

Milland shifted from ABC to syndication (Operation Prime Time) to appear briefly in *The Dream Merchants*, a two-part miniseries that also aired in May 1980 about the early days of Hollywood.

Based on Harold Robbins's 1949 best-seller, *The Dream Merchants* is a fictionalized biography of Universal Studios founder Carl Laemmle, foolishly renamed Johnny Edge and played by a young, callow Mark Harmon (Milland's *Love Boat* costar).

Though directed by Vincent Sherman, a sure hand from the studio days, *The Dream Merchants* received negative reviews and low ratings.

In Richard De Roy and Chester Krumholz's teleplay, Johnny Edge rises from nickelodeon operator to head of the first major Hollywood studio. Milland plays another wealthy and devious character, an investor who helps two rival studio heads (Howard Duff, Robert Culp) take over Edge's property. His appearance comes late in the story, and he looks either stoic or bored.

Milland was joined by Eve Arden (the best of the bunch as a Hedda Hopper type), Kaye Ballard, Fernando Lamas, Carolyn Jones, Red Buttons, and José Ferrer. That *The Dream Merchants* lightly critiques the old system is ironically undercut by the miniseries' inability to entertain like the better Golden Age products.

While Milland was making *The Dream Merchants*, the star of Vincent Sherman's *The Hasty Heart* (1949), Ronald Reagan, was running for president. Milland did not actively campaign for Reagan in 1980, but he and Mal were happy to see their old friend sworn in as the fortieth president of the United States in January 1981.

DANIEL

A short time later, on March 21, 1981, Ray received the worst news of his life. The police informed him over the phone that Danny fatally shot himself in the head. Apparently, the last time his friends had seen him, on the night before, Daniel was intoxicated. He was found in the West Los Angeles duplex he shared with two women, Jacqueline May, his fiancée, and Valerie Hartnett. A .22 caliber AK-7 "survival rifle" was lying next to his body, but no suicide note was found. A subsequent autopsy by senior coroner's investigator John W. Finken ruled forty-one-year-old Daniel Milland's death a suicide. The Milland family was devastated and did not issue a statement to the press.

In 2018, the anonymous entertainment lawyer at the crazydaysandnight.net website asserted a shocking revelation: Danny's death was the result of former child star Kim Richards turning a gun on Danny during her botched attempt to administer heroin into him the night of March 20, 1981. In this scenario, Danny's death was either a homicide or an accident but not a suicide. The anonymous blogger at foxella.com claims Richards did not deny the story when confronted about it by this second author. Still, no definitive proof of anything has emerged since 1981, and the case has never been reopened.

At the time, some columnists made connections between Danny's tragedy and the recent death of Mary Tyler Moore's son, Richie Meeker, also by a shotgun wound to the head, on October 14, 1980, and later the fatal drug overdose of Louis Jourdan's son, Louis Henry, on May 12, 1981. If the tabloids wanted to suggest an epidemic was starting among the offspring of the stars, they were ignoring a lengthy history of Hollywood deaths and suicides, most conspicuously by the sons of famous fathers: Charles Boyer's son, Michael

Charles, in 1965; William Powell's son, William Powell Jr., and Robert Taylor's son, Michael, both in 1968; Gregory Peck's son, Jonathan, in 1975; and Paul Newman's son, Scott, in 1978.

After a period of intense, unspeakable grieving, Milland was offered a showy part in a major studio comedy. Director John Landis was casting the big-budget *Trading Places* and wanted two elderly former stars to portray greedy, competitive brothers who bet against each other over whether two men from different social and racial backgrounds could switch places and survive. Eddie Murphy and Dan Aykroyd were cast as the young guinea pigs in this *Prince and the Pauper* meets *Pygmalion* screwball throwback. Milland, Landis's first choice as one of the older brothers, would have been perfect opposite Ralph Bellamy, but Milland was not feeling well, and he tried but failed to pass a physical exam to assure investors he could qualify for insurance to complete the film. Don Ameche, who had replaced Milland decades earlier in both *Midnight* and *Kiss the Boys Goodbye*, won the part in what turned out to be a box-office blockbuster in 1983 for Milland's one-time home studio, Paramount.

Though looking and feeling somewhat frail, Milland finally went back to work in the summer. He stole the show again in *Our Family Business*, an ABC pilot for a proposed series about the Italian mafia. As one of the many post-*Godfather* facsimiles, the September 1981 telecast did not garner enough attention for the network to greenlight the series. The formula worked better in 1990 with Martin Scorsese's *Goodfellas* and in 1999 with HBO's *The Sopranos*, primarily due to their darkly humorous approaches. *Our Family Business*, on the other hand, is deadly earnest, though respectably made.

The Lane Slate teleplay focuses on the generational conflicts within a mafia family. Sam Wanamaker plays a crime boss incarcerated for tax evasion who is released after six years. He immediately puts his two sons in charge of rebuilding the family empire, but neither heir (Ted Danson, David Morse) has any interest in mob activities.

Milland plays the grandfather and head of the family, a ruthless patriarch. Even in his weak-looking state, wearing a hearing aid in one scene, he has a commanding presence and alternates his dominant tone with quirky, puerile asides ("I'm so horny, I could honk!"). His final scene unveils Milland's character at its most malevolent, as he quietly, coldly tells his son (Wanamaker) how to handle a rival crime boss: "Burn him in public!"

Towards the end of 1981, Milland was invited back to the Aaron Spelling empire for a guest appearance on another long-running Spelling show.

Hart to Hart was the brainchild of Sidney Sheldon, the Oscar-winning screenwriter turned best-selling romance novelist. Sheldon developed this detective series in 1979 as a modernized *Thin Man*, centered around a well-heeled, Los Angeles–based crime-fighting couple, Jonathan and Jennifer Hart (Robert Wagner and Stefanie Powers).

The "My Hart Belongs to Daddy" episode, scripted by Rick Husky and directed by Dennis Donnelly, arrived midway through season 3, airing in January 1982, and it introduced a new character, Jennifer's wealthy father, Stephen Harrison Edwards (Milland).

In Husky's story, Jonathan and Jennifer spend a pleasant time with her father at his Maryland home, but they soon learn that he is besieged by a threatening person from his past. (The Warner Bros. soundstages and Los Angeles exteriors doubled for the Maryland locations.) In need of his daughter's help, Stephen reveals for the first time he was an OSS intelligence officer during World War II, and now the son (Kai Wulff) of a Nazi commander he captured wants to kill him in revenge for his father's death.

This typical episode is greatly enhanced by Milland's performance. He exhibits several characteristic traits—the wit, the disengagement, the fear—but also some genuinely felt familial emotion. Given his harrowing recent loss, Milland's scene with Stefanie Powers where he apologizes for working so much when she was growing up had to be a difficult one to perform. With a slight catch in his throat, Milland as Stephen says to his daughter, "Darling, please know I never meant to neglect you. You've always been the most important thing in my life." Both actors rise above the sentimental dialogue and make it heartrending and believable in a series that generally flaunts and promotes slick jet-set consumerism.

Milland's next TV film, *The Royal Romance of Charles and Diana*, required him to travel to London yet gave him far less to do dramatically than even *Hart to Hart*. Directed by journeyman Peter Levin in early 1982 and aired in September 1982 on CBS, the fictionalized romance between Charles, Prince of Wales (Christopher Baines), and Lady Diana Spencer (Catherine Oxenberg) was created to exploit the never-ending, world-wide fascination with the royal family in general and the July 1981 royal wedding in particular (excerpts of which appear toward the end of the movie).

Writers Robert L. Freeman, Selma Thompson, and Jonathan Platnick fabricated a fairy tale that could have been crafted by the p.r. team at Buckingham Palace. There are hints halfway through the narrative of some of the real-life anguish to come, but the conflicts are resolved by reaffirming the couple's strong bond of love.

For Ray Milland, another part of his career came full circle, this time from his Household Cavalry days of guarding Buckingham Palace and the royal family more than five decades earlier; now he was play-acting a Buckingham insider in a similarly menial position as Charles's elderly secretary, "Mr. Griffiths." Though he is a reassuring presence and the trip to England made the enterprise appealing to him, Milland seems completely detached emotionally, allowing some of the other actors, particularly Stewart Granger as Prince Phillip, to be much more colorful. Milland's reunion with a miscast Olivia de Havilland (as the Queen Mother), his 1946 *Well Groomed Bride* costar, is reduced to one short, undistinguished scene.

In any case, the trek to England for *Royal Romance* was Milland's first after Danny's death and allowed him to take a detour to his favorite pub in Wales, where he paid his respects and drowned his sorrows with friends.

Milland returned home after *Royal Romance* and spent a lengthy period without pursuing work. He still didn't feel physically well and was soon to find out why: after several diagnostic tests, his doctor informed him he was showing early indications of lung cancer. Milland shared the devastating news with only his immediate family, but it was clear to everyone who knew Ray Milland that he was genuinely moodier and finally willing to slow down professionally.

Then, a year-and-a-half after Danny's death, Milland was in for another shock. Along with the rest of the world, on September 14, 1982, he learned that Grace Kelly had died from injuries sustained in an automobile crash off a cliff near Monaco. She was only fifty-two. While past Kelly costars such as Cary Grant and Jimmy Stewart attended her funeral, for various and obvious reasons, Ray Milland did not.

By the end of year, a still shaken Milland returned to the TV disaster genre with *Starflight: The Plane That Couldn't Land*, which aired on ABC in late February 1983. Milland accepted producers Alan Manings and Henry Winkler's invitation to appear in a sort of turbocharged *Mayday at 40,000 Feet!*—with higher tech and less camp.

Manings and Winkler assembled an all-star cast of low rank (e.g. Lee Majors, Lauren Hutton), and *Starflight* was shot entirely at the Laird International Studio in Culver City. The post-*Star Wars* scenario by Peter R. Brook and Robert Malcolm Young (*Escape to Witch Mountain*) follows a space-age aircraft accidentally slipping out of the earth's atmosphere. This crisis leads to a race against time to get the plane out of its decaying orbit and back to earth before the oxygen supply is depleted.

Repeating the usual *Airport* formula, each passenger has a backstory, and in his last airborne movie, Ray Milland stays earthbound. As Q. T. Thornwell, he instigates the disaster by insisting his supersonic craft lift off even after his own son (Gary Bayer) warns him it might not be sufficiently tested. In true Milland fashion, his character eventually reveals he is more concerned about his investment in the plane than in the passengers' safety.

Starflight contains few of the dramatically extravagant moments that made *Mayday at 40,000 Feet!* enjoyably silly. Mostly, director Jerry Jameson keeps the theatrics in check, and this constrained style is helped by the moody sounds of Lalo Schifrin's compositions.

ABC thought well enough of *Starflight* to release it into theaters in some countries, including the United Kingdom, Australia, West Germany, and Austria, with forty minutes shorn from this version.

After *Starflight*, Milland flew on an actual aircraft for his annual visit to England and Wales. During his stay in London, he was asked by Malcolm Morris, the *This Is Your Life* producer, to appear on a March 1983 tribute to Anna Neagle (now Dame Anna Neagle). Milland gladly accepted the invitation to surprise the friend and costar he had known since 1927. Neagle was so beloved in England that this was her second *This Is Your Life* honor (the first came in 1958), and it was filmed at the Royal National Hotel. Milland looked noticeably older, but the reunion was a happy one.

In Los Angeles, Milland returned for his second and last appearance on *Hart to Hart*. "Long Last Love" aired in November 1983 and served as the series' Thanksgiving episode.

The show finds the sleuthing husband and wife again vacationing with Jennifer's father in Maryland. In the teleplay by Don Roos and Sidney Sheldon, Stephen has hidden from his family that he fathered a child before he met Jennifer's mother. Now, he must inform Jennifer that a woman (Samantha Eggar) claiming to be his daughter may very well be telling the truth. With little investigating, Stephen and the others welcome Jillian (Eggar) into the family, though Jonathan (Wagner) is skeptical and covertly investigates on his own.

"Long Lost Love" is a cut above many other episodes, not only because of Milland's work but also that of Eggar, who previously had a role (though no scenes with Milland) in *The Uncanny*. Karen Arthur's direction is assured, and for the single time in his career, Milland was directed by a woman. The best moment comes during another father-daughter scene between Milland and Powers where she is unable to tell her father the truth about the phony-daughter ploy because she knows how much it will hurt him. Milland's look of a man haunted by his past paints an indelible image, not dissipated by either the story's action-packed climax or overly cute coda.

This follow-up *Hart to Hart* episode is like a mini-retrospective of Milland's career, touching upon themes from *The Bachelor Father*, *Alias Mary Dow*, *The Uninvited*, and *Daughter of the Mind* (plus a photo of a young Stephen is actually a shot of Milland in military uniform from *Sealed Verdict*). Even the premise of a wealthy man's search for his long-lost daughter is similar to

Milland's *Charlie's Angels* episode, though the ending this time is much tidier and more upbeat.

Despite having a limited schedule, Milland was pleased to be invited as a guest speaker at the Film Society of Lincoln Center Annual Gala Tribute to Claudette Colbert. In April 1984, he flew to New York City to appear on the podium as one of a handful of colleagues (including Claire Trevor and Joshua Logan) honoring the life and career of his friend and former costar. Milland spoke glowingly about Colbert after movie clips from their films were shown.

Milland's very last project to be released to the public was shot next, also in April 1984, and it was seen more than a year later. Neither a feature film nor a TV movie, *The Gold Key* was an oddity, a videotaped murder mystery with an infuriating twist: the resolution was not included! Instead, the producers challenged buyers of the videocassette to figure out both the identity of the murderer and where the treasure mentioned in the story is hidden. This was the kind of gambit that could only have been released before the Internet age, when seeking information was far more difficult.

Was *The Gold Key* Milland's final gesture toward taking chances with different formats of entertainment or merely an exploitative commercial enterprise? Probably the latter since Milland indicated in an interview that he didn't know too much about the project or where it fit into his career. Milland told reporter Robert Cross, "They didn't give me the full script, and they shot other scenes outside of the scene [sic] I was in. I don't know what this is all about." In any case, he took the trip to Evanston, Illinois to film the curio.

Richard G. Kutok, the producer and director of *The Gold Key*, explained the "interactivity" that accompanied the videotape at an August press conference attended by Milland in New York City. The idea was that Embassy Home Entertainment would provide the videotape to twenty thousand store outlets across the United States in the fall of 1985, and the first viewer to submit correct answers to the questions would win $100,000.

The sixty-five-minute drama starts in traditional fashion—the reading of a wealthy man's will at the home of the man's colleague, a former movie executive, actor, and possible FBI agent (Milland). Clues about the man's mysterious death are either scattered or found by the various guests and relatives visiting the man's home. Thus, both the viewer and the characters are quickly involved in the treasure hunt dictated by the will.

Contest or not, *The Gold Key* is a depressing affair. Not only does Milland look somewhat sickly and uncomfortable, the production is as low budget as anything in his resumé, and the acting by most of the cast is downright incompetent. *Variety*'s dismissal characterized the few other reviews of the day: "Milland does handle his lines like the pro he is, but the rest of the acting falls somewhere between dreadful and amateurish. Overall, anyone just sitting through the program deserves a reward."

In one of the few interesting moments, Milland sits in a chair and gives a short soliloquy about his colleague's death that is moving, mainly because Milland's own death was imminent: "I'm certainly not fooling myself. People die all the time—war, accidents, for no reason at all—sometimes you notice, sometimes not."

As another plus, writer Paul A. Rambow tried to pay tribute to Milland by referring back to Milland's storied past using actual clips (from *Lisbon* and *Terror in the Wax Museum*) in a screening-room scene.

During the *The Gold Key* press conference at New York's Limelight nightclub, a reconverted church, Milland managed to inject some of his trenchant humor that was missing from the movie itself. When a reporter asked, "You must have big plans ahead. . . . Anything we should know about?," Milland answered, "Just to go home now and sit in my black leather chair and read. I've read everything, I think. I've got 3,000 books at home, and, believe it or not, I've read every one of them, including the Bible. It turned out to be a pretty dirty book."

What occurred next came about by chance—during the summer of 1984. For *The Masks of Death* (a.k.a. *Sherlock Holmes and the Masks of Death*) director Roy Ward Baker suggested getting Milland as a last-minute replacement for Sir John Gielgud, who suddenly became unavailable. Despite his weariness and health concerns, Milland flew from California three days before the start date. This trip allowed him to revisit England for his annual pilgrimage to Wales after quickly completing what would be his last film with a prominent director (Ward Baker) and distinguished cast (chiefly Peter Cushing as an elderly incarnation of Sherlock Holmes). He even managed to squeeze in a quick visit to Lancashire to see the restored Flying Scotsman, the train he had ridden in 1929 for the film of that title.

The Masks of Death was made for British television by Executive Producer Kevin Francis, who chose a newly created Holmes story. Milland shot his one scene at Twickenham Studios (other parts were done at Buckinghamshire and London). *Masks of Death* aired in the United Kingdom on Christmas Eve in December 1984, and it was only released in the United States through limited syndication, then video format.

Thus, few American audiences were able to see this modest yet above-average Holmes entry. In it, screenwriters Anthony Hinds and N. J. Crisp created an involved mystery set before World War I, when Holmes is alerted that three corpses have recently been found in London's East End but with few clues to explain why they all seemed to have died of fright. Interrupting

Revisiting the Flying Scotsman in Lancashire (1984).
Photo credit: Trinity Mirror / Mirrorpix / Alamy Stock Photo.

Holmes's new case is the presence of the British home secretary (Milland) introducing Holmes to a German diplomat, Count Felseck (Anton Diffring, a *Swiss Conspiracy* costar), who complains that a German envoy on a spy mission has vanished. With the help of his trusted sidekick, Doctor Watson (John Mills), Holmes looks into both matters and finds an unexpected connection.

Suspects and red herrings abound during the relatively short (eighty-two-minute) running time. The flashiest figure is the American-born Irene Adler (Anne Baxter, in her final performance). The home secretary might have been another suspect, but Ray Milland's character becomes an afterthought. His primary function is to prompt Holmes to look into the German spy matter. For those who enjoyed the byplay between Milland and Cushing in *The Uncanny* seven years earlier, there was little in their single conversation that measured up. Then again, both men were physically ailing at this point—and one could see it in their faces.

Apart from the cast, what keeps *Masks of Death* consistently entertaining is that the production values evoke Old World elegance: cinematographer Brendan J. Stafford covers the action with stately shots, and director Ward Baker pulls it all together with the expertise he had shown in both features (*Tiger in the Smoke* [1956]) and television (*The Avengers* [1965–68]).

Milland's final feature film and the last project he ever shot, *The Sea Serpent* placed him back in 1928's *Lady from the Sea* soup—with a monster replacing an exotic woman as the disrupting force of the narrative. In October 1984, Milland might have been lured by the promise of a trip to Spain, but on location, he and the cast and crew were transported to Sesimbra, Portugal (doubling for Spain) for the actual filming. In quite a contrast to *Masks of Death*, this production from Spanish independent Constan Films ranks as one of the silliest of all Milland movies.

In *The Sea Serpent*, Milland portrays a professor for the last time, a marine biologist who is confronted by a sea captain (Timothy Bottoms) and the captain's girlfriend (Taryn Power) who claim they have seen an enormous sea serpent emerge from the Spanish coastline, ready to kill anyone in its path. The professor is skeptical at first but finally convinced when he sees the creature himself and learns that an underwater atomic detonation has activated it out of its dormancy. The three try to warn others in the community and enlist some help in stopping the monster.

It is during the climax that Milland's grumpy but generally benign academic reveals the late career Milland signature of human indifference: he is more concerned about keeping the destructive "specimen" alive than about the people on a train passing over a bridge the serpent is about to demolish. Unlike the captain and his girlfriend, he is relieved when the creature eludes a fire bombing. Upon seeing the young lovers embrace while they ignore the serpent's getaway, Milland delivers his last on-screen quip: "Youth—no spirit of adventure!"

These moments with Milland are enjoyable, no matter how aged and slow moving he appears. The lengthy first half of the movie, though, has none of Milland's skills to buoy it since he only shows up later. Everything else is an embarrassment, from the inadequacy of the postdubbing to the murky lighting to the imitation-*Jaws* music themes. The "monster" itself is an obvious toy—but at least a cute one!

Sadly, *The Sea Serpent* marked the final film for both Ray Milland and the normally gifted director, Spanish-born Armando de Ossorio. Critic Thomas Scalzo took a positive view in 2013: "*The Sea Serpent* made me laugh time and time again, and kept me entertained from start to finish. For my money, that's what counts."

END TITLE

In 1985, Milland was not well enough to be interviewed for *Hitchcock: The Thrill of Genius*, an Italian documentary about Alfred Hitchcock. Though Janet Leigh, Farley Granger, Alida Valli, and a few others appeared, codirectors Francesco Bortolini and Claudio Masenza had to make do with footage from *Dial M for Murder* when Milland was referenced. The tribute was shown on Italian television in 1985 under the title *il brividio del genio*.

For the *All-Star Party for "Dutch" Reagan*, on the other hand, Milland made a point to show up in nearby Burbank. The TV special celebrated Reagan's reelection and promoted dozens of well-known stars from the Golden Age. Milland was lost in the sea of celebrities—some giving toasts from their appointed tables, others who sang on the ballroom floor, like Frank Sinatra and Dean Martin. This glitzy tribute, shot on December 1st, 1985, and airing on CBS on December 8, could be considered Milland's final *professional* full-circle moment: he was back to being a mere extra at a fancy-dress affair, just as he had been in his first film, 1929's *Piccadilly*, minus the artful touches of production designer Alfred Junge. In an additional connection to the past, Variety Club International hosted the event, the same organization that had been the subject of the all-star *Variety Girl* (1947), in which Milland appeared briefly (and, again, in a dress suit).

Later in December 1985, Milland traveled for the last time to his ancestral home in Neath, Wales. The few family and friends still alive were delighted to see him but probably sensed it would be his last trip anywhere. For Milland, the occasion was both bittersweet and exhausting, given his worsening condition.

Upon his return to Los Angeles, Milland rested as much as possible. Throughout the winter of 1986, he received chemotherapy treatments and made regular visits to Torrance Memorial Hospital. He withdrew entirely from the public during this time. On Thursday, March 6, he entered the hospital for good. Over the next few days, as family members visited, it was becoming clear he was not coming home. On Monday, March 10, 1986, Ray Milland died quietly in his sleep. He was seventy-nine.

Roland Leif, Milland's agent, announced on March 11, "He had a very full career and was very active to the end." Tributes, many from past costars, poured into the Associated Press and United Press International and were quoted in all the major newspapers. Barbara Stanwyck stated to UPI, "He was a very fine gentleman.... I enjoyed knowing him and working with him. He will be missed by all of us in the industry." Dorothy Lamour told the AP, "This is as bad as when Bing Crosby died, only worse.... I used to call him my jungle prince after the name of our picture. We've remained very good friends all these years. . . . He was a wonderful man."

Per Milland's instructions, no public funeral was arranged. Fans would have to mourn by themselves. After his body was cremated, the family gathered off the coast of Redondo Beach to scatter his ashes into the Pacific Ocean. It was a fitting gesture given Milland's lifelong fascination with the sea, his personal full-circle moment.

As a belated and subdued tribute by the city of Los Angeles, Milland's two stars on the Hollywood Walk of Fame were repaired after years of damage from foot traffic. In early November 1986, the restoration was completed with funding from the Hollywood Chamber of Commerce. Further repairs were made during more expansive rehab projects in both 2008 and 2019.

In late 1986, Mal Milland donated Ray Milland's papers, scrapbooks, photographs, articles he wrote, and other archival materials to the Margaret Herrick Library Special Collections in Los Angeles, a division of the Academy of Motion Picture Arts and Sciences.

Throughout 1986, it was clear that the overused "end-of-an-era" saying was more than appropriate in the world of show business, particularly regarding the Golden Age of Hollywood. The same year, in addition to Ray Milland, a number of people connected to him in one way or another also died: friend and *Blonde Crazy* (1931) costar Jimmy Cagney in the same month of March; costar of six Milland films Broderick Crawford in April; *My Fair Lady* lyricist Alan Jay Lerner in June; *Bugles in the Afternoon* (1952) costar Forrest Tucker in October; *Blonde Crazy* (1931) and *So Evil My Love* (1948) executive producer Hal B. Wallis, also in October; *Let's Do It Again* (1953) "ghost" and *Ray Milland Show* actor Paul Frees in November; and Cary Grant, also in November.

In 1988, the Millands' Los Angeles home was put on the real estate market, listed at $3,950,000. When rumors started spreading that Ray Milland's Oscar was lost, Victoria reassured the press that her son, Milland's grandson Travis, had been keeping it in a downstairs guest room.

Muriel "Mal" Milland lived for six more years after losing Ray Milland. She died on October 6, 1992, in Los Angeles at the age of eighty-three. A little later, Victoria's second child, Alexander, followed in his father, uncle, grandfather, and great-grandfather's tradition: he entered the military and was stationed at Fort Bragg, North Carolina, the state where his father, Edmund Lowell Graham, was born. In July 2005, Victoria lost Edmund, who was buried at Green Hills Memorial Park in California.

Occasionally, Victoria honors her father's legacy, such as when she appeared on the 2002 BBC documentary series *The Silver Screen*. In the hour-long Ray Milland episode, which aired in November that year, she spoke kindly of her father; the other guests included Roger Corman, Peter Falk, and Sylvia Syms, his *Hostile Witness* costar. David Howard wrote and directed the tribute.

As of 2024, Victoria lives in Rancho Palos Verdes and is eighty. Victoria Milland Graham's children are Travis, age fifty-three, and Alex Graham, age forty-eight, also living in Rancho Palo Verdes.

The Ray Milland legacy remains in an uncertain place. In recent years, more of his work has been revived or rediscovered, but there has been no major reassessment. In 2015, the Chapter Arts Centre in Cardiff celebrated with a season of his films, and in October 2022, Gwyn Hall in Neath showed *The Lost Weekend* as one of three films starring actors born in either Neath or Port Talbot. Beyond these local celebrations, there have been occasional DVD or Blu-ray restorations, anniversary screenings, and TCM's 2011 "Star of the Month" tribute.

EPILOGUE

In a late career interview, Milland combined his enthusiasm, modesty, and self-deprecation when he declared, "I've had a most wonderful life and as far I can see have done very little to deserve it." Elsewhere, he said, "I had a ball. But it all happened by luck, and I was just there at the right place and at the right time."

But was it only luck? Or did he determine much of his fate, however haphazardly? It would seem that more often than not, he did what he wanted to do, including much of the crapshooting with his life and career.

For Ray Milland, the movie business preoccupied much of his time as an adult, and he survived, even thrived, by his wits. As an adventurer, his profession afforded him a way to travel both outwardly to various locations and inwardly as a soul-searching actor.

For audiences, Milland's unusual approach to his cinematic archetype (the matinée idol) helped alter expectations and compel at least a degree of viewer self-reflection. Rather than take the easy path, Milland embraced experimental projects and roles that were definitely *not* designed to pacify his fans. In his later years, he was more than willing to risk alienating those who had once considered him a likable romantic hero. When Milland's

Grauman's Chinese Theatre prints (from 1947). Photo credit: Depositphotos.

envelope-pushing didn't succeed as he had hoped, the sheer fact he made the attempt was laudably daring. Perhaps in the future, artists willing to take chances and lay bare what is incongruous about themselves and the world will be better appreciated.

ACKNOWLEDGMENTS

THE PROCESS OF WRITING A BOOK HAS A GREAT NUMBER OF SOLITARY phases, but it is hardly a solo venture. Like the making of a movie, publishing a work usually requires a group effort.

Those I would like to thank the most for their contribution to and support of this project are my parents, Theo Sable and the late Jesse Sable, and my late wife, Kathi Patterson.

Naturally, I must thank everyone at the University Press of Mississippi, especially for maintaining the quality of the book and giving me so much help and guidance. On the top of my list is my eternally patient editor, Emily Snyder Bandy, as well as Carl Rollyson, Craig W. Gill, Laura Strong, Kristin Kirkpatrick, Cynthia Foster, Courtney McCreary, Amy Atwood, Joey Brown, Kathy Burgess, Jai Reaves, Rae Switzer, Jane McGregor, Lindsey Cleworth, Pete Halverson, and Camille Hale.

My interviews with those who knew Ray Milland were invaluable. For this project, it was an honor and a pleasure speaking and corresponding with Arlene Dahl, Louise Fletcher, Darryl Hickman, Marsha Hunt, Tina Louise, Debra Paget (Mrs. Debra Kung), Jeanette Sterke Michell, and Joan Van Ark; and I truly appreciate the interviews I conducted in the past with Louise Klos Steiner Elian (the former Mrs. Max Steiner), Joan Fontaine, Gary Graver, Dorothy Kingsley, Oswald Morris, and George Wells.

The people and places that helped me with contacts, tips, suggestions, permissions and access to research materials include the great Jane Klain, Manager of Research Services at the Paley Center for Media in New York City, and the staff of the Paley Center, including Patricia Lunde and Todd Kmetz; Kristine Kreuger, NFIS Coordinator, and the staff of the Margaret Herrick Library, Academy Picture Arts and Sciences, in Los Angeles; Ron Magliozzi, Josh Siegel, and Ashley Swinnerton of the Celeste Bartos International Film Study Center at the Museum of Modern Art in New York; John Calhoun and the Special Collections staff at the Library of the Performing

Arts in New York; Jasmine Sykes-Kunk and the staff at New York University's Bobst Library Special Collections; Ann Harris at New York University's Department of Cinema Studies; the staff at the Buncombe County Library of North Carolina; the staff at Manhattan's Film Forum theater: Bruce Goldstein, Steve Knudsen, Joe Berger, and Andrea Torres in the repertory division and Karen Cooper and Mike Maggiore in the contemporary division; the staff at Alamy; and the Photofest team, Howard Mandelbaum, Ron Mandelbaum, Derek Davidson, and Todd Ifft.

A number of individuals deserve special mention as well: Michael Almereyda, Donna Carlin, Jasmin Charles, Angelica Clark, John Cocchi, Harris Dew, Daniel de Wit and the De Wit family, Paul Donnelley, Anne Dean Dotson, Tim Faracy, Bart Farar, Robert M. Fells, Anthony Garofalo, Bernard Gertler, Eve Golden, Sid Gottlieb, David Greven, Molly Haskell, Clive Hirschhorn, Matthew C. Hoffman, Emily Hurst, George Johnson, Matthew Kennedy, Alain Kerzoncuf, Terry Kingsley-Smith, Michael Jay Klein, Kevin Lally, Elizabeth Lauritsen, Peter Lehman, Linda Lewis, Cheryl Lippert, William Luhr, Scott McGee, Patrick McGilligan, Marge, Dennis, Ginni and David Meisinger, Roger C. Memos, Toby Miller, Ben Monder, Harvey and Joan Monder, John-Luke and Samantha Montias, Gina Munz, Joy Nelson, Scott O'Brien, Patrick O'Dowd, Dennis Payne, Marc Rosen, Deborah Sable Garofalo, Andrew Sarris, Louise Spence, Gary Spero, Jon Spurny, Allan Taylor, Mary and William Truesdell, Elena Young, and Victoria Milland Graham.

Lastly, both Vincent Terrace's research assistance and James Robert Parish's support were immeasurably helpful.

APPENDIX 1

FEATURE FILM APPEARANCES

Note: Ray Milland was billed as *Ray Milland* unless otherwise indicated.

Moulin Rouge, 1928 (uncredited). British International Pictures.
Piccadilly, 1929 (uncredited). British International Pictures.
The Lady from the Sea a.k.a. *Goodwin Sands*, 1929 (as *Raymond Milland*). British International Pictures.
The Flying Scotsman, 1929 (as *Raymond Milland*). British International Pictures.
The Plaything, 1929 (as *Spike Milland*). British International Pictures.
The Informer, 1929 (uncredited). British International Pictures.
Way for a Sailor, 1930 (uncredited). MGM.
Passion Flower, 1930 (uncredited). MGM.
The Bachelor Father, 1931. MGM.
Strangers May Kiss, 1931 (uncredited). MGM.
Just a Gigolo, 1931. MGM
Bought!, 1931 (as *Raymond Milland*). Warner Bros.
Ambassador Bill, 1931. Fox Film Corporation.
Blonde Crazy, 1931. Warner Bros.
The Man Who Played God, 1932 (uncredited). Warner Bros.
Polly of the Circus, 1932 (uncredited). MGM.
But the Flesh Is Weak, 1932 (uncredited). MGM.
Payment Deferred, 1932. MGM.
Orders Is Orders, 1933. Gaumont.
This Is the Life, 1934. British Lion.
Bolero, 1934 (as *Raymond Milland*). Paramount.
We're Not Dressing, 1934 (as *Raymond Milland*). Paramount.
Many Happy Returns, 1934. Paramount.
Charlie Chan in London, 1934 (as *Raymond Milland*). Fox Film Corporation.
Menace, 1934 (as *Raymond Milland*). Paramount.
One Hour Late, 1934 (as *Raymond Milland*). Paramount.
The Gilded Lily, 1935. Paramount.
Four Hours to Kill!, 1935. Paramount.
Alias Mary Dow a.k.a. *Lost Identity*, 1935 (as *Raymond Milland*). Universal.
The Glass Key, 1935. Paramount.
Next Time We Love, 1936 (as *Raymond Milland*). Universal.

The Return of Sophie Lang, 1936. Paramount.
The Big Broadcast of 1937, 1936. Paramount.
The Jungle Princess, 1936. Paramount.
Three Smart Girls, 1936. Universal.
Bulldog Drummond Escapes, 1937. Paramount.
Wings over Honolulu, 1937. Universal.
Easy Living, 1937. Paramount.
Ebb Tide, 1937. Paramount.
Wise Girl, 1937. RKO.
Her Jungle Love, 1938. Paramount.
Tropic Holiday, 1938. Paramount.
Men with Wings, 1938. Paramount.
Say It in French, 1938. Paramount.
Hotel Imperial, 1939. Paramount.
Beau Geste, 1939. Paramount.
Everything Happens at Night, 1939. Twentieth Century-Fox.
French without Tears, 1940. Paramount.
Irene, 1940. RKO.
The Doctor Takes a Wife, 1940. Columbia.
Untamed, 1940. Paramount.
Arise, My Love, 1940. Paramount.
I Wanted Wings, 1941. Paramount.
Skylark, 1941. Paramount.
Sullivan's Travels, 1941 (uncredited). Paramount.
The Lady Has Plans, 1942. Paramount.
Reap the Wild Wind, 1942. Paramount.
Are Husbands Necessary?, 1942. Paramount.
The Major and the Minor, 1942. Paramount.
Star-Spangled Rhythm, 1942. Paramount.
Forever and a Day, 1943. RKO.
The Crystal Ball, 1943. United Artists.
Lady in the Dark, 1944. Paramount.
The Uninvited, 1944. Paramount.
Ministry of Fear, 1944. Paramount.
Till We Meet Again, 1944. Paramount.
The Lost Weekend, 1945. Paramount.
Kitty, 1945. Paramount.
To Each His Own, 1946 (trailer only). Paramount.
The Well Groomed Bride, 1946. Paramount.
The Imperfect Lady, 1947. Paramount.
California, 1947. Paramount.
The Trouble with Women, 1947. Paramount.
Variety Girl, 1947. Paramount.
Golden Earrings, 1947. Paramount.
So Evil My Love, 1948. Paramount.
The Big Clock, 1948. Paramount.
Sealed Verdict, 1948. Paramount.

Miss Tatlock's Millions, 1948 (uncredited). Paramount.
Alias Nick Beal, 1949. Paramount.
It Happens Every Spring, 1949. Twentieth Century-Fox.
Copper Canyon, 1950. Paramount.
A Woman of Distinction, 1950. Columbia.
A Life of Her Own, 1950. MGM.
Circle of Danger, 1951. Coronado Productions, RKO.
Night into Morning, 1951. MGM.
Rhubarb, 1951. Paramount.
Close to My Heart, 1951. Warner Bros.
Bugles in the Afternoon, 1952. Warner Bros.
Something to Live For, 1952. Paramount.
The Thief, 1952. Fran Productions, United Artists.
Jamaica Run, 1953. Paramount.
Let's Do It Again, 1953. Columbia.
Dial M for Murder, 1954. Warner Bros.
The Girl in the Red Velvet Swing, 1955. Twentieth Century-Fox.
A Man Alone, 1955. Republic.
Lisbon, 1956. Republic.
Three Brave Men, 1956. Twentieth Century-Fox.
The River's Edge, 1957. Twentieth Century-Fox.
High Flight, 1957. Warwick Films, Columbia.
The Safecracker, 1958. Coronado Productions, MGM.
King of Kings, 1961 (uncredited). MGM.
The Premature Burial, 1962. AIP.
Panic in Year Zero!, 1962. AIP.
X: The Man with the X-Ray Eyes, 1963. AIP.
The Confession, a.k.a. *Quick, Let's Get Married*, a.k.a. *Seven Different Ways*, 1964. Kay Lewis Enterprises, William Marshall Productions, Golden Eagle.
Hostile Witness, 1968. Caralan Productions, United Artists.
Company of Killers, 1970. Universal (originally shot in 1968 for NBC as *The Protectors* but not aired).
Love Story, 1970. Paramount.
Embassy, 1972. Hemdale, Triad Productions, Weaver Productions, K-Tel International.
Frogs, 1972. AIP.
The Thing with Two Heads, 1972. AIP.
The House in Nightmare Park, 1973. Anglo-EMI.
The Big Game, 1973. Comet.
Terror in the Wax Museum, 1973. Andrew J. Fenady Productions, Bing Crosby Productions, Cinerama Releasing.
The Student Connection, 1974. Cinema Shares International.
Gold, 1974. Allied Artists.
Escape to Witch Mountain, 1975. Walt Disney.
The Swiss Conspiracy, 1976. Warner Bros.
Aces High, 1976. Cinema Shares International.
The Last Tycoon, 1976. Paramount.
Oil, 1977. Casa de Filme Cinci, Spectacular Film Productions.

The Uncanny, 1977. Cinevideo, Rank Organization.
Slavers, 1977. Lord Film, ITM Releasing.
The Pyjama Girl Case, 1977. Zodiac Produzioni.
Blackout, 1978. Maki Films, DAI Productions, New World Pictures.
Oliver's Story, 1978. Paramount.
Spree, a.k.a. *Survival Run*, 1979. Film Ventures International.
Game for Vultures, 1979. New Line Cinema.
The Attic, 1980. Atlantic Releasing Corporation.
The Sea Serpent, 1985. Constan Films S.A., Calepas International.
The Gold Key, 1985. GeoQuest Productions.

APPENDIX 2

MAJOR TELEVISION APPEARANCES AND MADE-FOR-TV MOVIES

The Actor's Society Benefit Gala (4/18/49). NBC.
Civil Defense Week P.S.A. (10/17/51). Department of Defense.
The 25th Annual Academy Awards (3/19/53). NBC.
Meet Mr. McNutley, a.k.a. *The Ray Milland Show* (1953-55, 77 episodes). TV Series. CBS.
What's My Line? (10/31/54). CBS.
The Colgate Comedy Hour (10/23/55). NBC.
Screen Directors Playhouse: "Markheim" (4/11/56). NBC.
General Electric Theater: "That's the Man!" (4/15/56). CBS.
The Ford Television Theatre: "Catch at Straws" (10/3/56). ABC.
General Electric Theater: "Never Turn Back" (1/6/57). CBS.
Schlitz Playhouse: "The Girl in the Grass" (3/15/57). CBS.
General Electric Theater: "Angel of Wrath" (5/5/57). CBS.
Suspicion: "Eye for Eye" (6/23/58). NBC.
General Electric Theater: "Battle for a Soul" (11/2/58). CBS.
Goodyear Theatre: "A London Affair" (2/2/59). NBC.
What's My Line? (11/1/59). CBS
Markham (1959-60, 59 episodes). TV Series. CBS.
Celebrity Golf (4/9/61). NBC.
Trails West (1962 and other season rebroadcasts of *Death Valley Days*), host of several episodes. Syndication.
Alcoa Premiere: "Pattern of Guilt" (1/9/62). ABC.
Here's Hollywood (2/2/62). NBC.
Hollywood Come Home (1963). Documentary special. Syndicated.
The Alfred Hitchcock Hour: "A Home Away from Home" (9/27/63). CBS.
The Dupont Show of the Week: "The Silver Burro" (11/3/63). NBC.
The International Hour: "The Music from Hollywood" (5/21/64). CBS.
The Mike Douglas Show (6/1/64). Syndication.
What's My Line? (11/21/65). CBS.
The Tonight Show Starring Johnny Carson (11/24/65). NBC.
The Today Show (2/18/66). NBC.
The Ed Sullivan Show (3/6/66). CBS.
The Merv Griffin Show (5/19/66). Syndication.

The Twentieh Annual Tony Awards (6/16/66). CBS.
The Face Is Familiar (6/25/66). CBS.
The Mike Douglas Show (1/24/67). Syndication.
Dee Time (9/30/67). BBC.
The Hollywood Squares (8/23/68). NBC.
The Jackie Gleason Show (4/5/69). CBS.
The Merv Griffin Show (5/21/69). Syndication.
The Merv Griffin Show (6/16/69). Syndication.
Bracken's World: "Don't You Cry for Susannah" (10/10/69). NBC.
Daughter of the Mind (12/9/69). Made-for-TV movie. ABC.
The Mike Douglas Show (12/11/69). Syndication.
Bracken's World: "Focus on a Gun" (1/2/70). NBC.
The Name of the Game: "A Love to Remember" (9/25/70). NBC.
This Is Your Life: "Bob Hope" (11/25/70). Thames.
River of Gold (3/9/71). Made-for-TV movie. ABC.
Cinema (3/25/71). Documentary series. Granada Television.
The Merv Griffin Show (4/13/71). Syndication.
The Tonight Show Starring Johnny Carson (5/11/71). NBC.
Mantrap (8/10/71). Syndication.
The Tonight Show Starring Johnny Carson (8/11/71). NBC.
Night Gallery: "The Hand of Borgus Weems" (9/15/71). NBC.
Columbo: "Death Lends a Hand" (10/6/71). NBC.
Black Noon (11/5/71). Made-for-TV movie. CBS.
It's Your Bet (2/28/72). Syndication.
The Bob Hope Special (4/10/72). NBC.
The Tonight Show Starring Johnny Carson (6/23/72). NBC.
The Tonight Show Starring Johnny Carson (9/1/72). NBC.
Columbo: "The Greenhouse Jungle" (10/15/72). NBC.
Cool Million: "Hunt for a Lonely Girl" (10/25/72). NBC.
It's Your Bet (12/4/72). Syndication.
The Today Show (9/10/74). NBC.
The Mike Douglas Show (9/25/74). Syndication.
The Dead Don't Die (1/14/75). Made-for-TV movie. NBC.
Film '75 (3/4/75). BBC.
From Sea to Shining Sea: "The Unwanted" (3/16/75). Syndication.
The Book Programme (3/18/75). UK broadcast.
Ellery Queen: "Too Many Suspects" (3/23/75). NBC.
This Is Your Life: "Ray Milland" (11/19/75). Thames.
Rich Man, Poor Man (from 2/76 to 3/76). TV miniseries. ABC.
Rich Man, Poor Man—Book II (9/76). TV miniseries. ABC.
This Is Your Life: "Frankie Howerd" (10/27/76). Thames.
Look What's Happened to Rosemary's Baby (10/29/76). Made-for-TV movie. ABC.
Mayday at 40,000 Feet! (11/12/76). Made-for-TV movie. CBS.
Seventh Avenue (1977). TV miniseries. NBC.
Testimony of Two Men (1977). TV miniseries. OPT-TV.
Cruise into Terror (2/3/78). Made-for-TV movie. ABC.
The Hardy Boys/Nancy Drew Mysteries: "The Voodoo Doll" (2/12/78 part 1; 2/19/78 part 2). ABC.

Battlestar Galactica: "Saga of a Star World" (9/17/78). ABC.
Fantasy Island: "Nightmare" (11/4/78). ABC.
The Mike Douglas Show (12/11/78). Syndication.
The Darker Side of Terror (4/3/79). Made-for-TV movie. CBS.
The Love Boat: "Alaska Wedding Cruise" (parts 1 and 2, 9/79). ABC.
Charlie's Angels: "One Love . . . Two Angels" (part 1, 4/30/80). ABC.
The Dream Merchants (1980). TV miniseries. OPT-TV.
Our Family Business (9/21/81). Made-for-TV movie. ABC.
Hart to Hart: "My Hart Belongs to Daddy" (1/19/82). ABC.
The Royal Romance of Charles and Diana (9/22/82). Made-for-TV movie. CBS.
Starflight: The Plane That Couldn't Land (2/27/83). Made-for-TV movie. ABC.
This Is Your Life: "Anna Neagle" (3/9/83). Thames.
Cave-In! (6/19/83). Made-for-TV movie. NBC.
Hart to Hart: "Long Lost Love" (11/22/83). ABC.
The Film Society of Lincoln Society Annual Gala Tribute to Claudette Colbert (4/23/84). NBC.
The Masks of Death (12/23/84). Made-for-TV movie. KLV-TV.
All-Star Party for "Dutch" Reagan (12/8/85). CBS.

APPENDIX 3

MAJOR RADIO APPEARANCES

Just Suppose (12/1/36). Lux Radio Theatre. Scheduled but not aired.
Kraft Music Hall (11/11/37). NBC.
Morning Glory (3/24/40). The Gulf Screen Guild Theater.
Alexander's Ragtime Band (6/3/40). Lux Radio Theatre.
The Community Mobilization for Human Needs (11/40). Public Service Announcement.
Skylark (2/2/42). Lux Radio Theatre.
The Lady Eve (3/9/42). Lux Radio Theatre.
I Wanted Wings (3/30/42). Lux Radio Theatre.
Arise, My Love (6/8/42). Lux Radio Theatre.
The Kate Smith Hour (9/18/42). CBS Radio.
To Mary, with Love (11/16/42). Lux Radio Theatre.
Reap the Wild Wind (3/8/43). Lux Radio Theatre.
Submarine Astern (4/5/43). Cavalcade of America.
The Major and the Minor (5/31/43). Lux Radio Theatre.
This Thing Called Love (6/25/43). Philip Morris Playhouse.
Once upon a Honeymoon (7/26/43). Screen Guild Theater.
The Burns and Allen Show (9/21/43). CBS Radio.
The Gertrude Lawrence Show (10/6/43). Revlon Revue.
The Sorehead (11/17/43). Treasury Star Parade.
The Chase and Sanborn Hour (4/9/44). NBC Radio.
The Burns and Allen Show (5/9/44). CBS Radio.
The Uninvited (8/28/44). Screen Guild Theater.
Lady in the Dark (1/29/45). Lux Radio Theatre.
Standing Room Only (7/2/45). Screen Guild Theater.
Practically Yours (8/27/45). Lux Radio Theatre.
The Lost Weekend (1/7/46). Screen Guild Theater.
The Annual Film Critics Award (1/20/46). Radio Hall of Fame.
The Charley McCarthy Show (2/17/46). NBC Radio.
The Uninvited (2/19/46). Theatre of Romance.
The Lucky Strike Program Starring Jack Benny (3/10/46). NBC Radio.
The Mask of Kings (3/17/46). Theatre Guild on the Air.
The Fred Allen Show: "Candy Anonymous" (3/24/46). NBC Radio.
Arise, My Love (6/1/46). Academy Award Theatre.
Variety Girl (1947). Paramount Air Trailer.

The Jack Carson Show (1947). CBS Radio.
Alexander's Ragtime Band (4/7/47). Lux Radio Theatre.
Stairway to Heaven (10/27/47). Lux Radio Theatre.
The Trouble with Women (12/1/47). Screen Guild Theater.
Substitute Santa (12/11/47). Family Theatre.
The Sealtest Village Store (2/19/48). Sealtest Variety Theatre.
Grand Hotel (3/24/48). Theatre Guild on the Air.
The Perfect Marriage (4/12/48). Lux Radio Theatre.
The Last Frontier (6/7/48). Cavalcade of America.
For Bonnie Anne Laurie (7/8/48). Family Theatre.
Night Cry (10/7/48). Suspense.
Bing Crosby Philco Radio Time (10/13/48). ABC Radio.
Sir Lancelot of the Lake (10/16/48). Sealtest Variety Theatre.
Of Human Bondage (10/29/48). Ford Theater.
The Deeper Shadow (11/7/48). The Prudential Family Hour of Stars.
The Big Clock (11/22/48). Lux Radio Theatre.
The Constant Invader: "The Family Doctor" (11/26/48). New York Public Radio.
The Constant Invader: "Schools—Health Education" (12/2/48). New York Public Radio.
The Constant Invader: "Youth and Tuberculosis" (12/8/48). New York Public Radio.
So Evil My Love (1/13/49). Screen Guild Theater.
Shadow of a Doubt (2/18/49). Ford Theater.
The Leprechaun Who Didn't Listen (3/16/49). Family Theatre.
The Trouble with Women (5/1/49). Screen Directors Playhouse.
The Big Clock (7/8/49). Screen Directors Playhouse.
Chicken Feed (9/8/49). Suspense.
It Happens Every Spring (10/3/49). Lux Radio Theatre.
The Greatest Risk (11/15/49). Cavalcade of America.
The Uninvited (11/18/49). Screen Directors Playhouse.
The Constant Invader: "General Hospitals" (11/20/49). New York Public Radio.
Alias Nick Beal (12/8/49). Screen Guild Theater.
California (1/30/50). Lux Radio Theatre.
Academy Awards Program (3/23/50). ABC Radio.
It Happens Every Spring (4/14/50). Screen Directors Playhouse.
Pearls Are a Nuisance (4/20/50). Suspense.
Sir Galahad in Manhattan (11/14/50). Cavalcade of America.
After the Movies (12/7/50). Suspense.
Alias Nick Beal (12/28/50). Screen Directors Playhouse.
Cerebral Palsy Radio Spot Announcements (5/1/51). Public Service Announcement.
Mail Call (8/51). Armed Forces Radio Service (AFRS).
Strangers on a Train (9/3/51). Lux Radio Theatre.
Time for Defense (10/51). Department of Defense Public Service Announcement.
The Major and the Minor (10/14/51). Screen Guild Theater.
The Ship the Nazis Had to Get (10/16/51). Cavalcade of America.
Log of the Marne (10/22/51). Suspense.
Mississippi Bubble (11/15/51). Hallmark Playhouse.
Love from a Stranger (3/16/52). Theatre Guild on the Air.
The Devil's Staircase (4/1/52). Cavalcade of America.

Safari: "The Adventure of the Bull Elephant" (5/18/52). Hollywood Star Playhouse.
Close to My Heart (3/2/53). Lux Radio Theatre.
Meet Mr. McNutley (1953–54). Original episodes based on the TV series. CBS Radio.
The Winslow Boy (1/18/54). Lux Radio Theatre.
The Third Man (2/8/54). Lux Radio Theatre.
What's My Line? (10/31/54). CBS Radio.
Gentleman's Agreement (3/15/55). Lux Radio Theatre.
To the Rear March (1955). AFRS. A rebroadcast of *The Fred Allen Show* (1946)

APPENDIX 4

MAJOR STAGE APPEARANCES

The Woman in Room 13 (1930). Sources conflict as to how long Milland appeared in this stage production during his first return trip back to England. According to James Robert Parish and Don E. Stanke in *The Debonairs*, he was fired on opening night "for general incompetence" (244), but Milland himself asserts he was fired after two weeks and toured with the play for five full weeks until the company could find a replacement (*Wide-Eyed in Babylon*, 104).

My Fair Lady (Summer 1964). A Midwest and East Coast tour of a Kenley Players Production, starting at the Packard Music Hall in Warren, Ohio, and the Veterans Memorial Auditorium in Columbus, Ohio.

Hostile Witness (1966–1967). A January debut at the Hanna Theatre in Cleveland, Ohio, followed by a Broadway run at the Music Box Theatre (February 17–July 2, 1966) and an East Coast and Midwest tour, ending at the Studebaker Theatre in Chicago, Illinois (November 1966); later tours in Australia and the United Kingdom (1967).

Take Me Along (Summer 1969). A run at the Meadowbrook Theatre in Cedar Grove, New Jersey.

The Front Page (Fall 1969). A tour ending at the Parker Playhouse in Fort Lauderdale, Florida.

Critic's Choice (Summer 1970). A run at the Little Theatre on the Square in Sullivan, Illinois.

APPENDIX 5

DIRECTED BY RAY MILLAND

Alias Nick Beal (1949). Uncredited contributions. Paramount.
Meet Mr. McNutley and *The Ray Milland Show* (1953-55, also producer). Unconfirmed contributions to several episodes. CBS.
A Man Alone (1955). Republic.
Lisbon (1956, also associate producer). Republic.
General Electric Theater: "That's the Man!" (4/15/56). CBS.
The Ford Television Theatre: "Catch at Straws" (10/6/56). ABC.
General Electric Theater: "Never Turn Back" (1/6/57). CBS.
Schlitz Playhouse: "The Girl in the Grass" (3/15/57). CBS.
General Electric Theater: "Angel of Wrath" (5/5/57). CBS.
General Electric Theater: "Eyes of a Stranger" (12/8/57). CBS.
Suspicion: "Death Watch" (6/2/58). NBC.
General Electric Theater: "The World's Greatest Quarterback" (10/19/58). CBS.
General Electric Theater: "Battle for a Soul" (11/2/58). CBS.
The Safecracker (1958). Coronado Productions, MGM.
Goodyear Theatre: "A London Affair" (2/2/59). NBC.
Markham (1959-60, also producer). Unconfirmed contributions to several episodes. CBS.
Thriller: "Yours Truly, Jack the Ripper" (4/11/61). NBC.
The Dick Powell Theatre: "Open Season" (12/26/61). NBC.
Panic in Year Zero! (1962). AIP.
Hostile Witness (1968). Caralan Productions, United Artists.

NOTES

INTRODUCTION

4 **he appeared in more than 135 theatrical releases:** the 135-feature film total depends upon how one counts several latter-day TV projects that were eventually released into theaters.

4 **"When an actor is consistently good":** from "Ray Milland" by Leonard Maltin, *Film Fan Monthly*, 1968, 3.

5 **"[*The Lost Weekend*] was one of his last good films":** from *VideoHound & All-Movie Guide Stargazer*, 369.

5 **"[Milland] surprised many by becoming an actor":** from *Filmgoer's Companion*, 21.

5 **"[Milland] doesn't steal the film":** from *The Movie That Changed My Life*, 43.

6 **"[A]n actor of outstanding presence":** from *The Rise and Fall of the Matinée Idol*, 1.

6 **definition of this male species:** Of course, beyond the classical Anglo model, there were matinée idols in nearly every culture and language.

7 **"the best actor he'd ever seen":** from "Glamour and Catastrophe: Ray Milland, Irwin Allen Interviewed," by Gordon Gow, *Films and Filming*, September 1975.

7 **Milland and Grant as "Hitchcock's favorite male stars":** from "The Rhetoric of Hitchcock's Thrillers," by O. B. Hardison, *Man and the Movies*, 147.

8 **"Hollywood never quite knew what it had in Ray Milland":** from Frank Thompson, *International Dictionary of Films and Filmmakers*, as republished at Encyclopedia.com, 2019.

8 **"Milland suddenly revealed himself":** from prabook.com/web/ray.milland/1678021.

9 **the "irresistible lothario":** from "The Perfect Star," by Amy Fine Collins, *Vanity Fair*, April 23, 2010.

10 **he was "nice . . . maybe too nice":** from "Milland's Best Work Was Very, Very Good," by Michael Blowen, *Boston Globe*, March 12, 1986, 66.

10 **the "total prick" described by Tony Curtis:** from *Tony Curtis: American Prince*, 289.

10 **there never had been such a "sodden hero":** from *The Liveliest Art*, 246.

10 **"No other star played the spectrum of roles":** from TCM promo, April 2011.

10 **"The most sinister light comedian in Hollywood":** from "*Alias Nick Beal*," by Charlie Largent, trailersfromhell.com, June 26, 2021.

10 **"[Milland] never looked so at home":** from "*So Evil My Love*," by Largent, trailersfromhell.com, February 16, 2021.

344 NOTES

10   **"[H]is busy eyes [are] working overtime":** from *Ray Milland: The Films, 1929–1984*, 137.
11   **"[W]e go through life thinking we're very concerned":** from "Atom Menace: Survivors," by Joe Hyams, *New York Herald Tribune*, March 18, 1962.
13   **"I admired the frank theatricalism of March":** from "Wishing to Start from Scratch, He's Almost Left at the Post," *New York Herald Tribune*, June 16, 1940, G5.
13   **"Milland had a tendency to careen recklessly":** from "Frankly, Ray Milland Is No Press Agent's Dream," by Robert Cross, *Chicago Tribune*, August 30, 1985.
14   **"Perhaps, if he had retired in 1970":** from *Ray Milland: The Films, 1929–1984*, 2.

CHAPTER 1. THE CHILD WHO SAW TOO MUCH (1907–1929)

All books and certain articles are listed in the bibliography in full citation format; when mentioned in the notes, only the title and page numbers are cited. Otherwise, articles not listed in the bibliography are given full citations.

Shooting, release, and censorship information for most of the films in this book comes from catalog.afi.com/catalog (unless otherwise noted); budget and box-office (b.o.) information comes from sources listed at en.wikipedia.org/wiki and imdb.com (unless otherwise noted).

All quotes by Milland in chapter 1 come from *Wide-Eyed in Babylon* unless otherwise noted. Background about censorship and other production information throughout the book comes from the American Film Institute online site (afi.com), unless otherwise noted.

18   **Most summaries of Ray Milland's biography are scanty:** the three sources listing Milland's background incorrectly are *Movie Diary*, 42; *Movie Stars of the '30s*, 124; *Film Encyclopedia*, 943.
18   **The most definitive sources state:** a handwritten entry on March 15, 1907, in the Glamorganshire baptism records shows Milland's birth name beginning *Alfred Reginald*; much of Milland's family and background information in this chapter comes from *Wide-Eyed in Babylon* and has been cross-checked against such sources as *Ray Milland: The Films, 1929–1984*, *The Debonairs*, census records, myheritage.com, geni.com, studio press releases, press books, and a variety of Milland interviews, articles, and obituary notices; many sources reverse Milland's first names, calling him *Reginald Alfred*.
18   **"And don't make it 1905":** from "Soldier, Sailor, Jockey, Cook," by Max Breen, *Picturegoer Weekly*, April 15, 1939, 6.
19   **Some unfortunate, self-aggrandizing nicknames:** the nicknames *Ray the Magnificent*, *Hollywood's Master Actor*, and *Ole Milland* are listed at fold3.com/memorial/76842501/ray-milland.
19   **Reggie's parents:** Milland's early family heritage partially from ancestry.com and "Ray Milland—Report from Resolfen History Society," by Phil Davies, May 14, 2019 (resolvendistrictnews.co.uk/?p=4583).
19   **Jones established himself as a blacksmith:** Alfred Jones work history from ancestry.com (familysearch.org/tree/person/details/273J-6HH).
20   **Elizabeth had her third child:** the name of Milland's brother Leonard from a handwritten copy of the 1911 census; however, an England and Wales Civil Registration Death Index names him as Edward Brynmor Jones.
21   **his crush on a girl named Olwen:** the story about Olwen and "a very pretty daughter" quote from walesonline.co.uk/lifestyle/nostalgia/nostalgia-news-south-wales-1946-22026709.

NOTES

22 **he attended Mr. Jenkins's funeral:** from comment@jankench96226 http://www.youtube.com/watch?v=Jfi4xp UnHA
23 **singing in the boys' choir:** from "Actor Who Outgrew Reginald Dares Luck to Do Her Worst," by Beth Twiggar, *New York Herald Tribune*, April 21, 1941.
23 **a local steel-mill superintendent named Mullane:** Milland's new stepfather information from *The Debonairs*, 242.
23 **Among his parental figures:** Milland's relationship with his stepparents partially from a Twentieth Century-Fox press release, October 27, 1939.
23 **early signs of "wanderlust":** from "The Wanderlust," *Neath Guardian*, August 21, 1931.
24 **Reggie moved from school to school:** Milland's memories of being a teenage student from "My Regrettable Past," by Ray Milland, *Silver Screen*, November 1950, *Ray Milland, the Films, 1929–1984*, 5, and "Soldier, Sailor, Jockey, Cook," by Max Breen, *Picturegoer Weekly*, April 15, 1939.
24 **Reggie himself was entering contests:** a Twentieth Century-Fox press release (10-27-39) states he won cups and medals, but Milland himself says he "never won a race" in *Wide-Eyed in Babylon*, 35.
25 **"Even at a very early age":** Milland's mother quoted in "Soldier, Sailor, Jockey, Cook," by Max Breen, *Picturegoer Weekly*, April 15, 1939, 7.
26 **During a visit with his father:** differing from Milland's account, Parish and Stanke in *The Debonairs*, 242, state it was a friend in the Household Cavalry who suggested the idea of Milland joining the military.
26 **Reginald immediately wrote to Ramsey:** the sources for Milland applying for the King's Royal Guard include the *Chicago Tribune* Milland obituary, March 11, 1986, A6, and a Twentieth Century-Fox press release (10-27-39).
27 **his four separate uniforms:** Milland Cavalry uniform information from *The Debonairs*, 242.
28 **His partner was a lovely young woman:** Milland meeting Anna Neagle from *Nebraska State Journal*, June 9, 1940, 39.
29 **"One winter's morning, I was escorting the King":** from "New York Close-Up," by Tex McCrary and Jinx Falkenburg, *New York Herald Tribune*, October 17, 1951.
29 **to be honorably discharged from the army:** sources for Milland being discharged from the Cavalry include *Daily News*, September 22, 1946, 61, and "Ray Milland Hates Acting," by Elliseva Sayers, *Picturegoer*, February 25, 1950, 17.
29 **the very prestigious and expensive *Piccadilly*:** a 2004 crisply restored version from Milestone Films contains footage not seen in years, including tinted sequences.
30 **a film starring Nigel Barrie:** the "unreleased" film Milland mentions in *Wide-Eyed in Babylon*, 87, might be *The Plaything* starring Barrie, but he cites the director as Denison Clift, who was not the director of *The Plaything*.
31 **the producer of *The Informer* needed an expert marksman:** another story is that the producers found Milland through a recommendation by the War Office; the source for this version is *Ray Milland: The Films, 1929–1984*, 6; *The Informer* review: Hollywood 1930s, 90.
33 **Alfred Reginald John Truscott-Jones officially became Ray Milland:** Milland finalizing his name change from "The 'Two-Headed' Career of Ray Milland," Horror-Wood.com; "[T]hey said that only dogs were called Jack" and alternate name change story from "Ray Milland Dies of Cancer: Actor Won Fame for 'Lost Weekend' Role," *Los Angeles Times*, March 11, 1986; other versions of how "Milland" came about include his reworking his

stepfather's last name, Mullane, his remembering well-worn Milland Road in Neath, and his knowing of Milland Village in West Sussex.

33 **The Flying Scotsman was digitally restored:** reviews include the *Times of London*, February 28, 2011, 4, and *Kinematograph Weekly*, February 13, 1930, 49; there is some dispute as to which film was the true "first" British talkie since several films started out as silent and then had sound added later. Alfred Hitchcock's *Blackmail* is often cited as the first for this reason.

34 **Milland enjoyed going to the movies:** his leisure time described in "The Soldier from Neath Who Beat Catherine Zeta Jones and Sir Anthony Hopkins to become Wales' first Oscar Winner," by Jason Evans, walesonline.co.uk, April 30, 2019.

34 **"Life was just a bowl of cherries":** from *The Debonairs*, 279.

36 **the dance classes at the Max Rivers Dance School:** some sources say Milland danced in at least one London vaudeville revue but the name(s) and date(s) are never identified. A specific source for this is the *Philadelphia Inquirer* obituary, March 11, 1986.

37 **Rubin invited Milland to sign with the famed Hollywood studio:** according to his *Los Angeles Times* obituary, "Milland: 'Lost Weekend' Actor Dies," March 11, 1986, 18, Milland's contract pay is cited as $175 per week; other sources cite $150 per week.

37 **the termination of his *Charlot's Revue* contract:** both Milland himself and a Twentieth Century-Fox press release (10-27-39) say the screenwriter who helped him was Anita Loos, but other sources claim the help came from writer Adela Rogers St. Johns.

CHAPTER 2. FALSE STARTS, TRUE ROMANCE (1930–1936)

38 **"[The suburb] had gone against the haphazard planning":** from *Bring on the Empty Horses*, 3.

39 **"Greatest of all the studios was Metro-Goldwyn-Mayer":** from *Hollywood in the Thirties*, 16.

40 **"[B]oth studios were friendly":** from interview by the author with Marsha Hunt, June 24, 2021.

40 **[The building structure looked] "rather tacky":** from *Wide-Eyed in Babylon*, 120.

40 **studio cofounder, Louis B. Mayer, was a mere figurehead:** from *The Genius of the System*, 102.

40 **he was overshadowed by Robert Montgomery:** in *The Debonairs*, 314, Parish and Stanke tell the story of Robert Montgomery fighting with Louis B. Mayer over his perceived lack of professional perks; Mayer considered him an "ungrateful wretch" yet had to concede his movies made money.

41 **a scene chosen from DeMille's upcoming 1931 version of *The Squaw Man*:** screen test story from *Wide-Eyed in Babylon*, 121.

41 **One of Milland's other apprenticeship requirements:** the MGM drama coach story from *Wide-Eyed in Babylon*, 125.

41 ***Way for a Sailor* (1930) was built around John Gilbert:** *Way for a Sailor* review: *New York Herald Tribune*, December 13, 1930, 10.

41 ***Passion Flower*, directed by William C. DeMille, was somewhat better:** the *Passion Flower* budget came to $259,000, and the b.o. returns were $642,000, according to kayfrancisfilms.com by Michael O'Hanlon, January 1, 2009; review: *Variety*, December 24, 1930, 20.

42 **The Bachelor Father, a January 1931 release:** "I'm the girl on the right" quote from *Wide-Eyed in Babylon*, photoplate no. 2; rehearsals at San Simeon and Hearst as "strange and forbidding" from *Wide-Eyed in Babylon*, 127, 131; "Milland used to talk" from *The Times We Had: Life with William Randolph Hearst*, 129; Milland's account about Robert Z. Leonard is from *Wide-Eyed in Babylon*, 127, but in *The Debonairs*, 243, Parish and Stanke dispute that Milland liked Robert Z. Leonard, writing, "Leonard's impatience made him even more self-conscious" and that Davies helped Milland relax by teaching him to pretend that there was no director on the set; review: *Hollywood Daily Citizen*, March 6, 1931.

42 **and it was Milland's own idea to slash the name:** Milland name change from *The Debonairs*, 243.

43 **to report to the set of Strangers May Kiss:** censorship information from catalog.afi.com/Film/7193-STRANGERS-MAYKISS?sid=c2f23f14-d791-4b88-a9c4-1f234850426b&sr=12.645886&cp=1&pos=0.

44 **Milland worked on Just a Gigolo:** according to a *Hollywood Reporter* piece (May 21, 1931, 37), much of the film was reshot (and improved) after its poorly received previews; review: *Hollywood Reporter*, May 21, 1931, 37.

44 **Milland was assigned to Son of India:** story from *Wide-Eyed in Babylon*, 122–24.

45 **a friendly acquaintance named Bernadette Conklin:** story from *Wide-Eyed in Babylon*, 124–27, 209.

45 **Bought!, a downbeat melodrama released in August:** the film earned $777,000, well surpassing its $425,000 budget, according to the Warner Bros. financial information in the William Shaefer Ledger, appendix 1, *Historical Journal of Film, Radio and Television*, 1995, 15: sup1, 1–31, 11; review: *Los Angeles Evening Express*, August 14, 1931.

46 **Blonde Crazy was more typical:** "Del Ruth would really talk," from interview by the author with Dorothy Kingsley, April, 12, 1991; "a couple of goddam woodpeckers" from *Wide-Eyed in Babylon*, 142; Milland-Cagney friendship, ibid., 142–43; review: *New York Times*, December 4, 1931.

47 **Ambassador Bill, shot in August and September 1931:** review: *Variety*, November 17, 1931, 15.

48 **"I came back the cheapest possible way":** from *The Debonairs*, 244.

48 **"For months I made a living":** from *Ray Milland: The Films, 1929–1984*, 7.

48 **He learned her name was Malvina Muriel Weber:** meeting Mal Weber from *Wide-Eyed in Babylon*, 137–38; courtship, ibid., 139–41; Illinois, Cook County, Birth Certificates, 1871–1949, states Weber's birthdate as December 31, 1908.

49 **"A friend introduced me":** Mal Weber's quote from *The Debonairs*, 245.

49 **The Man Who Played God was the most popular of Arliss's string of films:** John Adolfi died of a brain hemorrhage within a year of the film's release; according to Bette Davis in *Mother Goddam*, 23, Arliss directed much of the film himself; Warner Bros. financial information is from the William Shaefer Ledger, appendix 1, *Historical Journal of Film, Radio and Television*, 1995, 15: sup1, 1–31, 13; "[Davis] was a very pretty and pleasant creature," from *Wide-Eyed in Babylon*, 142.

50 **the pro forma step of petitioning for him to become a naturalized citizen:** petition for naturalization information from ancestry.com.

50 **The Hollywood Reporter summarized:** from *Hollywood Reporter*, January 14, 1932, 3.

50 **Milland was assigned to Polly of the Circus:** Gable's role change from *Long Live the King*, 159; Milland knocking out Gable from *Wide-Eyed in Babylon*, 144–45; according to MGM records and the Eddie Mannix Ledger, *Polly of the Circus* earned $530,000 in the United

States and Canada and $170,000 elsewhere, resulting in a profit of $20,000; review: *New York Herald Tribune*, March 19, 1932, 8.

51 **But the Flesh Is Weak was MGM's adaptation:** the premise was borrowed for *Bedtime Story* (1964) and its remake, *Dirty Rotten Scoundrels* (1988); review: *New York Herald Tribune*, April 18, 1932, 10.

51 **an engagement party at her family home:** party information from "Troth Revealed at Luncheon: Bride-Elect Marlborough Graduate," *Los Angeles Times*, July 12, 1932.

51 **Milland's next picture for MGM,** *Payment Deferred*: according to the Eddie Mannix Ledger, the film grossed a foreign and domestic total of $304,000, resulting in a loss of $32,000; the Milland-Mendes relationship from *The Debonairs*, 246; reviews: *Variety*, November 15, 1932, 23; *New York Daily News*, November 13, 1932, 129.

53 **Ray Milland married Malvina Muriel Weber:** wedding and honeymoon information from *Wide-Eyed in Babylon*, 141.

53 **his studio option was not renewed:** after leaving MGM and before returning to England, Milland recalls appearing in an unreleased experimental film, but no trace of this film or information about it has been found; anecdote from *Wide-Eyed in Babylon*, 148.

53 **"I've heard it said that you insisted on divorcing":** from "Ray Milland's Rough Time," *Picturegoer Weekly*, April 29, 1939, 12.

53 **Milland's journey back to England:** from *Wide-Eyed in Babylon*, 150.

54 ***Orders Is Orders*, would be directed by Walter Forde:** reviews: *New York Daily News*, May 5, 1934, 168; *Life*, September 1933, 52.

54 **Milland became part of steeplechase lore:** Sandown Park steeplechase information from *The Debonairs*, 246.

54 **Milland was tapped by British Lion for *This Is the Life*:** review: *Kinematograph Weekly*, July 13, 1933, 45.

55 **an aspiring Viennese writer named Wilder:** Billy Wilder story from *Wide-Eyed in Babylon*, 4–5; if Milland sensed Hitler's growing menace during this particular trip, he doesn't mention it in his memoirs.

55 **Ray Milland's return to Hollywood:** while *The Mystery of Mr. X* is listed in some Milland filmographies, including imdb.com, as a 1934 feature he made in November 1933; it is highly unlikely Milland went back to his former employer, MGM, to appear in an uncredited bit part; the website, the Classic Movie Hub, states definitively, "Ray Milland is in the studio records for the role of 'Forbes', but he did not appear in the movie" (classicmoviehub.com/film/the-mystery-of-mr-x-1934/).

55 **an earthquake and its after-shocks startled Milland:** story from *The Debonairs*, 246.

55 **he attended a concert given by Ramon Novarro:** from "Ramon Novarro Gives Musicale in Own Theatre," *Los Angeles Examiner*, September 24, 1933.

56 **Milland was forced to ask friends:** borrowing money from friends story from "The 'Two-Headed' Career of Ray Milland," Horror-Wood.com.

56 **an upcoming picture called *Bolero*:** casting story from *The Debonairs*, 246; "stabbed by his boyfriend," from *Wide-Eyed in Babylon*, 162; review: *Life*, April 1934, 6.

57 **Milland had little to do in *We're Not Dressing*:** Lombard slapping Crosby story from *Bing Crosby*, 57–58; alternative sources say that director Wesley Ruggles, not Norman Taurog, was instrumental in having Milland signed to a long-term contract.

57 **he signed his contract:** Paramount contract information from *The Debonairs*, 246.

58 **they got hitched at the LA County courthouse:** the Milland remarriage information from familysearch.org/ark:/61903/3:1:3QSQ-G93H-S3XP?i=1880&cc=1804002.

58 **We're Not Dressing was at least well-received:** reviews: *Los Angeles Times*, April 19, 1934, 12; *New York Times*, May 6, 1934, X3.
58 **as a supporting player in *The Great Magoo*:** information from Elizabeth Yeaman, *Hollywood Citizen-News*, February 27, 1934.
58 **"Most of the big studios developed a distinctive style":** Paramount Studios in the 1930s described in *Hollywood 1930s*, 10; and *We're Not Dressing* as one of the "creaking horrors," ibid., 45.
59 **the three-story Dressing Room Row:** information from *My Side of the Road*, 51.
59 ***Many Happy Returns* blends comedy sketches:** review: *Los Angeles Times*, June 1, 1934, 12.
59 **Milland applied for his Declaration of Intention for Naturalization:** information from Declaration of Intention Form 65063.
60 **a Household Cavalry officer in the action-adventure *Lives of a Bengal* Lancer:** information from *Picturegoer Weekly:* "Soldier, Sailor, Jockey, Cook," by Max Breen, April 15, 1939, 7; Elizabeth Yeaman, *Hollywood Citizen-News*, August 30, 1934.
60 **one of the duties of a "Hollywood Wife":** baby shower information from "Hollywood Parade," by Reine Davies, *Los Angeles Examiner*, August 13, 1934.
60 **Luisa had died from injuries:** death information from *Wide-Eyed in Babylon*, 19.
60 **a serial entry, *Charlie Chan in London*:** review: *New York Times*, September 13, 1934, 26.
61 ***Menace* was shot quickly:** review: *New York Herald Tribune*, November 23, 1934, 12.
61 **Up Next: *One Hour Late*:** review: *Hollywood Reporter*, November 20, 1934, 3.
62 ***The Gilded Lily* was shot from early October:** Milland's description of Ruggles from *Wide-Eyed in Babylon*, 188; Milland's first reaction to Colbert from *The Debonairs*, 247; "Fred and I had been signed," from "Ray Milland," by Aljean Harmetz, *Architectural Digest*, April 1996, 190; reviews: *New York Times*, February 9, 1935, 11; *Chicago Daily Tribune*, February 2, 1935, 17 ("Mae Tinee" was actually a pseudonym for a group of critics at the *Tribune*).
63 **Milland was awarded the lead in *Lightning Strikes Twice*:** information from catalog.afi.com/Film/5527-HALF-ANGEL.
64 **Milland had little to do in *Four Hours to Kill!*:** "French kiss" story from *The Debonairs*, 247–48; reviews: *Variety*, April 17, 1935, 14; *Hollywood Reporter*, March 29, 1935, 3.
64 **as another murder victim in *The Glass Key*:** reviews: *Variety*, June 19, 1935, 21; *Billboard*, June 1, 1935, 22.
65 ***Alias Mary Dow*, was produced at Universal's B unit:** review: *Variety*, July 3, 1935, 14.
66 **to turn down the lead in *Hands across the Table*:** information from "Hands across the Table," by Paul Tatara, tcm.com/tcmdb/title/77277/hands-across-the-table#articles-reviews?articleId=139117, November 5, 2008, and *The All-Americans*, 258.
66 **another A picture, *Next Time We Love*:** reviews: *Chicago Daily News*, February 1, 1936, 17; *Billboard*, February 8, 1936, 20.

CHAPTER 3. IN THE SHADOW OF CARY GRANT (1936–1940)

69 **"By 1935, Cary Grant's willingness to continue":** from *Cary Grant*, 47–48.
69 **Grant moved onto a spectacular freelance career:** more accurately, Grant signed nonexclusive contracts with both Columbia and RKO rather than become a completely "free agent."
69 **"to continue in the footsteps of Cary Grant":** from *The Debonairs*, 241.

NOTES

70   **With *The Return of Sophie Lang*, a July 1936 release:** review: *New York Times*, July 24, 1936, 13.
70   **the Technicolor sound remake of *The Garden of Allah*:** information from *Casting Might-Have-Beens: A Film by Film Directory of Actors Considered for Roles Given to Others*, 95.
71   **Graham Greene's crime thriller *This Gun for Hire*:** information from "News of the Screen: Don Marquis and Friends Sell a Play–Akim Tamiroff a New Sherlock for the Screen," *New York Times*, August 22, 1936.
71   **Milland's October release, *The Big Broadcast of 1937*:** this edition arrived between *The Big Broadcast of 1936* (1935) and *The Big Broadcast of 1938* (1937); the use of *Murder in the Vanities* from catalog.afi.com/Film/6880-THE-BIG-BROADCAST-OF-1937; as an added incentive to theatergoers, Paramount installed a "Mirrophonic System" in some of its theaters, proclaiming it was the state of the art in sound clarity, according to *Boston Daily Globe*, October 10, 1936, 12; review: *Boston Daily Globe*, October 10, 1936, 12.
72   **the release of *The Jungle Princess*:** censorship issues and Breen quotes from catalog. afi.com/Film/4366-THE-JUNGLE-PRINCESS; the chimpanzee attack from *My Side of the Road*, 54; liquid dry cleaner incident, ibid., 55; "Ray was a genuinely unselfish actor," ibid., 53; "My Jungle Prince," from "Ray Milland, 78: Career Spanned 50 Years and 120 Films," *Philadelphia Inquirer* by Stan W. Metzler, March 11, 1986, 11-B; reviews: *New York Times*, December 24, 1936; *New York Herald Tribune*, December 24, 1936, 11; Milland's promotion of *The Jungle Princess* from metaunfolded.com/ray-milland.
74   ***Three Smart Girls*, which Milland filmed on loan out:** interview by the author with Louise Steiner Elian, March 13, 2001; the budget (over $300,000) and b.o. ($1, 635, 800) from "Three Smart Guys: How a Few Penniless German Émigrés Saved Universal Studios," by Helmut Asper and Jan-Christopher Horak, *Film History*, vol. 11, no. 2, January 1, 1999, 134; however, other sources state the budget and b.o. figures were higher; Louis Hayward's departure: the source citing Hayward as ill is "Around and About in Hollywood," by Kendall Read, *Los Angeles Times*, September 23, 1936, 15; the source citing Hayward as reluctant is Koster himself in *Henry Koster: A Directors Guild of America Oral History*, 51–52; the storyline had an obvious influence on Disney's *The Parent Trap* (1961); review: "Three Smart Girls/For Valour," by Graham Greene, *Spectator*, March 26, 1937.
75   **a large assemblage known as "The British Colony":** from *Laurence Olivier: A Biography*, 157, and *No Bed of Roses*, 116–17.
76   **to star in *Bulldog Drummond Escapes*:** information partially from "Heather Angel: What's in a Name?," by Barry Roberts, *Films of the Golden Age*, Summer 1996, 67; review: *Hollywood Reporter*, January 26, 1937, 3.
77   **Milland was sent back to Universal for *Wings over Honolulu*:** review: *Los Angeles Times*, June 1, 1937, A11.
77   **wasting his time in Paramount's inferior *Murder Goes to College*:** from "Karns Subs Milland," *Hollywood Reporter*, December 29, 1936, 3.
78   **his invitation from the Household Cavalry:** coronation information from "Ray Misses Coronation for Flying Movie Role," *New York Daily Mirror*, May 29, 1937.
78   **the school teacher falsely accused of murder in Mervyn LeRoy's *They Won't Forget*:** information from *They Coulda Been Contenders*, 265.
78   **a leading-man assignment in a major production titled *Easy Living*:** screenplay background from *Between Flops: A Biography of Preston Sturges*, 109; "By highlighting the extremes," from *Anatomy of Film*, 148; Milland's anxiety from *Wide-Eyed in Babylon*, 256; Milland's outward demeanor from author's interview with Marsha Hunt, June 24, 2021; review: *Variety*, July 7, 1937, 12.

NOTES

79 **Milland was paid by Lucky Strike:** information from "Hollywood Paid Fortune to Smoke," *BBC News*, September 25, 2008 (news.bbc.co.uk/2/hi/health/7632963.stm); Diamond Match Company information from metmuseum.org/art/collection/search/754365.

79 **Milland declined Howard Hawks's invitation:** *Bringing up Baby* information from *Cary Grant*, 61, and *Howard Hawks: The Grey Fox of Hollywood*, 247.

80 *Ebb Tide*, **a summer shoot:** there were previous black-and-white silent versions in 1915 and 1922, respectively; the "new Garbo" reference from *Frances Farmer: Shadowland*, 57; and "ill-defined bit," ibid., 61; budget information from the *Hollywood Reporter*, April 27, 1937, 2; review: *Newsweek*, November 29, 1937, 24.

81 **a small part in the original** *The Most Dangerous Game*: information from catalog.afi.com/Film/3937-THE-MOST-DANGEROUS-GAME.

81 *Wise Girl* **is nearly as good:** reviews: *Variety*, December 29, 1937, 17; *Hollywood Reporter*, December 23, 1937, 3.

82 *Roadshow*, **a low-budget screwball comedy:** information from "Milland-Sullavan Team Roach 'Roadshow' Plan," *Hollywood Reporter*, October 1, 1937, 1.

82 **to "keep title to the property":** Wales property information from "A Landed Gentleman of Hollywood," UPI report in the *New York Herald Tribune*, November 28, 1937.

82 **he attended Ray Milland movies:** Alfred Jones attending Ray's movies from "Actor Ray Milland Was Paid to Endorse Smoking," by Steffan Rhys, walesonline.co.uk/news/wales-news/actor-ray-milland-paid-endorse-2155062, September 26, 2008.

82 **Paramount commissioned** *Her Jungle Love*: review: *New York Times*, April 14, 1938, 27.

83 **Technicolor would have vastly improved** *Tropic Holiday*: review: *Variety*, July 6, 1938, 15.

84 **the massive Motion Picture Electrical Pageant:** information from "Stars Appear Tonight in Big Film Pageant," from *Los Angeles Examiner*, June 8, 1938.

84 **as a reporter tricked into marriage in** *Cafe Society*: information from "Dee, Hilliard, Milland Leads for 'Cafe Society,'" *Hollywood Reporter*, February 3, 1938, 1.

84 **a surprise birthday party for Joan Crawford:** information from *Hollywood Legends: The Golden Years of "The Hollywood Reporter*," 88.

84 **to submit his Petition for Naturalization:** information from Federal Naturalization Records, 1843, at ancestry.com.

84 **"The Ray Millands, who should know, insist that divorce gossip is untrue":** from "Behind the Makeup," by Erskine Johnson, *Los Angeles Examiner*, June 20, 1938.

85 **Milland started work in the spring on** *Men with Wings*: flying scenes information from "A Viewer's Guide to Aviation Movies," by Jack Hardwick and Ed Schnepf, *The Making of the Great Aviation Films*, General Aviation Series, volume 2, 1989; review: *Variety*, October 26, 1938, 13.

85 **in his upcoming blockbuster,** *Gone with the Wind*: information from *Memo from David O. Selznick*, 179 (memo dated November 18, 1938).

86 *Say It in French*, **was only a programmer comedy:** promotion of Olympe Bradna from "Chance Roles Turn Many Players into New Film Stars," by Mildred Martin, *Philadelphia Inquirer Public Ledger*, December 9, 1938, 17; review: *New York Times*, December 1, 1938, 29.

87 **Ernst Lubitsch green-lit remaking the 1927 silent classic** *Hotel Imperial*: *Invitation to Happiness* (*I Loved a Soldier*) information from *Marlene: The Life of Marlene Dietrich*, 118–20, and lastgoddess.blogspot.com/2014/06/dietrichs-unfinished-film-i-loved.html; Milland accident information and quote from *Wide-Eyed in Babylon*, 189; *Hotel Imperial* review: *Los Angeles Times*, May 8, 1939, A14.

89 ***Beau Geste* was a knockoff:** in 1939, the United Kingdom had its own self-serving patriotic warhorse, a fourth remake of *The Four Feathers*, produced by Alexander Korda, starring Ralph Richardson and concerning the 1882 battle in the Sudan; Milland-Donlevy fight information from "For the Cause!," *Variety*, March 1, 1939; review: "Newman's eerie, haunting music," from *The Complete Films of Broderick Crawford*, 131.
90 ***The Light That Failed*, costarring Ida Lupino:** information from *The Swashbucklers*, 150.
91 ***Elsa Maxwell's Hotel for Women*, a minor-league melodrama:** information from catalog. afi.com/Film/7768-ELSA-MAXWELLSHOTELFORWOMEN.
91 **the romantic lead in *Midnight*:** information from catalog.afi.com/Film/5067-MIDNIGHT.
91 **the Millands employed architect Robert Woolf:** the Beverly Hills Milland home information from "Ray Milland," by Aljean Harmetz, *Architectural Digest*, April 1996; and prabook.com/web/robert.woolf/1919801.
92 ***French without Tears* went into production:** traveling information from *Wide-Eyed in Babylon*, 193–94; the cartoon-ad cover art was completely misleading, depicting Milland's character seducing Drew's; the Milland-H. H. Asquith connection from a Paramount press release, July 1940; reviews: *Hollywood Reporter*, March 21, 1940, 3; *New York Herald Tribune*, April 29, 1940, 8.
94 **[Mal Milland had] "done a great deal":** Milland's mother's quote from *Picturegoer*, April 29, 1939.
94 ***Untamed* emerged as one more attempt:** Morison's working with Milland from "Patricia Morison: More Than Wonderful," by Colin Briggs, *Films of the Golden Age*, Fall 2005, 44; interview by the author with Darryl Hickman, September 15, 2020; review: *Variety*, June 26, 1940, 16.
95 **a Sonja Henie vehicle, *Everything Happens at Night*:** Robert Cummings's early attempts at acting British from Twentieth Century-Fox press release (10-27-39); review: *New York Times*, December 16, 1939, 12.
96 ***Irene*, yet another remake:** Wilcox proposing a follow-up film with Milland from the *Los Angeles Times* by Edwin Schallert, April 4, 1940, A10; review: *Los Angeles Times*, April 19, 1940, 17; budget and b.o. information from "RKO Film Grosses: 1931–1951," by Richard Jewel, *Historical Journal of Film Radio and Television* 14, no. 1 (1994): 55.
97 **Mal's girlfriends fêted her with a baby shower:** information from "Mrs. Wayne to Fete Mrs. Milland," by Sally Moore, *Los Angeles Evening Herald Press*, January 27, 1940.
99 ***The Doctor Takes a Wife* is lively:** reviews: *New York Times*, June 15, 1940, 12; *Los Angeles Times*, April 24, 1940, 13.
99 **"How could I help but have faith":** from *The Debonairs*, 252.
100 **Milland garnered not one but two separate fan clubs:** from "The 'Two-Headed' Career of Ray Milland," by Joe Winters, July 2006.
100 **Paramount itself scrapped plans:** unrealized Madeleine Carroll film information from "Griffith, Milland for Para. Brit. Pix," *Hollywood Reporter*, January 10, 1940, 1.

CHAPTER 4. A WAR BEGINS . . . A STAR IS BORN (1940–1943)

101 **"Mal honey, when this picture comes out":** from *Mitchell Leisen, Hollywood Director*, 142.
101 ***Arise, My Love* furthered his upward trajectory:** recasting from *Mitchell Leisen, Hollywood Director*, 134, and *The Debonairs*, 254; background from *Claudette Colbert: She Walked in Beauty*, 151.

NOTES

102 **his older sister, Olivia Charles, was killed:** Milland's sister's death from the *Hollywood Reporter*, July 15, 1940, 8.

102 **to join his British Colony compatriots:** meeting information from *Hollywood Legends: The Golden Years of "The Hollywood Reporter,"* 125.

102 ***Arise, My Love* as her personal favorite:** information about, 148, and censorship issues, 147, from *On Sunset Boulevard*; reviews: *Los Angeles Times*, October 30, 1940, 15; *Christian Science Monitor*, November 8, 1940, 8.

103 **Another kind of war, a private one, began:** Hedda Hopper fight from *Wide-Eyed in Babylon*, 202.

104 **an adaptation of 1938's *Alexander Ragtime's Band*:** information partially from *Alice Faye: A Life Beyond the Silver Screen*, 133.

104 **"Advertising companies ran the radio business":** *Lux Radio Theatre* information from George Wells and interview by the author with Wells, April 13, 1992.

104 **the movie translation of Clare Boothe Luce's *Kiss the Boys Goodbye*:** information from the *Hollywood Reporter*, July 3, 1940, 2.

105 **Milland's next picture, *I Wanted Wings*:** "[A] disastrous start," from *Between Flops: A Biography of Preston Sturges*, 153; "He went up with a pilot," and Milland's experience with DeMille from " Ray Milland: Against Type," *Films of the Golden Age*, 60; the burning plane story from "Milland Sacrifices His Own Eyelashes" (no author cited), *Zanesville Sunday Times-Signal*, April 27, 1941; Milland helping Lake from *Veronica: The Autobiography of Veronica Lake*, 54; other attitudes about Veronica Lake from *Between Flops: A Biography of Preston Sturges*, 154, and *Mitchell Leisen, Hollywood Director*, 145; review: *Los Angeles Times*, March 25, 1941, 8.

107 **"While they were making *Skylark*":** from "The Perfect Star," by Amy Fine Collins, *Vanity Fair*, April 23, 2010.

108 **"Milland remained an introvert":** from "Ray Milland Dies of Cancer: Actor Won Fame for 'Lost Weekend' Role," *Los Angeles Times*, March 11, 1986.

108 **When *Skylark* was released in November:** review: *New York Herald Tribune*, November 20, 1941, 31.

108 **Sturges thought he was "a bloated phony":** Sturges describing Leisen from *Between Flops: A Biography of Preston Sturges*, 110.

109 **the latter was Paramount's biggest money maker:** *I Wanted Wings* as the top-grossing Paramount film from *Mitchell Leisen, Hollywood Director*, 143.

109 **while preparing *How Green Was My Valley*:** information from *Memo from Darryl F. Zanuck: The Golden Years at Twentieth Century-Fox*, 43; *How Green Was My Valley* was put into production following two well-received 1940 Welsh coal-miner dramas out of Great Britain, Carol Reed's *The Stars Look Down*, shot mainly at several London studios, and Pen Tennyson's *The Proud Valley*, based on a true story and starring Paul Robeson, shot in Milland's hometown of Neath in 1939.

109 **in something called *Channel Port*:** information from "'Port' for Ray Milland," *Hollywood Reporter*, May 19, 1941, 1.

109 ***Lydia*, directed by Julian Duvivier:** information from "Milland Loaned Korda: Duvivier Nears Camera," the *Hollywood Reporter*, February. 23, 1941, 3.

110 **Milland and Goddard were first teamed in *Reap the Wild Wind*:** "He did not know a thing," from *The Debonairs*, 256; hoopskirt mousetrap story from "Filmland," by Hedda Hopper, *The Pittsburgh Press*, August 7, 1941, 11; DeMille and Paramount poll information from *The Debonairs*, 255; "They gave me women's permanents," from *The Debonairs*, 255

footnote; Milland's experiences from "Ray Milland: Against Type," *Films of the Golden Age*; Milland's fight with squid from "The 'Two-Headed' Career of Ray Milland," Horror-Wood.com (according to other sources the cost of the "red and blue devil fish" was considerably higher—as much as $70,000); DeMille donating "squid" rubber from *Hollywood Players: The Forties*, 11; reviews: *Variety*, March 25, 1942, 8; *New York Times*, November 30, 1941, BR 28; b.o. from "All-Time Top Grossers," *Variety*, January 8, 1964, 69.

113   **starring in the director's *Rurales*:** information from "Milland in Lead in DeMille's 'Rurales,'" the *Hollywood Reporter*, March 26, 1942, 2.

113   **the Milland-Wayne friendship was sorely tested:** Mexican vacation stories from *Duke: The Real Story of John Wayne*, 63; *John Wayne: The Man Behind the Myth*, 82; *John Wayne: The Life and Legend*, 115, 117; and historyonfilm.com/John-Wayne, a 2012 website.

114   **"I seldom have an open break with anyone":** from *The Debonairs*, 251.

115   **"[I] always liked working with Paulette":** from "Ray Milland: Against Type," *Films of the Golden Age*, 63.

115   **"[Sidney Lanfield] had a reputation":** from *They Coulda Been Contenders*, 275.

115   ***The Lady Has Plans* received favorable notices:** from *Christian Science Monitor*, March 13, 1942, 14.

115   ***Are Husbands Necessary?* was based on Isabel Scott Rorick's 1941 novel:** budget and b.o. from "101 Pix Gross in Millions," *Variety*, January 6, 1943, 58; review: *New York Times*, July 9, 1942, 17.

116   ***Frenchman's Creek*, a Technicolor adaptation:** information from "Milland 'Creek' Lead," *Hollywood Reporter*, March 23, 1942, 1.

116   ***The Major and the Minor* gave Milland a great part:** Wilder's casting of Milland from *Nobody's Perfect: Billy Wilder, A Personal Biography*, 102–10; salary information from *On Sunset Boulevard*, 174, and *The Debonairs*, 257; *Lolita* connection from allmovie.com/movie/the-major-and-the-minor-v101000/review; reviews: *Chicago Daily Tribune*, November 15, 1942, H6; *Variety*, September 2, 18; *New York Times*, September 17, 1942, 21; budget and b.o. from "101 Pix Gross in Millions," *Variety*, January 6, 1943, 58.

117   **the largest fine art collections in Hollywood:** Milland's collection information from *The Debonairs*, 257.

118   **an appearance in *Star-Spangled Rhythm*:** "If Men Played Cards as Women Do" was written by George S. Kaufman in 1929 for Irving Berlin's *Music Box Revue*.

119   **seen widely in early 1943 was *The Crystal Ball*:** review: *New York Herald Tribune*, February 19, 1943, 14; b.o. from "Top Grossers of the Season," *Variety*, January 5, 1944, 54.

119   **Milland's wandering eye fell upon De Carlo:** flirtation story from *Yvonne: An Autobiography* and "Yvonne De Carlo—A rare beauty," by Alan Royle at filmstarfacts.com; the "peccadilloes" quote is from *Wide-Eyed in Babylon*, 219.

121   **teaming him with Vera Zorina for W. Somerset Maugham's *Hour before the Dawn*:** information from catalog.afi.com/Film/944-THE-HOURBEFORETHEDAWN and "Zorina, Milland, Griffith Together," the *Hollywood Reporter*, August 12, 1941, 8.

121   **his forty-foot, high-powered speedboat:** information from "Ray Milland Gives His Speedboat to the Navy," *Hollywood Reporter*, August 19, 1942, 1.

121   **To Milland's chagrin:** Milland's attempt to join the draft from *The Debonairs*, 257.

121   **"On one such early outing":** from *The Debonairs*, 257; USO tour information from "Milland on Guadalcanal," *Hollywood Reporter* March 9, 1944, 4; and "Ray Milland," *Film Dope*, 16; Paulette Goddard war-bond tour information from *Paulette: The Adventurous Life of Paulette Goddard*. 122.

NOTES 355

122 **his father mailed Ray a frayed photograph:** story from Harrison Carroll's column, *Los Angeles Evening Herald Express*, December 20, 1943; one unsubstantiated rumor persisted for years that the FBI investigated Milland for a supposed wartime meeting in Mexico with a Nazi officer. One of the few places to find this allegation is the-solute.com/attention-must-be-paid-ray-milland. However, the website offers no details or sourcing.

122 ***Forever and a Day*, the all-star drama:** in an alternative reference regarding the donation of profits, Parish and Stanke claim the money went to the National Foundation for Infantile Paralysis, *The Debonairs*, 257; according to *Hitchcock Lost & Found: The Forgotten Films*, 126, Hitchcock worked on the script and other preproduction elements of the Lupino-Aherne segment.

123 ***A Farewell to Arms*, a tragic wartime romance:** information from "Forgotten Faces: Why Some of Our Cinema Heritage Is Part of the Public Domain," by David Pierce, *Film History*, vol. 19, no. 2, 2007, 135.

CHAPTER 5. AT PARAMOUNT'S PEAK (1944–1945)

124 ***The Crystal Ball* was produced at Paramount:** during this period, Paramount had an excess number of titles and United Artists had a deficit, per exhibitor quota rules, so even the Paramount A picture, *I Married a Witch*, was sold to United Artists for release in 1942.

124 **"Tracking the ups and downs":** from *The All-Americans*, 274.

125 **the long-delayed release of *Lady in the Dark*:** director Mitchell Leisen thought Irene Dunne would have been a better choice, and Dunne expressed interest, but Rogers had first right of refusal, from "Irene Dunne: Legendary Cool," by James Bawden, *Films of the Golden Age*, Fall 2012, 33; salaries: by 1945, Rogers earned $292,159, making her the highest paid Hollywood star, surpassing Deanna Durbin and earning the eighth largest salary in the United States, according to *Ginger Rogers*, 117; for this one film, Rogers was paid $122,500, whereas *Variety* reported Milland's cumulative annual salary at the end of 1943 was $169,000 (the former figure is noted in *The RKO Gals*, 222; the latter figure is noted in *The Debonairs*, 257).

125 **he prematurely plugged the film:** *The Revlon Revue* information partially from *The Debonairs*, 257.

125 **During the *Lady in the Dark* production itself:** "The Saga of Jenny" information from *Mitchell Leisen, Hollywood Director*, 186, and *Ginger Rogers*, 16 footnote; "She was physically competent," from *Mitchell Leisen, Hollywood Director*, 190; budget and b.o. from *The RKO Gals*, 222; reviews: *New York Times*, February 23, 1944, 17; *Variety*, February 16, 1944; Charley's mean-spirited remark, "Rage is a pretty good substitute for sex, isn't it?," is the first instance in a post-Code Hollywood film the term "sex" is used in its literal sense; additional cut sequences included Mischa Auer's "Tchaikovsky," as noted in *Mitchell Leisen, Hollywood Director*, 185, and Rogers's solo version of "Suddenly, It's Spring," as noted in *The Unkindest Cuts: The Scissors and the Cinema*, 163; Leisen claims he rewrote most of the screenplay himself—from *Mitchell Leisen, Hollywood Director*, 182.

127 ***The Uninvited*, which holds up well today:** Preproduction information from *"It's the Pictures That Got Small": Charles Brackett on Billy Wilder and Hollywood's Golden Age*, 215–16; Brackett's attempt to sign Hitchcock, ibid., 198, 199; Paramount's ad campaign from "Dial M For Milland: The Ray Milland Film Archive," Facebook; Del Toro's comments

were made in "Guillermo Del Toro: The Interview, Part II," by Ethan Gilsdorf, *The Daily Beast*, wired.com, August 11, 2011; Scorsese's list was part of his all-time list in the *Daily Beast*, October 28, 2009; Milland giving help to Gail Russell from "An Interview with Lewis Allen," by Tom Weaver, *The Uninvited* (booklet), The Criterion Collection, 2013, CC2328BD, 17–18; Paramount added "ghostly" special effects against the wishes of director Allen; they were removed in the prints sent to the United Kingdom, not out of respect to Allen's vision but because the "spectral" animation was thought to be too scary for audiences overseas; Leslie Halliwell quote from *Halliwell's Harvest*, 269; Patricia White's book, *Uninvited: Classical Hollywood Cinema and Lesbian Representability*, examines the lesbian theme in great depth (e.g. the Hays Office received complaints from the Catholic Legion of Decency regarding certain scenes, but it was too late for Paramount to change anything); preview screening information from *"It's the Pictures That Got Small": Charles Brackett on Billy Wilder and Hollywood's Golden Age*, 226.

129 **a promotional "Shiver Opera":** it is not entirely clear if this concert took place, but the date of the *Hollywood Reporter* announcement was March 23, 1943, 3.

130 **Milland worked on *Ministry of Fear*:** Lang's apology to Greene reported in "*Ministry of Fear*: Paranoid Style," by Glenn Kenny, The Criterion Collection essay, March 12, 2013; reviews: *Variety*, October 18, 1944; Kenny, "*Ministry of Fear*: Paranoid Style"; Kehr, *Chicago Reader*, October 15, 2014.

132 **Milland next shot *Till We Meet Again*:** regarding the title origins, another unrelated (and little seen) *Till We Meet Again*, a spy thriller, was produced by Paramount in 1936, starring Herbert Marshall; "On my way home," from '*Tis Herself*, 95; in her book, though, O'Hara sets the date of this event in February 1944, which conflicts with the shooting schedule at catalog.afi.com/Film/24213-TILL-WE-MEET-AGAIN; "Barbara was constantly aware," from *Hollywood Players: The Forties*, 100; reviews: *Variety*, August 30, 1944; "Jacob's Ladder, or Love and Adversity," by Hervé Dumont in *Griffithiana*, December 1992, 88; *New York Times*, August 30, 1944; according to tcm.com/tcmdb/title/17885/Till-We-Meet-Again/notes.html, Borzage replaced Irving Pichel as director.

134 **a musical-comedy version of Ferenc Molnár's play, *Olympia*:** information from *"It's the Pictures That Got Small": Charles Brackett on Billy Wilder and Hollywood's Golden Age*, 240–42.

134 **A heavy drama titled *Behold My Wife!*:** information from "Paramount Dusting 'Wife' for Milland and Russell," *Hollywood Review*, November 1, 1944, 1.

134 **the all-star *Duffy's Tavern*:** information from "Lamour, Hutton, Milland Line Up at 'Duffy's,'" *Hollywood Reporter*, August 16, 1944, 2.

134 ***The Lost Weekend* would be his next project:** Chandler's alcoholism from *On Sunset Boulevard: The Life and Times of Billy Wilder*, 214–15; according to Kevin Lally, however, Wilder's adaptation of the book was not influenced or inspired by his working with Chandler—*Wilder Times: The Life of Billy Wilder*, 145; the observations about Elizabeth Brackett from *On Sunset Boulevard*, 215, and *Inside Oscar: The Unofficial History of the Academy Awards*, 150; Wilder and Brackett manage to incorporate the gay subtext from Jackson's novel by having Don consistently avoid romantic involvement with Helen and also fail to be attracted to the very alluring prostitute character played by Doris Dowling; censorship information from *On Sunset Boulevard*, 222; "All the studio had was," from "Fame over a Weekend," by Lloyd Shearer, *Liberty Magazine*, March 9, 1946; "Read it. Study it," from *Wide-Eyed in Babylon*, 211; Ray and Mal Milland conversation, ibid., 212–13; and his "audition," ibid., 213–14; casting notes for "Helen" from *On Sunset Boulevard*, 217–18, and *"It's the Pictures That Got Small": Charles Brackett on Billy Wilder and*

Hollywood's Golden Age, 249–50; the Earl Warren banquet information, ibid., 253; least cooperative actor nomination from "Hollywood Today," by Sheilah Graham, *New York Daily Mirror*, February 21, 1945; Milland's preparations for role from *The Debonairs*, 260, and *Wide-Eyed in Babylon*, 215–16; traveling to New York from *On Sunset Boulevard*, 220, and *Wide-Eyed in Babylon*, 215; "[T]he company went on location," from *The Debonairs*, 260; location shooting notes also from *On Sunset Boulevard*, 221; incident with fan from *Wilder Times: The Life of Billy Wilder*, 145, and *Hollywood Anecdotes*, 347; incident with Mal's friend from *Wide-Eyed in Babylon*, 217–18.

138 **the biggest party in town:** Jack and Mary Benny party from *Hollywood Legends: The Golden Years of "The Hollywood Reporter,"* 155.

139 **Since the Milland separation took place:** rumored affair information from *The Debonairs*, 260; Gloria Vanderbilt information from *Sidney Lumet: A Life*, 172.

140 **Birnam swaps roles and prostitutes himself:** Milland's discussion about actors as prostitutes takes place with Cameron Mitchell in *Wide-Eyed in Babylon*, 235–38; "It had more sense of horror," from *The Lost Weekend*, introduction to the screenplay, 9; according to *Vintage Films*, 84, a sadder, more ambiguous ending (like the book's) was shot by Wilder and exists in some prints but has been rarely shown.

141 **to star in *The Last Man in the World*:** information from "Milland Atomized," *Variety*, December 26, 1945, 3.

142 **Bear offered a mammoth sum:** *The Lost Weekend*'s mobster influence to destroy the film from both *Wilder Times: The Life of Billy Wilder*, 150, and *Some Like It Wilder: The Life and Controversial Films of Billy Wilder*, 183; "Once we make a picture" and Santa Barbara and London preview information from *Inside Oscar: The Unofficial History of the Academy Awards*, 150; other screening information from *On Sunset Boulevard*, 231; "*The Lost Weekend* received the worst preview reactions," from *Academy Awards Illustrated*, 131; Robert Osborne further reports that well-received private screenings among "The Bel-Air circuit" helped encourage Paramount to proceed with the release, 131; reviews: *Variety*, August 15, 1945, 14; *New York Times*, December 3, 1945, 28; John F. Seitz comment from *The Debonairs*, 261; Hedda Hopper and "Most Widely Acclaimed" comments from *Inside Oscar: The Unofficial History of the Academy Awards*, 150.

143 **a ten-day fishing trip in Acapulco:** information from *Wide-Eyed in Babylon*, 224.

143 **"One Monday morning":** from *Wide-Eyed in Babylon*, 221.

144 **"I know that you're erratic":** from *Wide-Eyed in Babylon*, 226.

144 **"Ray Milland came [to the office]":** from "*It's the Pictures That Got Small": Charles Brackett on Billy Wilder and Hollywood's Golden Age*, 284.

144 **On Oscar night:** stories from *Inside Oscar: The Unofficial History of the Academy Awards*, 156; Wiley and Bona report Milland said nothing at the microphone, but newsreel footage exists of him accepting the award from Ingrid Bergman and saying, "Thank you. Thank you very much, indeed. I'm greatly honored." The footage appears to be a "recreation" done for the cameras after the ceremony; even in this case, the speech is exceedingly short.

146 **"I fell up the steps":** from "Real 'Weekend' Bar Draws Ray a Beer," by William Hawkins, *New York World Telegram*, March 16, 1946.

146 **"For Best Actor Ray Milland":** from *Inside Oscar: The Unofficial History of the Academy Awards*, 157.

147 **to appear in cigarette print ads:** from "Actor Ray Milland Was Paid to Endorse Smoking," *Wales News* by Steffan Rhys, September 26, 2008.

358 NOTES

147 ***The Lost Weekend* as "culturally, historically, or aesthetically significant":** the Library of Congress's National Film Registry quote, December 28, 2011.
148 **Despite all the success:** on a budget of $1.25 million, the film grossed $11 million at the box office ($4.3 million of which were US rentals), according to "60 Top Grossers of 1946," *Variety,* January 8, 1947.
148 **"If they would have given *me* the $5 million":** from *Wilder Times: The Life of Billy Wilder,* 150.

CHAPTER 6. DOWNFALL OF A HOMME FATALE (1946–1949)

149 **"[*California*] took three months to make":** from *Wide-Eyed in Babylon,* 228.
149 **Milland imprinted his hands:** Grauman's Chinese Restaurant information from *Hollywood at Your Feet: The Story of the World-Famous Chinese Theatre,* 203.
150 **Milland's actual crown was in need of padding:** toupée story from "*Casablanca*'s star's secret mistress dies; Humphrey Bogart carried on a seventeen-year affair with the woman known as 'Bacall's worst nightmare,'" by Vanessa Thorpe, *Observer,* February 10, 2008, 44; Milland's claim about his hair from *The Debonairs,* 255.
150 **Milland saw the release of *Kitty*:** budget and b.o. information from "60 Top Grossers of 1946," *Variety,* January 8, 1947, 8; 900,000 copies of the book were sold by the time of the film's release, according to the *New York Times,* January 31, 1946, 30; AMPAS recognized *Kitty,* but Best Art Direction-Interior Decoration was *Kitty*'s only Oscar nomination; Goddard trained extensively with both Phyllis Loughton, the dialogue coach, and Connie Emerald, Ida Lupino's mother, to master the Cockney dialect; Constance Collier helped Goddard with the formal English in the later scenes, according to Jeremy Arnold, tcm.com/this-month/article/276627%7C0/Kitty.html; reviews: *New York Times,* April 1, 1946, 24; *Variety,* October 10, 1945, 8; sensesofcinema.com/2005/great-directors/leisen.
152 ***The Well Groomed Bride* starts with Milland:** Milland's not wanting to make the movie from "*It's the Pictures That Got Small": Charles Brackett on Billy Wilder and Hollywood's Golden Age,* 257; review: *Variety,* January 30, 1946, 12.
154 **the Millands quietly looked into finding a sibling:** adoption attempt from *The Debonairs,* 262.
154 **The Millands next traveled to South Wales:** vacation information from walesonline.co.uk/lifestyle/nostalgia/nostalgia-news-south-wales-1946-22026709.
154 **"Everybody has to have a first sweetheart":** Mal Milland quote from "The Big Stories That Made the News in South Wales This Week in 1946," *Wales News,* and walesonline by David Prince, November 8, 2021; the Millands meeting with Alfred Jones and visiting Cardiff, ibid.
155 **"Right after [*The Lost Weekend*]":** from *The Debonairs,* 262.
155 **his salary was increased:** annual salary information from *The Debonairs,* 264.
155 **"I've always thought of directing":** Milland's attempt to be a director from Paramount press release, October 17, 1946.
155 ***California* was the most expensive:** the original plan was to remake *The Covered Wagon* (1923), according to zeusdvds.com/california-1947-dvd; "My son Danny was beginning to love John Wayne," from Paramount press release, December 19, 1947; it is very possible that by naming Milland's character Johnny Trumbo, the screenwriters were rallying behind their soon-to-be-blacklisted colleague, Dalton Trumbo, with the *Johnny* coming

NOTES

from *Johnny Got His Gun*, the author's controversial 1939 antiwar novel; Milland's quote about deleted sequence from *The Unkindest Cuts: The Scissors and the Cinema*, 101; review: *Variety*, December 18, 1946, 14; b.o. information from "Top Grossers of 1947," *Variety*, January 7, 1948, 63.

156 **The Imperfect Lady was not produced with the same care:** background, casting, and title changes from catalog.afi.com/Film/25212-THE-IMPERFECT-LADY; working titles included *I Take This Woman*, *They Met at Midnight*, *Lady 17*, and its UK release title was *Mrs. Loring's Secret*; review: *Variety*, March 12, 1947, 12; b.o. from *Variety*, January 7, 1948.

157 **a contemporary comedy titled *The Trouble With Women*:** production dates from catalog.afi.com/Film/25398-THE-TROUBLEWITHWOMEN; reviews: *Philadelphia Inquirer*, July 3, 1947, 23; *Newsweek*, August 4, 1947, 90.

158 **a cameo in the all-star *Variety Girl*:** the film was shot between mid-October 1946 and late January 1947, according to catalog.afi.com/Film/25413-VARIETY-GIRL.

159 ***Golden Earrings* was promoted as a major event:** budget from *Marlene: The Life of Marlene Dietrich*, 174; b.o. from "Top Grossers of 1947," *Variety*, January 7, 1948, 63; background from catalog.afi.com/Film/25183-GOLDEN-EARRINGS; "Ray Milland didn't want to make the picture," from *Mitchell Leisen, Hollywood Director*, 244; reviews: *New York Times*, December 4, 1947, 41; *Variety*, August 27, 1947, 16; information about the *Grand Hotel* radio show from en.wikipedia.org/wiki/Marlene_Dietrich#External_links.

161 **The first and best was *The Big Clock*:** Leslie Fenton had been first assigned to direct but was replaced by Farrow; *The Big Clock* grossed $2 million at the box office, according to "Top Grossers of 1948," *Variety* January 5, 1949, 46; Henry Luce story from crimereads.com/the-greatest-crime-magazine-that-never-was by Nathan Ward, April 19, 2019; review: *New York Times*, April 21, 1948; *Scandal Sheet* (1952) is actually based on a 1944 Sam Fuller novel, *The Dark Page*, which predates *The Big Clock* novel; the Dante remark quoted by Rob Thomas in *McClatchy-Tribune Business News*, November 7, 2011.

164 ***So Evil My Love* was a Gothic thriller:** reviews: *Variety*, March 10, 1948, 10, 22; *Spectator*, May 28, 1948, 645.

164 **"I was very glad to return to London":** from "Shop Talk of the Studios," 18.

165 **his next project, *Sealed Verdict*:** preproduction information from *Decatur Daily Review*, November 27, 1948, 4.

165 **Scott later recalled her costar as "amiable and charming":** Lizabeth Scott quote from *The Debonairs*, 264.

165 **the Millands attended a major social event:** Noël Coward party information from *Hollywood Legends: The Golden Years of "The Hollywood Reporter,"* 192–93.

165 **the studio sent Milland to Lima, Peru:** trip information from *The Debonairs*, 265.

165 **[*Sealed Verdict*] is flawed but certainly deserves some recognition:** "[*Sealed Verdict*] was Hollywood's first attempt," from *The Jewish Image in American Film*, 50; *Sealed Verdict* and HUAC connection from "Come in, Lassie," by Lillian Ross, *New Yorker*, February 21, 1948; reviews: *Washington Post*, November 5, 1948, B4; *Newsweek*, November 29, 87.

166 ***Miss Tatlock's Millions* debuted in theaters in November:** Milland casting from *"It's the Pictures That Got Small": Charles Brackett on Billy Wilder and Hollywood's Golden Age*, 321; "Saw the rushes with a gag scene," ibid., 334.

167 **"When I used to get burned up and disgusted":** from *The Debonairs*, 262.

167 **Mal's second pregnancy ended:** miscarriage information from *The Debonairs*, 264.

168 **"I high-tailed it to the front office":** from *Wide-Eyed in Babylon*, 200–201.

168 **Milland felt entirely miscast:** *A Mask for Lucrezia* and *Bride of Vengeance* information from *Wide-Eyed in Babylon*, 200.

168 **the studio released *Alias Nick Beal*:** reviews: *Los Angeles Times*, April 1, 1949, B6; *Washington Post*, May 3, 1949, C11; *New Republic*, March 21, 1949, 30; *Halliwell's Harvest*, 5; *The Devil on Screen: Feature Films Worldwide, 1913 through 2000*, 16; Milland calling it his favorite film from *The Debonairs*, 279–80; interview by the author with Darryl Hickman, September 15, 2020; the other two Hickman-Audrey Totter films that year were *The Set-Up* and *Any Number Can Play*; some Milland filmographies incorrectly state Milland appeared in the same role in a 1958 *Father Knows Best* episode titled "Mister Beal Meets His Match"; actually, Milland's *Dial M for Murder* costar, John Williams, plays Beal; Farrow allowing Milland to direct scenes from "Ray Milland," *Film Fan Monthly*, 8.

170 **"The studio began to treat me with a little more respect":** from *Wide-Eyed in Babylon*, 205.

170 **the upcoming *Copper Canyon*:** salary information from *Beautiful: The Life of Hedy Lamarr*, 244.

171 **One Milland turned down:** *Conspirator* information from *The Debonairs*, 266.

171 ***It Happens Every Spring*, a baseball comedy:** background and TV ratings information from *The Baseball Filmography, 1915 Through 2001*, 238, 240; interview by the author with Debra Paget Kung, February 5, 2021; "[That picture] nearly killed me," from "Back from Europe, Ray Wants to See U.S. Films," by Wanda Hale, Sunday News, September 17, 1950, 6; reviews: *Boxoffice*, May 14, 1949, A15, A16; *Variety*, May 11, 1949, 6; Hal Erickson, *The Baseball Filmography 1915 through 2001*, 237; Richard Carter, *New York Amsterdam News*, October 26, 2006, 10; b.o. from "Top Grossers of 1949," *Variety*, January 4, 1950, 59.

173 **Milland filmed *Copper Canyon* for the company:** "We were all miscast," from *Ecstasy and Me: My Life as a Woman*, 153; Milland "loathed" the movie, from "Ray Milland: Against Type," *Films of the Golden Age*, 66; reviews: *Washington Post*, October 20, 1950, 26; *New York Times*, November 16, 1950, 49.

174 **Ray and Mal Milland decided to adopt:** Victoria information and "We are very fond of the little girl" quote from *The Debonairs*, 266; "Her broad A's," from "Back from Europe, Ray Wants to See U.S. Films," by Wanda Hale, *Sunday News*, September 17, 1950, 6.

174 **Milland worked on *A Woman of Distinction*:** in the 1930s, the Connecticut-born Russell was often cast as an upper-class British "lady," whereas Milland would sometimes play American characters; back to their roots in *A Woman of Distinction*, Russell is a New Englander, and his character is described simply as "British"; background and casting from *Rosalind Russell*, 99, *Katharine Hepburn*, 84, and catalog.afi.com/Catalog/MovieDetails/26572; Buzzell's story about Milland from *Hollywood Anecdotes*, 132 (part of a July 17, 1982 interview, with a corroborating story by actor Walter Abel on January 5, 1979); review: *Christian Science Monitor*, May 6, 1950, 6.

176 **to star in *Jack of Diamonds*:** information from *The Debonairs*, 266.

176 **and the solitary film, *Of Men and Music*:** music film series information from "Milland Narrates 20th Music Pic," *Hollywood Reporter*, July 31, 1950, 5.

176 **"I'm trying to become a director":** from "Ray Milland Hates Acting," *Picturegoer*, February 25, 1950, 17.

CHAPTER 7. SHADOWS AND LIGHT (1950–1953)

177 ***A Life of Her Own* had a troubled production:** Milland salary from *Lana: The Lady, the Legend, the Truth*, 129; background and casting information from *The Films of Lana Turner*, 168, *George Cukor: Master of Elegance*, 189, catalog.afi.com/Catalog/moviedetails/2639, and *Lana: The Lady, the Legend, and the Truth*, 127; Milland and Corey later costarred in Milland's last contracted Paramount film, *Jamaica Run* (1953); censorship issues from catalog.afi.com/Catalog/moviedetails/2639 and *The Films of Lana Turner*, 169; according to MGM's records, the Eddie Mannix Ledger, the film earned $1,413,000 in the United States and Canada and $504,000 elsewhere, resulting in a loss to the studio of $679,000; reviews: *Chicago Daily Tribune*, September 26, 1950; *New York Daily News*, October 12, 1950, 393; *Cineaction*, September, 1999; *George Cukor: Master of Elegance*, 189.

179 **an invitation from the academy:** Academy Awards night information from *Inside Oscar: The Unofficial History of the Academy Awards*, 197–200.

179 **the Spanish Film Critics honored his body of work:** information from "State Dept. Forwards Bergman, Milland Awards," *Hollywood Reporter*, April 6, 1950, 10.

179 **Milland frequented the Bel-Air Country Club:** Milland's activities from interview by the author with Terry Kingsley-Smith, June 3, 2020.

179 **the undervalued *Night into Morning*:** "Here is something I can get my teeth into" from the *Night into Morning* pressbook; b.o. information from the Eddie Mannix Ledger: according to MGM records the movie earned $556,000 in the United States and Canada and $263,000 elsewhere, meaning a loss to the studio of $312,000; car accident information from *Belfast Telegraph*, November 29, 1950, 7; reviews: *Variety*, May 23, 1951, 6; *Los Angeles Times*, July 9, 1951; Nancy Davis calling the film her personal favorite is cited at tcm.com/tcmdb/title/346/night-into-morning.

181 **he further aligned himself:** Milland's Department of Defense p.s.a. from "Milland on Defense Airer," *Hollywood Reporter*, October 15, 1951, 22.

181 ***Circle of Danger* followed *Night into Morning*:** "They converged on me," from "Back from Europe, Ray Wants to See U.S. Films," by Wanda Hale, *Sunday News*, September 17, 1950, 6; interview by the author with Oswald Morris, January 12, 2001; reviews: *Variety*, March 28, 1951, 6; *New York Times*, July 12, 1951, 21.

183 ***Daddy Long Legs* was a 1919 silent classic:** remake information from *Astaire Dancing*, 365.

183 **Ray and Mal attended some functions:** Clark Gable party information from *Include Me Out*, 130.

184 **Milland shot the subpar *Rhubarb*:** b.o. from en.wikipedia.org/wiki/Rhubarb_(1951_film); production background from *The Baseball Filmography, 1915 through 2001*, 381; reviews: *Variety*, August 8, 1951, 6; *Picturegoer*, October 6, 1951, 18–19.

185 **Warner Bros. had announced:** deal announcement from "Milland to Make 3 Warner Movies," by Thomas F. Brady, *New York Times*, March 3, 1951, 8.

185 ***Close to My Heart* would be the first:** casting changes from *The Debonairs*, 267; interview by the author with Louise Steiner Elian, March 13, 2001 (The Steiners were divorced by 1951 but kept in touch about both professional and personal matters); "I had my best role," from *Self-Portrait*, 152; Tierney suffered lifelong angst about her own daughter being born with mental disabilities and was going through a painful divorce from Oleg Cassini during *Close to My Heart*; reviews: *Christian Science Monitor*, November 2, 1951, 5; *Washington Post*, November 17, 1951, 15.

187 ***Bugles in the Afternoon*, wasn't nearly as good:** shooting schedule and casting changes from "Drama: Breakston-Stahl Buy 'Primrose,' Barbara Bates Wins 'Best' Role," by Edwin Schallert, *Los Angeles Times*, April 24, 1951, 87, and "LIPPERT, PETRILLO IN ACCORD ON VIDEO," *New York Times*, April 24, 1951, 35; "Ray Milland was a jovial man," from "Helena Carter: The Colleen from New York," by Colin Briggs, *Films of the Golden Age*, Fall 2002, 69; reviews: *Chicago Daily Tribune*, March 13, 1952, B11; *New York Times*, March 5, 1952, 32.

188 **to release the director's long-withheld *Something to Live For*:** the studio shelving from *The Debonairs*, 267; "I think this is the best," from "Milland Finds 'Lost Weekend'" by Aline Mosby, UPI, June 3, 1952; for the record, Laurette Taylor never joined AA; Joan Fontaine's recollections from *No Bed of Roses*, 230, and through correspondence with this author, September 23, 2013; excerpts from *No Bed of Roses*, 230, 231; reviews: *New York Herald Tribune*, March 8, 1952, 7; *Variety*, January 30, 1952, 6; *New York Times*, April 29, 2012, AR17.

191 **his latest broadcast, *Safari*:** radio show information from archive.org/details/y7wdzbn sdkfcgtwyo428rslrr9yxzyuqi6bjpqcw.

192 **to star in Frederick Stephani's *The Roving Diplomat*:** information from "Popkin May Do 'Roving' for Para with Milland," *Hollywood Reporter*, June 2, 1949, 2.

192 **but now it was to produce *The Thief*:** "This is the most exiting thing," from "Actor Roams N.Y. 'Silently'" by Jack Gaver, UPI, May 23, 1952; Leavitt description from *A Star Is Born: The Making of the 1954 Movie and Its 1983 Restoration*, 128; reviews: *Ray Milland: The Films, 1929–1984*, 200; *New York Times*, October 16, 1952; *Variety*, September 26, 1951, 6.

195 **Milland's final Paramount film was *Jamaica Run*:** shooting schedule from catalog.afi.com/Film/50893-JAMAICA-RUN; interview by the author with Arlene Dahl and Marc Rosen, October 31 and November 1, 2021; review: *Chicago Daily Tribune*, September 3, 1953, B2.

195 **a Western called *Run for Cover*:** the film was eventually directed by Nicholas Ray in 1955 and starred James Cagney.

196 **the star-studded premiere of *Bwana Devil*:** information from *Hollywood Legends: The Golden Years of "The Hollywood Reporter,"* 239–40.

196 **The frivolous *Let's Do It Again*:** b.o. information from "Top Box Office Hits of 1953," *Variety*, January 13, 1954; Milland's singing "ghost" being Paul Frees is cited in *Jane Wyman: The Actress and the Woman*, 153; he was "ghosted" for his drumming by Johnny Williams according to janettedavis.net/Dubbers/dubberslist.php; reviews: *Variety*, June 17, 1953, 6; *Wide-Eyed in Babylon*, 254; Milland's quotes about Wyman from *Jane Wyman: The Actress and the Woman*, 153.

197 **a 1930s screwball classic—*My Man Godfrey*:** information from *The Debonairs*, 267.

CHAPTER 8. "FOR HIS SIN": GRACE AND TELEVISION (1953–1955)

198 **a proposed anthology series, *America's Finest*:** information from *Encyclopedia of Unaired Television Pilots, 1945–2018*, 283.

198 **to produce and star in his own show:** *Meet Mr. McNutley* salary figure from "The Man Who Hates to Act," by John Maynard, *Pictorial Review*, November 15, 1953, 10-P; "I went into television," from *The Debonairs*, 270.

200 **"[In a print] advertisement for a television set":** from "Dial M for Markham, McNutley and the Milland Show: Remaking and Reimagining Ray Milland's Established Cinematic Image for 1950s Television," by Gillian Kelly, *Stars en séries (Series and Stars)*, no. 20, 2022 (doi.org/10.4000/tvseries.5480).
201 **"I've been in 70 pictures":** from classicmoviefavorites.com/ray-milland-tv-appearances.
201 **Warner Bros.' musical remake of *A Star Is Born*:** information from *A Star Is Born: The Making of the 1954 Movie and Its 1983 Restoration*, 36, and *George Cukor: Master of Elegance*, 222.
202 **their own long-running series:** Robert Cummings first attempted a sitcom in 1952 called *My Hero*, but it was a single-season flop.
202 ***Dial M for Murder* did not start life as a play:** casting information from *Ray Milland: The Films, 1929–1984*, 207, and imdb.com/title/tt0046912; both sources confirm the Cary Grant casting; McKay states Hitchcock originally wanted Deborah Kerr as Margot, but she had a scheduling conflict, while imdb.com mentions that William Holden, Milland's *I Wanted Wings* costar, was penciled in as Mark but was also too busy, and Olivia de Havilland, Milland's *Well Groomed Bride* costar, was later offered the part of Margot but wanted too much money; "Milland did everything he was told," from "Milland's Best Work Was Very, Very Good," by Michael Blowen, *Boston Globe*, March 12, 1986, 66; "[I]t is curious to say the least," from *Hitch: The Life & Times of Alfred Hitchcock*, 224; the off-color jokes reported by Kelly from *High Society: The Life of Grace Kelly*, 118; "Admittedly, the part [in *Sleep, My Love*]," from *Anatomy of Film*, 195; *Dial M for Murder* production details from *The Dark Side of Genius: The Life of Alfred Hitchcock*, 365–69; Milland's salary from imdb.com/name/nm0001537; Cummings's salary from "Love That Bob: Robert Cummings," by James Bawden, *Films of the Golden Age*, Fall 2018, no. 94, 74; "There isn't very much we can say," from *Hitchcock by François Truffaut*, 156; "Hitch dismisses [*Dial M*]," from Bawden, 74; reviews: *Monthly Film Bulletin*, September 1954, 128; *Variety*, April 28, 1954; "This is one of the pictures," from *Hitchcock by François Truffaut*, 158; "*Dial M for Murder* is remarkable," from "The Old Broom That Knows the Corners Best," by Geoff Brown, *The Times*, August 5, 1983; "Rightly described as a director" from "Alfred Hitchcock Presents *Dial M for Murder*," by Ina Rae Hark, *Hitchcock at the Source: The Auteur as Adaptor*, 206–7; review: *Village Voice*, March 31, 1980; Warner Bros. released a 3-D version on Blu-ray in 2012; b.o. information from "Boxoffice Champs," *Variety*, January 5, 1955, 59.
203 **Whether or not Hitchcock remembered meeting Ray Milland:** *Elstree Calling* information from "Ray Milland," *Film Fan Monthly*, 12; historian Leonard Maltin is the only source that lists *Elstree Calling*, a 1930 music hall revue codirected by Hitchcock, as a Milland credit, but even Maltin writes equivocally that Milland "may have appeared in a brief bit." It would be interesting if director and star had worked together at this point, but Milland doesn't mention it in his memoirs, and he is not traceable when viewing the footage, so it is unlikely it happened.
207 **Grace Kelly had recently ended a romance:** "The rumor that Grace very nearly destroyed the Milland marriage" quote and skepticism about the affair from *High Society: The Life oof Grace Kelly*, 119, and "Hollywood Royalty: Two Sides of Grace Kelly," by Anthony Lane, *New Yorker*, January 4, 2010; "All the men fell in love," from *Grace*, 139; "I flew back from Hollywood," ibid.; "I'm not being catty here," from "Love That Bob: Robert Cummings," by James Bawden, *Films of the Golden Age*, Fall 2018, no. 94, 74; "When Joe Hyams went to interview," from *Grace*, 140; "My wife and I saw them," from "Grace Kelly and Ray Milland's Affair while Filming '*Rear Window*,'" from jamesspadashollywood.blogspot

.com/2013/02/grace-kelly-and-ray-millands-affair.html; "[Mal] feared it was true," ibid.; "I am sorry to have to print this," from "Serious Trouble: Millands Parted," by Louella Parsons, International News Service, October 21, 1953, and *The Debonairs*, 271; "hand-holding" comment by Skolsky in *Grace*, 142; Jack and Margaret Kelly's involvement, ibid., 143; "You go ahead and get a divorce," from filmsofthefifties.com/grace-kelly-and-ray-milland-dial-m-for-murder; "Skip" Hathaway recollections from *Grace*, 143; Rita Gam's story about becoming roommates is confirmed in *Biography: Grace Kelly "Hollywood Princess*," which aired on A&E on October 10, 1998; Ray's exit and return dates from *The Debonairs*, 271; "At times I think," from *Grace*, 144; "She was venomous, vicious," from *Wide-Eyed in Babylon*, 201; "In that era I was told," from *The Bridesmaids*, 57; "It was a bad mistake," ibid.; "Neither Bill Holden nor Ray Milland," from "The Grass Isn't Greener in Gracie Kelly's Backyard!," by Audrey Minor, *Confidential*, November 1954, 29; Kelly still pining for Milland from *Sex Lives of the Hollywood Goddesses*, 213; additional information from *The Shocking True Story: The Rise and Fall of Confidential, America's Most Scandalous Scandal Magazine*, 20–23.

210 **to accept an extraordinary offer:** *My Fair Lady* information and quote from "Milland Is Back and Frog's Got Him," by Gail Rock, *New York Times*, June 25, 1972, 34, and "'Writes Dramas' in His Sleep," by William Slover, *Newark Evening News*, January 9, 1966, and *The Debonairs*, 216, 275; Deanna Durbin casting consideration from "Deanna Durbin: She Never Looked Back," by David Zinman, *Films of the Golden Age*, Spring 2014, 46; alternate sources cite other stars who were offered the leads, including Noël Coward as Henry and Mary Martin as Eliza.

212 **"Like you and you":** from "The World Is My Mistress," by Ray Milland, excerpt from *Screenland*, 1954, as quoted in jake-weird.blogspot.com/2014/10/scandals-of-classic-hollywood-world-is.html.

212 **an abusive incident:** Ray Milland-Danny Milland fight detailed in *We Will Always Live in Beverly Hills*, 85 (Wynn does not give a date or even a year but suggests it took place around 1955).

213 **a visiting former Paramount colleague, Herbert Coleman:** story from *The Dark Side of Genius*, 371.

214 **Milland renamed the series *The Ray Milland Show*:** changes about and reviews from *Billboard*, September 25, 1954, 10, and "In Review: The Ray Milland Show," *Broadcasting*, November 29, 1954, 14; she "loved working with Ray Milland," from "Holiday Cheer," by Beverly Washburn, *Idaho Senior Independent*, December 20, 2023.

215 **by rereleasing *Reap the Wild Wind*:** information from *John Wayne*, 78.

216 **Brackett and Walter Reisch wrote *The Girl in the Red Velvet Swing*:** casting information from "Rambling Reporter," *Hollywood Reporter*, May 5, 1955; budget and b.o. from "The Top Box-Office Hits of 1955," *Variety Weekly*, January 25, 1956, and *Twentieth Century-Fox: A Corporate and Financial History*, 249; Nesbit's role in the film is described in *Backstory 2: Interviews with Screenwriters of the 1940s and 1950s*, 240–43; "I had very little to do with Ray Milland," from *Include Me Out*, 178; review: *New York Times*, October 20, 1955.

CHAPTER 9. THE COLD WAR AUTEUR (1955–1963)

219 **"[O]ne of the reasons why I want to become a director":** from "Ray Milland Hates Acting," *Picturegoer*, February 25, 1950, 17.

NOTES

219 **to adapt his short story "Room for Doubt":** information from *Hollywood Star* magazine, 1951.
219 **his plan to make *Stranger in Munich*:** information from *Hollywood Reporter*, December 11, 1952, 2.
220 **"It isn't easy for one actor":** from "Ray Milland, in Debut as Director, Embarrassed by His Actor Pals," *Variety*, February 9, 1955, 4.
220 ***A Man Alone* began production in March:** background from *The Debonairs*, 271, catalog. afi.com/Film/51578-A-MANALONE, and *Wide-Eyed in Babylon*, 243–46; the working titles for the film were *The Gunman* and *The Hostage*; Battle received uncredited help from Frank Burt and Talbot Jennings; the Republic-Yates deal information from "Drama: Milland Will Direct, Costar with Maureen," *Los Angeles Times*, October 27, 1955, A6; review: *Hollywood Reporter*, September 15, 1955, 3.
222 **they were about to sign the actor:** *The Story of Esther Costello* information from "Sympathy for Milland as a Meanie," by Louella O. Parsons, *New York Journal American*, April 23, 1955, 17.
222 ***Lisbon* would be Milland's second theatrical release:** background from *Wide-Eyed in Babylon*, 242–52; "a mean, ornery," ibid., 242; "I got to play the villain," from *'Tis Herself: An Autobiography*, 199; reviews: the *Hollywood Reporter*, August 1, 1956, 3; *Boston Globe*, August 17, 1986, 81.
224 **Milland's next project would be *Stockade*:** information from *Hollywood Reporter*, May 7, 1956, 2.
224 **he appeared in an episode:** "Markheim" had no connection to Milland's later TV detective series, the similar-sounding *Markham*.
225 **"That's the Man!" started things off:** background from "Milland to 'The Man,'" the *Hollywood Reporter*, February, 23, 1956, 8.
226 **"Catch at Straws" casts Milland:** review: the *Hollywood Reporter*, October 5, 1956.
226 ***Three Brave Men* held some promise:** despite all the sugarcoating, Chasanow remained as technical advisor throughout the production; reviews: *The Jewish Image in American Film*, 155; *New York Times*, March 24, 1957, 119.
227 ***The River's Edge*, premiering in April 1957:** Stanley Kramer goes Dwan one better in the tossed-dollars comedy climax of Cinerama's *It's a Mad, Mad, Mad, Mad World* (1963); interview by the author with Debra Paget Kung, February 6, 2021; reviews: *Variety*, March 27, 1957, 6; *New York Times*, April 12, 1957, 20; *New York Times*, July 11, 2006; *New Yorker*, movie-listings blurb, 2012.
229 **to enlist Milland in a follow-up, *White Shadows of the South Seas*:** background from "Bogeaus Dickering for Milland and Yamaguchi," the *Hollywood Reporter*, March 6, 1957, 2.
230 **to appear in the feature, *High Flight*:** review: *Variety*, September 25, 1957, 6.
231 **to star in James M. Barrie's *The Admirable Crichton*:** play announcement from *The Stage*, May 16, 1957, 1.
231 **at MGM's British studios in Borehamwood for *The Safecracker*:** background and budget from the Eddie Mannix Ledger, Los Angeles, Margaret Herrick Library, Center for Motion Picture Study and "Ray Milland Winds," the *Hollywood Reporter*, September 6, 1957, 10, and reelstreets.com/films/red-beret-the/; reviews: *Picturegoer*, March 22, 1958, 16; *Hollywood Reporter*, January 8, 1958, 3; *The New Biographical Dictionary of Film*, 596; *Films of the Golden Age*, Spring 2022, 11; interview by the author with Jeanette Michell (Jeanette Sterke), October 16, 2020.

233 **When David E. Rose announced:** unrealized Rose project discussed in "Pioneer Idea Luring Lana: Clown Kelly in 'Everglades;' Keel Will Star with Martin," by Edwin Schallert, *Los Angeles Times*, December 14, 1957, B3.
234 **He announced *No Holds Barred*:** information from "*No Holds Barred* as Milland Series," *Variety*, October 23, 1957, 48.
235 **to tell him their father had died:** Milland's father's death information from "Father of Neath Film Star Dies," *Neath Guardian*, August 15, 1958.
235 **His joining the Army continued:** Danny Milland's army enrollment information from *The Debonairs*, 274.
236 **"I was thinking about retiring":** from *The Debonairs*, 273.
236 ***Markham* was the brainchild:** review: *Variety*, May 6, 1959, 31; production background from *The Debonairs*, 273; several episodes are "unsigned," and it is likely a few were directed by Milland; Leisen's contributions are discussed by Milland in *Mitchell Leisen, Hollywood Director*, 299; interview by the author with Louise Fletcher, January 31, 2021.
238 **while Cary Grant was starring:** Grant's *Operation Petticoat* salary from *The Great Movie Stars: The Golden Years*, 265.
239 **"If you're counting my eyebrows":** from "Black Magic," by Valerie Steiker, *Vogue*, January 2008, 174.
239 **"to suspend his career and go back to college":** from "Ray Milland Planning to Get an Education," *Hartford Courant*, April 17, 1960, 10G.
239 **"My time is past":** from *The Debonairs*, 273.
239 **to write the screenplay for *Shadow of a Lady*:** information from "Lyndon Scripts Pic for Milland-Luber-Shlaes," *Hollywood Reporter*, August 5, 1960, 2; the screenplay appears to be based on Holly Roth's 1957 crime novel.
240 **a series pilot called *Count Your Chickens*:** information from markgoodson.fandom.com/wiki/Count_Your_Chickens.
241 ***King of Kings* (1961), produced by MGM:** originally, the film was going to be directed by John Farrow, Milland's friend and the director of *Nick Beal*; it is very possible the casting was first Farrow's idea, but Farrow was fired early on by producer Samuel Bronston.
242 **Ned Wynn turned twenty-one:** birthday party information from *We Will Always Live in Beverly Hills*, 175.
242 **the lead role in *Premature Burial*:** "I was planning to hire Vincent," from *How I Made a Hundred Movies in Hollywood and Never Lost a Dime*, 83; Samuel Arkoff saw the use of Vincent Price differently, feeling Corman and Pathé were betraying him by making *any* Poe-based movie, which he saw as the sole franchise of AIP; Arkoff tells his side of the story in *Flying Through Hollywood by the Seat of My Pants*, 116–18; Corman finally formed his own production company, New World Pictures, in 1970; "[He] was charming. We talked a lot," from *Asbury Park Press*, October 6, 1996, 70; *Premature Burial*'s connection to Hitchcock and *Dial M for Murder*: Hitchcock himself was a fan of Poe, and his *Alfred Hitchcock Presents* "Breakdown" (1955) episode contains similarities to "The Premature Burial" and other Poe stories; a far inferior version of "The Premature Burial" was shot for television in 1961 as part of Boris Karloff's *Thriller* series (with Sidney Blackmer playing Sir Guy); *Premature Burial*'s budget is disputed at imdb.com/title/tt0056368, which states it was an estimated $1,250,000 (which seems very unlikely given Corman's usual budgeting practices); $450,000 is mentioned at catalog.afi.com/Film/23327-PREMATURE-BURIAL; 'I felt Poe films," from *The Directors—Take Three*, 122; censorship information from imdb

.com/title/tt0056368; reviews: *Variety*, March 14, 1962, 6; *Monthly Film Bulletin*, January 1, 1962, 156; *Los Angeles Times*, March 30, 1962, C15.

245 **Samuel Arkoff and James Nicholson renamed it *Panic in Year Zero!*:** budget from imdb.com/title/tt0056331; "I play a father," from "Atom Menace: Survivors," by Joe Hyams, *New York Herald Tribune*, March 18, 1962; reviews: *Hollywood Reporter*, June 20, 1962, 3; *Box-Office*, July 2, 1962, B7, B8; a "right-wing director" from "Films on TV," by Jack Edmund Nolan, *Films in Review*, August/September 1972, 421; reviews: *Village Voice*, September 20, 2005; Llewellyn quote in "Dial M for Milland," *Western Mail*, July 11, 2015, 27; "TCM to air *Panic in Year Zero!*, the 'Walking Dead of 1962,'" *Daily Gleaner*, April 12, 2017, C1.

247 **a missing young woman seemed to involve Danny:** "Did Coed Elope to Spain with Ray Milland's Son?," by Alfred T. Hendricks, *New York Post*, November 4, 1962.

247 **he reluctantly moonlighted as the host:** *Trail's West* (*Death Valley Days*) information from classicthemes.com/50sTVThemes/themePages/deathValleyDays and "Milland for *Trails West*," the *Hollywood Reporter*, July 10, 1962, 7, which cites the dates of the Milland reruns as starting in July 1962 for 52 episodes; some other sources cite earlier start dates.

247 ***X: The Man with the X-Ray Eyes* was not greeted as a comeback:** regarding Floyd Crosby's contribution, AIP promoted the film as using "Spectarama," which was not a new technology but simply a name for Crosby's optical experiments; Milland praised Rickles on the June 23, 1972, episode of *The Tonight Show*; reviews: *Variety*, July 26, 1963, 6; *New York Times*, October 24, 1963, 37.

250 ***The Carpetbaggers*, a sprawling Hollywood saga:** information from catalog.afi.com/Film/23071-THE-CARPETBAGGERS.

250 **"A Home Away from Home" was an original work:** nominally, the producers of this episode were David Lowell Rich and Gordon Hessler, but according to Christina Lane in *Phantom Lady: Hollywood Producer Joan Harrison, the Forgotten Woman behind Hitchcock*, by the time of the *Alfred Hitchcock Hour*, Joan Harrison would "serve as producer on a limited number of shows each season but continue to play an essential role through the series' final installment in Spring 1965," 268–69; Bloch wrote the screenplay for a loose 1962 remake of *Caligari* called *The Cabinet of Caligari*; Bloch liked his "Home Away from Home" story enough to revive it as the frame for the multipart feature, *Asylum*, in 1972; review: "Films on TV," by Jack Edmund Nolan, *Films in Review*, August/September 1972, 422.

251 **Milland became tangentially embroiled:** the Duke and Duchess of Argyll scandal information from dailymail.co.uk/news/article-10359825/MICHAEL-THORNTON-lost-virginity-dazzling-Duchess-Argyll-defend-her.html.

CHAPTER 10. ENTR'ACTE (1964–1970)

253 ***The Confession* came about:** background from *The Films of Ginger Rogers*, 228, and imdb.com/title/tt0057961; Harold J. Kennedy's story in "Gingerly," by Harold J. Kennedy, *New York Magazine*, July 3, 1978, 35–38; Gould quote from "Elliott Gould on throwing his lunch at Robert Altman and *Saturday Night Live*'s Five-Timers Club," by Will Smith, avclub.com, July 26, 2013; "Among other things," from *Ginger: My Story*, 348; "I never in the world would have agreed," ibid., 348.

255 **a romantic comedy called *Brown Eye, Pic-A-Pie*:** background from catalog.afi.com/Film/54902-BROWN-EYE-EVIL-EYE?cxt=filmography.

NOTES

256 **to replace Brian Aherne in a road company tour of *My Fair Lady*:** background from "Milland Is Back and Frog's Got Him," by Gail Rock, *New York Times*, June 25, 1972, 34; and "Record 2,650 Fall in Love With Kenley's 'My Fair Lady,'" by Des Howe, *Warren Tribune Chronicle*, June 1, 1964; [H]e tackled a tremendous script," from "Kenley Musical Maestro Keeps the Stars on Cue," by Mary Jose, *Columbus Star*, August 15, 1964; review: "Ray Milland Sparkles at Warren," by Glenn C. Pullen, *Plain Dealer*, June 1, 1964; "[W]e got good notices," Rock, 34; "'To me, the stage is sheer hell,'" ibid.; "[T]he star told interviewers," from *Zachary Scott: Hollywood's Sophisticated Cad*, 192.

259 **Milland made his first visit to *The Tonight Show*:** FCC operating incident from "Did Johnny Carson Make a Risqué Remark about a Guest's Cat?," by David Mikkelson, snopes.com/fact-check/carson-cat-remark/, January 9, 2007.

259 **the Broadway version of *Hostile Witness* made its bow**: reviews: William Glover, Associated Press from *The Debonairs*, 276; *Los Angeles Times*, September 16, 1966, C13.

260 **Danny's first serious brush with the law:** Danny Milland arrest information from *The Debonairs*, 276.

260 **An incident in 1967:** Farley Granger story from *Include Me Out*, 224 (Granger cites the year as 1966, but *Laura* taped in October 1967).

261 **his intentions to lens *Hostile Witness*:** background from "Why Ray Milland Feels So Bad About Britain . . . ," by Paul Errol (a.k.a. Clive Hirschhorn), *The Sunday Express*, August 6, 1967.

261 **a musical version of Oscar Wilde's only novel, *The Picture of Dorian Gray*:** background from *The Debonairs*, 277.

262 **the first incarnation of *The Hollywood Squares*:** incident described in *The Debonairs*, 279, and "Films on TV," by Jack Edmund Nolan, *Films in Review*, August/September 1972, 421.

262 **his open support of Richard Nixon:** information from celeb-networth.com.

263 **and released it to theaters in August 1970 as *Company of Killers*:** reviews: Peter Hanson, every70smovie.blogspot.com; archive.usccb.org/movies/c/companyofkillers1970.shtml; Rose Thompson, radiotimes.com/movie-guide/b-285tfx/company-of-killers.

265 **and retitled it *Daughter of the Mind*:** "I played the crippled wife," from *Self-Portrait*, 221.

265 **Milland made two cameos on *Bracken's World*:** while several sources cite Milland being in "Don't You Cry for Susannah," the print viewed by this author did not include Milland; one possible explanation is that the print was incomplete; interview by the author with Dorothy Kingsley, April 12, 1992.

267 **Ray Milland appears on-screen in *Love Story*:** "When we did *Love Story*," from *The Directors—Take Two*, 286; during preproduction Arthur Hiller replaced director Anthony Harvey, who had replaced Larry Peerce; "if it isn't going to be too rough on you . . . ," from *Wide-Eyed in Babylon*, 259–60; "I loved working with [Ryan O'Neal]," from *Moving Pictures*, 13.

269 **Ray and Mal were delighted to see:** the Millands congratulating John Wayne and Wayne's response from "A Ray Milland Telegram, 1970," icollector.com.

269 **Milland considered some ambitious future plans:** his unrealized plans for the theater from *Film Fan Monthly*, 12.

271 **"One of the reasons I stopped":** Fontaine's quote from *The RKO Gals*, 503, and discussed by Fontaine in this author's correspondence (in September 2013).

271 **by the end of *Love Story*:** budget and b.o. information from *The Debonairs*, 278; TV ratings from "Alltime Top 20 Movies on TV," *Variety*, December 13, 1972, 26; rerelease b.o. information from the-numbers.com; reviews: *Los Angeles Times*, December 20, 1970, 29;

New York Times, December 18, 1970, 44; *From Reverence to Rape: The Treatment of Women in the Movies*, 333; *Washington Post*, December 26, 1970, B1; Thames interview at youtube .com/watch?v=22Sh7SA31Y4&t=111s.

CHAPTER 11. BABYLON REVISITED (1971–1977)

273 **"Do what you can with what you've got"**: from "Ray Milland Dies: Won Oscar for *Lost Weekend*," by Peter B. Flint, *New York Times*, March 11, 1986, D30.
273 **"How big is the part"**: from *Wide-Eyed in Babylon*, 235.
273 **"[He] was a man who was afraid"**: from "Milland's Best Work Was Very, Very Good," by Michael Blowen, *Boston Globe*, March 12, 1986, 66.
274 **"I always managed to have my salary"**: from *Wide-Eyed in Babylon*, 234.
274 **River of Gold would serve to complete:** despite the solid ratings, the TV movie did not become a TV series, as originally planned; review: *Los Angeles Times*, March 10, 1971.
275 **"The Hand of Borgus Weems" episode was completed:** one of the earliest realizations of the story was *Les Mains d'Orlac* (1920), a novel by Maurice Renard, adapted to film for the first time in 1924 as *The Hands of Orlac*; review: *Los Angeles Times*, September 16, 1971, H21.
275 ***Relatively Speaking***, **Ayckbourn's marital farce about "the swinging sixties":** background: *The Debonairs*, 278.
276 **a daytime Canadian talk show called *Mantrap*:** information from broadcasting-history .com/programming/television/mantrap and *Ray Milland: The Films, 1929–1984*, 306.
277 **a full-length TV movie, *Black Noon*:** reviews: *Variety*, November 10, 1971; *Gloria Grahame: Bad Girl of Film Noir*, 283.
278 ***Frogs*, filmed in November 1971:** interview by the author with Joan Van Ark, September 21, 2021; review: *Variety*, December, 31, 1971; "I just did that," from *The Debonairs*, 278; Milland leaving the production story is from delvallearchives.blogspot.com/2011/08/ frogs-melting-toupee-of-ray-milland.html and imdb.com/title/tt0068615.
280 ***The Thing with Two Heads* would be more outrageous:** "[The] *Defiant Ones* Gone Batshit," from "The Seriously Awesome Soul Music of NFL Legend Rosey Grier," by Nate Patrin, *Vice*, October 16, 2015; reviews: *Variety*, July 19, 1972, 14; *Los Angeles Times*, December 5, 1972, 21; "I saw old *Two Heads*," from *The Debonairs*, 278.
283 **to shoot the PG-rated *Terror in the Wax Museum*:** budget information from *The Complete Films of Broderick Crawford*, 209.
283 ***The House in Nightmare Park*, an original parody:** background from "Frankie Howerd," by Tony Williams, *Psychotronic Video*, 2001, no. 34, 62.
284 **the sci-fi adventure *The Big Game*:** he could tell *The Big Game* "smelled of disaster," from *Wide-Eyed in Babylon*, 233.
285 **to film his few scenes for *Gold*:** budget information from "Will 'Gold' bite the dust?: Hugh Hebert on the ACTT's attempts to black a film," by Hugh Hebert, *The Guardian*, November 24, 1973, 13; review: *Variety*, Oct. 2, 1974, 22.
286 ***Escape to Witch Mountain*, his first and only Walt Disney production:** review: *New York Times*, July 3, 1975, 21; rape accusation from "Four for Friday—She Killed Him," crazydaysandnights.net, May 4, 2018, and "She Killed Him," foxella.com.
288 **"Being a movie star's son":** from *The Debonairs*, 276 footnote.

289 **Wide-Eyed in Babylon reached bookstores:** reviews: *Kirkus Reviews*, September 9, 1974; "Ray Milland Range: Rides, Shoots, Acts, and Now Writes," *Variety*, September 18, 1974, 92.
289 **"I have a particular opinion":** from *The Debonairs*, 280.
289 **Bronson was "scandalously underestimated":** from *The Overlook Encyclopedia*, 365.
289 **a BBC radio show called *Nine-Five on Monday*:** information from *Neath Guardian*, February 14, 1975.
290 **"Funny thing, I never liked acting":** from *The Debonairs*, 279, 280.
290 **a short-lived TV series, *From Sea to Shining Sea*:** review: *New York Times*, April 16, 1975, 65.
293 ***Aces High* was released in Europe:** review: *New York Times*, December 7, 1979.
293 ***The Last Tycoon* became the final film:** budget and b.o. from *Final Cuts: The Last Films of 50 Great Directors*, 146–48; background from *Elia Kazan: A Biography*, 437; for some reason, Fleishacker does not appear in the 2016 Amazon Studios series remake of *The Last Tycoon*; "The greatest young actor" quote and Russell's claim from imdb.com/title/tt0074777; reviews: *Los Angeles Free Press*, November 26, 1976, 11; "A Stahr Is Reborn," by Andrew Sarris, *The Village Voice*, November 15, 1976; "the usurpers who were trying," from *Tony Curtis: American Prince*, 289; other Curtis stories, ibid., 190, 317.
297 **the similarly foolish *Look What's Happened to Rosemary's Baby*:** ratings and background information from *The Complete Films of Broderick Crawford*, 216–17; "[H]e was a remarkable actor" from interview by the author with Tina Louise, August 21, 2023.
298 **to film his few scenes for *Oil*:** the American and United Kingdom DVD releases of *Oil* changed the title to *The Billion Dollar Fire*, and a PAL version was retitled again to *Fireforce*, though it remains little known today.
298 **when he signed onto *The Uncanny*:** budget and background from *The Studio That Dripped Blood*, 153–54; Harry Waxman's story from imdb.com/title/tt0076853; review: Brunson, thefilmfrenzy.com, June 19, 2019.
299 **where he worked on *Seventh Avenue*:** review: *New York Times*, February 10, 1977, 78.
300 ***Testimony of Two Men* has been rightfully forgotten:** review: *New York Times*, May 9, 1977, 48.
301 **the Spanish- and Italian-financed production *The Pyjama Girl Case*:** reviews: Martyn, thesun.co.uk, September 14, 2018; Peirce, thecurb.com.au, August 3, 2019.
302 **to be interviewed for the documentary, *Once upon a Time . . . Is Now Grace Kelly*:** Milland's lack of participation is discussed at historyforsale.com 276785.jpg
302 ***Survival Run* (a.k.a *Spree*) was released in Europe:** review: *Variety*, March 5, 1980, 22.
304 **"I made this awful film called *Slavers*":** from *Trevor Howard: The Man and His Films*, 147; budget from *Ray Milland: The Films, 1929–1984*, 283; the story of the ferry drowning from imdb.com/title/tt0075230.

CHAPTER 12. THE LONG VOYAGE HOME (1977–1986)

306 ***Blackout*, a "ripped-from-the-headlines" thriller:** review: *Variety*, May 31, 1978, 26.
307 **a funny story in 1978 by old friend Ronald Reagan:** from *House of Representatives Congressional Record*, vol. 149, no. 21, February 5, 2003.
308 **the premiere episode of *Battlestar Galactica*:** review: Arthur Knight, *Hollywood Reporter* November 17, 1978.

NOTES

309 **a sequel to *Love Story* titled *Oliver's Story*:** postproduction and other details from catalog.afi.com/Film/56955-OLIVERS-STORY; reviews: *New York Times*, December 15, 1978; *Variety*'s review is dated at Variety.com as December 31, 1977, but must have been published in December of 1978.

310 **off to South Africa again for *Game for Vultures*:** filming took place predominantly near Pretoria and Johannesburg since Rhodesia was considered too dangerous, as noted in "BRIEFLY South Africa bans film," *Globe and Mail*, Toronto, June 1, 1979, 13; the film was "forgettable . . ." from *Past Imperfect*, 300; the connection between Milland and Harris extends to Rita Gam, who had been Milland's costar in *The Thief* in 1952 and Harris's girlfriend in the late 1950s, according to *Richard Harris: Sex, Death & the Movies*, 78–79.

311 ***The Darker Side of Terror*, a New Age Frankenstein tale:** review: *Hollywood Reporter*, April 3, 1979.

312 ***Cave-In!* was shot in 1979:** review: *Hollywood Reporter*, June 21, 1983.

314 ***The Attic* was something unique:** background from interview by the author with Gary Graver, May 15, 1998; review: *Boston Globe*, November 22, 1980, 11.

315 **In early 1980:** Milland may have started work in 1980 on Alberto Sordi's comedy, *Io e Caterina* (a.k.a. *Catherine and I*), but he apparently dropped out and was replaced by Rossano Brazzi, according to *Film Dope*, 18.

316 **Ray received the worst news of his life:** details regarding Daniel Milland's suicide from "Death of Milland's Son Ruled Suicide," UPI, March 26, 1981; additional information from "Four for Friday—She Killed Him," crazydaysandnights.net, May 4, 2018, and "She Killed Him," foxella.com.

318 **Milland's next TV film, *The Royal Romance of Charles and Diana*:** it competed with a 1982 ABC movie on the same subject, *Charles & Diana: A Royal Love Story*, which also aired that September.

321 ***The Gold Key* was an oddity:** production and press conference details from "Frankly, Ray Milland Is No Press Agent's Dream," by Robert Cross, *Chicago Tribune*, August 30, 1985; review: *Variety*, December 4, 1985, 102.

322 ***Masks of Death* was made for British television:** production background from *Sherlock Holmes on Screen*, 88.

324 **the last project he ever shot, *The Sea Serpent*:** review: notcoming.com/reviews/the seaserpent, October 2013.

325 **Milland traveled for the last time:** trip to Wales details from his *Variety* obituary, March 12, 1986, 4; "He had a very full career," from "Ray Milland, 78: Career Spanned 50 Years and 120 Films," by Stan W. Metzler, UPI, *Philadelphia Inquirer*, March 11, 1986, 11-B.

325 **"He was a very fine gentleman":** Stanwyck tribute from the Associated Press by Lynn Elber, March 11, 1986.

325 **"This is as bad as when Bing Crosby died":** Lamour tribute from Metzler, 11-B.

326 **Per Milland's instructions:** his burial at sea discussed at celeb-networth.com.

326 **When rumors started spreading:** Milland's "lost" Oscar story is told at imdb.com/name/nm0001537.

327 **"I've had a most wonderful life":** from "Ray Milland: Against Type," *Films of the Golden Age*, 69.

BIBLIOGRAPHY

BOOKS

Arkoff, Sam with Richard Trubo. *Flying through Hollywood by the Seat of My Pants*. Birch Lane, 1992.
Arnold, William. *Frances Farmer: Shadowland*. McGraw-Hill, 1978.
Balaban Quine, Judith. *The Bridesmaids*. NY: Pocketbooks, 1989.
Barbour, Alan G. *John Wayne*. NY: Pyramid, 1974.
Barnes, Alan. *Sherlock Holmes on Screen*. Reynolds & Hearn, 2002.
Basinger, Jeanine. *Gene Kelly*. NY: Pyramid, 1976.
Bauer, Barbara. *Bing Crosby*. NY: Pyramid, 1977.
Baxter, John. *Hollywood in the Thirties*. Oak Tree, 1968.
Behlmer, Rudy, ed. *Memo from Darryl F. Zanuck: The Golden Years at Twentieth Century-Fox*. NY: Grove, 1993.
Behlmer, Rudy, ed. *Memo from David O. Selznick*. Viking, 1972.
Boller Jr., Paul F. and Ronald L. Davis. *Hollywood Anecdotes*. NY: William Morrow, 1987.
Bryce, Allan, ed. *Amicus: The Studio That Dripped Blood*. Stray Cat, 2000.
Butler, Jeremy G., ed. *Star Texts*. Wayne State University Press, 1991.
Cagney, James. *Cagney by Cagney*. NY: Pocket Books, 1977.
Cawthorne, Nigel. *Sex Lives of the Hollywood Goddesses*. London: Prion, 1997.
Chandler, Charlotte. *Nobody's Perfect: Billy Wilder, A Personal Biography*. NY: Simon & Schuster, 2002.
Chierichetti, David. *Mitchell Leisen, Hollywood Director*. Photoventures, 1995.
Collins, Joan. *Past Imperfect*. NY: Simon & Schuster, 1984.
Conners, Mike, Beth A. Fhaner, Kelly M. Cross, eds. *The VideoHound & All-Movie Guide Stargazer*. Visible Ink, 1996.
Conrad, Peter. *The Hitchcock Murders*. London: Faber and Faber, 2000.
Corman, Roger with Jim Jerome. *How I Made a Hundred Movies in Hollywood and Never Lost a Dime*. NY: Random House, 1990.
Crowther, Bosley. *Vintage Films*. NY: G. P. Putman's Sons, 1977.
Curtis, Anthony, ed. *The Rise and Fall of the Matinée Idol*. NY: St. Martin's, 1974.
Curtis, James. *Between Flops: A Biography of Preston Sturges*. NY: Harcourt, Brace, Jovanovich, 1982.

Curtis, Tony. *Tony Curtis: American Prince*. NY: Harmony Books, 2008.
Davies, Marion. *The Times We Had: Life with William Randolph Hearst*. NY: Ballantine Books, 1975.
Davis, Ronald L. *Zachary Scott: Hollywood's Sophisticated Cad*. University Press of Mississippi, 2006.
De Carlo, Yvonne with Doug Warren. *Yvonne: An Autobiography*. NY: St. Martin's, 1987.
Dick, Bernard F. *Anatomy of Film*. 3rd ed. NY: St. Martin's, 1998.
Dick, Bernard F. *Claudette Colbert: She Walked in Beauty*. University Press of Mississippi, 2008.
Dickens, Homer. *The Films of Ginger Rogers*. Citadel, 1975.
Edwards, Anne. *Vivien Leigh: A Biography*. Simon & Schuster, 1977.
Eliot, Marc. *Cary Grant: A Biography*. NY: Random House, 2004.
Emery, Robert J. *The Directors—Take Three*. NY: Allworth, 2003.
Emery, Robert J. *The Directors—Take Two*. NY: TV Books, 2000.
Endres, Stacey and Robert Cushman. *Hollywood at Your Feet: The Story of the World-Famous Chinese Theatre*. Pomegranate, 1992.
Erickson, Hal. *The Baseball Filmography, 1915 through 2001*. McFarland, 2002.
Eyman, Scott. *Cary Grant: A Brilliant Disguise*. NY: Simon & Schuster, 2020.
Eyman, Scott. *John Wayne: The Life and Legend*. NY: Simon & Schuster, 2014.
Feeney Callan, Michael. *Richard Harris: Sex, Death & the Movies*. Robson Books, 2003.
Fleischer, Richard. *Just Tell Me When to Cry: A Memoir*. NY: Carroll & Graf, 1993.
Fontaine, Joan. *No Bed of Roses: An Autobiography*. NY: A Berkley Book, 1978.
Frank, Tom. *Fractured Karma*. Santa Rosa: Black Sparrow, 1990.
Friedman, Lester D. *The Jewish Image in American Film*. Citadel, 1987.
Granger, Farley with Robert Calhoun. *Include Me Out: My Life from Goldwyn to Broadway*. NY: St. Martin's Griffin, 2007.
Halliwell, Leslie. *The Filmgoer's Companion*. NY: Avon Books, 1975.
Halliwell, Leslie. *Halliwell's Harvest*. NY: Charles Schribner's Sons, 1986.
Hamann, G. D., ed. *Ray Milland in the '30s*. CA: Filming Today, 2011.
Hardy, Phil, ed. *The Overlook Film Encyclopedia*. NY: Overlook, 1998.
Haskell, Molly. *From Reverence to Rape: The Treatment of Women in the Movies*. Penguin Books, 1974.
Haver, Ronald. *"A Star Is Born": The Making of the 1954 Movie and Its 1983 Restoration*. NY: Alfred A. Knopf, 1988.
Higham, Charles. *Marlene: The Life of Marlene Dietrich*. Pocket, 1979.
Kerzoncuf, Alain and Charles Barr. *Hitchcock Lost & Found: The Forgotten Films*. University Press of Kentucky, 2015.
Knight, Arthur. *The Liveliest Art*. NY: A Mentor Book, 1957.
Knott, Frederick. *Dial "M" for Murder*. Dramatists Play Service, 1982.
Koca, Gary. *Forgotten Movie Stars of the 30's, 40's, and 50's*. CreateSpace Independent Publishing Platform, 2013.
Kofoed, William. *Movie Diary*. Wm. H. Kofoed, 1939.
Koster, Henry with Irene Kahn Atkins. *Henry Koster: A Directors Guild of America Oral History*. Scarecrow, 1987.
Lacey, Robert. *Grace*. NY: G. P. Putnam's Sons, 1994.
Lake, Veronica. *Veronica: The Autobiography of Veronica Lake*. NY: Bantam Books, 1972.
Lally, Kevin. *Wilder Times: The Life of Billy Wilder*. NY: Henry Holt, 1996.
Lamarr, Hedy. *Ecstasy and Me: My Life as a Woman*. A Fawcett Crest Book, 1966.
Lamour, Dorothy with Dick McInnes. *My Side of the Road*. Prentice-Hall, 1980.

Lane, Christina. *Phantom Lady: Hollywood Producer Joan Harrison, the Forgotten Woman behind Hitchcock*. Chicago Review, 2020.
Lentz, Robert J. *Gloria Grahame: Bad Girl of Film Noir*. McFarland, 2011.
Lenz Elder, Jane. *Alice Faye: A Life beyond the Silver Screen*. University Press of Mississippi, 2002.
Levy, Emanuel. *George Cukor: Master of Elegance*. NY: William Morrow, 1994.
Lewis, Judy. *Uncommon Knowledge*. NY: Pocket Books, 1994.
Lodge, Jack. *Hollywood 1930s*. Gallery Books, 1985.
MacGraw, Ali. *Moving Pictures*. Bantam Books, 1991.
Magill, Frank N., ed. *Magill Surveys: Cinema, Great Directors*. Salem, 1981.
Marill, Alvin H. *Katharine Hepburn*. NY: Galahad Books, 1973.
McBride, Joseph. *Orson Welles*. NY: Jove, 1977.
McCarthy, Todd. *Howard Hawks: The Grey Fox of Hollywood*. NY: Grove, 1977.
McClelland, Doug. *The Unkindest Cuts: The Scissors and the Cinema*. A. S. Barnes, 1972.
McGilligan, Patrick. *Ginger Rogers*. NY: Pyramid, 1975.
McGilligan, Patrick, ed. *Backstory 2: Interviews with Screenwriters of the 1940s and 1950s*. University of California Press, 1991.
McKay, James. *Ray Milland: The Films, 1929–1984*. McFarland, 2020.
Mell, Eila. *Casting Might-Have-Beens: A Film by Film Directory of Actors Considered for Roles Given to Others*. McFarland, 2004.
Michael Shearer, Stephen. *Beautiful: The Life of Hedy Lamarr*. NY: Thomas Dunne Books, St. Martin's Books, 2010.
Milland, Ray. *Wide-Eyed in Babylon*. NY: William Morrow, 1974.
Mitchell, Charles P. *The Devil on Screen: Feature Films Worldwide, 1913 through 2000*. McFarland, 2002.
Morella, Joe and Edward Z. Epstein. *Paulette: The Adventurous Life of Paulette Goddard*. NY: St. Martin's, 1985.
Mueller, John. *Astaire Dancing*. NY: Alfred A. Knopf, 1985.
Munn, Michael. *John Wayne: The Man behind the Myth*. London: Robson Books, 2003.
Munn, Michael. *Trevor Howard: The Man and His Films*. London: Scarborough House, 1989.
Niven, David. *Bring on the Empty Horses*. NY: G. P. Putnam's Sons, 1975.
O'Hara, Maureen with John Nicoletti. *'Tis Herself: An Autobiography*. NY: Simon & Schuster, 2004.
Osborne, Robert. *Academy Awards Illustrated*. Marvin Miller Enterprises, 1965.
Palmer, R. Barton and David Boyd. *Hitchcock at the Source: The Auteur as Adaptor*. State University of New York Press, 2011.
Parish, James Robert. *The RKO Gals*. NY: Arlington House, 1974.
Parish, James Robert and Don E. Stanke. *The All-Americans*. NY: Arlington House, 1977.
Parish, James Robert and Don E. Stanke. *The Debonairs*. NY: Arlington House, 1975.
Parish, James Robert and Don E. Stanke. *The Glamour Girls*. NY: Arlington House, 1975.
Parish, James Robert and Don E. Stanke. *The Leading Ladies*. NY: Arlington House, 1977.
Parish, James Robert and Don E. Stanke. *The Swashbucklers*. NY: Arlington House, 1976.
Parish, James Robert and Lennard DeCarl. *Hollywood Players: The Forties*. NY: Arlington House, 1976.
Parish, James Robert and Steven Whitney. *The George Raft File*. NY: Drake, 1973.
Pascall, Jeremy, ed. *Hollywood and the Great Stars*. NY: Crescent Books, 1976.
Phillips, Gene. *Some Like It Wilder: The Life and Controversial Films of Billy Wilder*. University Press of Kentucky, 2010.
Quirk, Laurence J. *Jane Wyman: The Actress and the Woman*. W. W. Norton, 1987.

Ragan, David. *Movie Stars of the '30s*. Prentice-Hall, 1985.
Ramer, Jean. *Duke: The Real Story of John Wayne*. NY: Charter Books, 1973.
Robinson, W. R., ed. *Man and the Movies*. Penguin Books, 1967.
Rogers, Ginger. *Ginger: My Story*. NY: HarperCollins, 1991.
Rosenberg, David, ed. *The Movie That Changed My Life*. Viking, 1991.
Russell Taylor, John. *Hitch: The Life & Times of Alfred Hitchcock*. A Berkley Book, 1978.
Sadoul, Georges. *Dictionary of Film Makers*. University of California Press, 1972.
Schatz, Thomas. *The Genius of the System*. University of Minnesota Press, 1988.
Schickel, Richard. *Elia Kazan: A Biography*. NY: HarperCollins, 2005.
Schiller, Ralph. *The Complete Films of Broderick Crawford*. A CP Book, 2015.
Scott, Henry E. *The Shocking True Story: The Rise and Fall of "Confidential," "America's Most Scandalous Scandal Magazine."* Pantheon, 2010.
Segaloff, Nat. *Final Cuts: The Last Films of 50 Great Directors*. Bear Manor Media, 2013.
Shipman, David. *The Great Movie Stars: The Golden Years*. Hill and Yang, 1979.
Sikov, Ed. *On Sunset Boulevard: The Life and Times of Billy Wilder*. New York: Hyperion, 1998.
Slide, Anthony, ed. *"It's the Pictures That Got Small": Charles Brackett on Billy Wilder and Hollywood's Golden Age*. NY: Columbia University Press, 2015.
Solomon, Aubrey. *Twentieth Century-Fox: A Corporate and Financial History*. Scarecrow, 1988.
Spiegel, Maura. *Sidney Lumet: A Life*. New York: St. Martin's, 2019.
Spoto, Donald. *The Dark Side of Genius: The Life of Alfred Hitchcock*. NY: Balantine Books, 1983.
Spoto, Donald. *High Society: The Life of Grace Kelly*. Three Rivers, 2009.
Spoto, Donald. *Laurence Olivier: A Biography*. NY: HarperCollins, 1992.
Stine, Whitney with Bette Davis. *Mother Goddam*. NY: Hawthorn Books, 1974.
Sumner, Robert L. *Hollywood Cesspool: A Startling Survey of Movieland Lives and Morals, Pictures and Results*. Sword of the Lord, 1955.
Terrace, Vincent. *Encyclopedia of Unaired Television Pilots, 1945–2018*. McFarland, 2018.
Thomson, David. *The New Biographical Dictionary of Film*. NY: Alfred A. Knopf, 2002.
Tierney, Gene with Mickey Herskowitz. *Self-Portrait*. A Berkley Book, 1979.
Tornabene, Lyn. *Long Live the King: A Biography of Clark Gable*. NY: G. P. Putnam's Sons, 1976.
Truffaut, François. *The Films in My Life*. NY: A Touchstone Book, 1985.
Truffaut, François. *Hitchcock by François Truffaut*. NY: Simon & Schuster, 1967.
Turner, Lana. *Lana: The Lady, the Legend, the Truth*. NY: Simon & Schuster, 1982.
Valentino, Lou. *The Films of Lana Turner*. Citadel, 1976.
Van Neste, Dan. *They Coulda Been Contenders: Twelve Actors Who Should Have Become Cinematic Superstars*. BearManor Media, 2019.
Vermilye, Jerry. *Cary Grant*. NY: Pyramid, 1973.
Viera, Mark A. *Sin in Soft Focus: Pre-Code Hollywood*. NY: Harry N. Abrams, 1999.
Wansell, Geoffrey. *Haunted Idol: The Story of the Real Cary Grant*. NY: Ballantine Books, 1983.
White, Patricia. *Uninvited: Classical Hollywood Cinema and Lesbian Representability*. Indiana University Press, 1999.
Wilder, Billy and Jeffrey Meyers. *The Lost Weekend: The Complete Screenplay*. University of California Press, 2000.
Wiley, Mason and Damien Bona. *Inside Oscar: The Unofficial History of the Academy Awards*. NY: Ballantine Books, 1986.
Wilkerson, Tichi and Marcia Borie. *Hollywood Legends: The Golden Years of "The Hollywood Reporter."* Tale Weaver, 1988.

Wlaschin, Ken. *The Illustrated Encyclopedia of The World's Greatest Movie Stars and Their Films.* NY: Harmony Books, 1979.

Wynn, Ned. *We Will Always Live in Beverly Hills: Growing Up Crazy in Hollywood.* NY: William Morrow, 1990.

Yanni, Nicholas. *Rosalind Russell.* NY: Pyramid, 1975.

SELECTED MAJOR ARTICLES AND WEBSITES

There are hundreds of articles about or interviews with Ray Milland and several pieces Milland himself wrote. The following list represents some of the more illuminating of the lot. Other articles cited throughout the text are referenced in the notes section.

Badder, David and Bob Baker, eds. *Film Dope*, no. 43, 1990, "Ray Milland" Entry 1143: 16–19.

Decaux, E. "Ray Milland." *Cinématographe*, April 1986.

"Dial M for Milland: The Ray Milland Film Archive" (https://www.facebook.com/groups/raymilland).

Doyle, Neil. "Ray Milland: Against Type." *Films of the Golden Age*, Summer 2002, no. 29: 56–69.

Errol, Paul (a.k.a. Clive Hirschhorn). "Why Ray Milland Feels So Bad about Britain." *The Sunday Express*, August 6, 1967.

Film Hub Wales: Chapter (http://filmhubwales.org/en/the-whole-story/), Ray Milland Season, Heno ("Tonight"), Welsh TV-Magazine, October 2015.

Gow, Gordon. "Glamour and Catastrophe: Ray Milland, Irwin Allen Interviewed." *Films and Filming*, September 1975.

Harmetz, Aljean. "Ray Milland: In Coldwater Canyon with *The Lost Weekend*'s Star." *Architectural Digest*, April 1996.

Hefner, Brooks E. "Milland Alone: The End of the System, Post-Studio Stardom and the Total Auteur." *Journal of Film and Video*, vol. 66, no. 4, Winter 2014: 3–18.

Kelly, Gillian. "Dial M for Markham, McNutley and the Milland Show: Remaking and Reimagining Ray Milland's Established Cinematic Image for 1950s Television." *Stars en séries (Series and Stars)*, no. 20, 2022, (https://doi.org/10.4000/tvseries.5480).

Krzisnik, David A. "Mr. Versatile: Ray Milland." *Screem*, April 2012, no. 24: 45–46.

Maltin, Leonard. "Ray Milland." *Film Fan Monthly*, July–August 1968, nos. 85-86: 3–15.

Milland, Ray. "How They Got into the Movies" (1950). *Film Parade*, London: Marks & Spencer: 30–31.

Milland, Ray. "Shop Talk of the Studios" (1948). *Hollywood in the 1940s: The Stars' Own Stories.* Ivy Crane Wilson, ed. New York: Frederick Ungar, 1980: 16–19.

Nolan, Jack Edmund. "Ray Milland on TV." *Films in Review*, 1972, vol. 23: no. 7, 64.

Piton, Jean-Pierre. "Ray Milland ou le charme trouble de l'ambiguïté." *Fantastyka*, October 1993, no. 1: 51–59.

#RayMilland on Twitter is not a formal group but has attracted many contributors with postings of interest.

"Ray Milland: Actor and Spirit of Rain" (https://www.facebook.com/groups/1646547425626387/).

Winters, Joe. "The 'Two-Headed' Career of Ray Milland." July 2006 (http://horror-wood.com/milland.htm).

INDEX

Page numbers in **bold** refer to illustrations.

Academy Awards, Oscars, and Oscar nominations, 3, 4, 5, 13, 75, 77, 85, 97, 99, 102, 107, 109, 113, 117, 124, 126, 129, 133, 143-46, **145**, 147, 148, 149, 150, 153, 159, 162, 165, 170, 179, 189, 194, 196, 197, 199, 210, 213, 224, 227, 238, 244, 247, 255, 269, 270, 280, 281, 285, 288, 289, 295, 312, 314, 317, 326
Academy of Motion Picture Arts and Sciences (AMPAS), 215, 326
Aces High, 293
Admirable Crichton, The (play), 57, 231
Adolfi, John G., 49
Adrian (costume designer), 55
Aherne, Brian, 6, 107, 108, 123, 256
Albert, Eddie, 287
Alcoholics Anonymous (AA), 146-47, 189
Alexander's Ragtime Band (1940 Lux Radio show), 104
Alfred Hitchcock Hour, The, "A Home Away from Home," 11, 250-51
Alias Mary Dow (*Lost Identity*), 65-66, 77, 320
Alias Nick Beal, 9, 11, 167, 168-70, **169**, 173, 221, 235, 241, 277, 282, 288, 292
Allen, Gracie, 57, 59, 71, 116, 173
Allen, Irwin, 312
Allen, Lewis, 127, 128, 130, 133, 157, 163, 165
Allyson, June, 197, 306, 307
Ambassador Bill, 47-48, 61
Ameche, Don, 5, 83, 91, 105, 204-5, 317
American International Pictures (AIP), 242, 245, 246, 247, 249, 278, 279, 280, 282
Angel, Heather, 76, 243, 244

Archainbaud, George, 70, 83, 95
Are Husbands Necessary?, 110, 115-16, 130
Arise, My Love, 101-4, 105, 107, 109, 114, 126, 168
Arkoff, Samuel Z., 242, 245
Arliss, George, 49
Arnold, Edward, 65, 78
Arthur, Jean, 78-79, **79**, 81, 136, 175
Arthur, Karen, 320
Asner, Ed, 265, 293
Asquith, Anthony, 93
Astaire, Fred, 6, 56, 96, 97, 183, 241
Attic, The, 14, **14**, 314-15
Aubrey Smith, C., 42, 44, 50, 62, 75, 122
Aumont, Jean-Pierre, 207, 306
Avalon, Frankie, 245, **245**, 246
Avery, Phyllis, 199, 200, **201**, 214
Awful Truth, The (1937 film), 196

Bachelor Father, The, 42-43, 50, 116, 320
Bacon, Lloyd, 171
Balaban, Barney, 70, 142, 210
Balaban Quine, Judith, 210
Ball, Lucille, 175, 199, 269
Bankhead, Tallulah, 233
Barbeau, Adrienne, 311
Barnes, Binnie, 75
Barrie, Nigel, 30
Barrie, Wendy, 77
Barrymore, John, 6, 160
Barrymore, Lionel, 39, 137
Barthelmess, Richard, 64
Barton, Charles, 199
Bassey, Shirley, **276**

379

Battlestar Galactica, "Saga of a Star World," 308
Beau Geste, 9, 13, 77, 89-91, **89**, 94, 157, 199, 210, 284
Behold My Wife!, 134
Belafonte, Harry, 238
Bel-Air Country Club, 60, 179
Bellamy, Ralph, 300, 317
Bellevue Hospital, 12, **12**, 135, 138, 139, 140
Benchley, Robert, 37
Bennett, Constance, 45
Benny, Jack, 71, 138, 148
Bergen, Candice, 309
Bergman, Ingrid, 123, 132, 134, 145-46, **145**, 164, 179, 280
Bernstein, Elmer, 235, 285, 290
Bickford, Charles, 41
Big Broadcast of 1937, The, 71-72, 83
Big Clock, The, 15, 30, 88, 154, 161-63, **163**, 167, 169, 170, 221, 282, 283
Big Game, The, 284-85
Bishop's Wife, The, 9
blacklisting, 166, 181, 226, 294
Blackmail (1929 film), 35
Black Noon, 277-78, 292, 296, 299
Blackout, 306-7, **307**
blaxploitation (film genre), 278, 280
Bloch, Robert, 240, 250-51, 288
Blonde Crazy, 8, 46-47, 48, 63, 178, 289, 326
Blondell, Joan, 46, 289
Blue Öyster Cult, 15
Blyth, Ann, 173
Bob Hope Special, The (1972 TV program), 280
Bogart, Humphrey, 15, 150, 173, 223
Bogeaus, Benedict, 227, 229
Bolero (1934 film), 56-57, 65
Bond, James (character), 230, 285
Bond, Ward, 113-14, 220, 221, 239
Borgnine, Ernest, 227
Borzage, Frank, 133, 224
Bought!, 8, 45-46, 63
Bouvaire-Thompson, Verita, 150
Boyd, Stephen, 285
Boyer, Charles, 71, 87, 119, 164, 316
Bracken, Eddie, 118, 135
Bracken's World, 265-66

Brackett, Charles, 92, 101, 116, 117, 127, 129, 134, 137, 140, 144, 145, 167, 203, 215-16
Brackett, Leigh, 234, 236
Bradna, Olympe, 86
Brando, Marlon, 7, 177, 221
Breen, Joseph, the Breen Office, 72, 74, 103, 160, 178
Bride of Vengeance. See *Mask for Lucrezia, A (Bride of Vengeance)*
Bringing Up Baby, 5, 80
"British Colony, The," 75-76, 84, 102, 183-84
British International Pictures (BIP), 30, 31, 33-34, 37
Britton, Barbara, 132-33
Broccoli, Albert R., 230
Brody, Estelle, 29, 31, 292
Brown Eye, Pic-a-Pie, 255
Bugles in the Afternoon, 187-88, 202, 220, 326
Bulldog Drummond Escapes, **4**, 76, 80, 244
Burns, Bob "Bazooka," 71, 83
Burns, George, 57, 59, 71, 116
Burton, Richard, 210, 284
But the Flesh Is Weak, 51
Buzzell, Edward, 175

Cafe Society, 84
Cagney, James, 7, 15, 46-47, 70, 173, 187, 326
Calhern, Louis, 46, 178
California, 149, 155-56, 161, 173, 174, 200, 220, 234
Capra, Frank, 174-75
Carey, Macdonald, 11, 234
Carpetbaggers, The, 250
Carradine, John, 56, 57, 66, 265, 283, 295
Carroll, Madeleine, 84, 100, 114
"Catch at Straws" (TV program), 225-26
Cave-In!, 312
Channel Port, 109
Charlie Chan in London, 60-61
Charlie's Angels, "One Love . . . Two Angels," 13, 315, 321
Charlot, André, 36-37
Circle of Danger, 179, 181-83, **182**
Citizen Kane, 287
Clark, Tom, 15
Close to My Heart, 11, 185-87, **187**
Cohn, Harry, 98, 196

Colbert, Claudette, 62–63, **63**, 77, 91, 101–4, 107–8, 114, 153, 204, 321
Coleman, Herbert, 213
Collins, Joan, 216, **216**, 310–11
Colman, Ronald, 6, 7, 40, 45, 76, 90, 184, 239
Columbia Pictures, 98, 106, 174–75, 196, 310
Columbo, 13, 290, 302; "Death Lends a Hand," 227; "The Greenhouse Jungle," 282–83
Company of Killers, 263
Confession, The, 253–55
Confidential (magazine), 209, 210
Congressman, The (proposed TV series), 229
Conspirator, 171
Cool Million, "Hunt for a Lonely Girl," 282, 293
Cooper, Gary, 66, 69, 70, **89**, 90, 123, 150, 158, 181, 183, 194, 210, 239
Copper Canyon, 171, 173–74, 179, 220
Corey, Wendell, 178, 195
Corman, Gene, 236, 242
Corman, Roger, 184, 242–44, 247–49, 306, 327
Cotten, Joseph, 109, 173
Country Girl, The, 210, 213
Count Your Chickens (proposed TV series), 240
Court, Hazel, 243
Coutard, Raoul, 278
Coward, Noël, 36, 165
Crawford, Broderick, 166, 283, 298, 326
Crawford, Joan, 15, 39, 84, 165, 198, 222, 252
Critic's Choice (play), 269–70
Crosby, Bing, 57–58, 59, 61, 119, 134, 144, 149, 158, 161, 175, 283, 325
Crosby, Floyd, 244, 249
Cruise into Terror, 305–6
Crystal Ball, The, 110, 119–20, 124
Cukor, George, 10, 177–79, 201
Cummings, Irving, 96
Cummings, Robert, 95–96, 121, 123, 202, 203, 204–5, **206**, 208, 250
Curtis, Tony, 10, 295–96
Cushing, Peter, 298–99, 322, 323

Dahl, Arlene, 195
Darker Side of Terror, The, 311–12

Daughter of the Mind, 265, 293, 320
Davies, Marion, 39, 42–43, 50–51, 239
Davis, Bette, 49, 223, 252
Davis, Nancy (Nancy Reagan), 181, 225
Dawson, Anthony, 203, **206**, 208, 273, 285
Dead Don't Die, The, 288–89
Dead Men Don't Wear Plaid, 15
Death Valley Days (*Trails West*), 247, 252
De Carlo, Yvonne, 119
De Havilland, Olivia, 153–54, 191, 319
Dellis, Bruce, 15
Del Ruth, Roy, 46–47
DeMille, Cecil B., 5, 41, 104, 110, 111–13, 118, 173, 195
DeMille, William C., 41
De Niro, Robert, 294–95, **295**
De Ossorio, Armando, 324
De Putti, Lya, 31
DeSylva, B. G. "Buddy," 109, 126, 132, 135
"Dial M for Milland: The Ray Milland Archive" (Facebook webpage), 15
Dial M for Murder (1954 film), 4, **7**, 9, 10, 13, 35, 96, 103, 123, 185, 195, 202–9, **206**, 212–13, 214, 225, 235, 240, 242, 244, 267, 273, 285, 289, 325; *Dial M for Murder* (play), 202, 203, 205–7, 259
Dick Powell Theatre, "Open Season," 240–41
Dieterle, Willliam, 253–54
Dietrich, Marlene, 70, 71, 86, 87–88, 159–61, **159**, 165
Dillman, Bradford, 282, 285
Disney, Walt, 286–87
Doctor Takes a Wife, The, 61, 98–100, 104, 174, 196
Donlevy, Brian, 13, 63, 90, 106, 157, 230
Double Indemnity, 134, 142
Douglas, Melvyn, 77, 107
Douglas, Paul, 171, 184
Dream Merchants, The, 315–16
Drew, Ellen, 92–93
Duffy's Tavern, 134
Dunne, Irene, 120, 165, 196
Dupont, E. A., 30
Durbin, Deanna, 75, 211
Dwan, Allan, 11, 227–29

Easy Living (1937 film), 8, 69, 78–79, **79**, 97, 249
Ebb Tide, 80–81, 224, 234, 305
Eden, Barbara, 253, 254, 256
Ed Sullivan Show, The, 259
Edwards, Blake, 238, 241
Edwards, George, 314
Eggar, Samantha, 320
Eilers, Sally, 65, 66
Ellery Queen, "Too Many Suspects," 290
Elliott, Sam, 279, **280**
Elsa Maxwell's Hotel for Women, 91
Elstree Studios, 29, 31, 35, 203
Embassy, 278, 311
Emmy Awards, 277, 292, 293, 299, 303
Escape to Witch Mountain, 286–88, **287**, 308, 319
Evans, Madge, 44
Evans, Robert, 267, 268, 309
Everything Happens at Night, 95–96, 121, 171, 204

Fairbanks, Douglas, Jr., 6, 40, 90
Falk, Peter, 277, 282, 327
Fannan, Cleo Janet (Mrs. Daniel Milland), 258, 260, 266
Fantasy Island, "The Nightmare," 309–10
Farewell to Arms, A, 123
Farmer, Frances, 80–81
Farrow, John, 155, 161, 162, 167, 169, 170, 173
Faye, Alice, 104
Fenady, Andrew J., 277, 283, 296
Fenady, George, 312
Ferrer, José, 135, 219, 316
Ferrer, Mel, 278
Feyder, Jacques, 44–45
Field, Betty, 115–16, 130
film noir, 4, 9, 10, 15, 88, 124, 128, 129, 130, 131, 147, 161, 162–63, 164, 168, 169, 178, 179, 180, 181, 182, 190, 192, 217, 223, 227, 228, 234, 236, 241, 277, 286, 288, 301, 313
Fitzgerald, Barry, 80, 81, 155, 158
Fitzgerald, F. Scott, 95, 293, 294, 295
Fitzmaurice, George, 43
Fleischer, Richard, 217
Fletcher, Louise, 238
Florey, Robert, 87, 88, 237, 238

Flying Scotsman, The (1929 film), 31–33, **32**, 34, 35, 36, 40, 322; The Flying Scotsman (train), 32, 322, **323**
Flynn, Errol, 6, 80, 85, 239
Fonda, Henry, 109, 256, 269
Fontaine, Joan, 76, 116, 134, 188–91, **191**, 259, 271, 275–76, 284
Ford, John, 31, 109, 112, 220, 221, 224
Foreign Affair, A, 165
Forever and a Day, 29, 97, 108, 122–23, 124
Forster, Robert, 311
Forsythe, John, 306, 315
For Whom the Bell Tolls (1943 film), 123
Foster, Lewis R., 195
Four Hours to Kill!, 64, 70
Four Sons, 100
Fox Film Corporation (Fox Studios), 47, 60, 63
Fractured Karma, 15
Francis, Kay, 41
Frees, Paul, 197, 326
Frenchman's Creek, 116
French without Tears, 91–93, 98, 100, 128, 164
Frogs, 278–80, **280**, 299, 310, 314
From Sea to Shining Sea, "The Unwanted," 290–91, 305
Front Page, The (play), 266, 267, 268, 269

Gable, Clark, 26, 40, 50–51, 61, 63, 77, 85, 112, 121, 183–84, 239
Gam, Rita, 181, 193, 209–10, 241
Game for Vultures, 310–11
Garbo, Greta, 39, 80, 160
Garden of Allah, The, 70–71
Garfield, John, 7
Gay, Maisie, 20
General Electric Theater (TV program): "Angel of Wrath," 230; "Battle for a Soul," 235; "Eyes of a Stranger," 233–34; "Never Turn Back," 229; "That's the Man!," 225; "The World's Greatest Quarterback," 235
Gentleman's Agreement, 147, 226
George, Christopher, 297, 306
George, Lynda Day, 306
Giallo (genre), 286, 301
Gibbons, Cedric, 55

Gielgud, John, 285, 322
Gilbert, John, 39, 41, 55
Gilded Lily, The, 62–63, **63**, 66, 68, 101, 102
Gilling, John, 231
Gilpin, Charles, 139
"Girl in the Grass, The" (TV program), 229–30
Girl in the Red Velvet Swing, The, 215–18, **216**, 221, 260, 310
Glass Key, The (1935 film), 64–65
Gleason, Jackie, 263, 264
Goddard, Paulette, 5, 103, 107, 110–15, **111**, 118–20, 122, 150–51, 153, 157, 168, 197, 215
Gold, 285–86
Gold, Jack, 293
Golden Earrings, 20, 71, 158–60, **159**, 214, 303
Golden Globes, The, 10, 144, 194
Gold Key, The, 321–22
Goldwyn, Sam, 40
Gone with the Wind, 5, 85–86, 105, 110, 271, 300
Goodman, Benny, 71
Gordon, Ruth, 297
Gould, Elliott, 253, 254, 255
Goya, Mona, 34, **35**
Grahame, Gloria, 277, 292, 299
Grand Hotel, 64, 160–61
Granger, Farley, 216, 217, 260, 325
Granger, Stewart, 177, 319
Grant, Cary, 5, 6–8, **7**, 9, 14, 55, 59, 60, 66, 68, 69–70, 75, 76, 79–80, 81, 82, 85, 90, 91, 93, 96, 117, 120, 123, 128, 135, 175, 177, 178, 183, 186, 196, 201, 203, 205, 213, 238, 260, 266, 319, 326
Grauman's Chinese Theatre, 144, 149, **328**
Graver, Gary, 314
Greene, Graham, 171, 75, 130, 270
Grier, Roosevelt "Rosey," **12**, 13, 281
Griffith, Edward H., 66, 67, 109
Gunga Din, 89–90, 91, 284
Gwenn, Edmund, 99, 175, 239

Hagen, Jean, 178, 180, 245, **245**
Haines, William, 44
Half Angel (1936 film), 64
Hall, Alexander, 196
Hamlet (1948 film), 164
Hammett, Dashiell, 64

Hands across the Table, 66
Hanson, Lars, 31
Hardwicke, Cedric, 76, 122
Hardy Boys/Nancy Drew Mysteries, The, "Voodoo Doll," 307–8
Harmon, Mark, 313, 315
Harrington, Curtis, 10, 288
Harris, Richard, 310–11
Harrison, Doane, 138, 141
Harrison, Joan, 181–82, 183, 204, 250–51
Harrison, Rex, 5, 211, 256–57
Hart to Hart: "Long Last Love," 320; "My Hart Belongs to Daddy," 318
Haskell, Molly, 272
Hathaway, Blanche "Skip," 209
Hathaway, Henry, 80, 87, 89
Hawks, Howard, 5, 79–80, 171, 223
Hays, Will, the Hays Office, 43–44, 72, 102, 137, 142, 150
Hayward, Louis, 36, 69, 75
Hayward, Susan, 90, 111, 147, 215
Hayworth, Rita, 106
Hearst, William Randolph, 42–43, 287
Heaven Forbid (1998 LP), 15
Henie, Sonja, 95–96, 204
Henried, Paul, 8, 265
Hepburn, Katharine, 79–80, 136, 174
Her Jungle Love, 82–83, 234
Herrmann, Bernard, 251
Hickman, Darryl, 94–95, 170
Hicks, Seymour, 6, 20
High Flight, 230–31
Hiller, Arthur, 267, 268, 270, 309
Hitchcock, Alfred, 35, 123, 127, 185, 202–5, 208, 213, 234, 250, 251, 302, 325
Hoffman, Matthew C., 15
Hogan, James, 76, 80, 81
Holden, Willliam, 106, 107, 109, 158, 161, 203, 210, 230, 302
Hollywood Revue of 1929, The, 39
Hollywood Squares, The, 13
Hollywood Walk of Fame, 239, 326
Homolka, Oscar, 80–81
Hope, Bob, 118, 121, 144, 149, 158, 161, 173, 215, 269, 270, 280, 291
Hopkins, Miriam, 81–82, 215

Hopper, Hedda, 13, 103–4, 143, 167, 181, 209, 210, 316
Hostile Witness (film), 261–64, **264**, 327
Hostile Witness (play), 258–61
Hotel Imperial (1939 film), 87–89, 121, 237
House in Nightmare Park, The, 283–84
House Un-American Committee (HUAC), 166, 181, 294
Howard, Leslie, 5, 6, 86
Howard, Norah, 35, 36
Howard, Trevor, 293, 303, 304
Howerd, Frankie, 283–84, 291
How Green Was My Valley, 5, 109
Hoyt, John, 165, 166, 237
Hunt, Marsha, 40, 79, 97
Hussey, Ruth, **127**, 128, 130
Huston, Walter, 45
Hutton, Betty, 118, 155, 158, 167

I Love Lucy, 115, 199, 200
I'm No Angel, 69
Imperfect Lady, The, 141, 156–57, 191
Informer, The (1929 film), 6, 31
Irene (1940 film), 29, 71, 79, 96–98, **98**, 122, 235, 277
It Happens Every Spring, 9, 171–73, **172**, 174, 184
I Wanted Wings, 105–7, **105**, 108, 109, 158, 230, 315

Jack of Diamonds, 176
Jackson, Charles, 134, 136, 137, 294
Jamaica Run, 192, 195–96, 202, 221, 274, 283
Janssen, David, 296, 297
Jason, Leigh, 82
Johnson, Kay, 41
Johnson, Rita, 161, 162
Johnson, Van, 262–63, 292
Jones, Jennifer, 136
Junge, Alfred, 29, 325
Jungle Princess, The, 69, 72–74, **73**, 76, 82, 83, 259, 315
Just a Gigolo (1931 film), 44, 50, 60

Karloff, Boris, 240
Kazan, Elia, 293, 294–95, 296
Keaton, Buster, 39

Keighley, William, 185, 186
Kellaway, Cecil, 151, 253
Kelly, Grace, 13, 202–3, 204, **206**, 207–10, 212, 213, 229–30, 243, 296, 302, 306, 319
Kelly, Lizanne, 208
Kenley Players, 256–57
King of Kings (1961 film), 9, 241
Kingsley, Dorothy, 46, 266
Kipling, Rudyard, 89, 90
Kiss the Boys Goodbye, 104–5, 317
Kitty, 134, 143, 150–52, **152**, 156, 157, 283
Knight, Castleton, 31–32, 33, 34
Knott, Frederick, 203, 206, 208, 258
Knowles, Patric, 151, 195, 283
Koscina, Sylva, 286
Koster, Henry, 75
Kowalski, Bernard L., 277
Krasna, Norman, 64

Ladd, Alan, 5, 65, 71, 130, 135, 155, 161, 176, 227, 250
Lady Eve, The (1942 Lux Radio show), 109
Lady from the Sea, The, 34–35, **35**, 324
Lady Has Plans, The, 110, 114–15, 119, 157, 214
Lady in the Dark, 77, 121, 124–27, 129, 155, 175, 234, 255
Lake, Veronica, 65, 71, **105**, 106, 119, 121, 132, 134, 158
Lamarr, Hedy, 173–74
Lamas, Fernando, 195, 316
Lamour, Dorothy, 72–74, **73**, 83–84, 94, 118–19, 158, 259, 291, 325
Lanchester, Elsa, 161, 283
Lanfield, Sidney, 115, 157
Lang, Fritz, 10, 130–32, 225
Last Man in the World, The, 141–42
Last Tycoon, The, 293–96, **295**
Latimer, Jonathan, 161, 165, 166, 168–69, 173, 176, 237
Laughton, Charles, 30, 51–52, **52**, 76, 161–62, 219
Laurel and Hardy, 39
Lawrence, Gertrude, 107, 125
LeBaron, William, 87, 109
Leif, Roland, 273, 325
Leigh, Vivien, 75, 93, 110

INDEX

Leisen, Mitchell, 10, 41, 51, 57, 58, 64, 66, 71, 78, 91, 92, 102, 105, 106, 108, 125, 126, 151, 152, 158, 159–60, 167, 168, 196, 237–38, 284
Lemmon, Jack, 147, 241
Leonard, Robert Z., 42, 43
Lerner, Alan Jay, 210, 256, 326
LeRoy, Mervyn, 252
Let's Do It Again, 196–97, 202, 326
Lewis, Kay, 254, 255
Life of Her Own, A, 177–79, 180
Lightning Strikes Twice. See *Half Angel*
Light That Failed, The, 90
Lillie, Beatrice, 36
Lindon, Lionel, 221, 235, 237
Lisbon, 132, 222–24, 226, 263, 322
Lives of a Bengal Lancer, 60
Loewe, Frederick, 210, 256
Lolita (1955 novel), 118
Lombard, Carole, 56–57, 59, 66, 197
"London Affair, A" (1959 TV program), 235–36
Look What's Happened to Rosemary's Baby, 297–98
Loos, Anita, 37
Lord, Pauline, 33
Lost Identity. See *Alias Mary Dow* (*Lost Identity*)
Lost Weekend, The, 4, 5, 8, 10, 12, **12**, 15, **16**, 42, 55, 129, 134–49, **140**, 152, 154, 155, 158, 161, 164, 180, 181, 184, 188, 189, 190, 191, 193, 194, 196, 198, 210, 212, 235, 237, 238, 244, 256, 272, 280, 283, 286, 290, 294, 297, 313, 327
Louise, Tina, 297
Love Boat, The, "Alaska Wedding Cruise," 305, 312–14, **313**, 315
Love from a Stranger (1952 *Screen Guild Players* radio version), 195
Love Story, 11, 14, 247, 255, 264, 266–72, **269**, 275, 285, 289, 305, 309, 313; royal film premiere, **276**
Loy, Myrna, 55, 77
Lubin, Arthur, 184
Lubitsch, Ernst, 58, 70, 87, 107, 159
Lund, John, 167, 168
Lupino, Ida, 71, 90, 123, 219, 224

Lux Radio Theatre, 104, 108, 109, 113, 116, 118, 120, 127, 156, 163, 165, 175, 204, 226
Lydia (1941 film), 109
Lynn, Diana, 263

MacGraw, Ali, 268, 270, 309
MacMurray, Fred, 62, 63, 66, 84, 108, 109, 113–14, 119, 124, 137, 173, 256
Macready, George, 161, 162, 169, 265
Maharis, George, 275, 292, 298
Major and the Minor, The, 55, 110, 116–18, **117**, 125, 161, 255, 263
Malone, Dorothy, 240
Mamoulian, Rouben, 58
Man Alone, A, 10, 88, 215, 218, 220–22, **222**, 223, 228
Mannix, Eddie, 40
Mantrap (TV program), 276
Man Who Played God, The, 8, 49–50, 185
Many Happy Returns, 59
March, Fredric, 13, 80, 139, 147
Markham (TV series), 11, 41, 88, 230, 234, 236–39, **237**, 240, 244, 306
"Markheim" (TV program), 224–25
Markle, Fletcher, 179, 180
Marley, Florence, 165–66
Marriott, Moore, 32
Marshal, Alan, 71, 97, 109, 235
Marshall, Don, 281–82
Marshall, George, 158
Marshall, Herbert, 6, 76
Marshall, William, 253–55
Marx, Zeppo (Herbert Manfred Marx), 101, 127, 170
Mask for Lucrezia, A (*Bride of Vengeance*), 167–68, 283
Masks of Death, The, 322–23, 324
Mason, James, 6, 147, 154, 177, 201, 213
matinée idol history, 6
Mature, Victor, 167
Mayday at 40,000 Feet!, 296–97, 306, 319, 320
Mayer, Louis B., 40, 177, 181, 294
Mayo, Archie, 45
McCambridge, Mercedes, 179
McCarey, Leo, 120, 224, 271
McCrea, Joel, 101
McDowell, Malcolm, 293

McLaglen, Cyril, 32
McLaglen, Victor, 32, 90
McLeod, Norman Z., 59
Meet Mr. McNutley, 9, 82, 198–202, **201**, 214–15, 236, 326
Menace, 8, 61, 65
Mendes, Lothar, 52
Menjou, Adolph, 82, 137, 181
Men with Wings, 77, 85, 90, 230
Merv Griffin Show, The, 263, 284
Metro-Goldwyn-Mayer (MGM), 3, 37–45, 48, 50, 51, 53, 55, 58, 59, 60, 72, 81, 85, 104, 105, 111, 118, 136, 146, 155, 165, 171, 177–81, 183, 225, 231, 233, 241, 254, 266, 294
Metty, Russell, 97, 277, 292
Mexican filming, 228–29, 274–75, 302–3
Michael, Gertrude, 61, 64, 70, 188
Midnight, 91, 105, 317
Mike Douglas Show, The, 260, 268
Milland, Danny (Daniel), **120**, 211; acting career, 224, 235, 241, 242, 247; death, 316; divorce, 266; marriage, 258
Milland, Mal (Muriel Weber), **120**, **211**; meeting and dating Milland, 48–49; Weber family background, 48–49
Milland, Ray, **4**, **7**, **12**, **14**, **16**, **21**, **28**, **32**, **35**, **43**, **52**, **63**, **67**, **73**, **79**, **89**, **92**, **98**, **105**, **111**, **117**, **120**, **127**, **131**, **140**, **145**, **152**, **159**, **163**, **169**, **172**, **182**, **187**, **191**, **194**, **201**, **206**, **211**, **216**, **222**, **232**, **237**, **245**, **250**, **257**, **264**, **269**, **276**, **280**, **287**, **295**, **301**, **307**, **313**, **323**; accidents and near-death incidents, 23–24, 25, 29, 53, 87–88, 106, 113, 121, 180, 231; alternate names and name changes, 11, 18–19, 33; antisemitism accusation, 295–96; birth date and place, 18; birth parents' background, 19–20; boxing, 26, 28, 29, 50; Broadway experience, 259–60; death, 325–26; directing philosophy, 155, 219, 220; education, 22–23, 24–25, 26; genealogical history, 19–20; golfing hobby, 86, 239–40; home sales and purchases, 92–93, **92**, 186–87, 273, 326; horse-racing and training, 24, 26, 27, 54; Household Cavalry service, 20–21, 26–29, **28**, 60, 78, 88, 318; marksmanship skills, 6, 31, 27, 32; marriage, divorce, and remarriage, 53, 58; marriage troubles, 84, 138–39, 202, 208–10, 212, 213, 221, 229–30, 243, 296, 302; the Method (acting style), 17, 137; New York City trips, 37, 74, 82, 137–38, 192, 259–60, 268, 321, 322; pets, 22, 92, **92**, 136; pilot hobby and flight instruction, 28, 61, 66, 85, 102, 121, 167, 230, 293; political views, 136–37, 181, 262, 276, 316, 325; religion, 19–20; retirement attempts, 236, 239, 290; sexual harassment experiences, 26, 41, 45; siblings, 20, 21, 24, 93–94, 102, 235, 291; smoking history, 79, 147; story writing, 219, 262, 326; toupée history, 8, 112, 150, 270–71, 273, 289; US citizenship, 50, 59–60, 84, 154, 181; World War II service, 121–22, 124
Milland, Vicki (Victoria), **211**; adoption, 174, 175, 186; Alexander Graham (son), 302, 326, 327; college years, 247, 258; Edmund Lowell Graham (husband), 266, 291, 326; Travis Graham (son), 280, 291, 326, 327
Ministry of Fear, 10, 124, 130–32, **131**, 225, 244, 270
Miranda, Isa, 87, 88
Miss Tatlock's Millions, 161, 166–67
Mitchell, Cameron, 285, 300
Mitchum, Robert, 294–95, **295**
Mogherini, Flavio, 301
Monroe, Marilyn, 216
Montgomery, Robert, 6, 40–41, 44, 49, 51, 59, 80, 147, 155, 181, 216
Moore, Roger, 6, 285
Morison, Patricia, 94–95, 116
Morris, Oswald, 182–83
Most Dangerous Game, The (1932 film), 81
Moulin Rouge (1928 film), 30
Moulin Rouge (1952 film), 183
Murder at the Vanities, 71
Murder Goes to College, 77
Murphy, Mary, 220, 221, 222
Murray, Don, 265
Music Corporation of America (MCA talent agency), 170, 198, 220, 231, 236, 242, 274
My Fair Lady (film), 256–57

My Fair Lady (stage musical), 5, 150, 174, 211, 256–58, **257**, 264, 326
My Favorite Brunette, 158
My Man Godfrey, 197

Name of the Game, The, "A Love to Remember," 270
Napier, Alan, 243, 244
Narrow Margin, The, 217, 241
Neagle, Anna (Margie Roberts), 28–29, 82, 96–98, **98**, 122–23, 320
Neath (Wales), 11, 18, 19, 20, 21, 88, 154, 289, 325, 327
Neumann, Kurt, 66
Next Time We Love, 8, 66–68, **67**, 69, 77
Nicholson, James H., 242, 245
Night Cry (1948 *Suspense* radio show), 168
Night Gallery, "The Hand of Borgus Weams," 275, 292, 298
Night into Morning, 147, 179–81, 185, 261
Niven, David, 6, 38, 69, 71, 165, 177, 183, 197, 274
Nixon, Richard, 262, 284
No Holds Barred (proposed TV series), 234
North by Northwest, 213, 238
Novarro, Ramon, 44, 55, 146
Novello, Ivor, 6, 51
Now, Voyager, 8

Oberon, Merle, 109, 123
O'Brien, Edmond, 219, 235
Of Human Bondage (1948 *Ford Theater* radio version), 161, 179
Of Men and Music, 176
O'Hara, Maureen, 132, 222, 223
Oil, 298
Oland, Warner, 60
Olive Oyl for President (1948 animated short), 161
Oliver's Story, 309
Olivier, Laurence, 75, 76, 164
Olympia, 134
Once upon a Honeymoon (1943 *Screen Guild Theater* version), 120
Once upon a Time... Is Now Grace Kelly (TV program), 302
O'Neal, Ryan, 268, **269**, 270, 309

One Hour Late, 61
Orangey (*Rhubarb* cat), 184–85
Orders Is Orders, 54
O'Sullivan, Maureen, 51, **52**, 161, 260
Our Family Business, 317
Out of the Past, 181, 236
Overman, Lynne, 74, 83, 119
Owen, Reginald, 88, 151

Paget, Debra, 171, 228–29
Panic in Year Zero!, 11, 142, 180, 245–47, **245**, 248, 250
Paramount Studios, 3, 5, 6, 8, 9, 10, 40, 41, 53, 210, 213, 214, 215, 217, 222, 236, 247, 250, 267, 268, 269, 270, 271, 283, 293, 297, 309, 317; Paramount Consent Decree, 168
Parker, Eleanor, 266, 313–14
Parsons, Louella, 209
Passion Flower, 41–42
Pasternak, Joe, 75
Patrick, Gail, 61, 99
"Pattern of Guilt" (TV program), 241–42
Payment Deferred, 30, 51–52, **52**, 61, 65, 161
Peck, Gregory, 144, 226, 317
Penny Serenade, 120, 186
Peters, Jean, 171
Phillips, Margaret, 178
Picture of Dorian Gray, The, 145, 261
Pidgeon, Walter, 5, 109, 264
Pinewood Studios, 163, 284, 298
Pinter, Harold, 294–95
Place in the Sun, A, 188
Plaything, The, 31
Pleasence, Donald, 287, **287**, 295, 299
Pleshette, Suzanne, 247, 275
Poe, Edgar Allan, 5, 242–43, 244, 245, 248
Polly of the Circus, 50–51, 183
Potter, H. C., 77
Powell, William, 6, 49, 197, 317
Power, Tyrone, 6, 78, 104, 121, 168, 239
Powers, Stephanie, 276, 318, 320
pre-Code movies (pre-PCA), 46
Premature Burial, 5, 76, 242–45, 248
Preminger, Otto, 168, 252, 269
Preston, Robert, **89**, 90, 187
Price, Vincent, 5, 15, 242, 243

Prince of Foxes, 168
Princess Margaret, **276**
Production Code Administration (PCA), 42, 47, 65, 72, 74, 102, 131, 157, 228, 267
Prohibition era, the, 42, 139
Protectors, The. See *Company of Killers*
Pygmalion (George Bernard Shaw play), 150, 151, 211, 317
Pyjama Girl Case, The, 14, 301-2, **301**

Quick, Let's Get Married. See *Confession, The*
Quinn, Anthony, 157, 228, 284

Raft, George, 56, 59, 65, 70, 150
Rains, Claude, 76, 122, 123, 223, 224
Rambeau, Marjorie, 44
Raye, Martha, 71, 83, 242
Ray, Nicholas, 9, 191, 220, 241
Ray Milland: Actor and Spirit of Rain (website), 15
Ray Milland Band, The, 15
Ray Milland Show, The. See *Meet Mr. McNutley*
Reagan, Nancy. See Davis, Nancy
Reagan, Ronald, 181, 225, 307, 316, 325
Reap the Wild Wind, 5, 110-13, **111**, 114, 150, 195, 215, 274, 305
Red, Hot and Blue, 167
Red Roses for the Fueher, 262
Reed, Theodore, 83, 105-6
Reiner, Carl, 15
Relatively Speaking, 275-76
Rennahan, Ray, 80, 234
Republic Pictures, 215, 220, 222-24, 225, 227, 231, 241, 261
Return of Sophie Lang, The, 70, 83, 95, 188
Rhubarb (1951 film), 184-85, 221, 291
Richards, Kim, 287, 288, 316
Rich Man, Poor Man, 292-93, 298, 299, 303
Rich Man, Poor Man Book II, 293
Rickles, Don, 249
Riding High, 174-75
River of Gold, 274-75
Rivers, Max, 36
River's Edge, The, 11, 171, 227-29, 230, 249
RKO Radio Pictures (RKO), 3, 80, 81, 89, 96, 122, 124, 165, 179, 181, 217
Roach, Hal, 82, 224

Roadshow, 82
Road to Bali, The, 215
Roberts, Ewan, **262**
Robinson, Edward G., 117
Robison, Arthur, 31
Roc, Patricia, **182**, 183
Rogers, Ginger, 56, 96, 97, 117-18, **117**, 119, 120, 121, 125-26, 127, 137, 165, 253-55, 260
Rogers, Will, 47
Romero, Cesar, 71
Roosevelt, Franklin D. (FDR), 56, 137, 139
Roots, 292, 299, 303
Rose, David E., 182, 231, 233, 261
Ross, Frank, 79
Ross, Shirley, 71
Roundtree, Richard, 278, 310, 311
Rowland, Roy, 187
Rowlands, Gena, 238
Royal Romance of Charles and Diana, The, 318-19
Rozsa, Miklos, 142, 145
"rubble" films, 165
Rubin, J. Robert, 37, 50
Ruggles, Wesley, 56, 62, 77
Rule, Janice, 235
"runaway" productions, 163, 223
Rurales, 113
Russell, Gail, 7, 127, 128, 130, 134, 239
Russell, Rosalind, 174, 175, 242

Safecracker, The, 231-33, **232**, 234, 261, 267
Sanders, George, 6, 260
Sandrich, Mark, 107
San Simeon (Hearst castle), 42, 287
Santell, Alfred, 50
Sarris, Andrew, 207, 295
Say It in French, 86-87, 96
Scala, Gia, 235-36
Schary, Dore, 177, 178, 180
Scorsese, Martin, 128, 317
Scott, Allan, 81, 82, 107, 253, 254, 255
Scott, Lizabeth, 156, 158, 165
Scott, Randolph, 85
Scott, Zachary, 258
Sealed Verdict, 165-66, 227, 237, 283, 320
Sea Serpent, The, 324

INDEX

Segal, Erich, 268, 270, 271, 309
Seitz, John F., 139, 142–43, 162
Selznick, David O., 70–71, 85–86, 104–5, 110, 123, 134, 136
Seven Different Ways. See *Confession, The*
Seventh Avenue, 299–300
Seventh Veil, The, 154
Shadow of a Doubt (1949 Ford Theater radio version), 173, 204
Shadow of a Lady, 239
Shane, 5, 176
Shearer, Norma, 39, 44, 138
She Done Him Wrong, 69
Shepperton Studios, 92, 261
Sherlock Holmes and the Masks of Death. See *Masks of Death, The*
Sherman, Vincent, 315, 316
"Silver Burro, The" (TV program), 252
Sinatra, Frank, 150, 325
Sirk, Douglas, 186, 191, 204
Skylark, 103, 107, 108, 200, 253
Slavers, 303–4, 305
Sleep, My Love, 204–5
Slick Hare (1947 animated short), 158, 161
Snodgress, Carrie, 14, **14**, 314
So Evil My Love, 9, 154, 163–64, 204, 225, 326
Something to Live For, 147, 158, 179, 188–91, **191**, 229
Son of India, 44–45
South Africa filming, 284, 285, 286, 310
Sparkuhl, Theodor, 33, 64
Spellbound (1945 film), 142, 145, 251
Spelling, Aaron, 242, 274, 305, 309, 312, 315, 317
Spencer, Douglas, 140, 239
Spiegel, Sam, 294–95, 296
Spree. See *Survival Run*
Squaw Man, The (1931 film), 41
Stagecoach, 5, 112
Stanwyck, Barbara, 84, 109, 155–56, 325
Starflight:The Plane That Couldn't Land, 319–20
Star Is Born, A (1954 film), 147, 201, 214
Star-Spangled Rhythm, 118–19, 158
Star Wars, 308, 319
Steiger, Rod, 225

Steiner, Louise (Louise Klos Steiner Elian), 75, 186
Steiner, Max, 75, 186
"Stella by Starlight" (melody), 129–30
Sterke, Jeanette (Jeanette Sterke Michell), **232**, 233
Sterling, Jan, 184, 291
Stevens, George, 90, 120, 189, 190, 191
Stevens, Stella, 306
Stevenson, Robert Louis, 80, 224–25
Stewart, James, 66–68, **67**, 78, 121, 144, 150, 221, 256, 302, 319
St. Leger, Margot, 29
Stockade, 224
Stokowski, Leopold, 71
Stone, Andrew L., 86
Story of Esther Costello, The, 222
Strange Case of Ray Milland, The, 15
Stranger in Munich, 219
Strangers May Kiss, 43–44, 51, 66, 138
Strangers on a Train, 203, 204, 216, 217
Strauss, Peter, 292, 295
Student Connection, The, 14, 286, 287
Sturges, Preston, 66, 78, 108–9, 118, 137
Sullivan, Margaret, 66–68, **67**, 82, 87, 239
Sullivan's Travels, 108–9
Survival Run, 302–3
Suspicion (TV series), 213, 234–35, 236; "Death Watch," 234–35, 241; "Eye for Eye," 234
Swiss Conspiracy, The, 296, 323
Syms, Sylvia, 261, 327

Take Me Along, 264
Tamiroff, Akim, 94–95
Tarantino, Quentin, 279
Taurog, Norman, 57, 115
Taylor, Dwight, 189, 229
Taylor, Elizabeth, 171
Taylor, Robert, 84, 171, 181, 317
Ten Nights in a Barroom (1926 film), 139
Terror in the Wax Museum, 24, 283–84, 296, 312, 322
Terry, Phillip, 237
Testimony of Two Men, 299, 300
Thalberg, Irving, 40, 55, 294
Thames Television, 272, 291

They Won't Forget, 78
Thief, The, 10, 89, 180, 192–95, **194**, 210, 241
Thiele, Wilhelm, 94
Thing with Two Heads, The, 12, **12**, 13, 275, 280–82, 311
This Gun for Hire, 71
This Is the Life, 54
This Is Your Life, 270, 284, 291, 320
Three Brave Men, 225–27
3-D format, 10, 202, 205, 207, 247–48
Three Smart Girls, 74–75, 76, 77, 211
Thriller, "Yours Truly, Jack the Ripper," 240, 283
Tierney, Gene, 185, 186, **187**, 265
Till We Meet Again (1944 film), 124, 132–34
To Catch a Thief, 213
Todd, Ann, 154, 164
To Each His Own, 153
Tone, Franchot, 6, 60, 62, 84, 119, 121
Tonight Show, The, 13, 249, 259, 272, 275
Totter, Audrey, 169, **169**, 170, 235, 250
Tourneur, Jacques, 181, 182, 183, 185
Trading Places, 5, 317
Tropic Holiday, 83–84, 105
Trouble with Women, The, 9, 141, 150, 157–58
Truffaut, François, 178, 205
Truscott-Jones, Alfred Reginald John. *See* Milland, Ray
Tugend, Harry, 118, 214
Turner, Lana, 177–78, 242
Turner Classic Movies (TCM), 3, 10, 132, 327
Tuttle, Frank, 64
Twelvetrees, Helen, 61
Twentieth Century-Fox Studios, 47, 91, 95–96, 104, 109, 132, 150, 168, 171, 176, 183, 215, 226, 227, 265, 312

Uncanny, The, 298, 299, 320, 323
Uninvited, The, 7, 10, 116, 127–30, **127**, 131, 132, 133, 203–4, 244, 265, 320
United Artists (UA), 109, 124, 192, 219, 261, 262, 264
Universal Studios, 65, 66, 74, 75, 77, 87, 91, 118, 197, 219, 238, 250, 263, 270, 275, 282, 288, 299, 300, 308, 315
"Unnoticeable Star, An" (poem), 15–16

Unseen, The, 129–30
Untamed (1940 film), 94–95, 116, 170

Valentine, Joseph, 77
Van Ark, Joan, 279, **280**, 300
Vanderbilt, Gloria, 139
Van der Vlis, Diana, 8, 248, 249
Variety Club International, 158, 325
Variety Girl, 158, 325
Virginia (1941 film), 109
Von Sternberg, Josef, 58, 159
Von Sydow, Max, 278

Wagner, Robert, 318, 320
Wallis, Hal B., 164, 326
Wanger, Walter, 101
Ward Baker, Roy, 322, 323
Warner Bros., 3, 33, 40, 45, 46, 49, 78, 85, 105, 118, 132, 136, 153, 153, 185, 187, 201, 202, 203, 205, 209, 256, 297, 310, 312, 318
Way for a Sailor, 41, 42, 47
Wayne, John, 5, 26, 53, 60, 99, 110–14, **111**, 155, 215, 227, 269, 312
Welles, Orson, 220, 241
Well Groomed Bride, The, 141, 150, 152–154, 319
Wellman, William A., 85, 90, 91
Wells, George, 104
Welsh history, customs, and culture, 6, 18–19, 21–22, 25–27, 82, 92, 102, 154–55, 243, 278–79
We're Not Dressing, 57, 58–59, 115, 231, 283
West, Mae, 59, 69
What's My Line?, 211–12, 238, 240, 259
White Shadows of the South Seas, 229
Whitman, Ernest, **12**, 13
Wide-Eyed in Babylon, 3, 19, 34, 42, 45, 197, 210, 274, 285, 289, 296, 302
Wilcox, Herbert, 96, 97, 122
Wilder, Billy, 4, 10, 55, 92, 101, 108, 116–17, 118, 134, 135, 136, 137, 138, 139, 140, 141, 142, 144, 145, 147, 148, 165, 167, 180, 190, 203, 214, 294
Wilding, Michael, 177, 262
William Morrow and Company, 3, 274, 285
Williams, John (actor), 203, 240
Williams, John (composer), 306
Wings over Honolulu, 77–78, 85, 230

Wise Girl, 69, 81–82, 107, 253
Woman in Room 13, The, 35–36, 256
Woman of Distinction, A, 9, 11, 99, 174–76, 179, 197
Wong, Anna May, 29, 30
Wood, Sam, 41
Wright, Teresa, 156, 157–58, 189, 191
Wyman, Jane, 136, 181, 196, 197–98
Wynn, Ned, 212, 242

"X-Ray Eyes" (song), 15
X: The Man with the X-Ray Eyes, 8, 15, 184, 234, 247–50, **250**, 285, 311

Yates, Herbert J., 215, 220, 221, 222–23, 224
Young, Loretta, 91, 99, 104
Young, Robert, 77
Young, Victor, 130, 132, 190

Zanuck, Darryl F., 95, 96, 100, 109, 252
Zinnemann, Fred, 224, 225

ABOUT THE AUTHOR

ERIC MONDER IS A WRITER AND LECTURER.

Eric was born in Manhattan and graduated from New York University. It was there he met his future wife, Kathi Patterson.

As a film and book critic, Eric has contributed hundreds of articles and reviews to such publications as *Film Journal International, Variety, Film Comment*, the *New York Times, The Motion Picture Guide, Cover Magazine*, the *Quarterly Review of Film and Video*, the *Oxford Dictionary of National Biography* and the *Hitchcock Annual*.

His first book, *George Sidney* (1994, Greenwood Press), was a study of the work of the Hollywood director.

Eric has given talks at the Museum of Modern Art, Lincoln Center's Walter Reed Theatre, the Film Forum in New York City, Eastman Kodak in New York, the McPherson Opera House in McPherson, Kansas, the Golden Anniversary Oscar Micheaux Festival in Great Bend, Kansas, the Buster

Keaton Celebration in Iola, Kansas, the Will Rogers Memorial Museum in Claremore, Oklahoma, Carolina Village in Hendersonville, North Carolina and the Bradford Film Festival in Bradford, England.

For several years, Eric was also a lecturer with the Kansas Humanities Speaker's Bureau, giving presentations throughout the state on such topics as "The Stars of Kansas" and "Censorship and Film."

Eric has taught film and media at Mercy College in New York, Sacred Heart University in Connecticut and, in Kansas, Bethany College, McPherson College and MindFire Academy. His courses have included "Religion and Film," "Philosophy and Film," "Popular Culture during the Great Depression," and "Horror Movies."

Eric has coproduced *Keaton Plus*, a 2001 documentary about Buster Keaton, distributed by Kino International, and he was a consultant on *Oil and Gold: the McPherson Globe Refiners Basketball Story,* an award-nominated 2012 short subject about the American basketball team that won an Olympic Gold Medal in Nazi Germany in 1936.

Eric currently lives in North Carolina.